CALIFORNIA

The Versatile Guide

FISHERMANS WHARF
OF SAN FRANCISCO
Sukiyaki
Tokyo
SUKIYAKI
yo Sukiyaki
HI BAR
GIFTS

CALIFORNIA

The Versatile Guide

Mick Sinclair

Duncan Petersen

This first edition published 1994 by
Duncan Petersen Publishing Ltd,
54, Milson Road,
London, W14 OLB

Sales representation in the U.K. and Ireland by

World Leisure Marketing,
117, The Hollow,
Littleover,
Derby, DE3 7BS.

Distributed by
Grantham Book Services

Conceived, edited, designed and produced by
Duncan Petersen Publishing Ltd from a concept by Emma Stanford

Typeset by Duncan Petersen Publishing Ltd;
film output by Reprocolor International, Milan

Originated by Reprocolor International, Milan

Printed by GraphyCems, Navarra

A CIP catalogue record for this book is available from the British Library

ISBN 1 872576 34 6

Editorial director Andrew Duncan
Assistant editors Mary Devine, Laura Harper
Art director Mel Petersen
Design assistants Beverley Stewart, Chris Foley
Maps by Chris Foley and Beverley Stewart
Illustrations by Beverley Stewart

Photographic credits
Francis Morgan: pp. 15, 17, 18, 20, 21, 24, 27, 29, 58, 66, 67, 70, 71, 73, 78, 83, 85, 89, 90, 94, 95, 96, 102, 106, 107, 113, 125, 131, 171, 172, 175, 187, 190, 199, 243, 255, 258, 259, 260, 263. **Marty Heinritz:** pp. 2, 38, 43, 49, 50, 51, 52, 76, 79, 82, 101, 118, 123, 126, 128, 130, 143, 150, 151, 154, 158, 166, 182, 183, 194, 196, 198, 203, 205, 206, 210, 211, 214, 215, 216, 234, 235, 238, 240, 246, 247. **Getty Museum:** p. 235. **Tim Fuller:** pp. 7, 19, 23, 34, 110, 111, 212, 218, 222, 223, 226, 232, 239, 254, 259. **Stephen Morgan:** pp. 115, 121. **Cindy Clark:** p. 103. **Mel Petersen:** 112, 224, 227, 247.

Born in England in 1956, **Mick Sinclair's** first experience of California was landing in Los Angeles after midnight and taking an unlicensed cab to a honeymoon suite booked by mistake in a Beverly Hills hotel. He spent most of the next day trying to walk to the end of the street; only much later discovering the street was 20 miles long.

Since then, he's been a regular California visitor and has traversed its many diverse regions variously by llama, horse and hot-air balloon as well as by more familiar modes of transportation. He's written three travel guides to the state – this is the first one to recommend specific tour routes – and other guides to New York, Florida and Scandinavia.

When not traveling or writing, he likes to spend his time telling Californians things they don't know about their own state. His ambition is to write an in-depth guide to California's "watering holes."

Master contents list

This contents list is for when you need to use the guide in the conventional way: to find out about where you are going, or where you happen to be. The index, pages 265-271, may be just as helpful.

HOWEVER...
There is much more to this guide than the region-by-region approach suggested by the contents list on this page. Turn to page 8 and see also pages 10-11.

Contents

California Overall
- *master map*

California Overall, pages 30-109, is a traveler's network for taking in the whole state, or large parts of it.

Each "leg" of the network has a number (i.e. California Overall: 1); you will also find it described as a Statewide Route, plus the number.

The term Statewide Route does *not* simply mean a line on a map. Each "route" leg features a whole region, and describes many places both on and off the marked route. Think of the Statewide Routes not only as physical trails, but as imaginative ways of connecting all the main centers of California, and of describing and making travel sense of the state as a whole.

They are designed to be used in these different ways:

1 *Ignore the marked route entirely:* simply use the alphabetically arranged Sights & Places of Interest, and the map at the start of each "route," as a guide to what to see and do in the region, not forgetting the hotel and restaurant recommendations.

2 Follow the marked route by public transportation (see the transportion box) or by car. You can do sections of the route, or all of it; you can follow it in any direction. Link the routes to travel the length and breadth of California.

San Francisco has a section of its own, pages 110-137.
For **Los Angeles**, see Local Explorations: 15 and 16.

The routes are broken down into manageable legs. Each leg has a section to itself, beginning with an introduction and a simplified map.

Always use the simplified maps in conjunction with detailed maps (suggestions are given on the introductory pages).

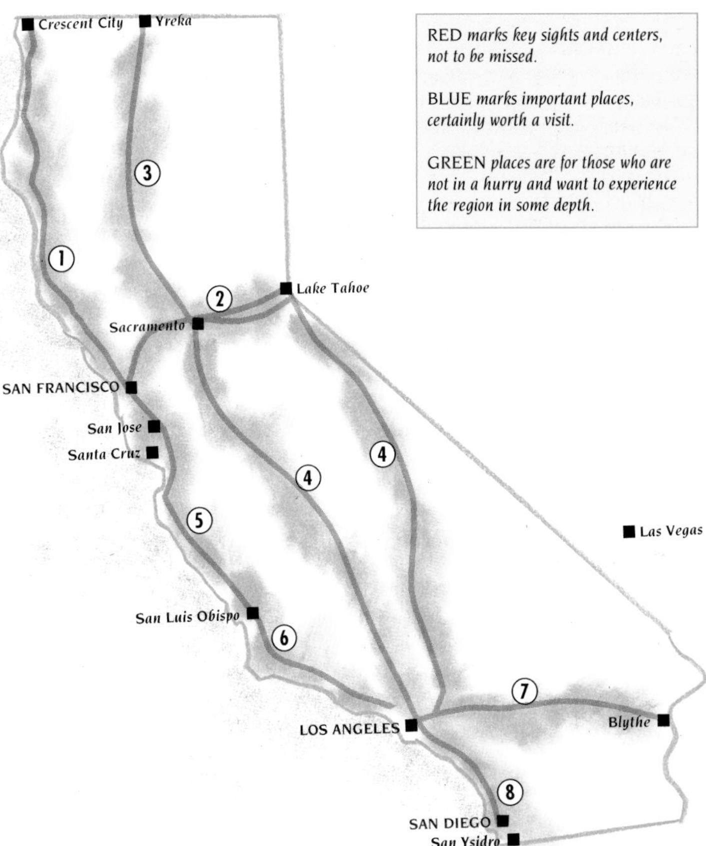

RED *marks key sights and centers, not to be missed.*

BLUE *marks important places, certainly worth a visit.*

GREEN *places are for those who are not in a hurry and want to experience the region in some depth.*

Some practical hints on how to travel red, blue and green are given in the introductory pages and the simplified maps, including key roads and their numbers. Generally, though, there are no absolute rules for going red, blue or green and you are meant to link the places in whatever way suits you best.

The *California Overall* section is ideal for:

- **Planning**, and undertaking, tours of the whole country, or parts.
- **Making the journey** to or from your eventual destination as interesting and as rewarding as possible.
- **Linking** the in-depth explorations of local sights provided by the Local Explorations section, pages 138-264.

Contents

The Local Explorations *- master map*

The Local Explorations are strategies for exploring all the interesting localities of California. Also described as Local Tours, they complement the National Routes, pages 30–98. **They are designed to be used in these different ways:**

1 *Ignore the marked route entirely*: simply use the alphabetically arranged Sights & Places of Interest, and the map at the start of each Local Exploration, as a guide to what to see and do in the area, not forgetting the hotel and restaurant recommendations.

2 Use the marked route to make a tour by public transportation (see the transportation box) or by car. You can do sections of the route, or all of it. (In the introduction it tells you how long you might take to cover everything the quickest way, by car.)

If you are driving, you can usually follow the tour in any direction; generally, the route as marked is an attractive and convenient way to link the places of interest; you may well find other ways to drive it. Always use our map in conjunction with a detailed road map (suggestions are given on each introductory page).

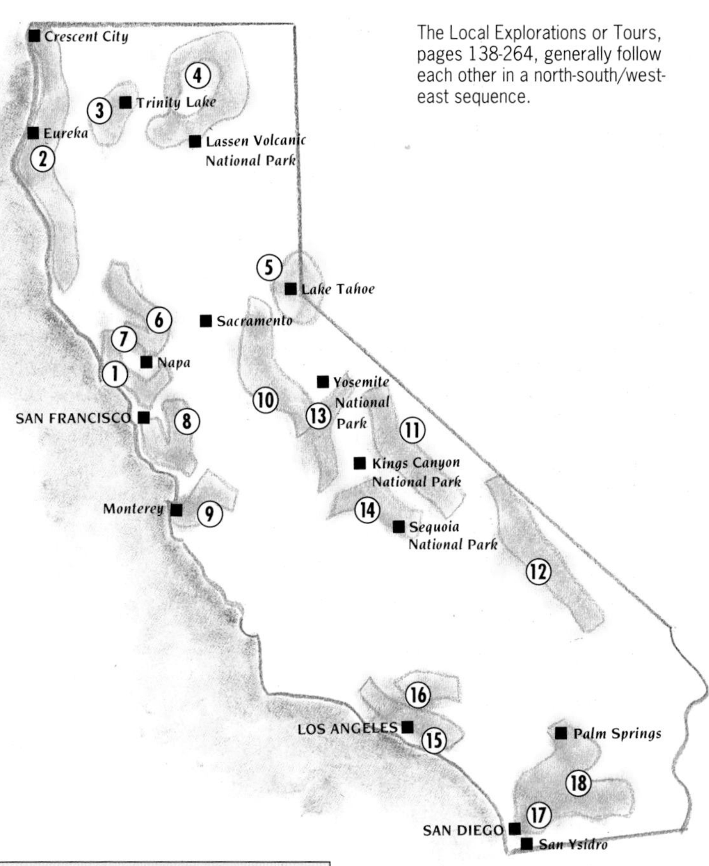

The Local Explorations or Tours, pages 138-264, generally follow each other in a north-south/west-east sequence.

The Local Explorations are ideal for:

■ **Planning single-destination vacations**: each Local Exploration encapsulates an area that would make a great vacation.

■ **Entertaining yourself while you are there**: each section is packed with ideas for things to see and do.

■ **Planning multi-destination vacations**. The map on this page shows you at a glance all the interesting parts of California. Combine them at will to experience the different faces of the state; or link them, by means of the national route network.

San Francisco has a section of its own, pages 110-137.
For **Los Angeles**, see Local Explorations: 15 and 16.

Conventions Used in this Guide

Opening times – hotels and restaurants
Assume, unless specifically stated, that **hotels** are open all year.

Also assume that the recommended **restaurants** open for lunch and dinner at normal hours, every day, unless specifically stated. Some diners and cheap eating places are open for breakfast as well as at lunchtime and in the evening: this is made clear in the entries.

Opening times – museums and tourist attractions
In California the traveler has the advantage of being able to rely on *relatively* consistent opening and closing times of museums and tourist attractions conforming to common sense general rules. This guide therefore avoids giving detailed opening and closing information except in a few instances where there are notable exceptions.

🛏 after a heading in **Sights & Places of Interest** means that there is an accommodation suggestion (or suggestions) for that place in **Recommended Hotels.**

✕ after a heading in **Sights & Places of Interest** means that there is a restaurant suggestion (or suggestions) for that place in **Recommended Restaurants.**

↗ After a place name on a map means that the sight or place of interest is covered in detail in another part of the book. To find out exactly where, look up the place in the **Sights & Places of Interest** gazetteer which follows the map: a cross-reference is given in every case.

The general rules are: major and state museums or attractions are usually open every day of the year except public holidays as listed on page 25. However, if your enjoyment of a day out is going to depend on access, you should consult the local telephone directory. This gives the opening and closing times for many of the museums and attractions, along with the telephone number. If the opening and closing information is not there, ring the museum.

Outside the major centers, opening and closing times of small-town museums and other tourist attractions are less predictable, but still tend to follow a set pattern of being open during normal working hours every day except Monday. Some also take Tuesday as a day off. Most are closed on public holidays. Again, if your enjoyment of a route or tour is going to depend on access to a museum or attraction, get the number from the local directory and find out in advance if it will be open.

A single dollar sign – **$** – or several dollar signs, such as **$$$,** in a hotel or restaurant entry, denotes a price band. Its object is to give an indication of what you can expect to pay, without wine.

Bear in mind that accommodation offered at any one place may well span two or more price bands. Similarly, the cost of a meal in a particular restaurant will vary according to whether you are nibbling a breakfast muffin or sitting down to a three-course dinner.

Hotels

$	Two people can stay for $25-45
$$	Two people can stay for $45-80
$$$	Two people can stay for $80-120
$$$$	Two people can stay for $120+

Restaurants

$	One person can dine for $5-12
$$	One person can dine for $12-19
$$$	One person can dine for $19+

Hotels and restaurants in this guide are a *selection* of personal recommendations – not exhaustive lists. They have been chosen to represent interest and quality, or to satisfy specific needs, at every price level.

Mileages for routes and tours are approximate. In the case of Statewide Routes, they represent the shortest distances you could expect to travel on the route, almost always the "red" option.

In the case of Local Explorations or Tours, they also represent the shortest possible distance you could expect to cover, excluding detours.

Since the routes and tours are designed to be traveled in whole, in part, or indeed not at all, the mileages are given as much for passing interest as for their practical value.

For routes and tours starting or finishing at Los Angeles, the mileages are measured from the edge, not the center, of that vast connurbation.

Something for Everyone

Getting the most from your guide

Here is a *small* selection of ideas for enjoying California opened up by this guide, aimed at a range of needs and tastes. The list is just a start: the guide offers many, many more ideas for what really matters: suiting *yourself*. You'll find that it takes into account not only your tastes, but how much time you have.

Sun, sand, surf and stars
Local *Explorations*: 15, 16 *and* 17.

The classic tourist experience
California Overall: 8.

California the social laboratory, plus natural California in a nutshell
San Francisco city section plus Local *Explorations*: 1.

Wine country
Local *Explorations*: 6 *and* 7.

The simple life, away from it all
Local *Explorations*: 18.

Walking, climbing, and the great outdoors
California Overall: 3 *plus* Local *Explorations*: 3.

Historical discovery, without the crowds
California Overall: 2, *in fall*.

Gastronomy, plus an obligatory national park
California Overall: 4 *plus* Local *Explorations*: 13 *and* 14.

Exhilarating coastal drive, magnificent landscape
California Overall: 5.

A taste of desert
Local *Explorations* 11 *and* 12.

CALIFORNIA: *an Introduction*

California has been exciting travelers since it was first sighted by Spanish explorers in the 16thC. The subsequent discovery of gold and the glory years of Hollywood did nothing to diminish the cherished notion of California as the land at the end of the rainbow: a place where fortunes could be made and where lives – be they astronomically wealthy, immeasurably decadent, or madly unconventional – could be lived to the full, with some of America's most beautiful scenery as a backdrop.

Described by author Tom Wolfe as America's "social laboratory," California gave birth to beatniks in the 1950s, hippies and mass political protest in the 1960s, gay and lesbian liberation in the 1970s, and the New Age during the 1980s. Through films, genre fiction and music, California has consistently set the agenda for modern American culture.

Yet there is far more history here than most people realize: the rock paintings and complex basketry of Native Americans; Spanish missions; the ghost towns of the gold rush; and even the remains of a 19thC Russian settlement among the remnants of earlier eras that take their place alongside the state's more modern images: the Golden Gate Bridge, Beverly Hills and Disneyland. What's more, in an area more than eight hundred miles long and over two hundred miles wide, California embraces beaches, forests, mountains, deserts, the most modern of modern cities and the most rural of rural towns – diverse and extreme landscapes which few other places can match.

I have been making regular visits to California for ten years and still find something to surprise me each time. The thoughtfully devised and exhaustively researched routes, explorations or tours described in this book are based on my experiences: following them will allow you to discover much more of the Golden State on a single trip than most people find over several visits.

Do any traveling at all in California and you will find the variations to be truly staggering. The state's two major urban areas alone could hardly be more different. In the south, Los Angeles sprawls over hills, through valleys, and alongside the ocean, making mincemeat of the usual definition of a city. Nonetheless, LA's affluent sections are, for many, what California is all about: million-dollar homes, swimming-pools fringed by palm trees, and beaches frequented by the bronzed and beautiful. Four hundred miles north, San Francisco is the total opposite: a compact, cultured and easily walked city that has a liberal and bohemian air, and rewards its residents with fabulous views every time they walk down the street.

Bear in mind that American cities can be dangerous places. Particularly in Los Angeles, you should take care to avoid the run-down areas where even the local police fear to tread. Always heed local advice and note the warnings given in this book.

• *Near Santa Barbara.*

Away from the state's big cities, the population thins remarkably. Journey along the coast and you'll pass from surfer-filled beaches to wave-lashed granite cliffs and secluded coves where seals are a more common sight than people. Head inland, passing immense swathes of farmland and groves of giant sequoia trees, and you will reach the Sierra Nevada mountains. Historically, the mountains were the great obstacle to migration into California from the east. They still form a formidable – but magnificent – natural barrier. From the mountains, Mount Whitney, the highest point in the continental U.S., looks down over the lowest – and often the hottest – place in the country: Death Valley, one of the strange and severe desert regions which stretch to the Nevada border.

Even if Californians have become oblivious to their state's extraordinary scenery, they still love to eat – and eating in California means never ordering the same meal twice. The state not only produces with finesse American staples such as ribs, steaks and burgers, but harbors the hallowed citadels of California cuisine, where the best of the state's home-grown produce is combined with the imaginations of some the world's most inventive chefs. In addition, every town has a plethora of quality Japanese, Chinese and Mexican restaurants, and spreading rapidly are the Salvadorean bakeries and Vietnamese fast-food stands that reflect just two of California's newer ethnic communities.

Food is invariably served in large amounts and at reasonable prices. To aid digestion, the state has native wines of a quality often matching those of France and dozens of micro-breweries producing beers of merit. Remarkably for such a unique and popular region, California does not burn a hole in the foreign visitor's pocket. Car rental is cheap, and whether you pass the night in a roadside motel or in a Victorian bed-and-breakfast inn overlooking the ocean, prices everywhere compare favorably – and standards are sky high.

Mick Sinclair

FOR OVERSEAS VISITORS

Climate: when and where to go

Forget everything you've heard about California being a subtropical paradise where the sun never stops shining and rainfall is unknown. The state is big and varied enough to span several different climatic zones and only southern California comes anywhere near matching the travel brochures' hyperbole.

Even in the south there are fluctuations. On the coast, San Diego and its surroundings enjoy very warm but largely humidity-free summers and mild winters. By contrast, Los Angeles has sunny days year-round but becomes unpleasantly hot and sticky during the summer, and in winter is prone to torrential rainfall. The city's notorious smog is at its worst from July to September. During the hot and dry summer months, the deserts of inland southern California veer from uncomfortable to intolerable; desert winters are well within human tolerance, though, and in springtime fabulous displays of blooming wildflowers bring many visitors to these severe regions.

In the north, San Francisco avoids extremes: its summers can be hot but are more often pleasantly warm; the winters are cool but seldom freezing. In common with the north coast, and much of the central coast, San Francisco is prone to fogs, which can bring a chilly, gray start to the sunniest day.

There is more fog, and generally colder and damper conditions, further north along the coast, although the summers here usually bring sunny, rain-free days. Inland, scorching summer temperatures are common in parts of the Gold Country, but winter can bring heavy snowfalls. Similar conditions prevail as you move east, rising through the foothills of the Sierra Nevada mountains. In these parts, the mild summer is the only time to enjoy walking and climbing in the alpine scenery; in winter, skiers take to the snow-covered slopes.

Overall, the best months to be in California are March to May and September and October, but don't despair if you cannot avoid the peak months of the summer or winter. Provided you pack a strong sunscreen for the southern summer and carry an umbrella in the northern winter, you will find that only the deserts (in summer) and the mountains (in winter, unless you plan to ski) are off-limits.

Clothing

If you intend to travel widely around the state, pack with the varying climates in mind. In the hotter, sunnier parts of the state, wear a hat, loose fitting clothes and smother yourself liberally with a powerful sunscreen. Farther north, a warm summer's day can give way to a surprisingly chilly evening; be sure to have a sweater or jacket handy.

Except in the most elegant restaurants, California dress is always casual, but barefeet and swimsuits are seldom acceptable away from the beach. The national and state parks, and much of the undeveloped coastline, are best seen by walking, so bring suitable footwear.

Documentation

Citizens of the U.K., and those of most Western European countries, need a full, valid passport to enter the U.S. Provided the trip is less than 90 days and you are in possession of a return ticket, it is not necessary to have a U.S. visa provided the visa-waiver form (issued on the plane) is completed. Customs and immigration forms are also given to passengers prior to landing.

These forms require simple information, such as the duration of your trip and the address where you are spending the first night. Provided it is clear that you are visiting the U.S. on vacation and are not planning to live or work in the country, there should be no problems when these forms are handed in at the immigration and customs control points on arrival.

Should you be arriving for an unusually long stay, it is likely that immigration officials will ask to see your return ticket and evidence of how you will be supporting yourself during your trip: a wad of credit cards and/or travelers checks is what they like to see. If you are intending to live or work in the U.S., you will need proof that you can do this legally.

Most major airlines on transatlantic routes run a computer immigration check of passengers' names as they check-in for the flight. Provided you're not a convicted criminal or have previously been refused entry to the U.S., a sticker will be attached to your passport which will speed your passage through immigration control when you land.

• *Lifeguards, Hermosa Beach, LA.*

Medical and travel insurance
Being covered by medical insurance is not compulsory when visiting the U.S., but it is an essential precaution. With no public health service to speak of, U.S. medical bills can quickly become astronomical for even minor medical attention. Most insurance policies combine health coverage with general travel insurance (which covers eventualities such as cancellations, delays and theft of luggage and valuables). Expect to spend around $45 per person for two weeks of adequate coverage.

Money
Before arriving in the U.S., convert most of your spending money to U.S. dollar travelers' checks and the remainder to American cash. Travelers' checks can be used as cash in most places of business: restaurants, hotels, shops and so on. Once in the U.S., trying to convert foreign currency to dollars is almost impossible outside the major international airports and a few banks in Los Angeles and San Francisco (see **Currency**, below). It can also be difficult to convert dollar travelers' checks to cash in a U.S. bank: if you try to do this you'll need to show ID and may have to pay a fee.

Currency
Notes are of identical size: $20, $10, $5 and $1; coins are variously-sized: 25¢ (a "quarter"), 10¢ (a "dime"), 5¢ (a "nickel") and 1¢ (a "penny").

Import duty
Duty-free allowances for non-U.S. citizens arriving in the U.S. include a quart (just under a liter) of alcoholic spirits or wine, 200 cigarettes or 50 cigars, and duty-free gifts to the value of $100. Anyone carrying duty-free alcohol into the country must be aged 21 or over (17 or over in the case of tobacco). Among a long list of items not permitted into the U.S. are meat, fruit and plants.

Local customs:
what to expect, how to behave
Americans in general are noted for their hospitality and Californians are no exception. Most of the people that you will encounter will be friendly and helpful, keen to tell you how wonderful California is.

Service in restaurants can be extremely prompt and efficient, and the person serving you will often appear to take a deep, personal interest in your enjoyment of the meal. This is largely due to the tip they are expecting you to leave – 15-20 percent of the bill is common. Tipping on a similar scale is also expected in bars and taxis; any porters who carry your luggage will expect around a dollar per bag.

In many situations, foreign visitors will find it helpful to speak (or to try to speak) some American-English. If not, the person with whom you're attempting to converse may fail to understand what you are talking about (in extreme cases, they may not even realize that you are speaking English). Among the most obvious language differences are "rest room" or "bathroom" for WC and "getting" the "check" for paying the bill once you are "through" (finished).

• *Landing at* LA – *for a bird's-eye-view of tailbacks.*

GETTING THERE

By air from outside the U.S.
Virtually all major scheduled airlines in Europe have non-stop services to Los Angeles, California's busiest international terminal. The best-priced fares from the European mainland will, however, involve a stop, and often a change of plane, in London.

From London, American, British Airways, United and Virgin airlines fly non-stop to Los Angeles (United also fly non-stop to San Francisco), and three other U.S. airlines – Continental, Delta and Northwest – have services from London to California which land at one or more U.S. cities on the way. Stopping obviously means a longer overall journey time (typically adding four or five hours to the ten hours of a non-stop trip) but can save money and bring greater flexibility as to where you land in California – many of the state's smaller towns being well-served by U.S. domestic flights.

Particularly in summer, charter companies have frequent flights from London and U.K. airports traveling non-stop to Los Angeles and, less regularly, non-stop to San Diego and Oakland (for San Francisco).

It is a money-saving rule to book through a travel agent or discount flight specialist rather than directly with an airline. Doing so enables you to sift through the various options on a route where competition between operators is intense.

Prices are seasonal (summer is most expensive, winter is least, fall and spring fall between), although not all airlines raise or lower their fares on the same dates: one may have implemented its top-rate summer fares while another is still offering cheaper spring fares, for example. Traveling on Fridays and weekends will always cost more than doing so during the week.

The various Apex fares, which usually entail booking and paying for your ticket a few weeks in advance and making a journey longer than a week but less than a month, are generally the cheapest type of scheduled fare. Charter fares (most prevalent in summer) can be lower than Apex fares, but offer less choice of travel dates.

Slack periods – typically January to March – may also see major airlines offering greatly reduced fares on certain flights: these are widely advertized in newspapers.

From within the U.S., by air
Most major U.S. airlines have non-stop flights from the East Coast to Los Angeles and to San Francisco, some also fly non-stop to San Diego. Fares vary greatly according to season, day and time of travel. Avoiding national holidays and weekends in high summer will reduce cost. Look through the Sunday newspaper travel section advertizements for the latest bargains.

The closer you are to California, the more choices there will be. A number of small airlines have strong route networks in the West Coast and Southwest states. These are also likely to bring extra choice of landing points within California, though fares are as variable as those from the East Coast.

By rail
More time-consuming and more expensive than air travel, but potentially much more memorable, several evocatively

• *Alternative transport, California style.*

named transcontinental train routes reach California from Chicago, calling at cities in the South and Midwest on journeys lasting two to three days. Daily from Chicago, the *California Zephyr* departs for San Francisco via Denver; the *Southwest Chief* leaves for Los Angeles via Albuquerque, and the *Desert Wind* sets off for Los Angeles via Denver and Las Vegas. Three times a week, the *Sunset Route* travels from Chicago to Los Angeles via St Louis, Dallas, New Orleans, Houston and El Paso.

The nationwide toll-free number for train information is 1-800 USA RAIL.

By bus

Long-distance bus travel in the U.S.A. is not for the faint-hearted. Greyhound buses have regular services to Los Angeles and San Francisco from all over the U.S. and from most of the rest of California. However, journey times are three long days and nights of continuous motoring from the East Coast – with the view restricted to dreary main highways and meals limited to run-of-the-mill Greyhound station cafeterias.

Periodic special deals, such as half-price midweek travel, can reduce costs but do nothing to improve comfort. More information on prices and schedules are available by calling the local Greyhound station.

• *Alternative transport, Julian style.*

GETTING AROUND

With car rental and gasoline costs far lower than they are in Europe, and the state's public transportation network woefully inadequate, traveling by car is undoubtedly the best way to see California.

Car rental

Almost always, it is cheapest and least problematic to arrange to rent a car before arrival (many airlines offer cut-rate car rental as an inducement to buying a transatlantic ticket from them) although all the major international car rental firms, and smaller local ones, have desks at the airports and offices throughout the state. It is at the airport that you will pick up your pre-booked car.

Driving in California (and the rest of the U.S.) is legal with a valid licence of most European countries, or with a valid International Driver's Licence. Be warned that would-be renters aged under 25, and anyone without a credit card to prove their credit-worthiness, may encounter problems when renting in the U.S.

When renting, always read the small print of the agreement, especially if you intend to leave California from a different city to that which you arrived (some companies don't allow for this and you might incur extra charges). Be aware, too, of the Collision Damage Waiver (CDW), a compulsory form of insurance that can add considerably to costs.

Roads and driving regulations

Generally, California's roads are of a high standard. Multi-laned Interstate Highways, free of traffic lights and gas stations (you'll need to leave the Interstate to refuel), are the speediest routes – though there is a speed limit of 65mph or 55mph throughout their length – between major cities. The forerunners of the Interstates, the State Highways, are still the main link between the minor communities. They are slower to drive on but are much more likely to pass through fine scenery. In very isolated areas, county roads – sometimes little more than bumpy dirt roads – carry a modest amount of traffic through forests, around mountains, and across stretches of desert.

At $1.20-$1.40 a gallon, gasoline is extremely cheap and service stations are common in all but the most sparsely populated regions. Distances are posted in miles, although distances may also be expressed in time – i.e. how long it takes to drive to a particular place. On-the-spot fines can be imposed for speeding and an extremely unfavorable view is taken of drinking and driving: do this and you could well find yourself in jail.

Domestic air travel

If you are a foreign visitor and California is only one of several stops on a trip around the U.S.A., it's worthwhile investigating the latest internal air pass deals offered by transatlantic airlines. These passes permit either a set number of domestic flights in the U.S. or an unlimited number of domestic flights within a certain time period.

Such passes are unlikely to save money on flights within California, however, where the local newspapers are full of discounted air fares for intra-state travel. If your car rental agreement makes it feasible, these flights can save much driving time. A remarkable number of small California towns are served by regular flights from Los Angeles and San Francisco and, to a lesser extent, from Sacramento, San Diego, and Fresno.

Public transportation

From motels to drive-in churches, everything in California is designed with the car – and drivers – in mind. Having learned to drive shortly after they learned to walk, many Californians have never been on a bus or a train and typically regard public transportation as being strictly for the very poor – or the very eccentric. It is possible to see much of California by public transportation, but it is not easy and is seldom cheap.

With some exceptions, such as between Los Angeles and San Diego, very limited train services operate in California and many of the towns linked to the rail network see just two or three trains a day (bizarrely, some of the train routes are actually covered by buses).

A more common form of long-distance travel is the Greyhound bus. While more widespread and frequent than trains, Greyhound services are skeletal in rural areas and often you will arrive (or have to depart) at inconvenient times. Also, many of the state's more spectacular regions are well off the Greyhound routes.

With the exception of San Francisco, which has an excellent public transportation network, getting around cities without a car is also difficult. This is especially true in Los Angeles – though not impossible, provided you study local timetables carefully.

Taxis

Taxis can be hailed in the street though it is more common to phone for one: many companies are listed in the Yellow Pages. Staff in hotels, restaurants and some bars will usually call a taxi for you. Fares are reasonable, averaging around $1.80 a mile, but are prohibitive over long journeys such as those from airports. Don't forget to tip the driver around 15 per cent of the fare.

• *On duty, San Francisco.*

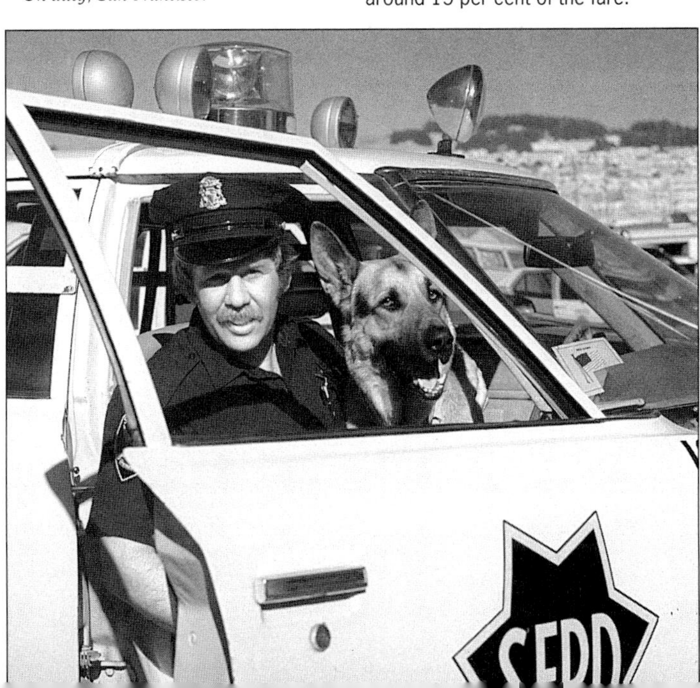

Banks and currency exchange
California's banking hours are Monday to Thursday 10 am to 3 pm, Friday 10 am to 5.30 pm. Some major branches also open on Saturday 10 am to 1 pm.

Bear in mind that very few banks will exchange foreign currency. Those that do, and other offices that will exchange currency are: **in San Francisco**: American Foreign Exchange, 315 Sutter St; tel. 415 391 9913; Bank of America, 345 Montgomery St; tel. 415 622 2451; Thomas Cook, 100 Grant Ave; tel. 415 362 3452; **in Los Angeles**: Bank of America, 555 S. Flower St, Downtown; tel. 213 228 2721.

Breakdowns
If your rented car breaks down, call the emergency number fixed to the dashboard. In most cases, someone will soon appear with a replacement car. To minimize the risk of breakdown in remote areas (this is essential in desert regions), you should ensure that the vehicle is running properly before starting out. Be certain, also, to carry adequate provisions to cover unscheduled delays – free checklists of essential supplies for touring remote areas are provided by local Visitors Bureaus.

Credit cards
Credit cards are a standard form of payment all over the U.S., and all the major ones – American Express (AE), Diners Club (DC) Mastercard (MC) and Visa (V) – are widely accepted; to a lesser extent, so are minor ones such as Carte Blanche (CB) and Discover (DS). In many instances, such as paying for accommodation or for a meal in an expensive restaurant (ordinary roadside diners often don't accept credit cards), it is more common to pay a bill with plastic than with cash. In fact, a person with no credit card/s is likely to be viewed with some suspicion.

Consulates
Most embassies in the U.S. are based in Washington D.C. For passport emergencies and other visitor's needs, most major countries have consular offices in San Francisco:
France 540 Bush Street; tel. 415 395 4330.
Germany 1960 Jackson St.; tel. 415 775 1061.
Ireland 655 Montgomery St., Suite 930; tel. 415 392 4214.
Netherlands 1 Maritime Plaza; tel. 415 981 6454.
Norway Two Embarcadero Center; tel. 415 986 0766.
U.K. 1 Sansome St., Suite 850; tel. 415 981 3030.
Sweden 120 Montgomery St.; tel. 415 788 2631.

Other consular offices can be found in Los Angeles and San Diego; their addresses are in the local phone books.

Drinking and smoking regulations
To buy and consume alcohol in California, you need to be aged 21 or over, and may well be asked for proof of age. Once it is established, you can imbibe legally. Most restaurants have full licenses, and, under California law, both restaurants and bars can serve alcohol daily from 6am to 2am; most, though, keep much shorter hours.

In health-conscious California, cigarette smokers tend to be regarded as extremely unevolved specimens. Smoking is strictly forbidden on all public transportation; many restaurants and movie theaters, and even some bars, consign smokers to designated areas. The good news for nictotine addicts, however, is that cigarettes are much cheaper in the U.S. than in Europe.

Electricity
The U.S. electrical supply is 110 volts (60 cycles) and appliances use two-prong plugs. European appliances are designed for 220 volts (50 cycles) and can only be used with an adapter. These can be bought before leaving (though first make sure the adapter is suitable for the U.S.) or in the U.S.

Emergencies
For fire, police or ambulance, dial 911 and ask for the service you require.

Free publications
Free publications on every subject under the sun are to be found on street corners, in hotels, bars and restaurants, and stacked high in bookstores. The least interesting among them are the ad-packed tourist-aimed magazines scattered through hotel lobbies: there is much more useful information to be

• *Opposite: advertising an annual festival.*

PEPSI
Pierfest
92
BEACH
HUNTINGTON
WARNING
BUSINESS WATCH
PROGRAM IN FORCE
PROHIBITED
BEYOND THIS POINT
BICYCLES, SKATEBOARDS,
SKATES OR OTHER
PEDESTRIAN OBSTRUCTIONS
ON SIDEWALKS;
H.B.M.C.
10.20.040 10.84.160 12.32.010

• *Souvenir license plates, Downtown San Francisco.*

gleaned from the newspapers which serve the local community. This is especially true in the major cities, where such publications carry comprehensive events listings. If you are in San Francisco, look for the *San Francisco Bay Guardian* and *SF Weekly*; in Los Angeles, for *LA Weekly*.

Lost checks, passports, luggage

Foreign visitors should read the instructions which come with their travelers checks: they explain exactly how to replace them if they are lost or stolen. Replacing a stolen passport is much harder and begins with a visit or phone call to the nearest appropriate consular office. Those in San Francisco are listed under **Consulates** (see page 22). Reclaiming lost luggage depends on where you lost (or think you lost) it. The local phone book will have a section listing the relevant numbers to trace luggage lost at airports, on city buses, Greyhound buses, and trains.

Maps and tourist information

Virtually every California community has a Visitors' Bureau or Chamber of Commerce able to provide free maps, brochures and information. These offices are usually easy to find and their addresses are always in the phone book. Most keep regular business hours; those in major cities also open at weekends.

In San Francisco, the central point for information is the Visitor Information Center, on the lower level of Hallidie Plaza by the junction of Market and Powell Streets (open Mon-Fri 9am-5.30pm, Sat 9am-3pm, Sun 10am-2pm; tel. 415 391 2000). Doing a similar job for Los Angeles is the Visitor Information Center, 695 S. Figueroa St., Downtown (open Mon-Fri 8am-5pm, Sat 8.30am-5pm; tel. 213 689 8822).

Maps and general information on the whole state are provided by the California Office of Tourism, 801 K Street, Suite 1600, Sacramento, CA 95814; tel. 916 322 2881.

Medical matters

Doctors are listed under "Physicians" in the phone book; most hospitals in major cities have emergency rooms, but if you're dealing with a serious injury call an ambulance by dialing the emergency number, 911. Dentists can be found by looking under "Dentist Referral Services" in the phone book, and calling the relevant number. You will have to pay for all of these services. Keep the receipts to make insurance claims when you return home. Information about late-night and (in the bigger cities) 24-hour pharmacies can also be found in the phone book.

Motor clubs

Most European motoring organizations have links with the American Automobile Association (AAA), to which both of California's main motoring clubs – the California State Automobile Association (CSAA) and the Automobile Club of Southern California (ACSC) – are affiliated. With offices in most towns (listed in the phone book), the CSAA and CSAA have an assortment of free maps and literature awaiting any suitably affiliated driver who asks for them.

Postal and telephone service

All California towns have post offices, most of them open Mon to Fri 8.30 am-5 pm, Sat 8 am-noon. As well as from post offices, stamps can be bought (slightly more expensively) from vending machines in some hotel lobbies and in some shops. To mail a letter, drop it into one of the blue mail boxes – which to foreigners can look suspiciously like rubbish bins – standing on most street corners.

Public telephones in working order are found on most streets and it's common to step into a restaurant, bar, or hotel lobby simply to use the public phone. By most foreign standards, local calls are very cheap – 20¢ for three minutes – although phoning a number just a few miles away will often be classed as a long distance call and will be much more expensive.

Some of the budget motels and hotels offer free local calls from their in-room phones. More commonly, though, in-room phone charges are much higher than those of public phones.

Emergency calls (dial 911) and calls to the operator (dial 0) or the international operator (dial 1 800 874 4000) are free.

Public holidays

Banks and all public offices will be closed on all the following holidays; however, some shops may be open on some of these days: New Year's Day (January 1), Martin Luther King's Birthday (third Monday in January), Lincoln's Birthday (February 12), Washington's Birthday (third Monday in February), Memorial Day (last Monday in May), Independence Day (July 4), Labor Day (first Monday in September), Columbus Day (second Monday in October), Veteran's Day (November 11), Thanksgiving Day (fourth Tuesday in November), Christmas Day (December 25).

Rush hours

Even the six-lane freeways of Los Angeles cannot allow traffic to move faster than a snail's pace when the California rush hour hits: 7.30 am to 9.30 am and 3.30 pm to 6 pm are the hours to avoid the main routes into and out of business areas. If you are using local buses at these times, be ready for a crush and a slow journey.

Sales tax

A state sales tax of 8.25 percent is added to the marked price of everything sold in California's shops.

Shopping and business hours

Going shopping in California can mean anything from cruising gigantic air-conditioned malls to stocking up with groceries from a corner store. Consequently, opening hours vary greatly but most shops in towns open Mon to Fri 9 or 10 am to 5 or 6 pm, with some also open during the evening and on Sat mornings. Office hours are typically Mon to Fri 8 or 9 am to 4 or 5 pm. For bank hours, see **Banks**.

Time

All of California uses Pacific Standard Time, three hours behind the East Coast, eight hours behind the U.K. and nine hours behind the rest of western Europe. Daylight Saving Time begins on the last Sunday in April (clocks go forward an hour) and ends on the last Sunday in October (clocks go back an hour).

Washrooms

Public washrooms are rarely seen in the streets but are plentiful (and free) in public buildings and in the developed sections of state and national parks. Look for a sign that says "rest room" or "bathroom," rather than "toilet."

A BRIEF HISTORY OF CALIFORNIA

The first Californians

Divided into more than a hundred linguistically and culturally diverse communities, their lifestyles designed to suit the varying local terrain and climate, it is believed that around 300,000 Native Americans lived in California in the period immediately prior to European discovery (their ancestors crossing from Siberia some 6,000 years earlier).

Despite the differences between them, the Native American communities traded peaceably with one another and there were none of the great tribal conflicts (in fact, the California settlements were too small to constitute "tribes" in the usual sense) that took place elsewhere in North America.

The native population was to decline rapidly through the first years of California's European settlement, chiefly through contact with diseases, such as measles and smallpox, to which the indigenous inhabitants lacked immunity. As California became a U.S. possession and the gold rush brought tens of thousands of new settlers, demand for land resulted in most Native Americans being forcibly removed from their ancestral homelands and resettled on reservations.

European sightings, landings and settlements

In 1533, a Spanish expedition under Hernando Cortés made the first European sighting of Baja (or "lower") California. Nine years later, Rodriguez Cabrillo became the first European to drop anchor off the present-day state of California, pausing first at what was later to be named San Diego Bay.

Believing California to be an island, the Spanish showed little interest in establishing settlements on the new land. In 1742, however, California was found to be part of the North American mainland and, in order to deter territorial advances by rival colonial powers, a series of 21 Franciscan missions was founded in California, part of the Sacred Expedition under the leadership of Padre Junipero Serra. Spread between San Diego and Sonoma, each mission was a day's horse-ride from the next. By co-opting Native American labor and importing vast herds of cattle, several of the Californian missions not only attained self-sufficiency but also became extremely rich.

Despite Russian, French and British (in 1579, Francis Drake had landed in California, claiming it for Queen Elizabeth I of England) interest in California, Spanish control was eventually ended by the *Californios*, mostly California-born Mexicans, who in 1822, with Spain too tied up in European conflicts to effectively govern its overseas possessions, declared themselves under Mexican rule. Subsequently, several *Californio* families attained great wealth as large land grants were handed out by the Mexican government. The Spanish missions were secularized in 1834.

American interest grows

Few U.S. citizens attempted to make the difficult journey from the eastern states to California (with no known routes across the Sierra Nevada mountains, the safest passage entailed a three-month sea voyage around Cape Horn) but those who arrived acquired great influence by marrying into the leading families and displaying the business acumen that the *Californios* lacked.

In June 1846, with the expansionist dreams of Manifest Destiny determining U.S. foreign policy, a band of U.S. soldiers took over a poorly defended fort in Sonoma and declared California an independent republic (the so-called Big Bear Republic). This state of affairs only lasted six days but, by July, U.S. troops had occupied most major Californian settlements, encountering minimal resistance.

California formally became a U.S. possession under the terms ending the American-Mexican War in 1847, part of a deal that gave the U.S. control over the American West for $15 million.

The gold-rush

The discovery of gold on January 24, 1848, 50 miles east of the future site of Sacramento, triggered one of the greatest population movements ever seen, increasing California's (non-native) population from 7,000 to 100,000 in four years, and setting it on the road to becoming a powerful, independently-wealthy region. Such were its riches that California was allowed to forego the usual transitional stage as a frontier territory and received full statehood in 1850.

• *Street politics, San Francisco.*

The need for men and mining machinery to be brought in by sea enabled San Francisco to grow into a major city, increasing its population fifty-fold within two years. Other settlements were founded on the sheltered bays of the north coast and inland river ports such as Sacramento and Stockton evolved into important centers.

In the gold-producing areas, chiefly in the western foothills of the Sierra Nevada mountains, scores of jerry-built new towns appeared. Getting rich quick was the sole concern in these rough-and-ready communities and what little law existed tended to be administered by vigilante mobs.

Within three years, however, the gold rush was over. The rivers where gold flakes had first been discovered had yielded all they were going to and it was company-owned mines – manned by a steady workforce – which provided the only access to the gold-bearing quartz still embedded in the hillsides.

The rise of southern California

As northern California enjoyed the sudden growth and vast profits of the gold rush, southern California remained a hot, dry and neglected outpost, where Los Angeles and San Diego each held populations of just a few thousand. Even the Big Four – a quartet of Sacramento merchants-turned-rail-barons whose transcontinental railway linked California to the rest of the nation in 1869, making them the richest and most powerful men in the state – saw little point (in other words, saw little profit) in developing the southern cities.

Seizing the initiative, a band of Angelenos bribed a rival railroad company to extend its tracks from Arizona to Los Angeles, and thereby to the Pacific. The line was duly completed in 1886. Accessible at last, southern California began vigorously promoting itself as a Mediterranean paradise, and heavily-subsidized rail fares brought tens of thousands of new settlers from the east.

In 1892, the discovery of oil near Los Angeles gave birth to what were to become gigantic aeronautical and automobile industries and helped bring about a sea-change in California's population pattern: the prospect of guaranteed employment convincing many northern Californians, rendered jobless by a post-gold rush depression, to move south.

Also eyeing southern California at this time were the visionaries and opportunists of the fledgling American film industry, hindered on the east coast by patent laws and a miserable climate. The film-makers, and subsequently thousands of would-be actors, writers and producers in search of fortune and fame, invaded a small farming town called Hollywood, then separated from Los Angeles by 8 miles of bean fields. By the 1920s, the Hollywood film industry was generating a billion dollars a year and employing 100,000 people. The new mansions spread across the Hollywood Hills housed the screen stars that made southern California synonymous with great wealth and physical perfection.

Recent California

Many of the social changes that shook American society during the 1960s had their roots in California. The Free Speech Movement, formed by students of the University of California at Berkeley in 1964, was the stimulus for nationwide campus revolts and anti-Vietnam War protests. San Francisco, where beatniks had shocked middle class society during the 1950s, became the world's number one hippie haven in 1967. And the ultra-militant Black Panthers was formed in neighboring Oakland in 1968.

However, in electing Ronald Reagan as state governor in 1967, Californians showed themselves in general to be less than the full-bloodied revolutionaries outsiders often took them to be.The grisly activities of the Charles Manson "family," recruited among San Francisco's street hippies, put paid to the peace and love movement, and the Watts Riot of 1965, when a black inner-city community of Los Angeles fought a six-day battle with police and the National Guard, was a sharp reminder that the wealth being accrued in the city of superstars was not percolating downwards.

With its abundant natural resources and reputation for technical innovation such as the booming computer industry of so-called Silicon Valley in the early 1980s – California has often seemed immune from economic recession. Lately, though, the loss of government contracts has forced the state's aerospace industries to reduce their workforces, California's major car manufacturers have made massive redundancies, while the high business taxes levied by the state government to help finance conservation have encouraged some Californian companies to relocate to other states. Silicon Valley, too, has suffered a downturn as the world computer market has matured.

KEY DATES

1533 First European (Spanish) sighting of California.
1542 First European (Spanish) landing in California.
1579 Francis Drake lands, claiming California for England.
1769 California's first Spanish mission founded at San Diego.
1846 The Big Bear Republic, proclaiming California as an independent republic, lasts six days.
1847 California becomes a U.S. possession.
1848 Gold discovered.
1850 California becomes a state.
1869 Completion of the transcontinental railroad, linking California to the rest of the U.S.
1892 Sierra Club formed, California's first organization dedicated to preserving the state's natural areas.
1906 A huge earthquake, followed by a three-day fire, destroys much of San Francisco.
1913 Cecil B. de Mille's, *The Squaw Man*, becomes the first feature film completed in Hollywood.
1932 Olympic Games held in Los Angeles.
1962 California becomes the nation's most populous state.
1971 Sixty-five killed when an earthquake rocks the San Fernando Valley, near Los Angeles.
1984 Los Angeles again hosts the Olympic Games, and breaks all records in the marketing of them.
1992 Following the acquittal of four white police officers accused of assaulting a black motorist, rioting in Los Angeles leaves 58 dead and causes $1 billion in damage.

The Californian Character

Due to Sierran gold, Hollywood movies, or Silicon Valley computer chips, California has long been regarded as the American promised land. The one thing that has always united its exceptionally transient population has been the search for a better life. The few Californians who can trace their lineage back to the early pioneers band together in special clubs and speak of nine decades of history as Europeans might speak of nine centuries. Rarely will you meet anyone whose links with the Golden State go back more than one generation and, among younger Californians, ethnic roots in south-east Asia or in south or central America are fast becoming more common than U.S. ancestry.

To most Californians, though, history really is bunk. The potential of the present has always been uppermost in the Californian mind. To get rich (once by panning for gold; lately on the money markets of the Pacific Rim); to become famous (traditionally through films, more recently via rock music); to reach a higher level of consciousness (California was embracing eastern mysticism by the 1920s; sixty years on, the New Age movement was in full-swing): California has been the place to do it, and to do it now while the rest of the world looks on.

From the surfers of the southern beaches to the plaid-shirted lumberworkers of the northern forests, Californians come in many guises. The typical face of California, though, is one you might never notice. It's the one that has provided the bedrock support for archly conservative politicians – California-born ones like Richard Nixon and adopted ones like Ronald Reagan – and it belongs to the white, Anglo-American middle classes who occupy the bungalow-lawn-and-two-car-garage tract housing estates of the Golden State's many square-miles of suburbia.

Key cultural themes

California has always been the place where anything is possible but many Anglo-American residents view the modern state as a land where nightmares, rather than dreams, are about to become reality. The riots that swept through Los Angeles in April 1992 stunned the outside world; to Californians, though, they were an inevitable expression of the rage that has built up behind the state's carefully nurtured facade of wealth and opportunity for all.

• *Busker, Fisherman's Wharf, San Francisco.*

It is not just violent civil disorder that makes Anglo-Californians, who have been the state's dominant group since the end of Mexican rule, feel threatened. Global recession and the job-losses following the post-Cold War reduction in weapons research – a mainstay of the Californian economy for years – have had an erosive effect on their free-spending lifestyles. Simultaneously, a decade of tax reductions has resulted in public services being pared to the bone and the state's educational system becoming severely under-funded. The solution for many has been simple: a move to Arizona or the states of the Pacific North West.

The growing exodus of Anglos is just one feature of contempory California's changing population pattern. Large sections of the major cities are entirely Spanish-speaking (Los Angeles, for example, holds the world's third largest Mexican community) while Laotians, Cambodians and Vietnamese are among the ethnic groups colonizing San Francisco's Chinatown district. The Chinese themselves have prospered sufficiently to start departing their traditional areas for middle-income suburbia.

Northern California

Between San Francisco and Crescent City
The Northern Coast

300 miles; map Kummerly + Frey California-Nevada

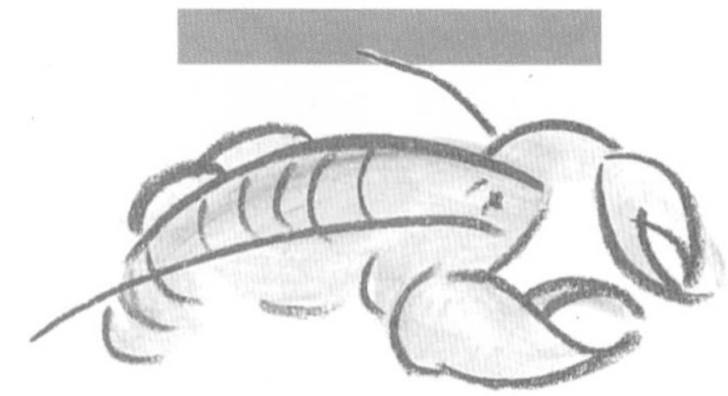

There is not a surfer-packed beach, a Spanish mission, a home of somebody rich and famous, or even very many sunny days to be found along California's North Coast. Instead, lonely coves, tortured bluffs and isolated fishing settlements – and fantastic groves of coastal redwoods, the world's tallest trees – fill the 400 miles between San Francisco and the Oregon border.

It is nature-loving adventurers who derive most enjoyment from the North Coast, and if the prospect of getting sweat on your brow or mud on your boots does not appeal, then you should spend your time elsewhere. Visitors should expect to get wet, too. The redwoods thrive because the North Coast has a cool, rainy climate, and the relatively dry period – from April to September – is the only sensible time to be here.

While this is one of the state's least-visited portions, the North Coast is by no means deserted. Many Californians arrive here for back-to-nature weekend breaks in rustic – but far from basic – country inns and to treat their tastebuds in the area's numerous award-winning restaurants. North Coast residents, on the other hand, are predominantly fishermen, farmers and lumber workers – the scourge of the North Coast's very active ecology movements. They who keep the region's archetypal American diners in business: places where I've often gorged on food at knock-down prices (especially seafood, served fresh and in very large quantities), while eavesdropping on scandalous small-town gossip.

Our fast route, Hwy-101, leaves San Francisco and clips the edge of the Wine Country – the Russian River Valley town of Healdsburg – before reaching rural inland towns such as Ukiah and Willits and continuing north through deepest redwood country. Switching between Hwy-101 and Hwy-1, our slower route, is relatively easy using one of the many minor roads linking Hwy-101 to the coast. Hwy-1 ploughs a continually engaging route beside the Pacific (where, in all but a few spots, the cold choppy waters are best left to the seals), linking small towns that hug sheltered bays but missing out on the redwoods until after merging with Hwy-101.

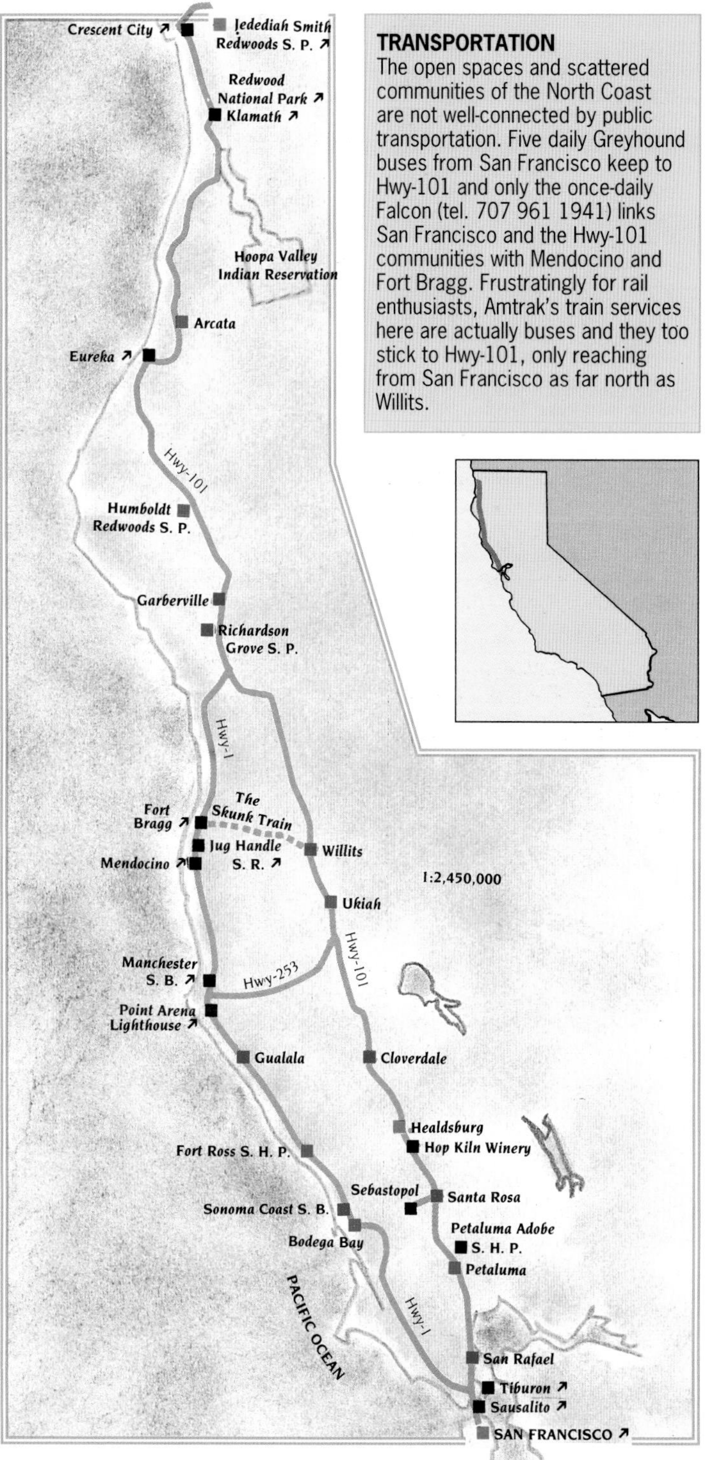

TRANSPORTATION

The open spaces and scattered communities of the North Coast are not well-connected by public transportation. Five daily Greyhound buses from San Francisco keep to Hwy-101 and only the once-daily Falcon (tel. 707 961 1941) links San Francisco and the Hwy-101 communities with Mendocino and Fort Bragg. Frustratingly for rail enthusiasts, Amtrak's train services here are actually buses and they too stick to Hwy-101, only reaching from San Francisco as far north as Willits.

SIGHTS & PLACES OF INTEREST

ARCATA 🛏 ✕

On Hwy-101, 7 miles N of Eureka Due to the students of Humboldt University, usually to be found patronizing the funky cafes and diners around the central plaza, diminutive Arcata has a zest that is rare along the north coast. Arcata might also be California's most ecologically-concerned town, with markers to its commitment to raising environmental consciousness easily found. As well as a large picnic area, the Arcata Community Forest has the **Historic Logging Trail**, which makes plain the detrimental impact of the lumber industry on California's woodlands. On Arcata Bay, a 75-acre waste dump has been transformed using treated sewerage into the **Arcata Marsh and Wildlife Preserve**, an animal and bird refuge viewable on several foot- and cycle-routes.

Less uniquely, Arcata was founded as a mining supply center during the gold rush and a sprinkling of its Victorian houses remains intact. Another remnant from these times is the three-story Jacoby's House, 791 Eighth Street, on the third floor of which the Redwoods Railroad Museum displays memorabilia from Arcata's formative years.

BODEGA BAY 🛏 ✕

On Hwy-1, 48 miles N of San Francisco. Home to a declining but substantial fishing fleet moored in its sheltered harbor, Bodega Bay is an affable little town

RECOMMENDED HOTELS

ARCATA

The Plough and the Stars, $$; *1800 27th Street; tel. 707 822 8236; credit cards, none.*

A small farmhouse, dating from 1862, converted into an atmospheric five-room (only two of which have private bathrooms) bed-and-breakfast inn. The 2-acre grounds unexpectedly include a croquet lawn, and the genial hosts serve brandy each evening.

BODEGA BAY

Inn at the Tides, $$$-$$$; 800 *Hwy-1; tel. 800 541 7788; credit cards,* AE, MC, V.

Spacious rooms equipped with fridges and coffee-makers – the more expensive ones have vaulted ceilings and fireplaces – in a series of lodges spread across a hillside overlooking the bay. A substantial breakfast buffet of fruit, croissants and rolls is included in the price. There is also a well-equipped health spa and a self-service laundry for guests' use.

Sea Horse Guest Ranch, $$; 2660 *Hwy-1; tel. 707 875 2721; credit cards,* MC, V.

A 700-acre working farm, complete with wandering chickens and fields of cattle, that offers a few tidy rooms in its main house. A great place for the back-to-nature experience without giving up too many modern comforts, the welcoming hosts also arrange guided horse rides for the truly adventurous, and provide a complimentary breakfast.

GARBERVILLE

The Benbow Inn, $$$-$$$; 445 *Lake Benbow Drive; tel. 707 929 2124; closed from Jan to April; cards,* MC, V.

A Tudor-style inn comes as a surprise in the northern California countryside, yet this riverside manor house 2 miles south of Garberville is exactly that, and it has been doing brisk business since the 1920s by catering to Americans who like pretending that they are English landed gentry. Besides the building itself and the complimentary afternoon tea and scones (and mulled wine on cool days), the big draw is the thickly-forested rural setting.

Herwood Forest Motel, $-$$; 814 *Redwood Drive; tel. 707 923 2124; credit cards,* MC, V.

The best motel option in motel-filled Garberville, the rooms are clean and comfortable. There is also a smallish pool and a self-service laundry.

GUALALA

Old Milano Hotel, $$-$$$; 99300 *Hwy-1; tel. 707 884 3256; credit cards,* AE, MC, V.

Opened in 1905 to provide accommodation for travelers on one of California's long-since vanished rail lines, the Old Milano Hotel enjoys a secluded bluff-top location and is stylishly furnished with carefully-selected which makes a decent overnight stop, and any visiting Alfred Hitchcock fans might amuse themselves by spotting the local buildings used by the director in his 1963 film, *The Birds,* although some of them are 5 miles inland, at the town of Bodega.

CLOVERDALE

On Hwy-101, 18 miles N of Healdsburg. Hwy-101 speeds through the center of Cloverdale, once a major producer of citrus fruits but now a rural hamlet better known for its January fiddle contest and its summer sheep-dog trials. The **Cloverdale Historical Museum**, 215 N. Cloverdale Boulevard, tenders the minutiae of days gone by, but if you like Californian wine, the tours and tastings at the Bandiera Winery, 115 Cherry Creek Road, are a greater temptation.

antiques. If the main building's rooms don't appeal, try the converted rail guard's van which sits in the gardens – it is big enough for a family of four and is equipped with a small kitchen.

HEALDSBURG

Madrona Manor, $$$ – $$$$; *1001 Westside Road; tel.* 707 433 4231; *credit cards,* AE, CB, DC, MC, V.

A hundred-year-old Gothic mansion set in an 8-acre landscaped estate drawing top marks for atmosphere and comfort. Of the main building's nine expansive rooms in-house, several have charming verandahs and even some of the furnishings of the manor's original owner. Slightly cheaper, though no less appealing rooms can be found in the converted out-buildings.

Healdsburg Inn on the Plaza, $$-$$$; *116 Matheson Street; tel.* 708 433 699; *credit cards,* AE, DC, MC, V.

From the floral prints on the walls to the claw-foot tubs in every bathroom, this completely renovated 1900 brick building on Healdsburg's main square is every inch the Californian bed-and-breakfast inn. The 12 antique-filled rooms lead off a large central staircase, at the top of which a roof garden provides a peaceful place in which to sun yourself. Besides the breakfast spread, complimentary afternoon coffee and cakes are served, followed by early-evening wine.

DETOUR – **HOP KILN WINERY**

Drive five miles south from Healdsburg to the **Hop Kiln Winery**, 6050 Westside Road, sited on a hillside above the Russian River and partly housed in a 1905 stone hop-drying barn. Try the wine and then enjoy a leisurely picnic beside the adjoining Griffin Vineyard – dating from 1880, it is one of California's oldest vineyards.

CRESCENT CITY

See Local Explorations: 2

EUREKA

See Local Explorations: 2

FORT BRAGG

See Local Explorations: 2

FORT ROSS STATE HISTORIC PARK

On Hwy-1, 27 miles N of Bodega Bay. As disparate imperial powers laid claim to various sections of California during the early 19thC, 95 Russians settled at what became Fort Ross. Growing vegetables for their scurvy-stricken countrymen in Alaska, hunting sea otters for their pelts and buying 125 miles of coastline from Native American tribes in return for three blankets and a few trinkets, the Russians aimed to establish a slavic toe-hold in the New World.

DETOUR – **HOOPA VALLEY INDIAN RESERVATION**

Sixty miles inland from Arcata, via highways 299 and 96, the Hoopa Valley Indian Reservation makes a worthwhile detour for the culturally curious. Be warned, though, that Indian reservations are rarely happy places, typified by poor housing and problems of alcoholism and unemployment. This one is no exception, although the collections of the Hoopa Tribal Museum (inside the Hoopa Shopping Center) go some way to justifying the journey. Sadly, perhaps, most white people come here solely to play high-stakes bingo – legal only on Indian reservations.

• *Fish-laden Northern California river.*

Building living quarters, warehouses and even an Orthodox Chapel in the traditional architecture of their homeland, the Russians also equipped the fort with sufficient weaponry to withstand attacks by the Spanish. As it turned out, the fort never fired a shot in anger. The colony was destroyed in 1841 by failing crops and otters being hunted to the point of extinction.

Ravaged by storms and earthquakes, the abandoned Fort Ross was eventually given state protection and its structures carefully restored to provide a fascinating glimpse into a forgotten facet of California's history. The isolated coastal setting can be very atmospheric, too, particularly when ocean mists rise over the fort's wooden fences and swirl about the park. One of the Russian-era cannons is fired, with an ear-splitting bang, daily at 3 pm.

GARBERVILLE 🛏 ✕

On Hwy-101, 62 miles S of Eureka. The fertile but hard-to-reach hillsides around Garberville became part of California's so-called Emerald Triangle during the 1970s and 1980s, a serious marijuana-growing area where cultivating the illegal crop promised profits far higher than traditional forms of agriculture. Following sustained Federal crackdowns, however, many of the more obvious trappings of the trade – such as Garberville's very specialized agricultural supply-shops – closed down.

More apparent for the casual visitor is Garberville's useful location between Humboldt Redwoods State Park and Richardson State Park, and the town has plenty of accommodation pitched at nature-loving tourists. Should you be heading north, the town also makes a useful starting point for an early morning assault on the Avenue of Giants (in Humboldt Redwood State Park). Hotel and motel space is at a premium only during the Garberville Rodeo, held each June, and the Rock and Reggae on the

DETOUR – **PETALUMA ADOBE STATE HISTORIC PARK**

Set on a low, barren hillside 4 miles east of Petaluma on Casa Grande Avenue, Petaluma Adobe State Historic Park holds the spacious two-story adobe building – restored and furnished in period style – raised in 1836 to sit at the heart of the 100-sq-mile land-holding of General Mariano Vallejo, a one-time commandant of San Francisco's presidio and among the richest and most powerful figures of California's Mexican era. The isolated adobe provides a moody impression of rancho life, but Vallejo himself is better remembered in Sonoma, a town which he founded (see Local Explorations: 7).

River music festival, which brings tens of thousands of revellers to Garberville during July.

GUALALA 🛏 ✕

On Hwy-1, 27 *miles* N *of* Fort Ross. Allegedly taking its name from a Spanish distortion of the Norse myth of Valhalla, isolated Gualala sits on a barren but oddly compelling stretch of coast. Other than the works of the town's surprisingly large artistic community on show in several galleries – and landmark buildings, such as the 1903 **Gualala Hotel**, now a popular bar – there's little to hold attention. Gualala is nicely placed, however, as an overnight stop between tours of Marin County and the Mendocino coast (see Local Explorations: 1 and 2).

HEALDSBURG 🛏 ✕

On Hwy-101, 20 *miles* N *of* Santa Rosa. With scores of beautifully restored century-old homes and a lovely Spanish-style plaza, Healdsburg makes a desirable short-term base before continuing north or winding coastwards to pick up Hwy-1. It also provides a genuine taste of the Wine Country that requires neither a detour off Hwy-101 nor doing battle with the crowds that pack the Napa and Sonoma Valleys (see Local Explorations: 6 and 7).

A dozen or so wineries lie in and around Healdsburg; one of the best is handily placed in the town center: **Clos du Bois**, whose award-winning vintages can be tasted – and, of course, purchased – at 5 Fitch Street (tours by appointment; tel.707 433 5576). Elsewhere, the **Healdsburg Museum**, 221 Matheson Street, stocks the usual historical bits and pieces and describes the wine-making process (something better discovered on a winery tour). However, anyone who prefers reading about wine to actually drinking it, will be at home inside the **Sonoma County Wine Library**, corner of Center and Piper streets, which holds more than 3,000 wine books available for browsing or for loan with a temporary library membership card.

HUMBOLDT REDWOODS STATE PARK

On Hwy-101, 68 *miles* N *of* Willits/41 *miles* S *of* Eureka. Found only in Oregon and northern California, the coastal redwood trees are the world's tallest living things and shouldn't be confused with the giant sequoias, a redwood species common to California's Sierra Nevada region which is larger in bulk but shorter than the coastal redwoods. Coastal redwood is a prized building material, and a century of commercial logging has greatly depleted stocks. Nonetheless, impressive numbers still cloak sections of the North Coast, including the 50,000-acre Humboldt Redwoods State Park.

Despite the tacky souvenir stalls which crop up along it, the **Avenue of the Giants** is a splendid 33-mile drive, clearly signposted from the Hwy-101, that weaves through several pockets of the mighty trees. For a fuller understanding of the remarkable redwoods, call into the Visitor Center, about halfway along the Avenue near the Burlington campground, and be sure to venture on foot through at least one of the groves (the redwoods cluster together in groves for mutual protection – their shallow root systems leave them vulnerable to high winds). The smart choice is Founders Grove, dedicated to the Save-The-Redwoods League, an environmental group active as early as 1918, where you will find the park's tallest tree – the 358-ft **Dyerville Giant** – and a self-guided trail describing the forest's ecology.

JEDEDIAH SMITH REDWOODS STATE PARK

See Local Explorations: 2

JUG HANDLE STATE RESERVE

See Local Explorations: 2

KLAMATH

See Local Explorations: 2

MANCHESTER STATE BEACH

See Local Explorations: 2

MENDOCINO

See Local Explorations: 2

PETALUMA

On Hwy-101, 35 *miles* N *of* San Francisco. Undecided whether to be a San Francisco suburb or a part of the Wine Country, Petaluma on first sight is an undistinguished little town with only a large dairy industry to boast about. A closer look reveals an impressive restoration of the town's early-1900s business strip beside the Russian River – an array of iron-fronted Victorians now mostly occupied by shops and restaurants that invite a lunchtime stroll. Petaluma's origins are chronicled inside the Historical Museum, 20 Fourth Street.

POINT ARENA LIGHTHOUSE

See Local Explorations: 2

REDWOOD NATIONAL PARK

See Local Explorations: 2

RICHARDSON GROVE STATE PARK

On Hwy-101, 7 miles S of Garberville. Sunlight becomes twilight as Hwy-101 passes through Richardson Grove State Park, where 800 acres of towering redwood trees form a natural canopy, blocking the sun and casting an evocative stillness. The park's three campsites, occupied by half a million visitors annually, do less for the peaceful mood. To enjoy the park fully, leave the busier parts and explore on foot. Details of the park's trails, varying from arduous hikes to short walks, are available from the Visitor Center beside the highway.

Despite the impression they give, the trees of Richardson Grove are not the State's tallest redwoods – even higher specimens occur in Humboldt Redwood State Park (see page 35) and Redwood National Park (see Local Explorations: 2).

SAN FRANCISCO

See pages 110-137.

SAN RAFAEL

On Hwy-101, 17 miles N of San Francisco. San Rafael began life in 1817 when it was chosen by the Spanish as a convalescence center for disease-stricken neophytes from San Francisco's Mission Delores. The mild climate and absence of fog did indeed prove to be beneficial to health and soon 2,000 neophytes were living in San Rafael's branch mission. A very modest replica of the **mission chapel**, at 1104 Fifth Avenue, and the few original artifacts stored there, are barely worth breaking a journey for, however. More significant is the **Marin County Civic Center**, a concrete and steel creation across three hilltops which you will see from Hwy-101 as you head north from San Rafael. Completed in 1957, the innovative structure was the last work of the influential architect, Frank Lloyd Wright. Free tours are available Mon-Fri 9am-3pm by appointment: tel. 415 499 6104.

THE SONOMA COUNTY WINE AND VISITORS' CENTER

Allows you to sample the output of virtually every vintner in the county. On Hwy-101 between Petaluma and Santa Rosa, this state-of-the-art center has a user-friendly computer which holds details of local wineries and which is programmed to supply you with a printed itinerary of those you choose to visit.

THE SKUNK TRAIN

The only way to penetrate the redwood groves between Willits and Fort Bragg is with the Skunk Train, which plies a steam-powered and extremely beautiful 40-mile route through forests, tunnels, and across trestle bridges high above the Noyo River. Built in 1885 to move lumber to the coast, the railway now limits its cargo to tourists, who can make a half-day ($16) or full day ($20) return trip. For details, tel. 707 964 6371.

SANTA ROSA

On Hwy-101, 17 miles N of Petaluma. Flattened by an earthquake in 1906, Santa Rosa has re-emerged as the epitome of comfortable Californian suburban living, a flat expanse of tract homes and shopping malls. By contrast, it is two altogether off-beat characters who provide reason to linger in the town.

Attracted by its mild climate and fertile soils, **Luther Burbank** arrived in Santa Rosa in 1875 and spent his remaining 50 years developing new types of plums, prunes and berries among a multitude of vegetable, fruit and plant hybrids that made him a legend in Californian horticulture circles. The **Luther Burbank Home and Memorial Gardens**, 415 Steele Lane, maintains his Greek Revival-style house and the gardens in which his creations first saw the light of day.

Born in Santa Rosa in 1908, **Robert**

L. Ripley acquired fame for his *Believe It or Not* cartoons which began documenting the world's most bizarre phenomena in the 1920s (and which later evolved into the present-day's *Believe It or Not* museums, scattered far and wide) and is remembered by the **Ripley Memorial Museum**, 492 Sonoma Avenue. The museum is actually less interesting than the building housing it: the Church of One Tree, a gothic-style chapel built from a single redwood tree, and the subject of an early *Believe It or Not* cartoon.

SAUSALITO

See Local Explorations: 1.

SONOMA COAST STATE BEACH

On Hwy-1, 2 miles N of Bodega Bay. Comprising 13 miles of separate and secluded beaches slotted between high, craggy headlands, the Sonoma Coast State Beaches are accessible by short signposted trails leading off Hwy-1. Gusty winds deter sunbathing, but the area finds favor with beachcombers, fishermen and tide pool enthusiasts. There is also much to be said for simply gazing at the surf crashing against the sea stacks and rock arches. Pull over at **Rock Point** for a terrific view.

TIBURON

See Local Explorations: 1.

UKIAH

On Hwy-101, 44 miles N of Healdsburg. A workaday lumber town occupying a deep, verdant valley, Ukiah unexpectedly harbors an outstanding art and ethnographical collection spread across the 4-acre site of the **Grace Hudson Museum and Sun House**, 431 Main St. Grace Carpenter Hudson won great acclaim for her emotive paintings of Pomo Indians, a selection of which is displayed here, while her husband's research into Native American cultures did much to foster a wider appreciation and understanding of the lifestyles of the earliest Californians.

WILLITS

On Hwy-101, 28 miles N of Ukiah. A down-to-earth country town set on a forested hillside, Willits marks the eastern end of the Skunk Train route from Fort Bragg (see page 36). Even if you arrive by car, take a look at the picturesque wooden railway station.

RECOMMENDED RESTAURANTS

ARCATA

Abruzzi, $$; *791 Eighth Street; tel.* 707 826 2345; *credit cards,* AE, MC, V.

Delicious and reasonably priced Italian cuisine from a restaurant that makes the most of locally-grown farm produce and freshly-caught seafood. A strong choice of vegetarian dishes is another plus point.

BODEGA BAY

Lucas Wharf, $$-$$$; 595 *Hwy-1; tel.* 707 875 3522; *credit cards,* MC, V.

The Bodega Bay fishing fleet supplies many of the North Coast's better eateries and the best of the day's catch often ends up as the daily special of this popular waterfront restaurant.

GARBERVILLE

Woodrose Cafe, $; 911 *Redwood Drive; tel.* 707 923 319; *breakfast and lunch only,* Mon & Tues; *cards, none.*

Dependable and very popular with locals, this simple diner serves thick breakfast omelettes with a variety of enticing fillings – spinach and feta cheese, for example – and immense sandwiches for ravenous lunch eaters. Vegetarians, too, are in for a treat with a strong assortment of meat-free meals from which to choose.

GUALALA

St. Orres Dining Room, $$$; 36601 *Hwy-1; tel.* 707 884 3303; *credit cards,* MC, V.

With its stained-glass windows and onion domes, St. Orres Dining Room has all the looks of a traditional Russian restaurant, but the food is a mix of French and Californian cuisines.

HEALDSBURG

Jacob Horner, $$-$$$; 106 *Matheson Street; tel.* 707 433 3939; *closed Sun and holidays; lunch only on* Mon; *credit cards,* AE, MC, V.

Californian and Italian cuisine – strong on seafood and pasta – served in an enjoyable informal setting.

Northern California

Between San Francisco and Lake Tahoe
Gold Country: The Northern Mines

150 miles; map Kummerley + Frey California-Nevada

Although hard to imagine today, there was a time when California was not the American promised land but an inaccessible backwater where farmland was handed out to more or less anyone who managed to arrive in one piece. That changed in 1848 when gold was discovered in the foothills of the Sierra Nevada mountains – the heart of what soon became known as the Gold Country.

Far from the state's present centers of power and occupying tranquil hillsides sloping steadily into the Sierras, the Gold Country's towns were hastily built to accommodate the biggest population shift ever known – 100,000 (the so-called 49ers) arriving during the peak year of 1849. Many lasted only as long as the gold around them. Those settlements which have endured take pride in their heritage: an impressive number of rough-hewn brick Victorian buildings remains, often lining cobblestoned streets where wooden awnings hang over wooden sidewalks. In some places, even the local gallows have been carefully preserved.

The Gold Country is fascinating to explore at any time, but my favorite period is early fall, when the high summer temperatures have eased, when the tourist crowds have thinned, and when the townsfolk start settling down for the winter. At that time, there are great bargains to be found among the dozens of well-restored hotels, where you can sleep in rooms once occupied by the desperate characters of what was the truly wild west.

Between Sacramento – thanks to its deep water port, California's state capital since 1854 but a small and easily explored town – and Lake Tahoe, the Gold Country really begins. The fast route, I-80, a lackluster interstate highway, touches only one gold rush town, Auburn. Our blue, medium-paced, route branches north off I-80 along a section of Hwy-49 to reach Grass Valley and Nevada City, two of the more elegant gold-rush survivors. With time in hand, pick and choose among the green suggestions: they involve substantial detouring on Hwy-49 – the road which is the key to visiting the gold-rush towns.

Further south on Hwy-49 are the more rural settlements of the Southern Mines, described in Local Explorations: 10.

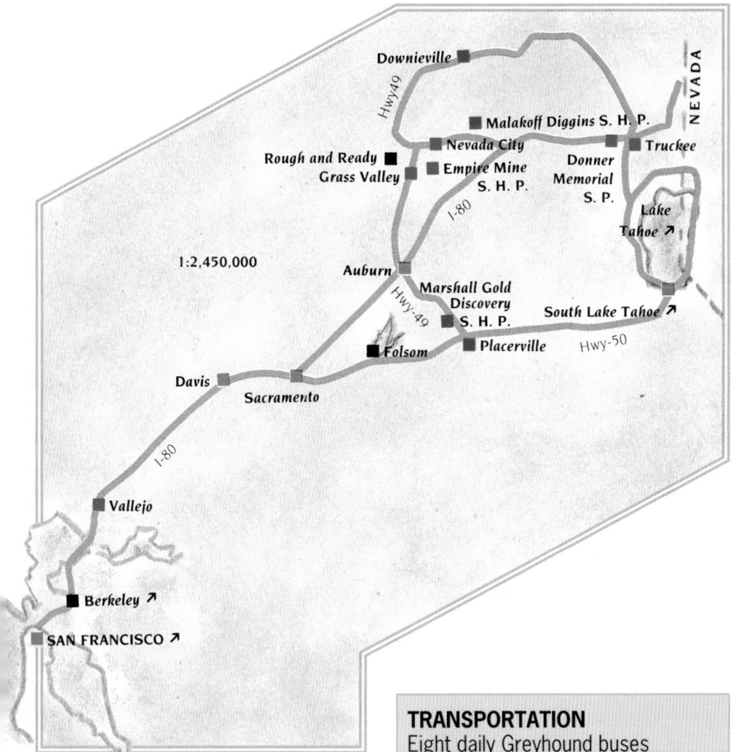

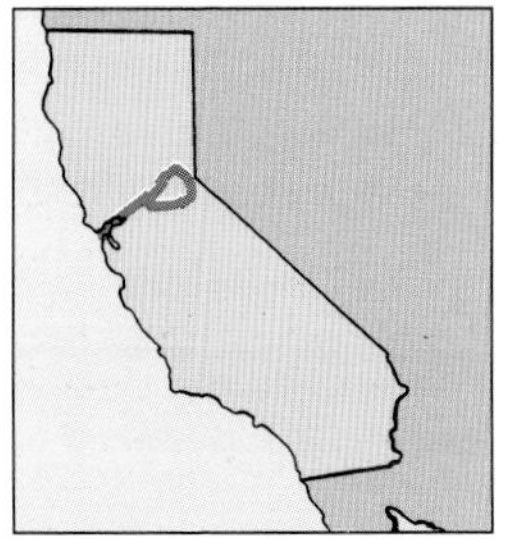

TRANSPORTATION
Eight daily Greyhound buses between San Francisco and Reno (in Nevada), call at Sacramento and Truckee, four a day also stop at Auburn.Travelling on Hwy-50 between Sacramento and South Lake Tahoe, seven buses a day call at Placerville. By train, Amtrak's cross-country California Zephyr connects Sacramento and Truckee once-daily in each direction with bus links to Grass Valley and Nevada City.

SIGHTS & PLACES OF INTEREST

AUBURN 🛏 ✕

On I-80 and Hwy-49, 26 miles E of Sacramento. Much of modern Auburn provides housing for Sacramento commuters and it is left to the commendable **Old Town** quarter to keep people aware of Auburn's roots as one of the Gold Country's more successful settlements. Alongside the inevitable antique shops, the Old Town's cobblestoned streets hold Auburn's 1892 fire station, the imposingly domed Placer County Courthouse, California's oldest continuously-used post office, and the tight alleyways of a former Chinatown district.

Just outside the Old Town, the **Gold Country Museum**, 1273 High Street, carries a better-than-usual stock of mining implements and explanatory displays, plus Native American exhibits and intriguing pieces from Auburn's early Chinese community. An annex of the main museum, the **Bernhard Museum**, does a fair job of replicating Auburn's Victorian times in several 19thC buildings.

BERKELEY

See Local Explorations: 8.

DAVIS

On I-80, 73 miles E of San Francisco/14 miles W of Sacramento. A small agricultural school founded in Davis in the 1920s has blossomed into a 1,000-acre regional campus of the University of California. Heaped with accolades for its research into environmental protection and clean forms of energy, the university – and its 20,000 students – set the tone for what must be the state's greenest community, one which has been recycling its waste for years and one where there is a bicycle for every inhabitant. Ponder these things as you drive through, but don't stop: eco-friendliness doesn't make for interesting viewing.

DONNER MEMORIAL STATE PARK

On I-80, 3 miles W of Truckee. At Donner Memorial State Park, the **Emigrant**

RECOMMENDED HOTELS

AUBURN

Auburn Inn, $$; *1875 Auburn Ravine Road; tel. 916 272 1444; credit cards,* AE, CB, DC, MC, V.

Although this is not the most atmospheric place to stay in the Gold Country, the soft colors and tasteful furnishings – plus the swimming-pool and jacuzzi – of this two-story motel combine to make this a relaxed overnight stop. A coin-op laundry is another useful feature.

GRASS VALLEY

The Holbrooke, $$-$$$; *212 W. Main Street; tel. 800 933 7077; credit cards,* AE, MC, V.

A delightfully restored mid-1800s hotel coupling period furnishings with all the necessary modern conveniences in rooms once occupied by various gold-rush heroes and villains. A great place to soak up the Gold Country ambience, either in the wood-panelled main building or in the more recent, circa 1870s, annex at the rear of the hotel.

NEVADA CITY

National Hotel, $-$$$; *211 Broad Street; tel. 916 265 4551; credit cards,* AE, MC, V.

A local landmark and claimed to be the oldest continuously operating hotel in the state. After seeing the wonderfully decorated lobby and bar area, you might be surprised to find the lower-priced rooms are rather spartan – though perfect for anyone wanting to believe they are back in the gold-rush days. Spending a few extra dollars brings copious antique furnishings and a private bathroom.

Northern Queen Inn, $-$$; *400 Railroad Ave; tel. 916 265 5159; credit cards,* MC, V.

A modern two-story motel located beside a river creek just might be an attractive alternative to the gold-rush-era accommodations being ruthlessly marketed a short walk away in the town center. The cheaper rooms here are the standard motel variety, although most include fridges. The cottages and chalets spread across the expansive and rural grounds are fitted with cooking facilities and are

Trail Museum recounts the sad tale of the Donner Party, a wagon-train of 89 men, women and children which set out in 1846 on the Emigrant Trail (the route crossing the northerly section of the Sierra Nevada mountains into California). Attempting to negotiate what is now the Donner Pass – part of which the park occupies – the party became trapped by snow and were forced to spend the winter without supplies. Forty people perished during the ordeal, some of the survivors resorting to cannibalism to stay alive. A 22-ft-high memorial **marker** reaches the height of the snow which filled the pass during that fateful winter: a scene difficult to imagine on a bright sunny day when the park, with its scurrying racoons and pine and fir trees, is a picture of natural beauty.

DOWNIEVILLE

On Hwy-49, 72 miles E of Auburn. Not content only to preserve many of its 1850s brick buildings, the people of Downieville also keep a shine on the gallows which brought the town the dubious distinction of being the one mining community ever to hang a woman. The town makes for an atmospheric stroll, even though the **Sierra County Museum**, inside a former Chinese store (and allegedly an opium den) on Main Street, carries merely the usual Gold Country complement of historical photographs and mining tools.

EMPIRE MINE STATE HISTORIC PARK

On Hwy-174, 1 mile E of Grass Valley. The biggest and most technologically innovative of the state's gold mines, the Empire Mine made Grass Valley one of California's richest communities in the late 1800s. A far cry from the romantic image of the lone placer miner panning the contents of a river bed, the Empire mine was the epitome of a company-run mine, with 367 miles of tunnels reaching 11,000 feet beneath the ground worked by an army of miners in round-the-clock shifts. The Empire Mine produced 5.8 million ounces of gold and only ceased production in 1956. Many of the buildings, including the opu-

well-suited to vacationing families.

PLACERVILLE

Chichester-McKee House, $$; 800 *Spring Street; tel.* 800 831 4008; *credit cards,* AE, DS, MC, V.

Despite the fact that it can no longer boast the only indoor plumbing in town, the three-room 1892 Chichester House makes an excellent bed-and-breakfast base, both for exploring Placerville and venturing further afield around the Gold Country. On days when you feel like doing nothing at all, there is a large garden waiting to be lounged in.

SACRAMENTO

Abigail's, $$$-$$$$; 2120 G *Street; tel.* 800 858 1568; *credit cards,* DC, DS, MC, V.

The six individually furnished rooms within this 1912 house, all but two of them with private bathrooms, overlook a peaceful garden in a quiet but convenient part of town. Come morning, descend the elegant stairway and you'll find fresh fruit juices, muffins and home-baked breakfast pastries awaiting you in the dining room.

Delta King, $$$-$$$$; 1000 *Front Street; tel.* 800 248 4354; *credit cards,* AE, DC, MC, V.

A 1920s paddle steamer now permanently moored in Old Sacramento, the vessel's cramped rooms do little to justify their "stateroom" description but if you want to stay somewhere unusual this surely fits the bill. A complimentary breakfast is served in the ship's saloon, overlooking the Sacramento River.

Vagabond Inn, $$; 909 *Third Street; tel.* 800 522 1555; *credit cards,* AE, DC, DS, MC, V.

A statewide chain of classy but affordable hotels with spacious, neatly (if usually blandly) furnished rooms, Vagabond Hotel's throw-in extras include complimentary morning newspapers and a good-sized swimming pool. Located on the edge of Sacramento's Old Town and within walking distance of virtually everything else, this one is well-placed for winding down after a day of pounding around the town.

lent English-style mansion belonging to the mine's owner, remain in the 13-acre park, and a short video film outlines the story of the mine.

GRASS VALLEY

On Hwy-49, 23 miles E of Auburn. Grass Valley grew fat on the profits of the Empire Mine (see above) in the late 1800s, even though many of its inhabitants were migrant Cornish tin miners who labored for a few dollars a day. Set in a lush meadow, today's Grass Valley is a pastoral town with many balconied 19thC buildings still lining its streets (several of them are appealing bed-and-breakfast spots: see hotels and restaurants). Another legacy of the mining times are the Cornish pasties – meat and potato wrapped in pastry which the miners munched underground – sold as an exotic dish in local shops and restaurants. Besides pasties, the Cornish arrivals brought new ideas in mining technology, the impact of which is assessed at the **North Star Mining Museum**, intersection of Highways 20 and 49. The museum carries detailed displays on mining techniques and also keeps a Pelton Wheel – an ungainly forerunner to modern water turbines – in working order.

An unlikely settler in Grass Valley was **Lola Montez**, a vivacious European dancer and a former lover of the King of Bavaria who toured her racy "spider dance" across the U.S. before arriving here in the 1850s (she moved on after her husband shot her pet bear). A replica of Lola's home at 248 Mill Street now houses the local tourist office and disappointingly few mementoes of her eventful life. Round out a day in Grass Valley by taking a snoop around the **Grass Valley Museum**, corner of Church and Chapel Streets, a collection of general historical displays inside the town's 1865 schoolhouse.

LAKE TAHOE

See Local Explorations: 5.

MALAKOFF DIGGINS STATE HISTORIC PARK

On Graniteville Road, 16 miles E of Nevada City. A massive gash on the side of a mountain caused by hydraulic mining – a form of gold mining that stripped away entire hillsides with high-pressure water hoses – has become a serene expanse of meadows and canyons populated by deer, coyote and squirrels. A few buildings dating from the mining settlement here have been restored, but it is the self-healing capacity of nature (for ecological reasons, hydraulic mining was banned as long ago as 1884) that impress most throughout the 3,000-acre park.

MARSHALL GOLD DISCOVERY STATE HISTORIC PARK

On Hwy-49, off I-80 or Hwy-50, 50 miles E of Sacramento. On January 24th 1848, James Marshall was building a sawmill for land owner John Sutter when he spotted flakes of gold in the American River on a site that is now the Marshall Gold Discovery State Historic Park. A museum tracing the colossal impact of Marshall's find stands in the park, as does a working replica of Sutter's Mill and the rustic cabin where a depressed James Marshall died broke in 1879 – never having benefited from the discovery that made millions of dollars and changed the entire course of California's history.

NEVADA CITY

On Hwy-49, 5 miles E of Grass Valley. Drunken brawling and public hangings were the order of the day in many gold rush towns, but Nevada City, with its white-painted two-story Victorian mansions, steepled churches and picket fences, was a cut above the rest. Being the seat of Nevada County, whose mines accounted for half the total gold yielded in California, Nevada City became one of the Gold Country's most affluent settlements.

On Nevada City's narrow tree-lined streets are scores of historic buildings.

DETOUR – **ROUGH AND READY**

Although little remains of the settlement, there is a curious site 4 miles west of Grass Valley just off Hwy-20, where Rough And Ready became the only town ever to secede from the U.S. Angry at the imposition of a miners' tax, its citizens elected to leave the union on April 7, 1850. Demoralized by an independent republic's inability to import liquor from the U.S., however, they rejoined on July 4th.

Take a walk beneath the fake gaslamps of Broad Street and you'll discover the **National Hotel**, no. 211, serving travellers since 1856 and claiming to be the West's oldest hostelry; also the **Old Nevada Theatre**, also thought to be the oldest of its kind in the West, which first raised its curtain in 1865 and saw author Mark Twain give his first public lecture. Close by, the **Firehouse Museum**, 214 Main Street, assembles an amusing collection of ageing articles inside an 1861 fire station, and the **Miners Foundry and Cultural Center**, 325 Spring Street, has turned the workshops that once produced mining tools into an arts and crafts showplace.

The informative Chamber of Commerce, 132 Main Street, issues free walking maps of all the town's notable buildings. There is something here which pre-dates by far the discovery of gold, however. To find it, walk for a few hundred yards east along Broad Street, to where the **Indian Medicine Rock** has stood since prehistoric times when it was revered by the Maidu people: they believed that whatever ailed them would be cured if they lay on the rock soaking up the rays of the sun.

• *Old Governor's Mansion, Sacramento.*

PLACERVILLE

On Hwy-50, 37 miles E of Sacramento. Once known as Hangtown for the eagerness of locals to execute alleged wrongdoers by hanging them two at a time from a tree, Placerville benefitted from its crossroads position during the goldrush and quickly expanded into a major trading center. Future rail magnate Mark Hopkins owned a grocery store here and John Studebaker spent his early years in Placerville perfecting miners' wheelbarrows before he found greater riches and fame producing cars. Placerville's main streets have the usual Gold Country conglomeration of restored Victorian buildings, and also the **El Dorado County Museum**, 100 Placerville Drive, which shows off a large horde of miners' tools and machinery. More unique to Placerville is **hangtown fry**, a dish of bacon, eggs and oysters served in several local eateries – it tastes better than it sounds.

SACRAMENTO 🛏 ✕

On I-80 and Hwy-50, 87 miles E of San Francisco/91 miles W of Lake Tahoe. In the 1850s, Sacramento was the gateway to California's gold mines and men, machinery – and millions of dollars – streamed through it. The town's selection as the state capital was crowned in 1874 when, at a cost of $2.5 million, the **State Capitol Building** was completed. A majestic expression of the Neoclassical style that typified U.S. public buildings of the period, the Capitol building was intended as a symbol of California's immense independent wealth – a pertinent gesture at a time when the rest of the U.S. was recovering from the Civil War.

Viewed from the grand Capitol Mall which leads to it, the Capitol Building – topped by a 120-ft-high rotunda – remains as impressive as ever. Inside, the State Legislature can be witnessed during its law-making sessions, though more appealing are the free guided tours of the building, departing hourly each day (weekdays only during winter) between 10am and 4pm.

The Capitol Building is a far cry from **Sutter's Fort**, 2701 L St, Sacramento's earliest fixed structure, erected in 1839 by German-born John Sutter. He acquired a considerable land grant (on which the first discovery of California gold was made, see Marshall Gold Discovery State Historic Park, page 42) from California's Mexican governors. Several reconstructed workshops stand in the fort's grounds, as does the **State Indian Museum**, with a fine stock of basketry, weapons, dug-out canoes, and ceremonial objects.

Up until 1967, when newly-elected state governor Ronald Reagan decided it was a fire hazard and spent several million dollars on a new ranch-style residence, 13 California governors had resided during their term of office at the **Governor's Mansion**, 1526 H St. Built in 1877, the house is a fine example of Californian gothic architecture and is enjoyably viewed on hourly guided tours (daily 10am-4pm).

The reason for Sacramento's success was the deep Sacramento River, which allowed ocean-going vessels to reach this close to the gold-producing areas. Many of the old riverside buildings, at the hub of local life a century ago, have been restored and turned into the **Old Town**, a strollable collection of museums, gift shops and cafes.

The main attraction in the Old Town

RECOMMENDED RESTAURANTS

AUBURN

Butterworth's Dining, $-$$; 1522 *Lincoln Way; tel.* 916 885 0249; *closed Mon; credit cards,* AE, MC, V.

The ample lunches and dinners served in this joyful 1885 mansion sited above old Auburn are rooted in traditional American meat and seafood recipes but enlivened by the inventiveness of California cuisine.

GRASS VALLEY

Main Street Cafe, $-$$; 213 W. *Main Street; tel.* 916 477 6000; *credit cards,* MC, V.

Be it spicy Cajun meat dishes that set the tastebuds alight, or fresh fish sandwiches so large they spill over the plate, this friendly restaurant works wonders with an impressively varied menu.

Marshall's Pasties, $; 203 *Mill Street; tel.* 916 272 2844; *credit cards, none.*

Six thousand miles from Cornwall it may be, but Grass Valley-style Cornish pasties, a legacy of the town's Cornish tin miners, don't come any better – or in greater variety – than those served at this cheap and cheerful eatery. They make a handy snack while seeing the town; look elsewhere for a full meal.

NEVADA CITY

Friar Tuck's, $$-$$$; 111 N. *Pine Street; tel.* 916 265 2262; *dinner only; closed Mon & Tues; credit cards,* AE, MC, V.

Dim lighting, brick walls, wood beams and secluded booths, bring about the sense of intimacy which makes this a favorite choice of locals in search of a special night out.

PLACERVILLE

Miners Cafe, $; 480 *Main Street; tel.* 916 622 6018; *credit cards, none.*

A no-frills spot which does a roaring trade in hangtown fry - eggs, bacon and oysters tossed in a pan, heated and served - a dish that has been a local favorite for over a hundred years (though the portions seem to have got smaller over the decades).

SACRAMENTO

The Firehouse, $$-$$$; 1112 *Second Street; tel.* 916 442 4772; *lunch and dinner only; credit cards,* AE, MC, V.

Sacramento's 1853 fire station is these days a very up-market restaurant, catering for a mixture of the gastronomically well-informed and the socially ambitious. Don your finery (casual clothes definitely not allowed) and come armed with a reservation if you want to spend an evening enjoying a formal French dinner.

Fox & Goose, $; 1001 R *Street; tel.* 916 443 8825; *credit cards, none.*

This would-be English pub not only offers a great selection of California-brewed and imported beers but also has a dining room serving excellent breakfasts and lunches, ranging from Welsh rarebit omelettes to banana-topped waffles.

TRUCKEE

Squeeze In, $; *Commercial Row; tel.* 916 587 9814; *breakfast and lunch only; credit cards, none.*

An unassuming little diner that prides itself on offering virtually every style of omelette or sandwich that customers can think of. Squeeze inside or stretch out on the patio.

CRUISING ON THE SACRAMENTO RIVER
One hour cruises along the Sacramento River aboard the *Spirit of Sacramento* – a vessel plying California's waterways since 1942 and once owned by actor John Wayne – depart daily Wed–Sun during the summer (Fri–Sun during the winter) from Old Sacramento's Front Street dock. The same boat offers dinner-, lunch-, Sunday brunch-, and happy-hour cruises, when food is included in the price. For details and reservations, tel. 800 433 0263.

is the **California State Railroad Museum**, 125 I Street, a dazzling collection of gleaming locos and imaginative displays clarifying the crucial role of railways in California's development. The railways were the first safe way to cross the mountains and deserts that divided California from the rest of the U.S., and their building was instigated by the so-called Big Four, a quartet of Sacramento merchants turned rail barons who outwitted the U.S. government on their way to becoming the state's richest and most powerful men during the late 1800s. Across the lawn from the railroad museum, the **Central Pacific Passenger Station** has been returned to its 1870 look, when it was the westernmost stop on the first transcontinental railway.

The California Supreme Court was originally housed in the 1854 B.F. Hastings Building, its offices and courtroom duly restored on an upper floor; more entertaining is the lower level **Communication Museum**, which describes the early days of Pony Express and Wells Fargo when sending a message from California to the rest of the country entailed a ten-day horse ride. Another Old Town call should be the **Sacramento History Museum**, 101 I Street, its hands-on high-tech exhibits relating California's past in several unusual ways.

The **Towe Ford Museum**, a short walk south of the Old Town, will undoubtedly delight any devoted American-auto buff, but the Model As, Model Ts and V-8s have little relevance to Sacramento. For anyone who is not a car enthusiast, a better bet might be the **Crocker Art Museum**, 216 O Street, whose crock of 19thC European and Californian art and contemporary photography catches the eye less than the tiled floors and curving staircases. The building is an 1873 Italianate villa financed by Edwin Bryant Crocker (a brother of Charles Crocker, one of the Big Four) and claimed to be the American West's first art museum.

SAN FRANCISCO

See pages 110-137.

SOUTH LAKE TAHOE

See Local Explorations:5.

TRUCKEE 🛏 ✕

On I-80 *and* Hwy-267, 78 *miles* E *of* Sacramento/14 *miles* N *of* Lake Tahoe. Workers on the transcontinental railway patronized the saloons and brothels of late-1800s Truckee, a town that only lost its reputation as a brash and boozy little place a few decades ago. Although it is within easy reach of busy Lake Tahoe, Truckee has an appealing time-locked quality instilled by its plethora of original wooden architecture and the community spirit of its inhabitants.

VALLEJO

On I-80, 28 *miles* NE *of* San Francisco. Dominated by a vast naval shipyard, Vallejo stands beside the junction of the Carquinez Strait and the Napa River, its links with the sea exhaustively – and not particularly interestingly – detailed in the **Naval and Historical Museum**, 734 Marin Street (closed Mon). Many vacationers, however, know Vallejo solely for **Africa USA/Marine World**, a large-scale tourist attraction beside I-80.

DETOUR – **FOLSOM**
Fans of Johnny Cash, who sang about Folsom State Prison's miserable qualities, may care to pay their respects to the forbidding penitentary, which lies 22 miles east of Sacramento on Placerville Road, between I-80 and Hwy-50. A more charitable reason to stop is to make a purchase at the prison shop which sells inmates' handicrafts, the proceeds going to the prisoners.

California Overall: 3

Northern California

Between Sacramento and Yreka
The Northern Interior

200 miles; map Kummerley + Frey *California-Nevada*

Forests of fir and pine, crystal-clear lakes and snow-covered mountain peaks fill the several hundred square miles that make up California's northern interior, a sparsely-populated largely alpine region that fully justifies its "empty quarter" nickname. This is not a place to visit half-heartedly. You have a 160-mile trek north along I-5 just to reach the region's nub and even then, while there is plenty to whet nature lovers' appetites beside the route – not least the moody profile of Mount Shasta – the Northern Interior's most pristine landscapes only reveal themselves to travellers sufficiently interested to make intrepid sojourns along winding, country backroads.

The climate of the Northern Interior also calls for respect. The area has some of the highest rainfall in the country and snow and freezing temperatures are regular features of the winter months. Visit from May to September and the region should be welcomingly warm and sunny – sometimes surprisingly hot in the lower-lying regions.

As my fast route I have taken I-5, the only major road to cross the whole Northern Interior and link the region's larger towns. Though short on sophistication, such communities provide food and accommodation at very fair prices. One or two also have intriguing museums providing glimpses into the past of one of California's most challenging regions, where several major confrontations between Native Americans and early white settlers took place. A few settlements with rather more character line my slower route, chiefly Hwy-70 and Hwy-99, which joins I-5 at Red Bluff.

To derive maximum enjoyment from the region's unique landscapes, it is essential to combine this statewide route with one or other of my local explorations in the area – numbers 3 or 4. These take in the bubbling mud pits and hot springs of Lassen Volcanic National Park and the lava formations of Lava Beds National Monument. Both will leave a lasting impression of the volatile geothermal forces beneath the state. And, for my money, one of the joys of journeying to such remote spots is later being able to brag about their awesome qualities to urban Californians, most of whom never venture anywhere near them.

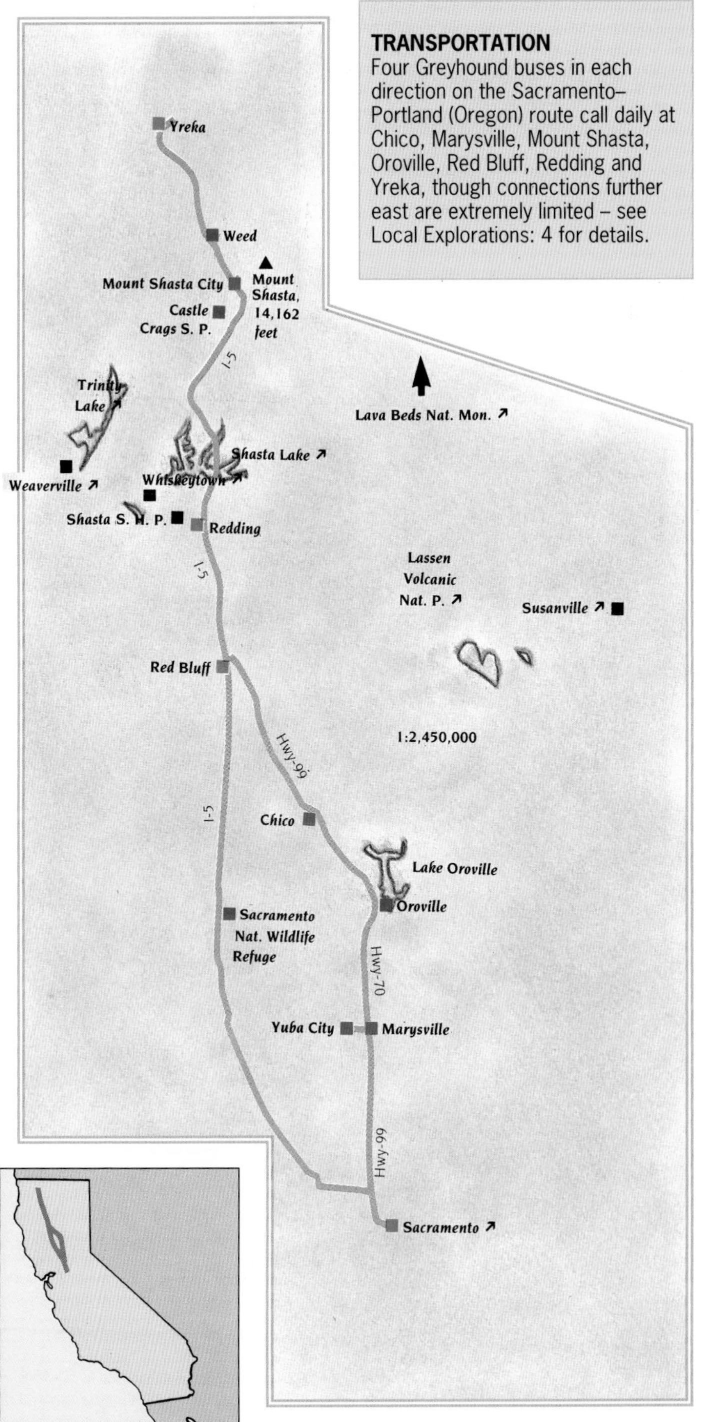

TRANSPORTATION
Four Greyhound buses in each direction on the Sacramento–Portland (Oregon) route call daily at Chico, Marysville, Mount Shasta, Oroville, Red Bluff, Redding and Yreka, though connections further east are extremely limited – see Local Explorations: 4 for details.

SIGHTS & PLACES OF INTEREST

CHICO ⛟ ×

On Hwy-99, 91 miles N of Sacramento. A small university town, Chico was founded by John Bidwell, who made a fortune from the gold rush but whose liberal attitudes – which would not be out-of-step with present-day Chico – stood in the way of the power-crazed rush into politics that was the path chosen by many of his peers. During the 1860s, in the heart of his fledgling town, Bidwell built an Italianate villa, a handsome three-story pile now preserved as the Bidwell Mansion State Historic Park, 525 Esplanade Avenue, and justifying a visit.

Also bearing the name of Chico's founder, **Bidwell Park** runs for 10 miles into the Sierra Nevada foothills: a picnic on its periphery gives a chance to contemplate the oak trees around which Errol Flynn played the part of Robin Hood in the 1937 film. A major event by local standards, the film is duly noted among the collections of the Chico Museum, corner of Second and Salem Streets.

CASTLE CRAGS STATE PARK

Off I-5, 48 miles N of Redding. Thrown up by volcanic activity 200 million years ago, the stark and dramatic granite spires of Castle Crags State Park loom above I-5. These forbidding 4,000-ft-high extrusions offer a stiff challenge even to experienced rock climbers. Several relatively easy **trails** pick through the lower elevations where the parks trees – oaks, firs, dogwoods and cedars – are clustered. The park ranger-led interpretive programs, on Saturdays evenings in summer (details; tel. 916 235 2684), are recommended. They outline the geology and natural history of the park and also describe the bloody battle fought here in 1855 between white settlers and the local Medoc Indians.

LASSEN VOLCANIC NATIONAL PARK

See Local Explorations: 4.

LAVA BEDS NATIONAL MONUMENT

See Local Explorations: 4.

DETOUR - **LAKE OROVILLE**
Seven miles east of Oroville (take Hwy-162 or Oroville Dam Boulevard), Lake Oroville was created by a damming project in the 1960s intended to aid irrigation of the Central Valley and southern California. The Lake Oroville Visitor Center provides a view of the dam and the lake (fishing and watersports) and carries low-key exhibits on the gold rush and on regional Native American cultures.

MARYSVILLE

On Hwy-70, 47 miles N of Sacramento. Founded by Chilean gold miners in 1850, little Marysville has but one tourist sight: the **Mary Aaron Museum**, 704 D Street, a Victorian dwelling holding very minor historical pieces. A lazy lunch beside Ellis Lake – the arm of water dividing Marysville from Yuba City, see page 53 – is a better option.

MOUNT SHASTA

8 miles E of I-5, 63 miles N of Redding. Thought by some to be inhabited by beings from a lost city of the Pacific and once attracting 3,000 brightly-robed devotees of the oddball I AM Foundation of Youth to a ritual on its slopes, perpetually snow-capped Mount Shasta, its peak, 14,162 ft high, is one of the most haunting sights in California. The nearest I-5 comes to the mountain is when passing through the town of Mount

CLIMBING MOUNT SHASTA
For anyone sufficiently fit, and with some hiking or back country experience, climbing Mount Shasta is by no means impossible. It is an arduous full-day ascent, using very steep trails – usually only passable without the aid of specialist equipment during August – beginning at Ski Bowl and Horse Camp, both reached by road from Mount Shasta City. Unpredictable weather and the prospect of avalanches are just two reasons for taking up-to-the-minute local advice from the nearest climbing/hiking supply shop before considering an attempt.

• *Antique farm machinery, Shasta* SH *Park.*

Shasta – officially entitled Mount Shasta City despite its population of a mere 3,000 – which serves as a supply base for the hikers and climbers aiming for the majestic mountain (if you are one, see the box on page 48). Only the geological and historical displays of the Sisson Hatchery Museum (actually part of a trout farm), on Old Stage Road, provide any incentive to pull yourself away from the hypnotic sight of the great peak.

OROVILLE

On Hwy-70, 26 miles N of Marysville. Erected in 1863, Oroville's **Temple of Assorted Deities**, 1500 Broderick Street, is a clear reminder that the Chinese played a significant role in early California: many arrived during the gold rush and it was they who later labored

> DETOUR – **SHASTA STATE HISTORICAL PARK**
>
> *Six miles west of Redding on Hwy-299,* Shasta State Historical Park holds remains and reconstructions of Shasta, a gold-rush town which flourished into the late 1800s but faded from the map as its gold mines closed down and is now intentionally preserved in its ruined state. Something of the desperate atmosphere of the gold-rush days can be experienced inside the former County Courthouse, which now functions as a museum, and behind it, where Shasta's ominous double gallows stand.

• *Oy-Vey's, Chico - see page* 52.

• *Opposite:* Bidwell Mansion, *Chico*.

on the transcontinental railway which linked the state to the rest of the U.S. A handy free leaflet describes the temples' three chapels and the furnishings donated to it by the Chinese Emperor.

RED BLUFF

On I-5, 136 *miles* N *of Sacramento*/25 *miles* S *of* Redding. A reward for venturing as far north as Red Bluff in the off-peak months of September or October are the jumping fish of the **Salmon Viewing Plaza**, on Sale Lane, where underwater video cameras capture the Sacramento River's ladder-climbing salmon as they return to their spawning grounds. Otherwise, only the adobe home of William B. Ide, at the eponymously-named state historic park on Adobe Road, merits a quick look. Ide was the first and only president of the 26-day Bear Flag Republic – created in 1846 when American settlers in California declared independence from Mexico, prior to joining the U.S. – and later erected this dwelling beside the Sacramento River. Ide's Adobe Ferry subsequently provided an important transportation link between the state's main gold-producing areas.

REDDING 🛏 ✕

On I-5, 161 *miles* N *of Sacramento*. Given the appeal of the great outdoors all around it, most people use Redding solely for food and accommodation – there are scores of fast-food joints and motels. If it's a rainy day, however, pass time at the town's **Carter House Natural Science Museum**, 48 Quartz Hill Road, providing a taster for the region's flora and fauna, or the **Redding Museum and Art Center**, 1911 Rio Drive, placing temporary local art exhibitions alongside permanent regional historical items, including a large collection of Native American basketry.

SACRAMENTO

See California Overall: 2.

SACRAMENTO NATIONAL WILDLIFE REFUGE

On I-5, 88 *miles* N *of Sacramento*. A five-mile car route and a one-mile foot-trail pass through sections of the 10,000-acre Sacramento National Wildlife Refuge, an undeveloped area where 175 migratory bird species have been sighted, among them many varieties of geese, egrets and herons.

TRAIN RIDE

From the Yreka Western Railroad Depot, 300 Miner Street, the Blue Goose Excursion Train, complete with 1915-vintage carriages, begins a three-hour tour through the Shasta Valley. The trips run daily Wed-Sun in summer; the fare is $9; details, tel. 916 842 4146.

SUSANVILLE
See Local Explorations: 4.

TRINITY LAKE
See Local Explorations: 3.

WEAVERVILLE
See Local Explorations: 3.

WHISKEYTOWN LAKE
See Local Explorations: 3.

WEED
On 1-5, 64 miles N of Redding. For the most part as exciting as its name suggests, the tiny community of Weed boasts the worthy **Weed Historic Lumber Town Museum**, 303 Gilman Avenue, a collection and celebration of the industry which brought the town into existence during the 1920s. Also here, the **Black Butte Saloon**, 259 Main Street, stores motley items of 1920s memorabilia and stakes its claim to have been Weed's first bank.

YREKA
On 1-5, 88 miles N of Redding. Unless you're heading for Oregon, there is little point in coming this far north, but Yreka,

• *Cow Patty Palace, with its life and soul.*

RECOMMENDED RESTAURANTS

CHICO
Oy-Vey Cafe, $; 146 W. *Second Street; tel.* 916 891 6710; *credit cards, none.*
Fresh-baked bagels, homemade soups, large omelettes and a range of vegetarian dishes are all reasons to visit this popular, centrally-placed eaterie. The outdoor tables are prime vantage points for watching Chico go by.

MOUNT SHASTA
Marilyn's, $; 1136 S. *Mount Shasta Boulevard; tel.* 916 926 9918; *credit cards, none.*
Housed in a former stagecoach stop and adorned with photos of Shasta's frontier times, Marilyn's serves a filling and fair-priced selection of staple American diner fare for breakfast and lunch; the blow-out, three-course dinners are the best deal for miles.

Michael's, $-$$; 313 N. *Mount Shasta Boulevard; tel.* 916 926 5288; *lunch and dinner only, closed Sun; credit cards*, AE, DS, MC, V.
The delicious homemade pastas and generously-sized burgers are the star choices from a large and varied menu and bring this laid-back restaurant a devoted local clientele.

REDDING
Andy's Cow Patty Palace, $; 2105 *Hilltop Drive; tel* 916 221 7422; *breakfast and lunch only; closed Sun; credit cards, none.*
Sumptuous omelettes, burgers and sandwiches prepared and served by a one-time Hollywood-based stand-up comic. The food is great and the jokes are not bad either – though the host's singing is a bit much first thing in the morning.

J.D.Bennetts, $-$$; 1800 *Churn Creek Road; tel.* 916 221 6177; *lunch and dinner only; credit cards* AE, MC, V.
A few Mexican and Italian dishes show up on the wide-ranging menu, but what this place does best is straightforward American staples such as steak and grilled seafood. For many, the setting – turn-of-the-century saloon-style decoration, with dark woods, stained glass, and fake gaslights – makes the meal.

just 22 miles short of the border, holds plenty to fill a day pleasantly. The discovery of gold provided the impetus for the town's founding in 1857, and a prosperous period ensued as local mines gorged forth the precious metal that kept the community on its feet for years. If you have ever wanted to see what a gold nugget actually looks like, step into the foyer of the **Siskiyou County Courthouse**, 311 Fourth Street, which displays them in all shapes and sizes. Gold is just one facet of Yreka's past touched on by the **Siskiyou County Museum**, 910 S. Main Street, a comprehensive and entertaining gathering which chronicles everything from local geological formations and Native American tribes, to the arrival of white fur-trappers and the rise of the post-gold logging industry. Some of Yreka's 19thC commercial buildings can be seen in the **Historic District**, where lack of development has left many early structures not only still upright but still carrying on business; a free leaflet from the Chamber of Commerce, 1000 S. Main Street, provides an amusing, anecdotal guide to them.

YUBA CITY

On Hwy-70, 47 miles N of Sacramento. Only the modest Native American and pioneer-period artifacts at the **Community Memorial Museum**, 1333 Butte House Road, provide any reason to break a journey in Yuba City, although the banks of picturesque Ellis Lake, which divides the town from Marysville (see page 48), make a commendable picnic spot.

RECOMMENDED HOTELS

CHICO

Safari Garden Motel, $-$$; 2352 *Esplanade; tel.* 916 343 3201; *credit cards,* AE, DC, DS, MC, V.

Chico is unrivalled for budget-range accommodation and only gets busy when special events take place at the university. The Safari Garden is clean, tidy and quiet, appealingly priced, and well-placed for touring the town.

MOUNT SHASTA

Mount Shasta House B&B, $$-$$$; 113 A *Street; tel.* 916 926 5089; *credit cards,* MC, V.

A lumber-workers' boarding house erected in 1925 which now offers cozy bed-and-breakfast lodgings in one of five rooms (two of which have private bathrooms). Plus points are the great views of Mount Shasta and, when the temperature drops, a blazing fireplace. The hosts can arrange white-water rafting trips on local rivers and even llama trips into the wilderness.

Swiss Holiday Lodge, $-$$; 2400 S. *Mount Shasta Boulevard; tel.* 916 926 3446; *credit cards,* AE, DC, MC, V.

A great place to stay with very reasonable rates, provided you don't mind a northern California hotel that masquerades as an Alpine hostelry. There are tremendous views from every window, a heated pool and covered jacuzzi, a communal kitchen for preparing picnics, and a lounge for swapping back country hiking yarns with other guests.

REDDING

Best Western Ponderosa Inn, $$; 2220 *Pine Street; tel.* 800 528 1234; *credit cards,* AE, CB, DS, MC, V.

Unelaborate, sound-value motel with spacious rooms, a swimming-pool, and a location close to the town center.

Red Lion Motor Inn, $$-$$$; 1830 *Hilltop Drive; tel.* 800 547 8010; *credit cards,* AE, CB, DS, MC, V.

A sensible choice in this traveller-friendly town, the inn (more accurately described as a motel) is a large and often busy facility but the large patio area and the neatly landscaped and wooded grounds – which include a putting green – make for a relaxing atmosphere. There's a swimming-pool, too.

BUDGET ACCOMMODATION

MOUNT SHASTA

Alpenrose Cottage Hostel (AYH); 204 E. *Hinckley Street; tel.* 916 926 6724.

Central California

Between Sacramento and Los Angeles
The Central and Owens Valleys

330 *miles miles; map* Travel Vision *California*

The Central Valley is a mind-numbingly flat expanse of land filling the 150-mile gap between the foothills of the Sierra Nevadas and the coastal mountains. It was once barren but – thanks to decades of ecologically ruinous diverting of rivers – it has been turned into one of the world's most productive agricultural areas. Our fast and medium routes, I-5 and Hwy-99 respectively, pass through the Central Valley beside mile after mile of raisin and almond groves (just two of the many money-spinning crops), encountering a change of scene only in the south, where hundreds of oil derricks litter the area around Bakersfield.

Agriculture and oil may make money but they don't make for exceptionally interesting towns. Central Valley accommodation is uninspiring as well, limited to ordinary mid-range chain hotels and two-a-penny motels. Consequently it is easy to see why Californians who live elsewhere spend more time joking about the Central Valley than touring it. Nonetheless, I feel a couple of well-chosen days here are a chance to discover a different side of the state – one where prices and pretensions are low, and the mood is more middle-America than wacky, surf-and-sun Californian.

Furthermore, the region's own produce and the culinary skills of farmworkers settling from Europe mean that there is some damn fine eating to be done in the Central Valley, the Basque restaurants being particularly worth sampling. A more practical consideration is that the valley is on the route to the tremendous Yosemite National Park and the under-rated Kings Canyon and Sequoia national parks – three places which should be on the itinerary of every California visitor.

Unlike the sedate Central Valley, the Owens Valley (on the eastern side of the Sierra Nevadas) is a geological wonderland, regarded as the most geologically active area in North America. Bubbling springs, basalt formations, and eerie bristlecone pine forests are among the strange phenomena within reach of our slow route, Hwy-395 (parts of which may be blocked by snow in winter). In general, the communities strung along Hwy-395 are no more memorable than their Central Valley counterparts but the scenery around them is second to none and they provide the only food and shelter for those who come to marvel at it.

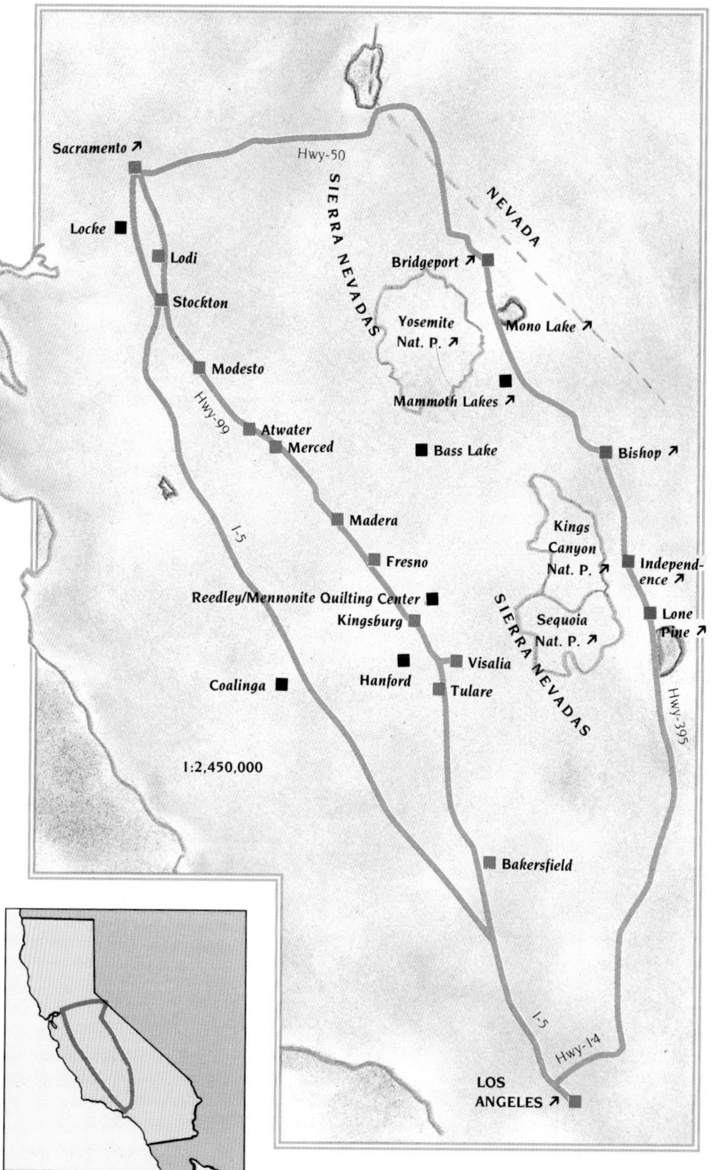

TRANSPORTATION

In the Central Valley, eight trains a day travel between Stockton and Bakersfield, making stops at Madera, Merced and Hanford. Onward links to Sacramento, Visalia and Los Angeles are by Amtrak bus (which meets the trains). Ten Greyhound buses operate daily between Sacramento · and Los Angeles, making stops at Stockton, Modesto, Fresno and Bakersfield on the way; a few of these services also stop at Atwater, Madera and Visalia. The only public transport in the Owens Valley is a daily Greyhound bus between Reno (in Nevada) and Los Angeles, linking the communities along Hwy-395.

SIGHTS & PLACES OF INTEREST

ATWATER
On Hwy-99, 7 miles N of Merced. Life in the little community of Atwater revolves around the Castle Air Force Base, a military flying school opened during the 1940s and currently training the crews of the U.S. Air Force's long distance bombers. Clearly not first choice among pacifists as a place to spend an afternoon, the **Castle Air Museum** displays dozens of aircraft which dropped their explosive loads in conflicts from the Second World War to Vietnam, and quite a few from later years which never had the chance to take off in anger.

BAKERSFIELD 🛏 ✕
On Hwy-99, 108 miles N of Los Angeles. Country music fans take a shine to Bakersfield, a dour and lackluster town where legends such as Merle Haggard and Buck Owens first made their names, and where dozens of honky-tonks feature the best of the local talent every weekend. Don't expect the show-biz trimmings of Nashville: Bakersfield country music is earthy and raw, and so are its venues. After a night spent carousing, visit the **Kern County & Pioneer Museum**, an engrossing collection of the town's historic buildings restored on a 15-acre site, where you will also find the **Country Music Museum** outlining the origins of the "Bakersfield Sound" and the success of its proponents.

BISHOP
See Local Explorations: 11.

BRIDGEPORT
See Local Explorations: 11.

FRESNO 🛏 ✕
On Hwy-99, 168 miles S of Sacramento/215 miles N of Los Angeles. Anonymous office blocks wedged between a freeway and a web of railway tracks are not a happy first impression of Fresno – a town famously at the butt of Californian jokes. But three miles north of the featureless center, close to the local university campus, the Tower District holds the Central Valley's trendiest few blocks, with cafes, bookshops and antique shops, plus several decades worth of California architecture – from Monterey-style homes to the streamlined modernity of the Tower Theater (from which the compact area takes its name) – to be explored and enjoyed.

Elsewhere, the diverse displays and interactive exhibits of the **Metropolitan**

DETOUR – **HANFORD**
Fifteen miles south of Fresno, turn off Hwy-99 on to Hwy-43 and continue for 20 miles to Hanford. Once a major stop on the Los Angeles-San Francisco railway and holding one of the state's largest Chinese communities, Hanford is now a sedate and extremely rural place, with a wealth of 1920s façades and a grand neoclassical courthouse. Another, far more intriguing, remnant of the old days is the Taoist Temple, on China Alley, at the center of Hanford Chinese life from 1893.

RECOMMENDED HOTELS

BAKERSFIELD
Econo Lodge, $-$$; *200 Trask Road; tel.* 805 764 5221; *credit cards,* AE, DC, MC, V.

Situated a few miles west of town, this branch of the nationwide chain can keep its rates below those of its local rivals. It has no great character but simply offers straightforward value for money.

La Quinta Motor Inn, $$; *3232 Riverside Drive; tel.* 805 325 7400; *credit cards,* AE, DC, DS, MC, V.

A large, recently-built hotel adjacent to Hwy-99 with amply-sized rooms grouped around a heated swimming-pool. The bar is a lively country music venue on Friday and Saturday nights.

FRESNO
Chateau Inn, $$-$$$; *5113 E. McKinley Avenue; tel.* 800 445 2428; *credit cards,* AE, DC, DS, MC, V.

Fresno has scores of ordinary motels along the appropriately-named Motel Drive just west of the Tower District. Even on a tight budget, however, you may be tempted by the Chateau Inn's greater level of comfort at a price far less than what you would

DETOUR – **BASS LAKE**

The great draw at the end of Hwy-41, which branches from Hwy-99 at Fresno, is Yosemite National Park. Follow the road as far as Oakhurst, however, and you will soon be surrounded by the water-sports fanatics and fishermen who prefer to spend their vacations at Bass Lake, reached from Oakhurst by a well-signposted side road. Around the lake, a number of pleasant walking trails pick through the pine-cloaked hillsides separating the lake from the more serious slopes of the Sierra Nevada mountains. Boats and jet-skis can be hired at most of the lakeside marinas, for other information contact the Mariposa Ranger District Office in Oakhurst (tel. 209 683 4665).

Museum , 1555 Van Ness Avenue, are less stimulating than the contemporary exhibitions of the **Fresno Art Museum**, 2233 N. First Street, or a guided tour around the **Meux Home**, 1007 R Street, a wooded Victorian gem whose playful arches and turrets originally belonged to a wealthy Fresno doctor.

An important figure in turn-of-the-century Fresno was M. Theo Kearney, an agricultural entrepreneur who made a fortune from raisins and sunk some of his money into a grand abode now preserved as the **Kearney Mansion Museum**, 7 miles west of central Fresno on Kearney Boulevard. With its European wallpaper and art-nouveau light-fittings, Kearney's French Renaissance-style home was an incongruous Fresno sight when it was built – and it still is today. Forty-five-minute guided tours reveal the details of the house and of Kearney's life, and a few of the secrets of successful raisin raising.

pay in areas more popular with tourists.

LODI

Wine & Roses Country Inn, $$-$$$; 2505 W. *Turner Road; tel.* 209 334 6988; *credit cards,* AE, MC, V.

An exceptionally friendly bed-and-breakfast inn dating from 1902, with its full quota of antiques and ornaments – and two acres of land: if you can't relax here, you can't relax anywhere. The helpful hosts also take delight in offering extras, such as horse and carriage rides at sunset.

MODESTO

Mallard's Inn, $$$; 1720 *Sisk Road; tel.* 209 577 3825; *credit cards,* AE, CB, DC, MC, V.

Stylishly designed and furnished rooms that constitute a very reasonable mid-range option: all are equipped with coffee-makers and 60-channel TVs; morning sees a newspaper delivered to your door and a sumptuous breakfast buffet laid out in the restaurant. If you can't sleep, try counting duck motifs – they appear all over the hotel.

Malaga House, $$; 2828 *Malaga Way; tel.* 209 523 9009; *credit cards, none.*

Bed-and-breakfast being a rare commodity in the Central Valley's larger communities, this provides a much needed break from the ubiquitous hotel and motel chains. Unusually, it is not an antique-filled Victorian house, but a tastefully appointed modern dwelling with several guest rooms, a private pool, and a hearty home-cooked breakfast each morning.

STOCKTON

Holiday Inn – Plum Tree Plaza, $$–$$$; 111 E. *March Lane; tel.* 800 234 5568; *credit cards,* AE, DC, MC, V.

While Holiday Inns have a reputation for blandness, this one stands out from the rest by setting its reasonably-sized rooms around a pool framed by pleasant grounds. Also offers complimentary fruit and morning coffee.

Motel Orleans, $; 3951 *Budweiser Court; tel.* 209 931 9341; *credit cards,* AE, DC, MC, V.

Handy, budget-priced three-story motel within easy reach by car of central Stockton and the whole Sacramento Delta area.

VISALIA

Oak Tree Inn, $; 401 *Woodland Drive; tel.* 209 732 8861; *credit cards,* AE, MC, V.

A quiet, town center location makes this easy-going smallish motel a good-value base for seeing Visalia and its immediate surroundings.

• *The Graffiti U.S.A. Festival, Modesto.*

INDEPENDENCE
See Local Explorations: 11

KINGS CANYON NATIONAL PARK
See Local Explorations: 14.

KINGSBURG
On Hwy-99, 20 miles S of Fresno. When 50 Swedish settlers founded Kingsburg in the late 1880s, few of them could have predicted that a century later the town's typically Californian buildings would be redesigned to ape traditional Swedish architecture, or that the place would be permanently festooned with yellow and blue Swedish flags. The idea is a bit daft but the results are entertaining, and it does give Kingsburg a character quite different to other Central Valley towns. There are certainly few better places in California to purchase a Dala Horse – a quaint wooden ornament originally made for bartering purposes by 17thC carpenters in the Dalarna district of Sweden. Kingsburg's Swedish Festival, held each May, is a spirited event; also worth dropping in for is the distinctly non-Swedish Watermelon Festival held in July, when40 tons of melon slices are handed out to thirsty visitors.

DETOUR – **COALINGA**
Aware that oil pumps are not the world's prettiest things, the schoolkids of Coalinga, 64 miles south of Madera on Hwy-145, painted a group of them to resemble clowns, animals and various imaginary creatures – their heads bob up and down in a steady rhythm. The site, nine miles north of the town center, is now known as the Iron Zoo.

LODI
On Hwy-99, 35 miles S of Sacramento. Lodi itself is of minor appeal but its surroundings are noted for their grapes and several wineries can be found close by. For tours and tastings, the best of the bunch is the **Oak Ridge Vineyards**, 6100 E. Hwy-12, where the tasting room (open 9 am-5 pm) is located inside a 50,000-gallon storage tank. Just south of town, the expansive **San Joaquin County Historical Museum** will prove to anyone in any doubt that farming is what makes the Central Val-

DETOUR – **MENNONITE QUILTING CENTER**
Five miles east of Kingsburg at Reedley, the Mennonite Quilting Center, 1010 G Street, offers a rare opportunity to observe slow and steady Mennonite weavers at their craft. Mennonites belong to a Protestant sect which rejects the usual church organizations, infant baptisms, and the swearing of oaths (thereby precluding its members from military service and holding public office).

Made from cast-off materials to prevent wastefulness, Mennonite quilts are works of imagination and enterprise: after seeing the care which goes into making them, you may well be tempted to buy one in the adjoining shop – which also sells assorted Third World crafts.

ley tick – every implement that ever turned the region's sod seems to be gathered here. The museum also features accounts of regional Native American history and gives a potted account of local wine production.

LONE PINE
See Local Explorations: 11.

LOS ANGELES
See Local Explorations: 15 *and* 16.

MADERA
On Hwy-99, 146 miles S of Sacramento.
Few people stay in Madera longer than it takes to drive through or swing east towards Hwy-41 and Yosemite National Park. While here, though, find an hour for the deserving Madera County Museum, 210 W. Yosemite Avenue, which does a more than adequate job of remembering the town's pioneer days. Alongside a welter of knick-knacks of early settlers and re-creations of a blacksmith's workshop, a miners' cabin and a county store, there is a partially rebuilt flume – a construction used in the transportation of lumber, which was the reason for Madera's founding on the Fresno River in 1876.

MAMMOTH LAKES
See Local Explorations: 11.

MERCED
On Hwy-99, 113 miles S of Sacramento.
When California's spit-and-sawdust pioneer communities decided to join the civilized world, their wealthiest citizens clubbed together and financed huge courthouses to show that law and order was now being practiced. Merced was no exception, and the Italian Renaissance job raised in 1875 still forms a striking centerpiece to the town. Nowadays the dispensing of justice takes place elsewhere and within the courthouse's simulated marble exterior lie the collections of the Merced County Museum – interesting enough for half an hour.

MODESTO 🛏 ✕
On Hwy-99, 74 miles S of Sacramento.
Founded in 1872, Modesto was intended to bear the name of William C. Ralston, a San Francisco banker. Ralston's graceful decline of the offer resulted in the town instead being named Modesto, the Spanish word for modest. Famous Modestons include champion swimmer Mark Spitz and film director George Lucas, who used the town as the inspiration for his celebration of smalltown America, *American Graffiti*. Each June, Modesto stages the Graffiti U.S.A. Festival, a very well-supported classic car show with many participants – and spectators – decked out in early-1960s regalia.

An earlier local hero was Robert McHenry, a successful wheat farmer who subsequently became head of the Modesto bank and a pillar of the community. The Italianate **McHenry Mansion**, 906 15th Street, in which McHenry and his family lived from 1883, has been extensively restored to its Victorian style (it suffered considerably after being converted to apartments during the 1920s). A short walk away, a Greek Revival building was financed by the McHenry family in 1912 as a home for the town library. Subsequently, the library gave way to the **McHenry Museum**, 1402 I Street, where several rooms store oddments from, and re-create scenes of, early Modesto life.

Other echoes of the past are provided by the murals which decorate the Depression-era **El Viejo Post Office**, 1125 I Street, and the 1912 **Modesto Arch**, above the corner of 9th and I Streets, which welcomes visitors to the

DETOUR – **LOCKE AND THE SACRAMENTO DELTA**
Between Stockton and I-80, the tiny towns and islands forming the Sacramento Delta make for an intriguing detour. For a taste, drive 18 miles north from Stockton on I-5 and turn east onto Walnut Grove Road, passing Walnut Grove on the way to Locke. Described as the last rural Chinatown in the U.S., Locke's frail-looking wooden buildings and sidewalks were erected in 1915 for a 2,000-strong Chinese community, many of whom were employed building levees on the delta. Up until the 1940s, many non-Chinese arrived in Locke each weekend to gamble and utilize the town's brothels and opium dens. The Dai Loy Museum occupies the premises of one former gambling club and there is more memorabilia – and a magnificent collection of moose heads – at Al's, a restaurant-cum-bar that has long been the fulcrum of local life. Some elderly Chinese, looking as frail as the buildings, still live here and seem somewhat bemused by Locke's growing popularity as a tourists' photo opportunity.

town with the promise of "Water Wealth Contentment Health."

MONO LAKE
See Local Explorations: 11.

SACRAMENTO
See California Overall: 2.

SEQUOIA NATIONAL PARK
See Local Explorations: 14.

STOCKTON 🛏 ✕
On Hwy-99 and I-5, 46 miles S of Sacramento. Sited at the junction of the Sacramento and San Joaquin rivers, Stockton grew rich and strong as a gold-rush supply center, miners and mining machinery coming ashore at its deep-water harbor on the way to the Gold Country.

Except for some mildly interesting murals depicting the community's growth and ethnic diversity inside the 1920s **City Hall**, Downtown Stockton has little appeal. Nearby, at 1201 Pershing Avenue, the **Haggin Museum** has – of all things – a strong selection of 19thC European art alongside the more predictable stash of ageing farming tools. A better way to pass an hour, though, is by strolling the campus of the **University of the Pacific** – a private university with a history stretching back to 1851 – with the aid of the free walking tour pamphlet available from the information desk inside Burns Tower, off Pacific Avenue a few miles north of Downtown.

TULARE
On Hwy-99, 46 miles S of Fresno. Anxious to entice passing tourists, dot-on-the-map Tulare spent half-a-million dollars on its **Tulare Historical Museum**, 444 W. Tulare Avenue, during the 1980s. Money cannot buy history, though, and the collections don't differ wildly from those in any other Central Valley museum. The diorama of a Yokut Indian village carries some interest, however, and you should also look out for Chum, a fox terrier belonging to an early Tulare surgeon who frequently accompanied his master to the operating theater: both Chum and master are dutifully re-created in wax.

VISALIA
Off Hwy-99, 43 miles S of Fresno. Visalia was one of the earliest Central Valley settlements, its first inhabitants including a band of Confederate sympathizers who published a pro-slavery newspaper during the Civil War. Such times seem far removed in the placid, present-day Visalia, where a trip to the local shopping mall is considered a big event and the smalltown America mood is all encompassing. Pick up the free walking tour map from the Chamber of Commerce, 720 W. Mineral King Avenue, and you will be able to stroll around the town's shady, oak- and eucalyptus-lined streets locating the older homes. Five miles south, **Mooney Grove Park** holds the worthy local history exhibits of the **Tulare County Museum** and James Earle Fraser's emotive End of the Trail statue – originally cast for the 1915 World Fair in San Francisco – depicting the sad plight of the west's Native Americans.

YOSEMITE NATIONAL PARK
See Local Explorations: 13.

RECOMMENDED RESTAURANTS

BAKERSFIELD

Maitia's, $$-$$$; *3535 N. Union Avenue; tel.* 805 324 4711; *lunch and dinner only; credit cards,* MC, V.

The best of several Basque restaurants in Bakersfield, with a mouthwatering choice of main courses (mostly beef and lamb, although the frogs' legs might tempt the adventurous diner), all of which are served with gluttonous portions of green beans, potatoes and mushrooms.

Zingo's, $; *2625 Pierce Road; tel.* 805 324 3640; *credit cards, none.*

Possibly the last genuine truck stop in California, Zingo's is open around the clock with bee-hived waitresses delivering substantial helpings of anything American – meatloaf, ham, eggs any style, and much more. On weekends after the local honky-tonks close, you'll find local country musicians munching their supper here and gossiping through the small hours.

FRESNO

Butterfield Brewing Company Bar & Grill, $–$$; 777 *E. Olive Street; tel.* 209 264 5521; *credit cards,* AE, MC, V.

The excellent selection of beers brewed on the premises is reason enough to make a call, but the lunches and dinners – a wide selection of salads and pastas and more, served by a friendly staff – makes this an essential Tower District stop.

George's Shish Kebab, $-$$; 2405 *Capitol Street; tel.* 209 264 9433; *breakfast and lunch only; credit cards, none.*

Best place in town to sample inexpensive Armenian fare, served alongside assorted Middle Eastern and more familiar American dishes. Lamb shanks and chicken kebabs are the house specialities; there's limited scope for vegetarians.

Santa Fe, $; 935 *Santa Fe Avenue; tel.* 209 266 2170; *lunch and dinner (served to 8.30pm) only; closed Mon; credit cards, none.*

Wonderful Basque food – and plenty of it – served at ridiculously low prices to diners seated along an enormous bench table.

MODESTO

Greenhouse Dining Room, $$-$$$; 1990 *N. Divanian Drive; tel.* 209 634 4947; *lunch and dinner only, no lunch at weekends; credit cards,* AE, DC, MC, V.

A highly-rated gourmet restaurant where everything served is grown or raised in and around Modesto; even the chocolate, into which the dessert strawberries are hand-dipped, comes from the local Hershey's factory.

STOCKTON

The Fish Market, $$-$$$; 445 *W. Weber Avenue; tel.* 209 946 0991; *lunch only on Mon; credit cards,* AE, DC, MC, V.

The seafood is excellent but the attractive waterfront location makes prices a touch higher than they ought to be. Nonetheless, a very popular place and reservations are a wise precaution for evening eating.

Le Kim's, $; 631 *N. Center Street; tel.* 209 943 0308; *credit cards,* MC, V *(cards accepted only with a* $10 *minimum order).*

Don't be put off by the pokiness of this tiny Vietnamese eaterie: there may only be five tables but everything on the lengthy menu is sure to be first-rate. While here sample the Vietnamese coffee.

VISALIA

Kay's Kafe, $; 215 *N. Giddings Ave; tel.* 209 732 9036; *breakfast and lunch only; credit cards, none.*

Early-rising farm workers are stuffing themselves with American breakfast fry-ups here even before dawn. Later in the day, a varied clientele drops by for the best-value lunches in town.

Vintage Press, $$-$$$; 216 *N. Willis Street; tel.* 207 733 3033; *lunch and dinner only; credit cards,* AE, CB, DC, MC, V.

Among the region's top restaurants, the Vintage Press features California cuisine and creates tempting gourmet-standard variations on traditional Cajun dishes. The wine cellar is impressively stocked, too.

Central California

Between Santa Cruz/San Jose and San Luis Obispo
The Northern Central Coast

180 miles; map Travel Vision California

The Northern Central Coast is natural California at its most inspiring. Big cities, smog, and even theme parks, suddenly become a distant memory as the landscape becomes one of scrub-covered mountains and rugged cliffs pounded by crashing ocean surf. Barely changed for millennia, this is California as it was when the Spanish arrived and several of the missions they erected remain here, some completely renovated, others reduced to ruins.

Visit this part of the coast between May and September: the weather is liable to be inclement even then; winter is sure to bring rain and vicious gales. The routes I have devised, based on two separate highways, have no links between them other than at their start and end points. Therefore you will need to decide in advance which course has most appeal.

The faster route, Hwy-101, is generally the least interesting, traveling inland to link dull farming towns and separated from the majestic coastline by a mountain range. In its favor, however, is the fact that Hwy-101 follows a section of El Camino Real, the old route linking the 21 California missions, and Mission San Antonio de Padua (one of two recommended detours), is the one I've long considered the most evocative of the lot. You'll also find the pick of the state's smaller wineries in the southerly portion of this route.

Hwy-1 is slower but overall far more impressive, hugging the magnificent coastline and providing plenty of scope for dining in hillside restaurants above the ocean and spending nights in rustic lodges or small-town inns. With Monterey, a one-time California capital, and the beautifully restored mission at Carmel, this route earns high marks for its historical interest, too. Hwy-1 also passes Hearst Castle, a testament to human indulgence on the scale of the infinite and second only to Disneyland in popularity among visitors to California.

Unfortunately, Hwy-1 is no secret. A twisting, two-lane road, it's bumper-to-bumper with tourists throughout the summer (weekends in particular should be avoided), when I've often spent more time anxiously watching the over-sized motor home in front rather than enjoying the view all around.

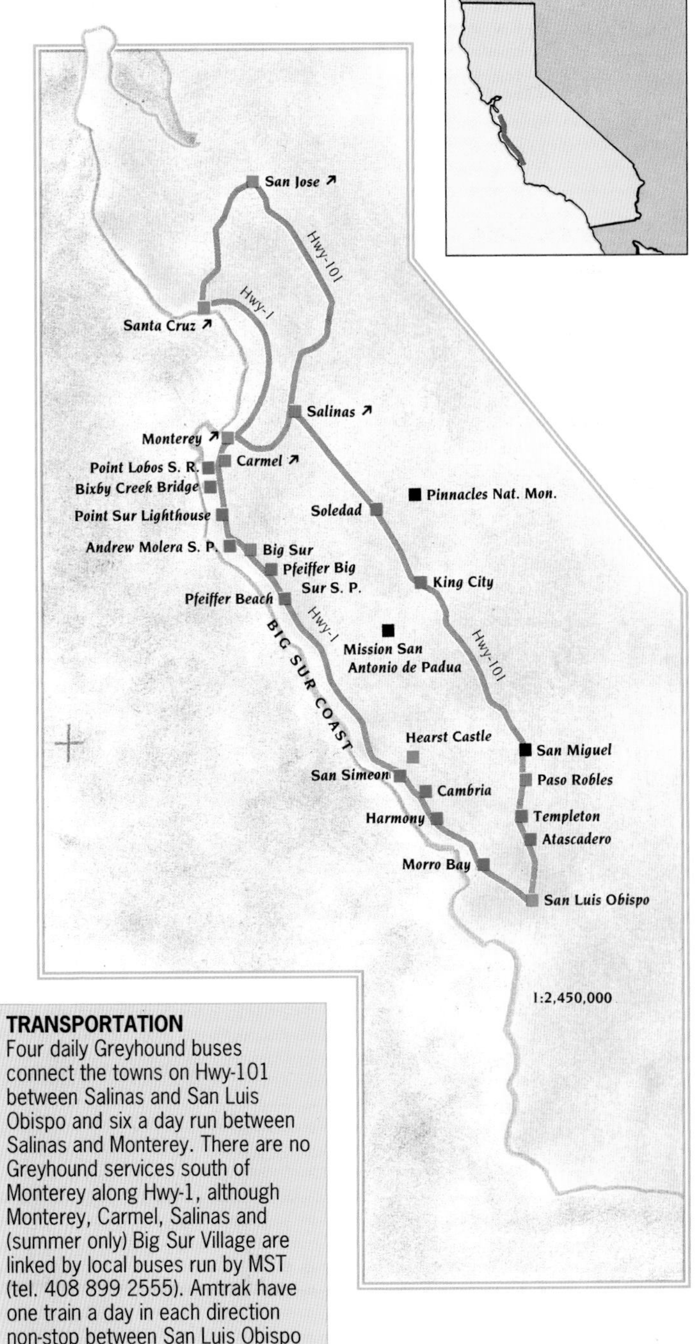

TRANSPORTATION
Four daily Greyhound buses connect the towns on Hwy-101 between Salinas and San Luis Obispo and six a day run between Salinas and Monterey. There are no Greyhound services south of Monterey along Hwy-1, although Monterey, Carmel, Salinas and (summer only) Big Sur Village are linked by local buses run by MST (tel. 408 899 2555). Amtrak have one train a day in each direction non-stop between San Luis Obispo and Salinas.

SIGHTS & PLACES OF INTEREST

ANDREW MOLERA STATE PARK

On Hwy-1, 21 miles S of Carmel. From a slender beach fringing a lagoon at the mouth of the Big Sur River, Andrew Molera State Park rises through groves of sycamore and oak to views of the Pacific from towering bluffs. Easy walking trails, endowed with picnic tables at particularly attractive spots, follow the river, weave around meadows, and climb through the woodlands to the upper elevations.

ATASCADERO

On Hwy-101, 15 miles N of San Luis Obispo. Founded in 1913 as a utopian farming community and bestowed with an elaborate Italian-Renaissance-style civic center shortly before its benefactor, one E.G. Lewis, was imprisoned for fraud, the origins of pastoral Atascadero are chronicled by the Historical Society Museum, inside the civic center.

BIG SUR ×

On Hwy-1, 23 miles S of Carmel. Sixty unforgettable miles of God's own landscaping, Big Sur is the most dramatic coastal strip in the U.S: the rugged Santa Lucia mountains meeting the Pacific in a series of surf-pounded granite cliffs and weather-beaten outcrops. The views are gasp-worthy all along Hwy-1, which dips and weaves through the folds of the mountains, ploughs through canyons (their sides coated with colorful wildflowers in springtime) and soars over high, narrow bridges.

Several parking spots offer brief opportunities to pull over and savor the scenery (while doing so, don't underestimate the Big Sur wind), but the diversity of Big Sur is best discovered in the state parks such as Andrew Molera and Pfeiffer Big Sur (see the separate entries), which make much of the region's natural splendour accessible on foot – or even on horseback.

The limited commercial services are strung along Hwy-1 at **Big Sur Village**, the only built-up section of Big Sur, where the population of 1500 mostly live in homes set back from the highway along twisting lanes. While passing through, look out for the **Henry Miller Memorial Library** (opening hours erratic; tel. 408 667 2574) beside Hwy-1, in which a small collection of artifacts recalls one of the many writers who have drawn inspiration from Big Sur's savage beauty.

Another Big Sur landmark is the **Esalen Institute** (no casual visitors; for information tel. 408 667 3000), pre-empting the New Age movement by providing a full range of mind-and-body-improving experiences from holistic medicine to gestalt therapy – in a back-to-nature setting since 1962.

HORSEBACK TOURS

The memorable way to tour Big Sur is on horseback. Lasting between a couple of hours and several days, guided horseback tours through Andrew Molera and Pfeiffer Big Sur state parks are run by Big Sur Trail Rides; tel.408 667 2666.

BIXBY CREEK BRIDGE

On Hwy-1, 5 miles N of Andrew Molera State Park. The tallest of a series of hair-raising bridges carrying Hwy-1 across the deep canyons of Big Sur – and much the most photographed – the Bixby Creek Bridge was completed in 1932. A small car-park on the north side is alive with the sound of clicking shutters.

CAMBRIA ×

On Hwy-1, 40 N miles of San Luis Obispo. The preponderance of half-timbered gift shops can be off-putting, but Cambria repays a leisurely exploration on account of its rural serenity and for the commendable work of a small band of local artists and artisans displayed in a dozen galleries along Main Street. Country lodges, bed-and-breakfast inns and good quality restaurants are another feature of this pine-shrouded town, and it has some fine beaches off which seals – and surfers – can often be seen.

CARMEL

See Local Explorations: 9.

HARMONY

On Hwy-1, 26 miles S of Cambria. A privately-owned hamlet, most of Harmony's tiny population are glass-blowers, potters or jewellery-makers who sell their wares from roadside shops. Standards are high and prices can be low.

While passing through, survey the local fields for Arabian horses, bred and trained on ranches owned by the Hearst family.

HEARST CASTLE

Off Hwy-1, 88 miles S of Carmel/40 miles N of San Luis Obispo. Set on a hilltop above the village of San Simeon, Hearst Castle was the part-time home (and, some would say, the full-time folly) of controversial media magnate William Randolph Hearst – the role model for Orson Welles' *Citizen Kane* – erected at an estimated cost, at today's prices, of $400 million.

Work began on Hearst Castle in 1919 and architect Julia Morgan spent the next 28 years coping with Hearst's constantly changing ideas and the five-ton wagonloads of Flemish tapestries, French fireplaces, Italian ceilings, Persian carpets, candelabras and coats-of-arms, which he spared no expense in gathering up from the great houses of Europe to be incorporated into the design.

As the castle took shape, the likes of Charlie Chaplin, Greta Garbo and Clark Gable (friends of Hearst's long-time companion, actress Marion Davies) escaped Hollywood's maddening crowds to spend their nights occupying the palatial guest villas and their days enjoying the swimming-pools and tennis courts, or admiring Hearst's collection of lions, cheetahs and zebras, among the residents of the world's largest privately-owned zoo.

Plagued in his later years by debts and astronomic tax bills, Hearst died in 1951 and six years later the Hearst family donated the castle to the state in return for a $50 million tax write-off.

It's impossible not to be struck by the incongruity of a would-be medieval palace appearing mirage-like on the rugged slopes of a Californian coastal mountain (land which Hearst inherited from his father), or be less than awed by the sheer scale and extravagance of the place, which compensates for its lack of style, finesse or continuity.

From the Visitors' Center beside Hwy-1, telescopes offer tantalising glimpses (fogs permitting) of the hill-top structure, which can only be properly seen on one of three 90-minute guided tours, each of which visits different sections of the castle.

First-time callers should take Tour 1, which includes the marble-lined Neptune Pool fringed by million-dollar classical statuary, the Gothic-style dining room, the Guest Hall, and the gold-leaf decorated Roman Pool. A fourth (summer-only) tour concentrates on the lavish gardens. Tour reservations are recommended, and are essential in summer (tel.1 800 444 PARKS).

KING CITY

On Hwy-101, 22 miles S of Soledad. A market town for the produce of the south-

DETOUR – **PINNACLES NATIONAL MONUMENT**

Scenery is not a strong point of Hwy-101 but there is some spectacular geology to be found by driving east from Soledad on State Road 146, which leads into the lunar-like landscapes of Pinnacles National Monument. Thrown up by volcanic activity 23 million years ago, these immense rock extrusions, gnarled by erosion into bizarrely-shaped towers, spires and pinnacles, lie on and around a 1,000-ft-high ridge running across the monument.

A network of walking trails makes the ridge top accessible with comparatively little effort (though some sections are steep enough to make handrails necessary), bringing breathtaking views of the monument and far beyond, across the Salinas River Valley to the mile-high Santa Lucia mountains flanking the coast.

Bear in mind that this is a severe and isolated place: rattlesnakes are not unknown, venturing off marked paths can be dangerous, and you should never enter a cave – many of which have been formed by streams cutting through the ridge – without a flashlight and helmet. Be sure to stop at the Visitors' Center for free maps and information.

Note, too, that visitors with RVs should enter the monument using the eastern section of State Road 146, which leaves Hwy-25 31 miles south of Hollister.

• *Hearst Castle, from the coastal side.*

ern Salinas Valley, King City doesn't have much to recommend it save for a chance to buy gasoline and stretch your legs. It does, however, mark the junction of Hwy-101 and Jolon Road, the start of the route to Mission San Antonio de Padua, for which see the detour below.

MONTEREY
See Local Explorations: 9.

MORRO BAY 🛏 ✕
On Hwy-1, 14 miles W of San Luis Obispo. Some very agreeable seafood restaurants cook up the daily catch of the local fishing fleet in Morro Bay, an otherwise only moderately interesting town whose best feature is the imposing volcanic hunk of Morro Rock, a near-vertical slab rising 576 feet immediately offshore.

Morro Rock is a protected nesting ground for peregrine falcons and climbing it – once a popular local pastime – is prohibited.

Just south of the town, **Morro Bay State Park** extends across inland hills and around coastal marshlands. Home to an abundance of great blue herons, among many other species, this is one of California's foremost bird-watching spots. The **Museum of Natural History,** opposite the park's entrance, engagingly recounts the earliest human settlements in the area and explains the intricacies of local ecology.

• *The Neptune Pool, Hearst Castle.*

PASO ROBLES
On Hwy-101, 26 miles N of San Luis Obispo. Surrounded by fertile vineyards owned by some of the state's best

DETOUR - **PFEIFFER BEACH**
Turn off Hwy-1 a mile south of the entrance to Pfeiffer Big Sur State Park along Sycamore Canyon Road and you'll wind up at Pfeiffer Beach, ideal for a picnic. The white-sanded beach is sheltered from ocean winds by a large offshore rock formation, the colors of which alter subtly as the prevailing light changes. Enjoy the solitude but don't try swimming here: the water's cold and the riptides are dangerous.

small wineries, Paso Robles – a popular up-market health resort until its elegant spa hotel burnt down in 1941 – draws plenty of wine-loving Californians but is happily spared the tourist crowds which flock to the state's better-known wine-producing valleys (see Local Explorations: 6 and 7).

The Wine Tasting in Paso Robles' leaflet, free from the Chamber of Commerce, 548 Spring Street, lists more than 20 quality local wineries (particularly recommended is the Estrella River Winery 5640 Hwy-46 E, for its award-winning Cabernet Sauvignon), and details of the town's frequent summer events, such as May's wine festivals and August's San Luis Obispo County Fair.

PFEIFFER BIG SUR STATE PARK

On Hwy-1, 26 miles S of Carmel. Beside Hwy-1 as it swings inland – forsaking ocean views but often finding the sunshine that is obscured by fog along the coast – Pfeiffer Big Sur State Park occupies a section of the Big Sur River Valley and protects some of California's most southerly Coastal Redwood trees.

Around the stately trees are a plethora of marked picnic spots and several excellent – and fairly simple to negotiate – trails. Ascending from the redwoods to a grove of tanburn oaks (their

RECOMMENDED HOTELS

BIG SUR

Big Sur Lodge, $$-$$$; *Hwy-1 in Pfeiffer Big Sur State Park; tel.* 408 667 2171; *credit cards,* MC, V.

Comfortable and well-equipped two-bedroomed cabins – the pricier ones include a fully-equipped kitchen – on a hillside studded by pine and redwood trees. Being part of a state park – there's a restaurant and a general supplies shop on the site – results in the cabins being quickly snapped up during the summer. If you're arriving between May and September, book at least three months ahead.

Ventana Inn, $$$$; *half a mile east of Hwy-1, 28 miles S of Carmel; tel.* 800 628 6500; *credit cards,* AE, CB, DC, MC, V.

Ultra-pricey accommodation in wooden cottages high above the stupendous Big Sur coastline. This is a place for those who like roughing it in style: rewarding but sometimes arduous hiking trails are within easy reach. But it will also appeal to those who simply aspire to pampering themselves in the jacuzzis and saunas. The day begins with an enormous breakfast buffet; complimentary refreshments are served in the afternoon.

CAMBRIA

Cambria Pines Lodge, $$-$$$; 2905 *Burton Drive; tel.* 805 927 4200; *credit cards,* MC, V.

The accent here is on rural relaxation: peacocks strut across the leafy 250-acre site and you can choose a room in the main building or take one of the individual cabins scattered throughout the grounds. Most rooms and cabins are fitted with a woodburning-fireplace, a welcome addition during the cool Central Coast nights, and there's also a fitness center, heated indoor swimming-pool, jacuzzi, and a sauna for guests' use.

Olallieberry Inn, $$$; 2476 *Main Street; tel.* 805 927 3222; *credit cards,* MC, V.

Being a two-story, Greek Revival-style home dating from 1873 makes this one of the more authentic old houses providing bed-and-breakfast along the coast. Stuffed to the rafters with turn-of-the-century antiques and curios, the house has six guest rooms, all of them non-smoking and each with a private bathroom. The hosts are friendly and the atmosphere is mellow.

MORRO BAY

The Inn at Morro Bay, $$$-$$$$; 19 *Country Club Drive; tel.* 800 321 9566; *credit cards,* AE, DC, CB, MC, V.

A sizeable hotel but one with the ambience of a small bed-and-breakfast inn. The rooms are in single-story wooden buildings spread across Cypress-tree-lined grounds. Almost all have brass beds and a pleasant French rural decoration, some have gas-burning fireplaces. Spending an extra few dollars brings views of the town's harbor and its famous rock.

tanning once used commercially), the short but steep Valley View Trail reveals the park's best panoramas. Combine this with the less tiring trail to Pfeiffer Falls, where the Pfeiffer-Redwood Creek plummets 60 feet, and you'll feel the day has been well spent.

Named after a homesteading family who eked out an existence here in the mid-19thC, the origins of the park, and its geology and ecology, are cogently outlined in the Nature Center.

POINT LOBOS STATE RESERVE

On Hwy-1, 3 miles S of Carmel. A sanctuary for a multitude of sea creatures and seabirds, the caves, coves and slender beaches of Point Lobos State Reserve also provide a happy hunting ground for humans with half a day to spare and a hankering to discover one of the wildest and prettiest sections of the Central Coast.

The 450-acre promontory, its granite headlands dotted with wind-tortured Monterey cypress and pine trees, is criss-crossed by easy walking trails. The pick of these, the Headland Trail, passes Sea Lion Point, where the honks of sea lions join the sound of crashing surf, and continues to Headland Cove, where sharp eyesight and luck might reveal sea otters feeding from a kelp bed.

PASO ROBLES

Paso Robles Inn, $$; 1103 *Spring Street; tel.* 805 238 2660; *credit cards,* AE, MC, V.

A fetching Spanish Colonial-style creation, complete with verandah and fake bell tower, erected on the site of the town's famed spa resort. The Inn lacks the glamour associated with its predecessor but is a likeable low-key and well-priced place to stay in this enjoyable small town, particularly if you can get a room facing the lovingly-tended gardens.

SAN LUIS OBISPO

Adobe Inn, $$; 1473 *Monterey Street; tel.* 805 549 0321; *credit cards,* AE, DC, MC, V.

What looks like a standard motel from the outside is actually a competitively-priced bed-and-breakfast option. The 15 rooms belie their uniform exterior appearance, being furnished with a sense of style and economy – and there's a window seat and rocking chair in each. The civilized atmosphere is maintained by the serving of afternoon tea in the dining room. Very friendly owners, and within easy walking distance of the town center.

Peach Tree Inn, $$; 2001 *Monterey Street; tel.* 800 227 6396; *credit cards,* AE, DS, MC, V.

A welcome inexpensive find on the town's motel-lined approach road, the pick of the Peach Tree Inn's simple but comfortable rooms are those described as "creekside": they are adjacent to a stream and abundant vegetation at the foot of a steep hill.

SAN SIMEON

San Simeon Lodge, $$-$$$; 9520 *Castillo Drive; tel.* 805 927 4601; *credit cards,* AE, CB, DC, MC, V.

Accommodation this close to Hearst Castle is bound to be costlier than its equivalent elsewhere. The rooms are not spectacular but they are clean, tidy and among the most fairly-priced in the vicinity (rates drop appreciably in the October to April off-season). Spend a night here and make an early-morning assault on the castle, thereby avoiding the crush.

TEMPLETON

Country House Inn, $$; 91 *Main Street; tel.* 805 434 1598; *credit cards,* DS, MC.

The spirit of small-town California is evoked by this tiny place: only five guest rooms, with just one with en suite bathroom. The garden is guarded by a white picket fence. The owner-host is always on hand to welcome guests, wax lyrical to them about local attractions, and send them on their way with a hearty country breakfast.

• *Sebastian's General Store, San Simeon.*

DETOUR – **MISSION ANTONIO DE PADUA**

To find one of the state's most atmospheric missions, leave Hwy-101 just west of King City along Jolon Road, after 11 miles arriving at the all-but-deserted village of Jolon and veer right along Mission Road. In this secluded and enchanting river valley in the midsts of the vast Fort Hunter-Liggett military base (ID must be shown at the gates), the 1810 church and – more unusually – many of the outbuildings of the Mission San Antonio de Padua remain in good states of repair. It is the tranquillity of the setting, however, and the sight of robed Franciscan monks moving quietly through the grounds, that make this detour such a pleasure.

POINT SUR LIGHTHOUSE

Off Hwy-1, 16 miles S of Carmel. Set on a tall basalt outcrop and operational since 1889, Point Sur Lighthouse originally utilized a whale-oil lantern to ward ships away from what was known to seafarers as the Graveyard of the Pacific. The lighthouse still earns its keep, these days automatically with a computer-controlled beam. Informative guided tours (tel. 408 625 4419) explore the stone buildings, which comprised the former living quarters, and describe the deprivations of the earliest attendants.

SALINAS

See Local Explorations: 9.

SAN JOSE

See Local Explorations: 8.

• *Madonna Inn, San Luis Obispo.*

SAN LUIS OBISBO

On Hwy-1, 189 miles S of San Jose/174 miles S of Santa Cruz. An ideal base for visiting Hearst Castle and a great place to be on a Thursday evening when the Farmer's Market brings the town's entire population to impromptu food stands along Higuera Street, San Luis Obispo grew up around Mission San Luis Obispo de Tolosa, founded by Junipera Serra in 1772.

The fifth of the 21 California missions, **San Luis Obispo de Tolosa** was the first to acquire thick adobe walls and a red-tiled roof, necessary alterations if it were to withstand attempts by Native Americans – often forcibly co-opted as mission labor – to burn it down. Falling into disrepair after secularization, extensive restoration has brought the mission back to something approaching its Spanish-era appearance. Inside, though, only the mildly atmospheric chapel and a museum with a copious stock of Native American arrowheads and handicrafts make the token admission fee worth paying.

On the other hand, Mission Plaza, on which the mission stands, is a lively spot: set beside the small river creek which runs through the town, it's a popular place for al fresco dining. Nearby at 969 Monterey St., the **County Historical Museum** puts the community's past on show with the furnishings and knick-knacks of pioneer-period families; another historical marker is the r[illegible] brick **Ah Louis General Stor[illegible]**, 800 Palm St., the only reminder of a sizeable Chinese community which lived in San Luis Obispo during the late 1800s, mostly men employed in constructing the state's first railways.

San Luis Obispo can also boast the world's first motel, opened here in 1925 and currently a private residence, and (possibly) the world's most kitsch hotel: the shocking-pink **Madonna Inn**, complete with more than a hundred tastelessly-themed rooms, beside Hwy-101.

SAN MIGUEL

On Hwy-101, 52 miles S of King City/10 miles N of Paso Robles. Surviving the ravages of weather and secularization – when many mission buildings were given over to public use – and thereby requiring minimal renovation, the 1797 **Mission San Miguel Arcangel** (just north of the hamlet of San Miguel) is among the most authentic of California's missions with an impressive number of its original features – including some striking frescos by the acclaimed Esteban Munras – intact. Now maintained by Franciscan monks, the buildings do much to evoke the early days and the museum offers factual insights into what was, with 24,000 sheep and cattle, and land stretching to the ocean, among the state's wealthiest missions.

Directly across Hwy-101, the 1850 **Rios-Caledonia Adobe** originally housed Petronillo Rios, the owner of the mission following secularization, and later became a stagecoach stop on the

Los Angeles–San Francisco route.

SAN SIMEON

On Hwy-1, 65 *miles* S *of* Big Sur Village/40 *miles* N *of* San Luis Obispo. William Randolph Hearst built Spanish Colonial-style homes in San Simeon for the staff of Hearst Castle, sited on the hill above the village. More in evidence today are rows of undistinguished hotels and motels catering to Hearst Castle visitors. Pause to take a look at **Sebastian's General Store**, in business since 1852 though these days proffering a rather bland line in souvenirs, and press swiftly on to San Simeon Bay, where William Randolph Hearst State Beach offers some of the best swimming on the Central Coast. Dominated by a 1,000-ft-long wooden pier, the beach is where many of the Hearst Castle treasures were unloaded.

SANTA CRUZ

See Local *Explorations*: 8.

SOLEDAD

On Hwy-101, 25 *miles* S *of Salinas*. Soledad is a small and placid farming town that grew up in the shadow of a mission, Nuestra de Soñora de Soledad, completed in 1797. Never

RECOMMENDED RESTAURANTS

BIG SUR

Fernwood, $; Hwy-1, *northern edge of* Big Sur Village; *tel.* 408 667 2422; *credit cards, none.*

Budget-priced food of acceptable quality isn't exactly abundant along the Big Sur coast, but the burgers and fish-and-chips served at this likeable log cabin eaterie are cheap and tasty; and just the ticket for a filling lunch before hitting one of the classier options further along the coast for dinner.

Nepenthe, $$-$$$; Hwy-1, 30 *miles* S *of Carmel*; *tel.* 408 667 2345; *credit cards,* AE, DC, MC, V.

Few restaurants enjoy a more splendid location. Nepenthe is perched in a forest above the Big Sur coast in a architecturally-impressive, split-level building which also houses an art gallery and bookshop. Lunch and dinner are served inside, beneath a redwood- and pine-beamed ceiling or, more popularly, on the patio overlooking the ocean. There is a choice of well-prepared soups and salads, and the Ambrosia burger – a cheeseburger given the gourmet treatment – has thrilled many educated eaters over the years. Make a reservation if you come for dinner.

CAMBRIA

The Brambles Dinner House, $$-$$$; 4005 *Burton Drive*; *tel.* 805 927 4716; *dinner only*; *credit cards*, AE, DC, MC, V.

Atmospheric and relaxed dining in an 1874 cottage decorated with assorted antiques and a prized collection of clocks. Yorkshire pudding features as part of the English slant given to the lamb and beef courses, although the best choice is the broiled salmon, fresh from the Pacific. The soups and the multifarious forms of bread are homemade.

The Chuck Wagon Diner, $; 5670 *Moonstone Beach Drive*; *tel.* 805 927 4644; *credit cards, none.*

As you might expect from an all-you-can-eat buffet restaurant, the emphasis is on quantity rather than quality. Nonetheless, the meat, fish and the copious varieties of vegetables on offer here are a cut above what you'll usually encounter in such establishments. There's also an impressively large salad bar and a good choice of desserts.

MORRO BAY

Dorn's Original Breakers Cafe, $-$$; 801 *Market Street*; *tel.* 805 772 4415; *credit cards*, AE, DC, MC, V.

Cheaper and of no lesser quality than this fishing town's pricier seafood outlets, you'll find sizeable seafare sandwiches forming the core of the lunchtime menu and a couple of noteworthy daily specials complementing the dinner selection. Breakfast is served, too: a tempting variety of omelettes, pancakes and waffles that finds favor with many locals.

Rose's Landing Restaurant, $$; 725 *Embarcadero, Morro Bay*; *tel.* 805 772 4441; *credit cards*, AE, MC, V.

prosperous, the frequent flooding of the Salinas River and various epidemics contributed to the mission's swift demise, while the isolation of its setting did little to endear the mission to its Spanish incumbents; one visitor describing it as "the gloomiest, bleakest, and most abject looking spot in all California."

Restoration work has been limited to the chapel and a wing of the inner courtyard (holding a small museum), easily toured in a few minutes, while the ruins keep the sense of desolation as strong as ever.

TEMPLETON ×

Off Hwy-101, 6 miles S of Paso Robles. Swedes arriving from Minnesota founded Templeton in 1887, taking advantage of the new Southern Pacific Railroad which linked the town to San Francisco and all points east. Templeton retains its original Lutheran church and more than a small town's share of antiques shops. The Country House Inn (see hotels) makes a cozy overnight stop, and three miles west of the town center at 2900 Vineyard Drive, the Pesenti Winery, offers free tours and tastings of its noted Zinfandel.

The almost inevitable wait for a table at this immensely popular bayside restaurant is worth enduring. There are steaks and pasta options, but it's the fresh seafood, ranging from lobster to albacore tuna, that stands out. The portion are large: have lunch here and you won't need dinner.

SAN LUIS OBISPO

Apple Farm, $$; *2015 Monterey Street; tel. 805 544 6100; credit cards,,* MC, V.

Traditional American fare is served in this elegantly furnished restaurant throughout the day. Breakfast includes apple dumplings and cinnamon rolls alongside a fair choice of omelettes. Later in the day, the dinner features no-nonsense fare such as fried chicken with dumplings, roast turkey, prime ribs, or fried trout. A sizeable salad bar provides an alternative for those with lighter appetites, but the desserts are strictly for gluttons.

Kyoto/China Brown, $; *685 Higuera Street; tel. 805 546 9700; credit cards,* AE, MC, V.

As the name suggests, a combined Chinese and Japanese restaurant offering best value with its health-concious (plenty of fresh fruit and meat-free fare) lunch and dinner buffets, which include everything from sushi to spicy "country-style" bean curd.

Margie's Diner, $-$$; *1575 Calle Joaquin; tel. 805 772 2510; credit cards, none.*

Prides itself on offering value-for-money, healthy food while retaining the atmosphere of a traditional American diner. Drop in to sample the wonderful milkshakes and you might well find yourself staying for an unplanned meal. Breakfast options include glorious buttermilk pancakes, lunch can be a generously proportioned sandwich or a burger topped with avocado, and the various steak dinners (there is also a vegetarian dinner special) will satisfy the most demanding appetite.

• *The pier, San Simeon.*

Central California

Between San Luis Obispo and Los *Angeles*

The Southern Central Coast

150 *miles; map* Travel Vision *California*

The differences between northern and southern California well and truly strike home along this stretch of the coast. Within a few miles, the towering bluffs, fogs, and slow-paced rural living of the north give way to the palm trees, expansive beaches, and high-priced luxury lifestyles typical of the south. The contrasts stem from simple geography: between San Luis Obispo and Santa Barbara the coastline turns a corner, becoming south-facing rather than west-facing, thereby catching the full rays of the sun and not allowing ocean fogs to fill its inland canyons.

I've made this journey many times but the sheer speed and completeness of this change never fails to surprise. Head south after eating lunch in a fog-cloaked beach-side diner outside San Luis Obispo and you'll be in Santa Barbara in time for an elegant patio dinner – and have time for a leisurely ocean dip on the way.

Unlike the northern Central Coast, there are no mountain ranges to complicate touring. Our fast route, Hwy-101, unfussily links the region's (mostly undistinguished) main towns – and for many miles is joined by our blue route, Hwy-1. In its more adventurous sections, Hwy-1 also passes some tiny coastal settlements before reaching Lompoc, where you'll discover the most comprehensively restored mission in California. Lompoc is also a feature of our green route, which in part follows century-old stagecoach roads as it meanders through inland valleys. The numerous pastoral villages within the valleys include Solvang, which makes a meal of its Danish origins, and Ojai, which turns up unexpected links with Indian mystics.

The region's one essential stop is Santa Barbara, packed with historical and architectural interest and – in my view – summing up everything that's good about southern California. The town also has a pleasing number of inexpensive eating places, although accommodation costs are high. If you can tear yourself away (I usually can't) there are lower-priced overnight options within easy reach.

Santa Barbara can be visited at any time, but be cautious if you're touring the northern part of the region during winter, when the climate can be less than inviting.

TRANSPORTATION

Greyhound buses are frequent between Santa Barbara and Los Angeles, and most make stops at Oxnard, Ventura and Thousand Oaks. Slighter fewer buses – usually 18 a day – run between Santa Barbara and San Luis Obispo, all of them calling at Santa Maria and six a day also calling at Lompoc, Solvang, Buellton and Pismo Beach. Four daily trains link San Luis Obispo and Los Angeles, all calling at Santa Barbara. Santa Barbara has a further four daily train connections with Los Angeles, and an Amtrak bus service which carries passengers on to San Luis Obispo

• *Chumash vessel, Ventura Archaeological Museum.*

SIGHTS & PLACES OF INTEREST

AVILA BEACH

Off Hwy-101/Hwy-1, 11 miles SW of San Luis Obispo. A beach of white sand, three fishing piers, and a knack of being sunny when neighboring beaches are shrouded in fog, helps make Avila Beach a sound bet for a restful day of ocean-gazing and snacking from seafood stands. Expect a rowdier ambience at weekends, when the beach-side boardwalk is chocked with the fun-seeking, sun-tanned students of nearby Cal Poly. If you're staying in San Luis Obispo, **rent a bike** for the day and pedal here along the back roads.

BUELLTON

Junction of Hwy-101 and Hwy-246, 31 miles S of Santa Maria. Surrounded by thoroughbred-horse farms and verdant hillsides, Buellton looks pleasant but won't detain you for longer than it takes to drive through. As you pass, however, take a look at **Pea Soup Andersen's**, now a Best Western-owned hotel and restaurant, but the site of the original Pea Soup Andersen's – a budget-priced eatery opened by a Dane and his French wife in 1924. Their split-pea soup served with endless refills became a California legend.

CARPINTERIA

On Hwy-101/Hwy-1, 12 miles E of Santa Barbara. A pleasant but thoroughly unexciting community, Carpinteria has little to suggest that it was once a Chumash Indian village, renamed by Spanish explorers impressed by the canoe-making skills of the natives. Modern visitors tend to be keener to swim than to learn about local history. At **Carpinteria State Beach**, three miles away, an offshore reef keeps the water free of rip tides, enabling bathers to enjoy some of the safest swimming anywhere on the Central Coast.

CHUMASH PAINTED CAVE

Off Hwy-154, 10 miles N of Santa Barbara. Living in the coastal hills between Ventura and San Luis Obispo, the Chumash Indians were much admired by the earliest Spanish arrivals for their technical skills – notably their canoes, made from lashed-together planks caulked with asphalt. The Chumash also had great artistic skills, expressed through basketry and ornament-making, and also in their cave paintings. Protected by an anti-vandal mesh, this cave holds an excellent example of the tribe's artistry.

EL CAPITAN STATE BEACH

Off Hwy-101, 19 miles W of Santa Barbara. Occupying a slender headland cloaked with sycamore trees and ending in spectacular bluffs, El Capitan State Beach is the most popular of several south-facing beaches lying west of Santa Barbara. The waters are ripe for swimming and surfing, and there's a well-equipped campsite for those who like to be soothed to sleep by the sound of ocean waves. A 2-mile cycle and foot-path leads west to Refugio State Beach, described on page 79.

GAVIOTA STATE PARK

On Hwy-101, 30 miles W of Santa Barbara. As the southbound Hwy-101 swings east to follow the coast, it passes through Gaviota State Park, which encompasses a small beach enclosed by rocky outcrops and extends inland across 3,000 acres of chaparral-covered slopes. Hiking trails lead to **Gaviota Hot Springs** and to **Gaviota Peak**, the summit of which gives views clear along the coast to Santa Barbara and beyond: a rewarding target for a day's hike. Also within the park are **Las Cruces Hot Springs**, two pools of warm, mineral-rich water, easily reached by following a short trail from a car-park near the junction of Hwy-101 and Hwy-1.

LOMPOC

On Hwy-1, 66 miles S of San Luis Obispo. Californians know Lompoc for two things: the 100,000-acre Vandenburg Air Force Base, where missile and satellite guidance systems are tested (launches are frequent, look for the vapor trails above the ocean in the evening sky); and flowers, grown for the commercial potential of their seeds and covering the gently undulating terrain around the town each summer. The **Lompoc Museum**, 200 S. H Street, has a little on Chumash Indian life and plenty on the founding of the town, also its development. The catalyst for Lompoc's creation was **Mission La Purisima Concepcion**, founded in 1787 in the present town center but, following an earthquake, subsequently moved to a location 4 miles east.

Don't feel bad about missing the town, but if you miss the mission you should kick yourself. Although the second mission crumbled to ruins, a major restoration project on its site, **La Purisima Mission State Historic Park**, began during the Depression and has resulted (so far) in 21 buildings being rebuilt by hand, using traditional methods and materials. The upshot is the most complete mission complex in the state, and one that concentrates on the secular aspects – such as the bakery, the soap factory, the weaving room, the grain mill and the workshops – of mission life.

LOS ALAMOS 🛏

Off Hwy-101, 17 miles S of Santa Maria. Nestled in a valley of cottonwood trees, the hamlet of Los Alamos has cultivated an Old West appearance, its main street being one long row of preserved wooden façades. The place is easily admired without stopping, but you might fancy pausing long enough to push through the swing-doors of the 1850s mahogany bar of the **Union Hotel**: see Recommended Hotels.

LOS ANGELES

See pages 230-249.

LOS OLIVOS

On Hwy-154, 6 miles N of Santa Ynez. In Los Olivos, **Mattei's Tavern** makes much of its roots as a one-time stage-coach stop. The restaurant still occupies the two-story wooden building erected by local big-wig Felix Mattei in 1886. Just outside the village, at 5017 Zoca Station Road, the **Firestone Vineyard** was the first Santa Ynez Valley winery to crush local grapes – and today it uses them to produce some notable wines.

MALIBU

See Local Explorations: 15.

OJAI 🛏 ✕

On Hwy-150, 20 miles E of Carpenteria. Surrounded by orange and avocado groves and set in the secluded crescent-shaped valley that played the part of Shangri-La in the 1937 film, *Lost Horizon*, serene and beautiful Ojai (say "O-hi") casts an instant spell. This being

DETOUR – **NIPOMO DUNES PRESERVE**
South of Pismo Beach, this reserve protects several miles of large (some are 500-ft-high) and ever-moving sand dunes, which fulfil an important ecological role: they allow numerous species of coarse vegetation to thrive and provide a habitat for brown pelicans and California least terns. In one dune, director Cecil B. de Mille buried the entire set of his 1923 film, *The Ten Commandments*. In 1990 excavation work commenced on the "Ten Commandment Dune" (near the entrance just west of the village of Guadalope, on Hwy-1) with the intention of unearthing the evidence of one of Hollywood's greatest cinematic excesses – the four-ton plaster sphinxes emerging from the sands are just the start.

California, though, much of the magic is being packaged and sold off as desirable real estate: sprawling luxury homes dot the hillsides, as do tennis courts, golf courses, and the spa resorts that pamper the bodies of rich visitors from Los Angeles. A cheaper way to keep trim while exploring the valley is by **cycling**: there are plenty of bike rental outlets in the town and several signposted cycling routes.

Ojai's background is described in the **Ojai Valley Historical Museum**, 109 S. Montgomery Street, where you will become aware of the numerous writers, artists and musicians who have settled in the town over the years – and of the Indian mystic, Krishnamurti, who lectured here during the 1920s. Krishnamurti's presence gave rise to the **Krishnamurti Foundation**, 1130 MacAndrew Road, which is open for tours. An equally esoteric stop is the **Krotona Institute**, across town on Krotona Hill, its mission-style buildings holding the West Coast's largest library of theosophical tomes.

OXNARD

On Hwy-1, 11 miles S of Ventura. Unfortuitously placed between the beautiful Central Coast and the multifarious charms of Los Angeles, Oxnard has several miles of beaches and a large marina, but little else to call its own. A beach-side stroll here does bring great

• *The red-tiled roofs of Santa Barbara.*

views of Anacapa, the nearest of the Channel Islands, but less interesting are the souvenir shops and tourist-aimed restaurants of Oxnard's Fisherman's Wharf.

PISMO 🛏 ✕

On Hwy-101/Hwy-1, 12 miles S of San Luis Obispo. The local Chamber of Commerce describes Pismo Beach as "friendly and old fashioned," as fair a description as any of this small coastal community, filled each summer by the vacationing pensioners who can't afford California's more famous retreats. There was a time when succulent **Pismo clams** could be dug up from the sands forming Pismo State Beach, running either side of the town. Threatened with extinction, the creature is now under state protection.

REFUGIO STATE BEACH

Off Hwy-101, 23 miles W of Santa Barbara. Flanked by rows of palm trees, the broad cove that holds Refugio State Beach makes a relaxing picnic stop. Once here,

• *Refugio Beach.*

it is tempting to do nothing but gaze for hours at the pretty beach. Should you be feeling energetic, explore more of the coastline on the 2½-mile cycle and footpath which runs to El Capitan State Beach, described on page 77.

SAN LUIS OBISPO

See California Overall: 5.

SANTA BARBARA 🛏 ✕

On Hwy-101/Hwy-1, 93 miles S of San Luis Obispo/96 miles N of Los Angeles. Santa Barbara captures the spirit of southern California completely. A wealthy and conservative community with an enviable natural setting – the heart of the town lies between a palm-lined beach and forested hillsides – yet it is also a place where the pace is slow, the mood informal, and visitors immediately feel welcome. Quite deliberately, Santa Barbara also looks exactly how a southern Californian town ought to look. After an major earthquake in 1925, the local authorities took the state's mission-style Spanish colonial architecture to heart, reconstructing the whole place with white plaster walls and red-tiled roofs, fitting arches and fake bell towers wherever space permitted.

Ironically, the one major building which deviates from this style is the **Santa Barbara Mission**, founded in 1786. At first a series of simple adobe structures, the mission underwent repeated modification until 1820 when, following substantial earthquake damage, it was rebuilt with the twin towers and columns which distinguish it today. There are also unusual neo-classical features, derived from a book on Roman architecture found in the mission's library. This is the tenth link in the Californian mission chain, and it has a majestic presence rarely matched by its counterparts. After the proud façade, the interior is rather disappointing, as is the museum with its small collection of ageing objects and reconstructed rooms. But take a look inside the serene chapel and then walk through the cemetery, bearing the unmarked remains of 4,000 Chumash neophytes alongside the elaborate tombs of Spanish notables.

More can be learned about the Chumash and about past and present Californian wildlife – close to the mission at the **Museum of Natural History**, 2599 Puesta del Sol Road. If spending a day in the open air holds more appeal, aim instead for the **Botanical Gardens**, 1212 Mission Canyon Road. "Gardens" is an inadequate title for this imposing chunk of land with five miles of foot trails winding through canyons and creeks, passing a thousand different species of native Californian vegetation – from towering redwood trees to the bright orange California poppy.

RECOMMENDED HOTELS

LOS ALAMOS

Union Hotel, $$$; 362 *Bell Street; tel.* 805 344 2744; *weekends only; credit cards,* AE, DC, MC, V.

A bizarre re-creation of a hotel that stood on this site in 1880, the Union Hotel is made up of odds and ends from various periods – an upright piano here, a jukebox there: what the place lacks in authenticity is more than compensated for by its eccentricity. An adjoining house, the Victorian Mansion, is even weirder, offering six windowless "themed" rooms, ranging from a 19thC Parisian artist's loft to a Spanish galleon.

OJAI

Ojai Valley Inn & Country Club, $$$$; *Country Club Road; tel.* 800 422 OJAI; *credit cards,* AE, CB, DC, DS, MC, V.

As luxurious (and as expensive) as they come, the original mission-style buildings date from 1923 but, several million dollars and several owners later, the 200-acre grounds are dotted by fully-equipped cabins, several tennis courts, and an 18-hole golf course.

PISMO BEACH

Knights Rest, $$; 2351 *Price Street; tel.* 805 773 4617; *credit cards,* AE, DC, MC, V.

On weekdays, when prices are reduced, you will find here the best value for money in this town of (seemingly) a million motels. Most of the rooms are large, some have two separate bedrooms, and most are equipped with coffee makers and fridges; in the grounds are a swimming-pool and a sauna.

SANTA BARBARA

Casa Del Mar; 18 *Bath Street; tel.* 808 433 3097; *credit cards,* AE, MC, V.

Generously-priced bed-and-breakfast accommodation in rooms grouped around a Mediterranean-style courtyard, at the center of which is an inviting jacuzzi. Within easy reach of the beach and Downtown, but a peacful and relaxing spot in which to unwind.

Hotel State Street, $-$$; 121 *State Street; tel.* 805 966 6586; *credit cards,* AE, MC, V.

One of a very limited batch of budget-priced hotels in Santa Barbara, these no-frills rooms are within easy walking distance of the beach and about half-a-mile from the downtown area; for the lowest rates, you'll have to share a bathroom.

Santa Barbara Inn, $$$-$$$$; 901

The Spanish often erected their missions hand-in-hand with a *presidio*, or fortress, serving an administrative as well as a military role. In Downtown Santa Barbara, **El Presidio State Historic Park**, 123 E Cañon Perdido, holds what little remains of the Santa Barbara *presidio* and is the site of a 40-year project to produce a detailed replica of the *presidio*. So far, only a very fine reconstruction of the chapel, decorated by numerous 17thC and 18thC religious objects and paintings, has been completed. The next major task involves restoring the gloomy and easily missed 1788 El Cuartel adobe, across the road from the chapel, part of the *presidio*'s residential quarters. A few minutes' walk away, the rich and entertaining clutter of the **Historical Museum**, 136 E De La Guerra Street, provides a fuller record of Santa Barbara's past.

There is no single example of Santa Barbara's fixation with Spanish Colonial architecture more deserving of attention than the **County Courthouse**, 1120 Anacapa Street. Finished in 1929 at a cost of $1.5 million and built around a sunken courtyard, the courthouse's lobby features fine Tunisian tilework, Moorish ceilings and Italian urns. On the second floor, pass beneath Byzantine arches and Romanesque windows while tracing the history of California depicted by a vast mural, and then continue by elevator to the top of the El Mirador belltower for a fabulous view across the whole town. Around the corner, the **Museum of Art**, 1130 State Street, devotes three floors to a small but mostly high quality collection ranging from Greek and Roman statuary to the artists of the American West and the California avant garde.

Despite being in plentiful supply, art,

Cabrillo Boulevard; tel. 805 966 2285; *credit cards*, AE, CB, DC, MC, V.

Facing the ocean but about a mile from the beach's busier sections, with fair-sized rooms and suites (the less expensive ones face inland), an inviting pool, plus complimentary continental breakfast and afternoon snacks.

Simpson House Inn, $$$-$$$$; 121 E. *Arrellaga Street; tel.* 805 963 7067; *credit cards*, MC, V.

An 1874 home built for two Scottish settlers, this tranquil bed-and-breakfast inn packed with frilly lace, flowers and antique furnishings – is only a couple of streets from the heart of downtown Santa Barbara. There is a minimum stay of two nights (three during public holidays) and you'll need at least that long to get through the complimentary decanter of sherry brightening every room.

SANTA MARIA

Santa Maria Inn, $$-$$$; 801 S. *Broadway; tel.* 805 928 7777; *credit cards*, AE, CB, DC, MC, V.

Among Santa Maria's oldest and most attractive buildings, this vine-covered early 1900s hotel comes rich in atmosphere and country-town charm. It also has handy modern conveniences such as video players and fridges in the bedrooms.

SOLVANG

Alisal Guest Ranch, $$$$; 1054 *Alisal Road; tel.* 805 688 6411; *credit cards*, AE, DC, MC, V.

A 10,000-acre former cattle ranch where guests can ride horses over hilltops and across meadows to a large lake teeming with bass and trout, waiting to hop out of the water and into frying pans; square dances, hay rides and barbecues complete the cowboy mood. Substantial ranch-style breakfasts and dinners are included in the sky-high rates – but stetson hats are not.

VENTURA

Doubletree, $$-$$$; 2055 *Harbor Boulevard; tel.* 805 643 6000; *credit cards*, AE, DC, DS, MC, V.

A branch of the nationwide chain that is fast becoming a byword for high standards in comfort and service. Just a block from the beach, with facilities that include a heated swimming-pool, sauna and whirlpool, and a well-equipped exercise room.

BUDGET ACCOMODATION

SANTA BARBARA

International Backpackers Hostel; 409 *State Street; tel.* 805 963 0154.

• *The mission at Ventura.*

architecture and history are far from the minds of many who visit Santa Barbara. For them, the town begins and ends with the lovely stretch of beach a mile west of Downtown. Along the beach-side path, joggers and skaters glide beneath the palm trees, often dodging homeless people pushing their worldly possessions in carts – a juxtaposition of California's hedonistic and poverty-stricken lifestyles much loved by TV news crews.

At the center of the beach, the 19thC **Stearns Wharf**, once part-owned by actor James Cagney, offers a dreary selection of gift shops and seafood restaurants. The wharf's Nature Conservancy Sea Center is an exception, providing useful information on visiting the Channel Islands National Park and on other issues of ecological importance.

Perversely, perhaps, it is very easy to eat well and inexpensively in Santa Barbara but much harder to find low-cost accommodation. If costs are a problem, spend a day (or two) here and sleep elsewhere.

SANTA MARIA 🛏 ✕

On Hwy-1, 31 miles S of San Luis Obispo. A commercially important agricultural town with a surprisingly high cultural profile – the highly-rated Pacific Conservatory of the Performing Arts is based here – Santa Maria nevertheless holds little that will set visitors' pulses racing. Should you be passing through,

THE CHANNEL ISLANDS NATIONAL PARK

From Ventura, and less frequently from Santa Barbara, there are boat trips to the Channel Islands National Park, comprising five of the nine volcanic islands which lie some 15 miles off the coast between Los Angeles and Morro Bay. The Chumash people once settled the larger islands, California's first Spanish visitors landed on one of them, and 19thC fur trappers devastated their colonies of sea otters, seals and sea lions. Since becoming partly protected in 1938, the islands' unique plant and birdlife have flourished. Rugged and uninhabited, the Channel Islands have no tourist facilities and can be explored only on the marked hiking trails. Trips are run by Island Packers, 1867 Spinnaker Drive, Ventura (tel. 805 642 1393), the Nature Conservancy, Stearns Wharf, Santa Barbara (tel. 805 962 9111).

however, the **Santa Maria Valley Historical Museum**, 616 S. Broadway, provides an excuse to dally.

SANTA MONICA

See Local Explorations: 15.

SANTA PAULA

On Hwy-126, 15 miles E of Ventura. Using computer simulations and a working model of an oil rig, Santa Paula's **California Oil Museum** describes the discovery of oil in California and the subsequent rise of the state's oil industry. Predictably, it is a celebratory display and from it you wouldn't suspect that drilling for oil (and particularly offshore drilling) is one of the hottest environmental issues in California.

• *Solvang, a little piece of Denmark in California.*

SANTA YNEZ

On Hwy-154, 34 miles S of Santa Maria. In Santa Ynez, the **Valley Historical Society Museum**, 3596 Sagunto Street, allocates a room to the Chumash Indian life, highlighting their basketry and canoe-making skills, and stocks several of the wagons, stagecoaches and buggies that were used locally from the late 19thC. Within a few minutes' drive, the Gainey Vineyard (a mile east) and the Santa Ynez Winery (2 miles south) both offer tours and tastings.

SOLVANG

On Hwy-246, 3 miles E of Santa Ynez. Solvang was founded in 1911 by Danish professors based in Illinois, hoping to establish a college to pass on Danish traditions in the style of Denmark's folk high schools. What they would make of

the fake-thatched roofs, wooden storks, windmills and souvenir shops that fill the moderately-sized town today is anyone's guess. Nonetheless, Solvang is an amusing phenomenon – take a peek at the **Hans Christian Andersen Museum**, 1680 Mission Drive, then sample the produce of the bakeries.

On the eastern edge of Solvang and predating the arrival of the Danes, **Mission Santa Inez** was founded in 1804 as part of a plan to convert the Chumash living in the inland valleys. Sheer isolation meant that the mission never thrived, though a large cattle holding enabled it to survive. The mission's small museum and its church's *trompe-l'oeil* paintings merit a quick visit.

THOUSAND OAKS

On Hwy-101, 33 miles S of Ventura. A leafy, valley community separated from Los Angeles by the Santa Monica Mountains, Thousand Oaks was a stop on the LA to Santa Barbara stagecoach route during the late 1800s. In a reconstructed Monterey-style building, the **Stagecoach Inn Museum**, 51 S. Ventura Park Road, records the early days of southern Californian long distance transportation – and assorted other historical interludes – with a large stack of diverse memorabilia.

VENTURA ⛟ ✕

On Hwy-101/Hwy-1, 32 miles S of Santa Barbara/64 miles N of Los Angeles. A large oil refinery does substantially less for Ventura's scenery than it does for the town's economy, but several miles of beaches patronized by surfers and water-sports enthusiasts give the town some appeal – as do the historical remnants found around **Mission San Buenaventura**, 211 E. Main Street, from which Ventura derived its name.

Of the mission buildings, only the small church, completed in 1809, survives intact. More promising are the numerous finds from the time of Spanish settlement and Native American items dated to 1600 BC (predating the better-known Chumash peoples), unearthed on local archaeological digs, and on display at the **Albinger Archaeological Museum**, 113 E. Main Street. The **Ventura County Museum of History & Art**, 100 E. Main Street, documents the diverse nationalities who settled in and farmed the Ventura region from the late 19thC. From a slightly earlier period, when California was still a Mexican possession and divided into vast ranchos, stand the **Ortega Adobe**, 215 W. Main Street, and, across town, the **Olivas Adobe Historical Park**, 4200 Olivas Park Drive, with a Monterey-style adobe home packed with fixtures and fittings of the time.

RECOMMENDED RESTAURANTS

OJAI

Soda Bar & Grille, $; 219 E. *Matilija Street; tel.* 805 646 7632; *cards, none.*

Simple selection of burgers, sandwiches and omelettes in a 1950s-style setting. The desserts are wicked and highly calorific.

PISMO BEACH

McLintock's Saloon & Dining House, $-$$; 750 *Mattie Road; tel.* 805 773 1892; *lunch and dinner only on weekdays; credit cards,* MC, V.

It may be a mile north of Pismo Beach (at Shell Beach), but everybody who stays in the area visits this long-established bar and eatery at least once. Served as steaks or burgers, the meat is exceptionally well prepared and the seafood, too, is sure to be fresh. For good food in large amounts, the prices are reasonable – expect to wait for a table if you don't make a reservation.

SANTA BARBARA

Andria's Harborside Restaurant, $-$$; 336 W. *Cabrillo Boulevard; tel.* 805 966 3000.

One of the best locations close to the beach for large energy-giving breakfasts, also a dependable stop for lunch and dinner.

Cajun Kitchen, $; 1924 *De La Vina Street; tel.* 805 687 2026; *breakfast and lunch only; credit cards, none.*

A great place for a spicy, Louisiana-style snack – choose from chili, red beans and rice, blackened fish or shrimp creole.

Esau's Coffee Shop, $; 403 *State Street; tel.* 805 965 4461; *closes 1pm; credit cards, none.*

Also in Ventura, the Channel Islands National Park Visitors Center, 1901 Spinnaker Drive, provides useful background on the Channel Islands National Park, described on page 82.

• *Branding calves, Ventura County.*

Fans of the great American breakfast will be right at home here. Breakfast is all that's served in various combinations of corned beef, ham, sausage and eggs, or as ambrosial omelettes with a host of enticing fillings. Included are homemade jam and salsa, and you can even try your luck with grits.

Joe's Cafe, $-$$; 536 *State Street; tel.* 805 966 4638; *credit cards,* AE, DC, MC, V.

A local institution as a great place to gorge on simple, well-cooked American food – the multi-course steak and seafood dinners are enormously popular – and as a jolly place to drink and socialize into the small hours.

Main Squeeze, $; 138 E. *Cañon Perdido; tel.* 805 966 5365; *evenings only at weekends; credit cards, none.*

A very southern Californian health food restaurant with a lengthy and tempting seafood, pasta and vegetarian menu that includes some tremendous salads. At weekends, the eating is done to the accompaniment of live music.

SANTA MARIA

China Brown, $-$$; 1206 S. *Broadway; tel.* 805 925 0041; *credit cards, none.*

A large range of regional Chinese dishes making the most of California's abundant supplies of fresh meat and vegetables – and the chef's pleasure in concocting hot and spicy sauces – and served in a very informal setting.

SOLVANG

Danish Inn Restaurant, $$; 1547 *Mission Drive; tel.* 805 688 4831; *credit cards,* AE, DC, DS, MC, V.

Although it is a Swedish, not a Danish, speciality, the lunch and dinner smorgasbord offered here is great value for its artfully presented array of meat and fish. Pick and choose from the open table as much and as often as you want; alternatively, order from the extensive menu.

The Mustard Seed, $; 1655 *Mission Drive; tel.* 805 688 1318; *credit cards, none.*

Easy-going mixture of regular American and Danish-influenced fare served throughout the day (no dinners on Mon). The Danish-style breakfast omelettes are worth trying; for dinner, sample chicken pot pie – the house speciality.

VENTURA

Yolanda's Mexican Cafe, $-$$; 2753 E. *Main Street; tel.* 805 643 2700; *lunch and dinner only; credit cards,* AE, MC, V.

The fiery specialities of Mexico and the American southwest presented in a vibrantly decorated room.

Southern California

Between Los Angeles and Blythe/Las Vegas
The Inland Empire and the High and Low Deserts

180/200 *miles; map Kummerley + Frey California-Nevada*

Few parts of California evoke such excitement – or such apprehension – as the deserts, which cut a great swath across the state's eastern and southern extremities. Not unusually, my first sight of the California desert was bitterly disappointing: instead of rolling dunes and fantastic cacti, all that lined the dusty interstate was open scrubland and abandoned tires. The great vistas are there, but an effort is needed to find them.

To make this easy, I have devised a two-in-one route across the desert that leaves you with just one decision: whether to take the northerly I-15, the main road between Los Angeles and Las Vegas, or the more southerly I-10, which connects LA and Palm Springs and has easy links with Local Explorations: 17 and 18 before it continues into Arizona.

The only area touched by both I-10 and I-15 is the Inland Empire (part of our medium, blue route) between the deserts and Los Angeles. Here, fertile soils stimulated a turn-of-the-century citrus boom and made this one of the state's busiest, richest regions. The citrus industry is still going strong, but the Inland Empire towns have seen better days, and much of their historical appeal has been swamped by creeping suburbia.

Above the Inland Empire, our green route explores the un-desert-like alpine scenery of the San Bernardino Mountains on the so-called Rim of the World Drive.

Otherwise, our red and blue routes stick close to either the I-15 or the I-10. As if designed for drivers with roulette wheels on the brain, I-15 has few distractions all the way across the Nevada border to Las Vegas. One exception is Barstow, close to which a prehistoric lake bed creates a scene of geological strangeness and an archaeological site has revealed evidence of a 200,000-year-old settlement.

If gambling does not feature on your agenda, you are better off exploring the desert with the I-10, finding time to visit some or all of our blue places, which are reached by branching off the I-10 through the Coachella Valley, a palm-dotted oasis holding the famed Palm Springs and an ideal base for visiting the incredible Joshua Tree National Monument: a place that you'll remember long after you have forgotten what the rest of California looks like.

TIPS FOR DESERT TRAVEL

The best months for desert travel are September to March: the high desert summers are too hot for comfortable touring, although the low desert summers are more bearable. Whenever and wherever you go, carry a detailed map, ample drinking water and supplies, and seek and heed the advice given by local visitor centers. If you plan to venture off the major routes, first inform the local visitor center – or another relevant authority – of your plans.

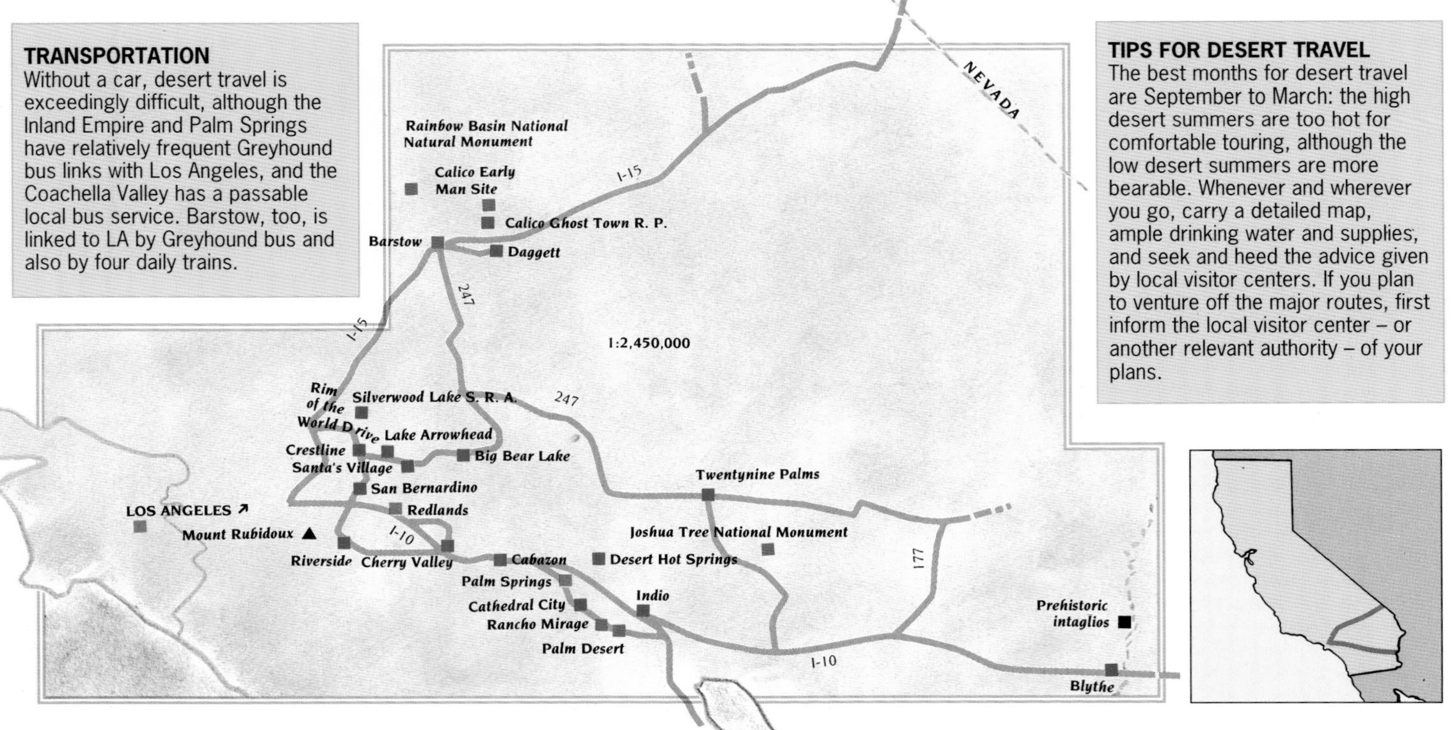

TRANSPORTATION

Without a car, desert travel is exceedingly difficult, although the Inland Empire and Palm Springs have relatively frequent Greyhound bus links with Los Angeles, and the Coachella Valley has a passable local bus service. Barstow, too, is linked to LA by Greyhound bus and also by four daily trains.

SIGHTS & PLACES OF INTEREST

BARSTOW 🛏 ✕

On I-15, 113 miles NE of Los Angeles. Barstow originated as a railroad junction in 1886 and even today most people who arrive in the town are in transit – pausing just long enough to buy gasoline and a snack before continuing through miles of empty desert on the way to Las Vegas. More surprisingly, Barstow has earned a cult following among Los Angeles shoppers, who think nothing of a five-hour round-trip drive to reach the discounted designer-label clothes sold at the town's **Factory Merchants Outlet Plaza**. Should desert touring, rather than gambling and shopping, be top of your agenda, make use of the town's **Desert Information Center**, 813 Barstow Road (tel. 619 256 8617) for the latest on desert weather and road conditions.

BIG BEAR LAKE 🛏 ✕

On Hwy-18, 30 miles E of Lake Arrowhead. When Angelenos and residents of the Inland Empire want to escape the dusty flatlands, they make for Big Bear Lake, a year-round recreation spot 7,000-ft-up in the San Bernardino Mountains. The 7-mile-long reservoir here is enclosed by dense woodlands, and activities include hiking, horse-riding, boating and fishing (and, in winter, skiing). Fresh air and invigorating alpine landscapes are here for the taking, but don't rely on solitude – this is a very popular place.

> DETOUR – **RAINBOW BASIN NATIONAL NATURAL MONUMENT**
>
> Drive north from Barstow on Fort Irwin Road, after about five miles turning left on to Fossil Beds Road and following the signs for Rainbow Basin National Natural Monument. Some 15 million years ago, this now barren and arid area was lush and fertile, and held several enormous lakes. Over tens of thousands of years, a changing climate caused the lakes to dry up, exposing their varied layers of sediment and the fossils of prehistoric creatures – such as three-toed horses, dog-bears and various gigantic insects. Take the signposted drive and feast your eyes on an other-worldly landscape of strangely-shaped, brightly-colored rocks that seem to glow in the sun.
>
> Fossils, too, are easily found, with a bit of exploration on foot, though removing them is forbidden.

BLYTHE

On I-10, 230 miles E of Los Angeles. Succinctly described by one guide as a "useful freeway stopover town," Blythe is a speck on the California–Arizona border surrounded by a slender band of fertile farmland, the ground being irrigated by the Colorado River which marks the border. With great optimism and not much success, Blythe is attempting to sell itself as a desert resort town but there's nothing – except distance from anywhere else (and the detour described below) – to encourage a stop.

CABAZON ✕

On I-10, 33 miles E of Redlands. Evidence of prehistoric habitation is scattered throughout California's desert regions. Two of the least authentic examples stand beside I-10 at Cabazon: 40-ton replicas of a brontosaurus and a tyrannosaurus rex, inside the former a collection of odds and ends described as a desert museum. Fans of Pee Wee Herman are likely to remember the creatures from their part in the cult actor's film, *Pee Wee's Big Adventure.*

CALICO GHOST TOWN REGIONAL PARK

Off I-15, 7 miles E of Barstow. Genuine ghost towns, their ruined buildings inhabited only by wind-blown tumbleweed, are dotted across California. Like many of them, Calico thrived in the late 1800s when five years of mining in the nearby Calico Hills yielded $86 million-worth of precious minerals, notably gold and silver. To all intents and purposes, as soon as the mines were finished, so was the town, and what's here now is a re-creation of an Old West boom town, complete with reconstructed saloon, general store and school house. The park is enjoyable and popular, but the accent is firmly on entertainment rather than historical accuracy.

CALICO EARLY MAN SITE

Off I-15, 14 *miles* E *of* Barstow. A parched spot in the Calico Hills might be the last place you'd expect decades of established historical thinking to be overturned. However, over the last 30 years, archaeological excavations here have revealed scrapers, cutters, saws, axes, and other primitive tools believed to be 200,000 years old. If the age is correct, this is the oldest known site of human habitation in North America and one that proves settlement took place long before the arrival of the people previously thought to have been the first Americans (those who crossed the Bering Straits from Siberia 10-20,000 years ago). Marked walkways make the dig-site accessible, though there is more to be gleaned in the visitors' center and museum, where many of the finds are exhibited and their significance explained.

CATHEDRAL CITY ×

On Hwy-111, 8 *miles* SE *of* Palm Springs. The least up-market of the towns grouped close to Palm Springs in the Coachella Valley, Cathedral City is uninteresting in itself but when you tire of the glamor (and the sometimes inflated prices) of its more famous neighbor, the town is a likely stop for an inexpensive bite to eat; see hotels and restaurants.

DETOUR – **PREHISTORIC INTAGLIOS**

A few miles east of Blythe on I-10, turn north on to Hwy-95 and continue for 15 miles until you reach a signposted side road. This leads to a set of prehistoric intaglios, or ground figures, made by removing the top-layer of rocks and gravel to expose lighter-colored sand beneath. Whether these figures – the larger ones resemble a human and a four-legged animal – were intended as art, for use in rituals, or served some other purpose, can only be guessed at. One curious fact, however, is that the figures are much clearer from the air than from the ground.

• *Dinosaurs off* I-10, *near* Palm Springs.

• *Joshua Tree National Monument.*

CHERRY VALLEY

Off I-10, 12 miles E of Redlands. Old World culture unexpectedly rears its head in the rural hamlet of Cherry Valley, where the **Edward Dean Museum of Decorative Arts**, 9401 Oak Glen Road, carries a striking collection of European and Asian decorative art from the 17thC to the 19thC, and numerous pieces of handcrafted antique furniture.

CRESTLINE

On Hwy-18, 10 miles N of San Bernardino. The rustic community of Crestline, mostly concealed along winding forested lanes, is of no appeal whatsoever except as a start (or end) point of the Rim of the World Drive. From here, heading left (through the Valley of Enchantment) leads to Silverwood Lake State Recreation Area, turning right (through the Valley of the Moon) leads to Lake Arrowhead.

DAGGETT

Off I-40, 6 miles E of Barstow. Named after a man who walked from Ohio to California in 1850, Daggett is a dusty village of a few streets and the Stone Hotel, dating from 1875. A more bizarre sight stands just east, where hundreds of mirrors sticking out of the ground are actually heliostats belonging to the Solar One Power Plant. Call at the plant's visitor center for an explanation of the intriguing process which turns sunshine into electricity.

DESERT HOT SPRINGS

Off I-10, 12 miles N of Palm Springs. Desert Hot Springs lacks the allure of nearby Palm Springs but its residents make a fuss about their extra hour of daylight (unlike Palm Springs, there's no mountain to block the sunset), which makes possible an extra set of tennis or an extra few holes of golf – paramount local concerns.

Besides sport, and several spa resorts, the town has one place of special curiosity. **Cabot's Old Indian Pueblo Museum,** 67616 E. Desert

View Avenue, was built (but never finished) single-handedly over 20 years by an early local settler. The ramshackle four-story building, packed with Hopi Indian handicrafts and desert oddments, can be fully comprehended on the guided tours (Wed to Sun only).

INDIO

On I-10, 18 miles E of Palm Springs. Tourism is the key factor in most economies in and around Palm Springs. In hard-working Indio, however, it is agriculture that rules the day. Locally-grown melons, grapefruits and strawberries all pass through this commercial base, as does an incredible $30-million worth of dates. The **National Date Festival**, held in Indio each February since 1921, celebrates the crop with ostrich and camel races, and provides opportunities to sample rich and delicious varieties of date which you would otherwise never dream existed. That aside, the only other object of attention is the **Coachella Valley Museum and Cultural Center**, 82616 Miles Avenue, a comprehensive gathering of paraphernalia covering 70 years of local life.

JOSHUA TREE NATIONAL MONUMENT

Off Hwy-62, 2 miles E of Twenty Nine Palms; also off I-10, 20 miles E of Indio. UFO-logist George Adamski claimed to have been carried above the Joshua Tree National Monument in a craft piloted by "long-haired Venusians" – just one of the numerous weird tales which have grown up around the Joshua Tree National Monument. Indeed, it was a persecuted religious group, the Mormon Battalion, on the journey that eventually led to the founding of Salt Lake City, that helped give the place its name in the 1850s. They believed that the upturned branches of the strange trees (actually a species of giant yucca) matched a passage in their Book of Joshua – "thou shalt follow the way pointed for thee by the trees."

Whatever you think of the stories, there's no debating the fact the Joshua Tree National Monument is an extraordinary place. It is also incredibly big – covering 870 square miles – and there's no way you're going to see all of it unless you're a seasoned desert adventurer armed with a tent and supplies to last several months. It is quite feasible, however, to spend a day driving across the monument between Hwy-62 and I-10. Before entering, call at the Oases Visitors' Center, off Hwy-62 just outside Twentynine Palms (or the Cottonwood Visitor Center off I-10), and study the free map and brochures. Pick out the vantage points, the picnic spots and special sites of interest – which might be a prehistoric rock pictograph or a 19thC gold mine – that appeal most and make for them.

Try to avoid walking in the midday heat (especially in the lower, southerly part of the monument) and aim to be in the north-westerly section – where the wondrous trees are situated – at sunrise or sunset. At these times, the Joshua trees cast long, eerie shadows and the huge quartz boulders behind them are bathed in various shades of red, orange and gold – as mystical a landscape as you are ever likely to see.

LAKE ARROWHEAD 🛏 ✕

Off Hwy-18, 4 miles W of Crestline. Los Angeles high-flyers buy weekend retreats on Lake Arrowhead where they can imbibe crisp alpine air and gaze contentedly across a wide expanse of privately-owned water fringed by fir and pine trees. It's a lovely setting but unless you're very well connected the most you can expect from it is an enjoyable narrated cruise on the *Arrowhead Queen*, a paddle-wheel vessel departing

DETOUR – **INDIAN CANYONS**

Five miles from the center of Palm Springs, a toll-gate on S. Palm Canyon Drive gives access to the Indian Canyons, a series of palm-filled canyons within the stark folds of the San Jacinto Mountains. The toll is paid to the Agua Caliente people and the canyons form part of their tribal homelands. The Agua Caliente operate a trading post here, selling arts and handicrafts, and the maps which are essential for visiting the canyons. On a first trip, Palm Canyon is the simplest to explore: a paved footpath leads from a car-park through the canyon – which holds the world's largest single gathering of palm trees, around 7,000 at the last count – and reaches several points where prehistoric desert people have left their mark.

several times daily from Leroy's Sports, in Lake Arrowhead Village (for details: tel. 714 336 6992).

LOS ANGELES

Local Explorations: 15 and 16.

PALM DESERT

On Hwy-111, 12 miles SE of Palm Springs. The leading names of international haute couture have outlets in Palm Desert's **El Paseo**, a high class shopping mall with a Spanish architectural style. Even if you can't afford a downpayment on a Polo Ralph Lauren tie pin, there's no charge for looking in the windows and seeing what the well-dressed, well-heeled Palm Springs socialite is wearing. For considerably less money, a different side of local life is on show at the **Living Desert Reserve**, 47900 S. Portola Avenue, where 6 miles of pathways pass through re-creations of California's diverse desert landscapes. Besides a copious amount of cacti and hardy desert plants, the reserve holds live coyotes, owls, bats, snakes and bighorn sheep, and many other desert-dwelling creatures.

PALM SPRINGS 🛏 ✕

On Hwy-111, 103 miles E of Los Angeles. Internationally famous as a desert playground for the rich and famous, Palm Springs may well be America's most sybaritic community – but it's also far smaller and less elitist (and much less expensive) than its high rolling reputa-

RECOMMENDED HOTELS

BARSTOW

Astro Motel, $; 1271 E. *Main Street; tel.* 619 256 2204; *credit cards,* AE, DS, MC, V.

Accommodation in Barstow begins and ends with the rows of clean, functional motels on or close to Main Street. You will be hard pushed to find a better-priced one than this.

BIG BEAR LAKE

Knickerbocker Mansion, $$$; 869 S. *Knickerbocker Road; tel.* 714 866 8221; *credit cards,* MC, V.

A rustic and comfortable bed-and-breakfast inn occupying the gigantic log cabin which Mr. and Mrs Knickerbocker began building in 1917 to house their growing brood of little Knickerbockers. Remnants from the Knickerbockers' time lie scattered through the ten pleasantly furnished guest rooms, some of which overlook the lake.

Cozy Hollow Lodge, $$-$$$; 40409 *Big Bear Boulevard; tel.* 714 866 8886; *credit cards,* AE, DC, DS, MC, V.

Spread across 4 acres of pine-studded grounds, Cozy Hollow Lodge comprises a series of cabins – some fairly simple, others well-equipped suites with two bedrooms – complete with an outside barbecue area where you can gut and cook the fish you've just caught on the lake.

LAKE ARROWHEAD

Bluebelle House Inn, $$$; 263 *Route* 73; *tel.* 714 336 3292; *credit cards,* MC, V.

One of several appealing bed-and-breakfast options around Lake Arrowhead: five cozy rooms, two with private bathrooms and all pervaded by the invigorating scent of pine trees.

PALM SPRINGS

Casa Cody Country Inn, $-$$$$; 175 S. *Cahuilla Road; tel.* 619 320 9346; *credit cards,* AE, MC, V.

The one- and two-bedroom suites are exceptional value for money and ideal if you're planning a lengthy stay. Like the cheaper rooms, they are decorated in Santa Fe style, and are equipped with wood-burning fireplaces for cool desert evenings.

Mira Loma, $$-$$$; 1420 N. *Indian Drive; tel.* 619 320 1178; *credit cards,* AE, MC, V.

Twelve rooms grouped around a pool and decorated in 1940s Art Deco style, with fridges and coffee-makers, and a free newspaper delivered each morning. Be a devil and ask for Room 3, that's (allegedly) where Marilyn Monroe used to stay.

Motel 6, $; 595 E. *Palm Canyon Drive; tel.* 619 325 6129; *credit cards,* CB, DC, MC, V.

Only the prices – the lowest in town – distinguish this branch of the very plain nationwide budget-chain. Often fully booked, but last minute cancellation would have you believe. In fact, much of what the outside world thinks of as Palm Springs includes the other Coachella Valley communities – such as the truly wealthy Rancho Mirage – grouped shoulder-to-shoulder along Hwy-111. Palm Springs itself extends for only a few square miles and its south-western edge is walled by the San Jacinto Mountains, so close you could reach out and touch them.

For years a forlorn, barely-populated desert outpost, Palm Springs got into gear in the 1930s when the screen stars of Hollywood began arriving in droves. Attracted by the warm climate, the (then) cheap land and the chance to escape the Hollywood paparazzi, Humphrey Bogart, Clark Gable and Marlene Dietrich were among the first big names to have homes built here. They have since been followed by a veritable *Who's Who* of the entertainment industry (including the town's long-serving mayor, Sonny Bono) plus numerous ex-presidents and countless millionaires. Remarkably, though, Palm Springs major land owners are the Agua Caliente Indians, a section of the Cahuilla tribe who were granted parcels of the area (even though they'd lived on it for countless generations) in a chessboard-style arrangement with the Southern Pacific Railroad in 1870.

The town makes the most of its delightful setting. Palm fronds are arranged over traffic lights to prevent glare diminishing the clarity of the star-

tions can sometimes be snapped up.

Spa Hotel & Mineral Springs, $$-$$$$; 100 N. *Indian Avenue; tel.* 800 854 1279; *credit cards*, AE, CB, DC, MC, V.

One of the oldest and, for many people, still the best of Palm Springs's numerous spa resorts, and one that offers aromatherapy and eucalyptus vapor inhalation alongside the more customary massage, gym and solarium – and, of course, dips in a hot mineral pool.

Villa Rosa Inn, $-$$; 1577 S. *Indian Trail; tel.* 619 327 5915; *credit cards*, MC, V.

Friendly, small motel at the south end of town with regular rooms and kitchenettes; a light complimentary breakfast is served at the poolside.

Villa Royale, $$-$$$$; 1620 *Indian Trail; tel.* 800 245 2314; *credit cards*, AE, MC, V.

A very stylish but low-key bed-and-breakfast inn where the rooms – each one tastefully decorated in the style of a European country – face on to small courtyards, which in turn lead to a 3-acre Spanish-style garden complete with splashing fountains.

RIVERSIDE

Hampton Inn, $$; 1590 *University Avenue; tel.* 714 683 6000; *credit cards*, AE, CB, DC, MC, V.

Part of the nationwide chain offering fair-sized, well-equipped rooms at a reasonable price. Set on the edge of town, this one is awkward to reach if you're not driving.

The Mission Inn, $$$-$$$$; 3649 *Seventh Street; tel.* 714 784 0300; *credit cards*, AE, DC, MC, V.

An historic local landmark (see Sights & Places of Interest) recently treated to a $40-million renovation: quite the most elegant place for miles around, though not reaching the decadent heights of luxury it once attained.

TWENTYNINE PALMS

Econo Lodge, $; 72562 29 *Palms Highway; tel.* 800 874 4556; *credit cards*, AE, DC, DS, MC, V.

Just right for a budget-priced night's rest before an early morning visit to the Joshua Tree National Monument.

Oases of Eden Motel, $$–$$$; 56377 *Twentynine Palms Highway; tel.* 619 365 6321; *credit cards*, AE, MC, V.

A choice of regular motel rooms, some of which have kitchenettes, and five imposingly-themed suites varying from a 1920s Art Deco job to a re-creation of Ancient Roman living quarters. Outside, a heated pool and a jacuzzi ease the rigors of desert travel. Actually situated 20 miles east of Twentynine Palms, in Yucca Valley.

filled night sky; micromist systems spray fine jets of water on restaurant patios to cool (but not soak) diners; and the golf courses, more than 70 of them, are irrigated by recycled water.

Undoubtedly a great place in which to do absolutely nothing, Palm Springs does have a couple of places worth making the effort to see (though both are closed during summer): the **Desert Museum**, 101 Museum Drive, an ultra-modern facility with changing exhibitions of western and desert art, natural history and anthropology – the sculpture-filled garden was financed by Frank Sinatra; and **Moorten's Botanical Garden**, 1701 S. Palm Canyon Drive, a bird and wildlife sanctuary with a mesmerizing stock of desert plants and cacti.

Spotting celebrity's homes is a popular Palm Springs pastime. The necessary map is available free from the Visitor Information Agency, 2781 N. Palm Canyon Drive (tel. 619 774 8418), though you'll have more fun seeing the same houses with the commentary provided by Desert Adventures (tel. 619 324 3378) who also lead tours into the surrounding desert and canyons. By contrast, nobody famous ever lived in the 1884 McCallum Adobe, the oldest house in Palm Springs and, filled with remnants of the town's earliest days, forming part of the **Village Green Heritage Center**, 221 S. Palm Canyon Drive. On this briefly diverting historical plot, you'll also find the "Little House," built in 1893 of old railway sleepers, and Ruddy's General Store Museum, a detailed reconstruction of a 1938 if-they-make-it, we'll-sell-it shop.

For a bird's-eye view of Palm Springs and a chance to escape the desert floor heat, take the **Aerial Tramway** – off Hwy-111 just west of town – and rise 6,000-feet in 20 minutes to **Mount San Jacinto State Park**, a sub-alpine landscape covered by 50 miles of hiking and horse trails (which the winter snows transform into ski-trails). One of the trails leads to the 10,000-ft summit of Mount San Jacinto and gives unparalleled views over the Coachella Valley and far beyond. A sight which pioneering California naturalist John Muir described as "the most sublime spectacle to be found anywhere on this earth."

RANCHO MIRAGE

On Hwy-111, 11 miles SE of Palm Springs. Contrary to popular belief, those greats of American showbiz such as Frank Sinatra and Bob Hope don't actually have homes in Palm Springs but live in Rancho Mirage, a community composed of guarded estates, ultra-exclusive country clubs and very well maintained (thanks to astronomical membership fees) golf courses. Being incredibly rich and famous can have its pitfalls, however, as demonstrated by the presence of the **Betty Ford Clinic**, a high-cost detoxification facility named after the wife of former president, Gerald Ford – who also happens to live in Rancho Mirage.

REDLANDS

On I-10, 7 miles E of San Bernardino. Today it is hard to believe, but long before anybody had heard of Palm

• *Aerial Tramway, off Hwy-111, west of Palm Springs.*

• *A cultural oasis in the desert, Palm Springs.*

Springs, Redlands was a booming citrus farming town and the apple of the eye of many rich Easterners seeking a warm place to spend their winters. Their patronage resulted in the construction of dozens of gabled and turreted wooden houses, many of which still stand (mostly along Olive Street), in what is now a fast-growing suburban town.

Redlands holds several curious items. Behind the Moorish-style public library, the **Lincoln Shrine Memorial** is devoted entirely to Abraham Lincoln, with a collection of photos, letters and memorabilia mostly detailing his role in leading the Union side to victory in the Civil War. And while the extensive collections and displays of the **San Bernardino County Museum**, 2025 Orange Tree Lane, could easily consume an hour, a more atmospheric record of times past is provided by the two-room museum of the restored **San Bernardino Asistencia**, 26930 Barton Road, built in 1830 as a branch of Mission San Gabriel Archangel.

RIVERSIDE

On Hwy-215, 6 miles S of San Bernardino. In 1895, Riverside could boast of being the wealthiest city – per capita – in the U.S., a fact entirely due to the rich soils and balmy climate that made the town a center for citrus growing, including the raising of the newly-developed navel orange, uniquely able to ripen in winter. Easily the grandest of several old buildings in the present town center is the **Mission Inn**, 3649 Seventh Street, designed in flowing Spanish Revival manner by Frank A. Miller, who moved to Riverside in 1873 when his father was appointed chief engineer. The inn's lavishly furnished bedrooms, music rooms and patios were enjoyed by several generations of the country's rich and powerful. Discover more about the inn, and much more about oranges, at the **Municipal Museum**, 3720 Orange Street, occupying a pretty Italianate building of 1912.

A recent boost to civic pride was the acquisition of the **California Museum of Photography**, 3824 Main Street, an outstanding collection which documents the development of photography with an absorbing cache of old cameras and modern hands-on exhibits. The actual photographs on display range from the 1800s to the present day, and there are temporary shows of a high standard.

SAN BERNARDINO

On I-10, 62 miles E of Los Angeles. Easily the least appealing settlement of the Inland Empire, San Bernardino was founded by a Mormon colony in the 1850s and has evolved into an unattractive combination of citrus-packing center and smog-bound suburbia. Proximity to Crestline (see page 90) and the Rim of the World Drive is the only reason to pass through.

SANTA'S VILLAGE

On Hwy-18, 4 miles E of Lake Arrowhead. An underwhelming collection of pretend sleigh rides, revolving Christmas trees and other lightweight amusements linked by a Santa Claus theme. Don't stop at Santa's Village unless you have a perverse sense of humor or some very restless kids on board.

• *Snowy egret, Silverwood Lake State Recreation Area.*

RECOMMENDED RESTAURANTS

BARSTOW

Idle Spurs Steak House, $-$$; *29557 Hwy-58; tel. 619 256 8888; lunch and dinner only; credit cards, MC, V.*

A few miles west of Barstow, this Old West-style eatery delivers steak, ribs and seafood meals in large portions and without pretensions.

BIG BEAR LAKE

Boo Bear's Den, $-$$; *572 Pine Knot Boulevard; tel. 714 866 2932; credit cards, MC, V.*

A reliable stop for straightforward, inexpensive dishes such as omelettes, soups and burgers; open all day but the best deals are at breakfast time.

The Iron Squirrel, $$$; *646 Pine Knot Boulevard; tel. 714 866 9121; dinner only; brunch on Sunday; credit cards, AE, MC, V.*

The wonderful French country cooking is enough to draw discerning diners from LA up into the mountains, but the atmosphere is far from formal; a dinner here is an excellent last-night treat before departing Big Bear Lake.

CABAZON

Wheel's Inn, $; *on I-10 at Cabazon; tel. 619 849 7012; credit cards, none.*

An open round-the-clock truckstop, whose owner is responsible for the two replica dinosaurs in the grounds (see Sights & Places of Interest). Even if you don't feel up to tackling a full meal (if you do, you won't need to eat again all day), sample one of the delicious desserts – and load the jukebox to hear your favorite Country & Western tunes.

CATHEDRAL CITY

Stuft Pizza, $-$$; *67-555 Hwy-111; tel. 619 321 2583; lunch and dinner only; credit cards, MC, V.*

An establishment which takes great pride in its crusts – fresh, chewy ones that form the base of Chicago-style pizzas served with a multitude of toppings. The calzone is worth trying, too.

Marie Callender's, $; *69830 Hwy-111; tel. 619 328 0844; lunch and dinner only; credit cards, AE, MC, V.*

A chain well-known throughout California for its sinful fruit pies that also plies a decent assortment of lowish-priced, simple main meals: omelettes, chili, burgers and the like.

LAKE ARROWHEAD

Heidi's, $; *Lake Arrowhead Village; tel. 714 336 1511; Sun-Fri breakfast and lunch*

SILVERWOOD LAKE STATE RECREATION AREA

On Hwy-18, 8 miles NW of Crestline. Vacationing northern Californians find their enjoyment of the picnicking, hiking and swimming at Silverwood Lake State Recreation Area tempered by the fact that the artificial lake is filled with water from the north's rivers, stored here on its way to lubricating the farmlands and homes of southern California. What upsets the north's ecology has done wonders for the south's birdlife, however: great blue herons, snowy egrets, western grebes, and a variety of waterfowl are among the species likely to divert amateur ornithologists at the lakeside.

DETOUR – **MOUNT RUBIDOUX**
Named after Louis Rubidoux, an 1840s rancher whose land holdings encompassed all of what is now Riverside, Mount Rubidoux rises above western end of the town. At its 1,200-ft summit stand the Serra Cross, remembering the founder of the California missions, and the World Peace Tower, commemorating Frank A. Miller. To reach the top, take the winding lane which begins at the junction of Ninth Street and Mount Rubidoux Drive.

TWENTYNINE PALMS

On Hwy-62, 43 miles W of Palm Springs. Twentynine palms did indeed surround Twentynine Palms when the community was named in the 1870s. Today there are far more palms, but only a few thousand people living in a settlement that is best utilized as an overnight base for early morning trips to the nearby Joshua Tree National Monument. With time to spare, take a look around the **Historical Society Museum**, 6136 Adobe Road, delving into the darkest corners of small-town desert life.

only, dinner also served on Sat; credit cards, AE, DC, MC, V.

Inspired by its alpine setting, Heidi's decor suggests a Swiss/Bavarian mountain-top restaurant. The food is genuinely American, though, and features a wide range of soups, sandwiches, pasta and chicken dishes, and substantial salads.

PALM SPRINGS

Bono's, $$-$$$; *1700 N. Indian Canyon Drive; tel. 619 322 6200; credit cards,* AE, CB, DC, DS, MC, V.

The cuisine of southern Italy is the speciality in this attractively designed restaurant, but plenty of vacationing diners come here less for the classy food than the chance of glimpsing the owner, Palm Springs' mayor and showbiz superstar, Sonny Bono.

Las Casuelas, $; *368 N. Palm Canyon Drive; tel. 619 325 3213; lunch and dinner only; credit cards,* AE, MC, V.

A long-established Mexican restaurant that has recently opened branches in a couple of more fashionable Palm Springs locations, but this is still the one that the locals choose for wholesome, home-cooked food at friendly prices.

Louise's Pantry, $; *124 S. Palm Canyon Drive; tel. 619 325 5124; closed in summer; credit cards, none.*

Poky diner with a wonderful atmosphere and great-value all-American breakfasts, lunches and dinners served with a smile to appreciative regulars.

Nate's Deli, $; *100 S. Indian Avenue; tel. 619 325 2506; credit cards,* AE, DC, DS, MC, V.

A perfect example of the American Jewish delicatessen, since 1948 serving chopped liver, corned beef, pastrami and salami (with limited vegetarian alternatives) in stomach-filling sandwiches. Gastronomic wimps can order a "half-sandwich". Come here in the evening and you'll be offered a nine-course dinner at an irresistible price.

Sorrentino's, $$-$$$; *1032 N. Palm Canyon Drive; tel. 619 325 2944; dinner only; credit cards,* AE, CB, DC, MC, V.

A relaxing atmosphere and fine food make this the choice for a couple of hours of leisurely dining. Fresh seafood in diverse mouth-watering styles is the main feature of the menu, but there is also a selection of inventive veal and lamb dishes.

California Overall: 8

Southern California

Between Los Angeles and San Ysidro The Southern Coast

90 miles; map Travel Vision *California*

Passing a photogenic coastline and the kind of suburbia that gives town-planners a bad name, the journey between Los Angeles and the border town of San Ysidro crosses the state's most heavily-populated region.

Our fast route, I-5, is a godsend to anyone itching to test their driving skills and temper on California's busiest stretch of six-way freeway. Tail-backs permitting, I-5 whizzes above the tract housing and shopping malls of Orange County, a vast middle-income dormitory of Los Angeles, and continues to the slightly less homogenized hinterland of San Diego, California's second-largest city.

For some, I-5 begins and ends with a trip to Disneyland, the theme park about which everyone has an opinion but in which few visitors ever fail to enjoy themselves. The other important stop on I-5 could hardly be more different: the mission at San Juan Capistrano, a mix of haunting ruins, lush gardens and impressively-restored buildings that serve as a reminder that the Spanish had a toe-hold here long before Mickey Mouse showed up.

Just south of San Juan Capistrano, I-5 combines with our medium route, Hwy-1, a two-lane road following the coast and linking the shoulder-to-shoulder settlements south of Los Angeles, varying from the surfer-packed Huntington Beach to the millionaires' lair of Newport Beach. Hwy-1 also, albeit intermittently, reveals landscapes of rugged beauty to rival those of the state's central and northern coasts.

Bizarrely, though, you need to cross a vast military base – which I-5 does – to really see how the southern coast looked before the property developers arrived. From the base, I-5 speeds towards San Diego, but branch off on our slow route (Hwy-21) and you'll discover a string of small coastal towns north of San Diego, including the exquisite La Jolla, which can brighten anyone's day.

The weather in this region is welcoming year-round, but expect to pay $15–25 extra a night for accommodation if you're passing through during the summer.

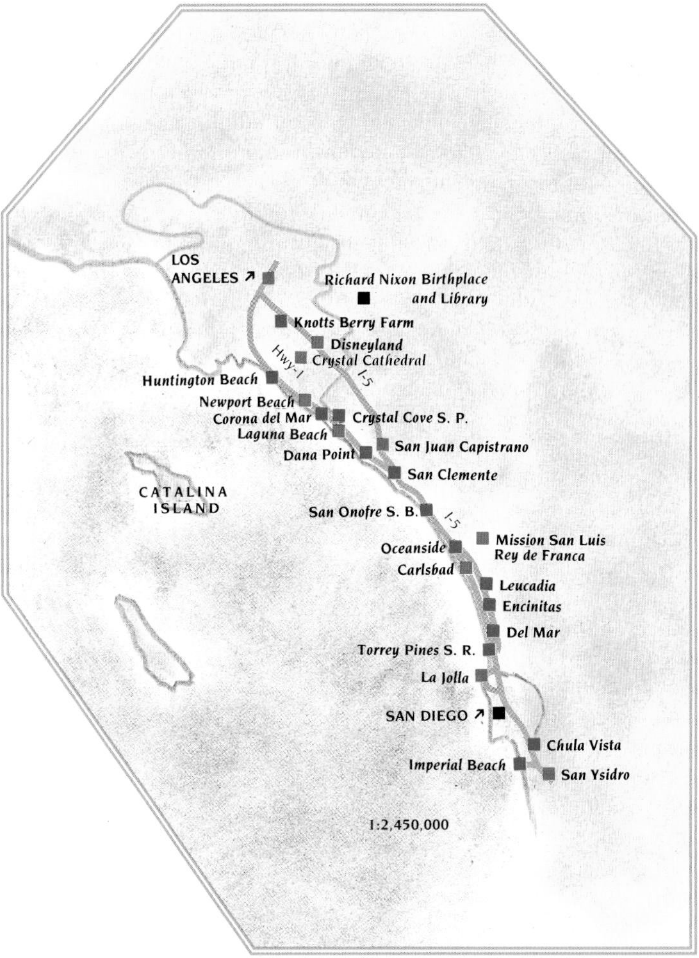

LOS ANGELES ↗
Richard Nixon Birthplace and Library
Knotts Berry Farm
Disneyland
Crystal Cathedral
Hwy-1
I-5
Huntington Beach
Newport Beach
Corona del Mar
Crystal Cove S. P.
Laguna Beach
Dana Point
San Juan Capistrano
San Clemente
CATALINA ISLAND
San Onofre S. B.
I-5
Oceanside
Mission San Luis Rey de Franca
Carlsbad
Leucadia
Encinitas
Del Mar
Torrey Pines S. R.
La Jolla
SAN DIEGO ↗
Chula Vista
Imperial Beach
San Ysidro
1:2,450,000

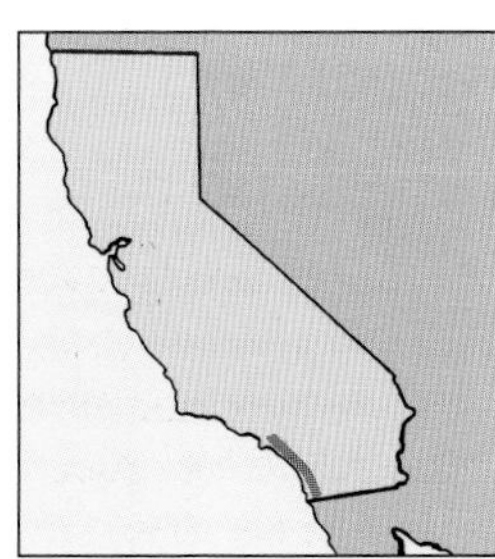

TRANSPORTATION

With more than 20 services a day, the train service between Los Angeles and San Diego (from where trams and local buses continue to San Ysidro) is the busiest in the state, and much of the route is a scenically-appealing coastal run. Greyhound bus connections are good too, if less pleasing to the eye. All buses, except the non-stop express services between Los Angeles and San Diego, call at Anaheim and Oceanside; a few also stop at San Juan Capistrano and San Clemente, and two a day connect Del Mar, Encinitas and Solana Beach.

SIGHTS & PLACES OF INTEREST

CRYSTAL CATHEDRAL

Off I-5 in Garden Grove, 22 miles SE of Los Angeles. Designed by noted architect Philip Johnson for top-rating TV evangelist Robert Schuller (who began his preaching career in a disused drive-in cinema) and completed in 1980, the steel trusses of the Crystal Cathedral support 10,000 panes of tempered silver glass. With shafts of sunlight bouncing around the 12-story interior, the effect as you step inside is indeed like entering a giant crystal. Much of the multi-million dollar cost of the cathedral was raised by donations from faithful followers of Schuller's weekly cable-TV show – the *Hour of Power.*

CARLSBAD ✕

Off I-5, 3 miles S of Oceanside. Growing up around a natural mineral spring discovered in 1886, which caused the town to be named after a Bohemian spa resort, Carlsbad is swift to make the most of its European connections – however tenuous they may be. Over the now dry well from which the mineral waters were drawn, the timber-framed **Alt Karlsbad Hanse Gift Shop**, 2802 Carlsbad Boulevard, doubles as a souvenir shop and a small museum. A building more typical of early California is the 1880s Sante Fe depot, the one-time train station, which now houses the local Convention and Visitors Bureau. Central Carlsbad's has some strolling appeal, but the town's major plus is **Carlsbad State Beach**, a handsome strand – despite the power plant which blights the view at one end – with plenty of spots to camp, have barbecues, rent surfboards, or simply laze in the sun.

CHULA VISTA

On I-5, 6 miles S of San Diego. Wedged between metropolitan San Diego and Imperial Beach (see page 102) at the southern end of San Diego Bay, Chula Vista is perhaps an unlikely place to find one of the last salt marshes remaining on the Pacific Coast. Salt marshes may be short on visual appeal, but they have profound ecological importance, not least in providing a habitat for some 200 species of bird. Salt marsh novices will find a trip around the **Nature Interpretive Center**, 1000 Gunpowder Point Drive, a fruitful undertaking.

CORONA DEL MAR

Off I-5, 2 miles S of Newport Beach. Palm-tree-lined Corona Del Mar State Beach is a lovely place in which to picnic, sunbathe and swim. While in this small oceanside community, find time to tour the **Sherman Library and Gardens**, 2764 E. Coast Highway, where 2 bright acres of sub-tropical plants surround a library devoted to the history of the American South West.

CRYSTAL COVE STATE PARK

On I-5, 5 miles S of Newport Beach. Undeveloped coast is a rare sight in this part of California, which makes the rough-and-tumble greenery of Crystal Cover State Park a welcome sight. Pick through the scruffy vegetation to reach the beach – seldom holding more than a few souls – or venture inland on one of several hiking trails into the San Joaquin Hills and ascend the slopes once grazed by the cattle of Mission San Juan Capistrano.

DANA POINT

On Hwy-1, 7 miles S of Laguna Beach. Much of the undramatic town of Dana Point perches on a dramatic headland named after Richard Henry Dana, author of *Two Years Before the Mast*, published in 1840 and including a description of cow hides being tossed over this cliff to trading ships waiting beneath. The bulging headland shelters a quiet cove which holds the rest of the town – and a very large marina packed with expensive private yachts.

DETOUR – **RICHARD NIXON BIRTHPLACE AND LIBRARY**

Where the Orange County suburban sprawl hits the Santa Ana Mountains (take almost any major road heading east off I-5) you'll find Yorba Linda and the Richard Nixon Birthplace and Library, holding the simple wooden house where the 37th President of the U.S.A. was born in 1913; also the elaborate multi-million dollar complex stuffed with memorabilia, and an extremely hagiographical account of Nixon's topsy-turvy political career.

• *La Jolla.*

DEL MAR

On Hwy-21, 25 miles N of San Diego. Even if you're not planning any long stops between LA and San Diego, set aside an hour for the easily-walked Del Mar, an instantly likeable resort town that strives to project a cultured European look with its "Tudor-style" town center and the **Del Mar Plaza**, an ultra-ritzy shopping mall with stonework walls. Del Mar's many pricey shops and boutiques do most of their trade during the summer, when LA socialites and celebrities arrive for the race meetings at the **Del Mar Racecourse,** one of the most architecturally attractive race tracks in the U.S. (thanks to a major injection of funds during the 1930s from actor Bing Crosby and singer Pat O'Brien). Next to the racecourse, the Del Mar Fairgrounds provide the setting for one of California's largest and most enjoyable County Fairs, held annually in the second half of June.

DISNEYLAND

Off I-5 in Anaheim, 25 miles SE of Los Angeles. The booming aerospace industry certainly played its part, but another contributor to Orange County's incredible growth was Disneyland – the mother of all theme parks – which opened in 1955 and transformed a patch of bean fields into the greatest tourist attraction ever known. The dense jungle of over-priced hotels and restaurants that surround Disneyland are proof of the enduring popularity of the park, which has been visited by more than 300 million people. Yet, provided you choose the right time – a midweek day between mid-September and mid-June is recommended – you can enjoy Disneyland without enduring its notoriously long lines.

Should the admission fee seem extortionate, remember that it does entitle you to go on every ride in the park as many times as you want to – be it a spine-jolting space trip based on the Star Wars film, a death-defying ride on the runaway train of Thunder Mountain Railroad, being tickled by the spooks of the Haunted Mansion or casting off with the Pirates of the Caribbean (to mention but a few of the attractions). Most first-timers are surprised to find Disneyland is much less the glorified childrens' playground than is commonly believed, and that it holds plenty that is designed – through technical innovation or clever psychology – to appeal to adults.

ENCINITAS

On Hwy-21/off I-5, 25 miles N of San Diego. Approaching Encinitas takes you through many acres of poinsettia, a shrub of Central American origin with a red, yellow and white bloom. During the May to September blooming period, the sight of the flowers might well awaken dormant horticultural interests. If so, pay a call on **Quail Botanical Gardens**, 230 Quail Gardens Drive, where beds of madly exotic plants give way to pine-cloaked hillsides and untouched chaparral, preserved as a bird and animal refuge. Just north of the town center, the towers of the **Self Realization Fellowship**, a meditation-based sect founded in India at the turn of the century and settling here in the 1930s, overlook yet more well-tended gardens.

• A *perennial Disneyland favorite.*

HUNTINGTON BEACH

On Hwy-1, 22 miles S of Los Angeles. A major international surfing tournament takes place here each September, but come to Huntington Beach on any weekend and you'll find scores of surfers – some highly-skilled, some just beginning – riding some of the best waves in the state. Imported from Hawaii, surfing first appeared in California in 1907 but didn't achieve wide popularity until the invention of the lightweight, fiberglass surfboard during the late 1950s. If you fancy your chances in the water, there are plenty of surfboard rental outlets around the entirely beach-focused town. At night, the biggest party for miles takes place around the 500 fire rings which line the sands: a scene of barbecues, rowdy behaviour, and much anecdote-swapping in impenetrable surfers' slang.

IMPERIAL BEACH

Off I-5, 12 miles S of San Diego. Long the downbeat domain of ex-patriot Mexicans and the personnel of the town's U.S. Navy helicopter base, Imperial Beach is in the throes of some rapid social climbing. Its ocean-front properties are being swiftly snapped up by affluent southern Californians seizing their last chance of an affordable beachside home. You can't cross into Mexico at Imperial Beach, although it is possible to peer into Mexico from the town's **Border Field State Park**, in which a marble obelisk marks the spot of the 1851 United States–Mexican border survey – responsible for drawing up the present boundary between the countries.

KNOTTS BERRY FARM

Off I-5 in Buena Park, 20 miles SE of Los Angeles. Older, homier and less expensive than the nearby Disneyland, Knotts Berry Farm, 8039 Beach Boulevard, is an amusement park which began life as a fruit farm and first drew crowds to the 65¢-chicken dinners offered by the farmer's wife during the Depression. A replica California ghost town built on the farm to amuse the diners has evolved into a series of high- and low-tech thrills-and-spills rides, and Camp Snoopy, where younger visitors are entertained by characters of the Peanuts cartoon strip.

LAGUNA BEACH 🛏 ✕

On Hwy-1, 11 miles S of Newport Beach. Unlike the flat and sprawling coastal towns which precede it on the route from Los Angeles, Laguna Beach emerges from the canyons of the San Joaquin Hills and spills around a

Mediterranean-like series of coves, inlets, and sandy beaches. It's a landscape worth lingering over and also one that encouraged an artistic community – of writers, painters, and even a few Hollywood stars – to settle during the early decades of the 20thC. These days, the art and handicrafts sold from the town's many street stalls and galleries tend to be quaint rather than creative, but a look around the **Museum of Art**, 307 Cliff Drive, can turn up some of the best local – and statewide – artists, and is easily combined with a walk along the coastal boardwalk which reveals the weather-sculptured intricacies of the shoreline. For six weeks each summer, Laguna Beach plays host to the **Pageant of the Masters**, a bizarre festival (originating during the Depression as a money-raiser for local artists) which features world-famous works of art re-created with local people posing as the central figures.

LA JOLLA 🛏 ✕

Off I-5, 9 miles N of San Diego. Sandy coves and tiny bays form a picturesque coastline at La Jolla, a town set on a low-rise cliff-top and with main streets lined by chic boutiques, trendy restaurants, jewellery shops and up-market art galleries. Enticingly, La Jolla combines its obvious affluence with tremendous visual appeal – few buildings rise above the palm trees, postcard-perfect ocean views are everywhere, and a relaxed, seaside charm pervades.

For such attributes, La Jolla is indebted to **Ellen Scripps**, a wealthy philanthropist who moved to the town in 1896 and bought large tracts of land, placing them under public ownership. Scripps also commissioned architect Irving Gill to raise several buildings in what became his acclaimed and distinctive style, which fuses a Cubist-influenced modern technique with the traditional California mission look. One such building, originally Ellen Scripps' home, is now the **Museum of Contemporary Art**, 700 Prospect Street, a renowned showcase of post-war works, chiefly from the California minimalist and Pop Art schools, and a setting for notable temporary exhibitions.

Scripps' money also helped finance La Jolla's other main tourist draw: the **Scripps Aquarium**, north of the town center at 8602 La Jolla Shores Drive, where dozens of tanks re-create marine habitats – from kelp forests to coral reefs – and display many curious crea-

• *The Scripps Aquarium, La Jolla.*

tures of the deep. The aquarium is run by the Scripps Institution of Oceanography, a branch of the University of California, which occupies a sprawling (and intensely uninteresting) campus above La Jolla.

Overlooked by many visitors due to its unlikely setting in the University Towne Center shopping mall, 4405 La Jolla Drive, is the **Mengei International Museum of World Folk Art**, whose stimulating exhibitions highlight some of the world's disappearing cultures. One culture that shows few signs of disappearing can be seen in its natural habitat just south of La Jolla at Tourmaline and Windansea beaches, where the hardcore surfers are descendants of those described in Tom Wolfe's 1968 book, *The Pump House Gang*.

LEUCADIA

On Hwy-21, 6 miles S of Carlsbad. Like neighbouring Encinitas, Leucadia is a major flower-growing center but in itself has little appeal. More intriguing, perhaps, is the fact that it was named by two English settlers in 1885 after the Ionian island from which 6thC poet Sappho leapt to her death. Flanking Leucadia are two beckoning beaches: **Leucadia State Beach** and **Moonlight State Beach**, both reached by staircases hewn into high bluffs.

RECOMMENDED HOTELS

CARLSBAD

La Costa Hotel & Spa, $$$$; *Costa del Mar Road; tel.* 800 854 5000; *credit cards,* AE, DC, MC, V.

Four hundred acres of luxury where the overpaid and overweight of southern California come to shed a few pounds and many hundreds of dollars. The complex includes tennis courts, two 18-hole golf courses, a fully-equipped spa, a cinema and eight restaurants. If you have time to rest, you'll find the rooms are decorated in reposeful, pastel shades.

Surf Motel, $-$$; 3136 *Carlsbad Boulevard; tel.* 619 729 7261; *credit cards,* AE, DS, MC, V.

With rooms overlooking the ocean and one of the area's best beaches within a few minutes' walk, this is a perfect base if surf and sand are your prime concerns. There is complimentary fresh-brewed coffee each morning, and a heated pool for when the ocean turns chilly – plus a coin-operated laundry.

DEL MAR

Del Mar Inn, $$$; 720 *Camino Del Mar; tel.* 619 755 9765; *credit cards,* AE, CB, DC, MC, V.

Designed in Tudor style to match the rest of Del Mar and serving tea and cakes each afternoon to evoke an Olde English ambience, the Del Mar Inn is a much-admired resting place; get an ocean-view room and you'll be able to sit on your balcony gazing into the sunset.

Rock Haus, $$-$$$; 410 *15th Street; tel.* 619 481 3765; *credit cards,* AE, MC, V.

A far cry from the mock-Tudor that dominates much of Del Mar, this is a genuine 1911 Craftsman-style house – once used as an illegal gambling den – which offers beds in ten individually-furnished rooms and a tempting breakfast of home-baked muffins and strudels.

DISNEYLAND

Disneyland Hotel, $$$-$$$$; 1150 *W. Cerritos Avenue; tel.* 800 854 6165; *credit cards,* AE, CB, DC, MC, V.

The official Disneyland hotel with all the features you'd expect: 4 acres of immaculately-maintained grounds which include colorful gardens and a marina filled by remote controlled boats, a massive video-game arcade, a monorail link to Disneyland itself, and a "gold-rush-style" saloon for making merry when the park closes. The rooms themselves are fairly ordinary, but guests aren't expected to spend much time using them.

Econo Lodge, $$; 1914 *S. Anaheim Boulevard; tel.* 714 533 2666; *credit cards,* AE, CB, DC, MC, V.

By a whisker, the cheaper of two Econo Lodges close to Disneyland and, like the rest of this dependable nationwide chain, offering decently-furnished rooms at a fair rate.

ENCINITAS

Moonlight Beach Motel, $$; 233 *Second Street; tel.* 619 753 0623; *credit cards,* AE, MC, V.

There are cheaper motels than this

LOS ANGELES
See Local Explorations: 15 and 16.

NEWPORT BEACH
On Hwy-1, 7 miles S of Huntington Beach. Anyone who doesn't own a yacht, drive a sports car, or drink champagne for breakfast is likely to feel out of place in Newport Beach, a securely bank-rolled community sometimes referred to as Beverly Hills-by-the-Sea. Unsurprisingly, the town doesn't gladly open its arms to tourists, although plenty arrive for the three miles of stunning sands which line the **Balboa Peninsula**. Elsewhere, the **Newport Harbor Art Museum**, 850 San Clemente Drive, merits a call for its excellent temporary exhibitions and permanent selections of contemporary Californian art, and the high-fashion clothing outlets of the stultifying landscaped Fashion Island (off Hwy-1) are where you'll find the locals nonchalantly exceeding their credit limits.

OCEANSIDE
On Hwy-21/Off I-5, 18 miles S of San Clemente/32 miles N of San Diego. Crew-cuts and military uniforms are common sights in Oceanside as the town is neighbored by the vast Camp Pendleton Marine Corp Base, which uses 125,000 acres of untamed coastal land for practising amphibious landings. Oceanside's

one in Encinitas, but only here will you find in-room fridges and ocean-view balconies at visitor-friendly rates barely more than a frisbee's fling from an excellent beach.

LAGUNA BEACH
Casa Laguna Inn, $$$-$$$$; *2510 S. Coast Highway; tel. 800 243 0339; credit cards, AE, DC, DS, MC, V.*
Individually decorated rooms and suites fill the main building, or opt for a fully-equipped cottage in the rambling, landscaped grounds. Many rooms have ocean views, as does the heated pool; breakfast and afternoon tea and snacks are included in the price.

Eiler's Inn, $$$-$$$$; *741 S. Coast Highway; tel. 714 494 3004; credit cards, AE, MC, V.*
A peaceful retreat despite being located on Laguna Beach's busy main road, the 12 rooms are arranged to face the inner courtyard where a buffet breakfast and afternoon wine and cheese are served. You'll need to book well ahead to be sure of a room here – the reward is a complimentary bottle of champagne on arrival.

LA JOLLA
The Bed-and-breakfast Inn at La Jolla, $$$-$$$$; *7753 Draper Avenue; tel. 619 454 2066; credit cards, MC, V.*
An Irving Gill-designed residence dating from 1913, most of the 16 guest rooms – six of them in the more recent annex – are fitted with a fireplace, a four-poster bed and a decanter of sherry. Breakfast is served in the garden and a short video film describing the building's history can be watched in the book-lined lounge.

La Jolla Travelodge, $$; *1141 Silverado Street; tel. 800 255 3050; credit cards, AE, DC, DS, MC, V.*
Perfectly adequate rooms just a short walk from lively Windandsea Beach; the lowest rates in town but none of the character that makes La Jolla so enjoyable.

La Valencia Hotel, $$$-$$$$; *1132 Prospect Street; tel. 619 454 0771; credit cards, AE, DC, MC, V.*
A La Jolla landmark as soon as its pink walls were raised in 1926 and a by-word for glamor since silent-era screen star Marion Davies became the first Hollywood celebrity to vacation here. La Valencia's under-stated charm keeps it among California's most elegant and enjoyable hotels. A stay here is a must if you can afford it.

NEWPORT BEACH
Countryside Inn, $$$; *325 Bristol Street; tel. 714 549 0300; credit cards, AE, CB, DC, MC, V.*
Being 3 miles inland allows this very comfortable facility – all rooms have video-players, a few even have microwave ovens – to offer considerable savings on Newport Beach's overpriced ocean-side resort hotels; a breakfast buffet is another advantage.

• *Mission San Juan Capistrano.*

pier has acquired cult status among local anglers, but otherwise the town is worth being in only long enough to make the detour to Mission San Luis Rey, described on page 107.

SAN CLEMENTE

On Hwy-1, 8 miles S of Dana Point. A dull town but with great ocean views from its hill-top location, San Clemente is primarily remembered as the site of Richard Nixon's 25-acre Casa Pacifica estate, known as the Western White House during his presidency and becoming his place of refuge after the Watergate scandal. The estate, no longer owned by Nixon, can be glimpsed from **San Clemente State Beach**, a fine white-sanded strand at the foot of towering bluffs.

SAN DIEGO

See Local Exploration: 17.

SAN JUAN CAPISTRANO

On Hwy-74/I-5, 3 miles E of Dana Point. Easily among the most impressive of California's 21 Spanish missions, **Mission San Juan Capistrano** – in the eponymously-named town – shouldn't be missed. Founded in 1776, the complex was devastated by an earthquake in 1812 which felled the enormous seven-domed Great Stone Church. (A modern church just north of the mission is a re-creation of the lost masterpiece.) The Spanish priests were so upset that they never attempted to rebuild. Subsequently, the ruins became entwined with bougainvillaea and acquired a romantic appearance much-loved by camera-carrying tourists.

A more practical appreciation of mission life is provided by a small museum and several reconstructed workshops – but don't leave before taking a meditative stroll around the beautiful gardens, or without spending a few contemplative minutes inside the Serra Chapel. Simply decorated by Indian frescos and 17thC Spanish reredos, the tiny chapel is the only surviving church in which Junipero Serra (the leader of the mission-founding Sacred Expedition) said Mass – and, dating from 1777, is believed to be the oldest building in California.

Come to the mission during March and you'll be regaled with tales of the Capistrano swallows, which legend (and a hit song of 1930) describes as returning from their annual migration on March 19th, St Joseph's Day. Sometimes the swallows do return that day; usually they don't – but there's a welcome home carnival nonetheless.

DETOUR – MISSION SAN LUIS REY DE FRANCA

Five miles inland from Oceanside on Hwy-76, Mission San Luis Rey de Franca, founded in 1798 and saved from ruin by the Franciscan Order which has occupied it since 1893, was the largest link in the California mission chain. It housed nearly 3,000 neophytes and owned 50,000 cattle and sheep. The mission museum's artifacts, and re-created living rooms and workshops, give a reasonable insight into mission life but can't draw attention away from the sheer size of the building: originally part of a complex that covered 6 acres. To guard the unusually large mission, an unusually large barracks was built, the extensive ruins of which can be seen beside Hwy-76.

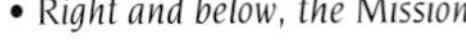

• *Right and below, the Mission.*

Most visitors don't see any more of San Juan Capistrano than the mission – and frankly they're not missing much. Those who arrive by train, however, have little excuse for not noticing that the station has been restored to something approaching its 1895 appearance – of Spanish-Moorish arches and tilework – or for failing to make the short walk to the **Los Rios Historic District**, where several adobe houses almost as old as the mission can be seen.

SAN ONOFRE STATE BEACH

Off I-5, 4 miles S of San Clemente. Comprising a great stretch of beach fringed by open country, San Onofre State Beach would be a peach of a place were it not for the nuclear power station which, since 1968, has overlooked these inviting vistas. Foolhardy as it may seem, some locals actually like to swim here on cool days – when discharge from the power plant keeps the ocean waters warm.

SAN YSIDRO

On I-5, 7 miles S of Chula Vista. San Ysidro, the world's busiest border crossing, is not a pretty sight: a constant flurry of cars, buses and people crossing the United States–Mexican border. Within walking distance on the Mexican side, the city of Tijuana makes an interesting day out. Packed with Californians on shopping sorties, however, Tijuana is hardly typical of Mexico. There are no formalities when you cross from the U.S. but returning non-U.S. and non-Canadian citizens face the usual border checks.

TORREY PINES STATE RESERVE

On Hwy-21, 4 miles N of La Jolla. Covering a 1,000-acre headland site purchased by Eileen Scripps (see La Jolla, page 102) and donated to the state, the Torrey Pines State Reserve protects one of the few remaining groves of the Torrey pine – the U.S.'s rarest pine tree. A few walking trails – the best is the half-mile **Guy Fleming Trail** – bring close-up views of the trees, many of them twisted into strange shapes by ceaseless ocean winds, and ravishing views of the coastline. The same winds provide uplift for hang-gliders, who launch themselves over the near-vertical cliff-face and hover above the ocean, just south of the reserve.

RECOMMENDED RESTAURANTS

CARLSBAD

Pollos Maria, $; *3055 Harding Street; tel. 619 729 4858; closed Mon; credit cards, none.*

Tasty, very inexpensive Mexican delights served fast-food style and eaten on a sunny terrace – and don't neglect the delicious homemade desserts.

Andersen's, $-$$; *850 Palomar Airport Road; tel. 619 438 7880; credit cards,* AE, CB, DC, MC, V.

Part of the Pea Soup Andersen chain offering filling and highly nutritious salads and a wide range of sandwiches, steaks and burgers, as well as the split-pea soup which has been revitalizing tired travellers since 1924.

DEL MAR

The Old Del Mar Cafe, $-$$; *Flower Hill Center, 2730 Via de la Ville; tel. 619 755 6614; lunch and dinner only; credit cards,* AE, MC, V.

A choice of well-priced burgers, omelettes and sandwiches make this a likely lunch spot; the dinner menu is more eclectic but costlier – live entertainment is another evening feature.

Sushi Bar Genji, $-$$$; *Del Mar Plaza; tel. 619 755 5589; lunch and dinner only; credit cards,* MC, V.

Succulent sushi morsels can be enjoyed from the counter while more serious eating – which might be the chef's soft-shell crab roll speciality or simply a bowl of miso soup – is done at the tables. Between 5pm and 7pm, snacks, beer and sake are half-price and the sunset views are free.

DISNEYLAND

Belisle's, $; *12001 Harbor Boulevard, Garden Grove; tel. 714 750 6560; credit cards,* MC, V.

Big portions – such as 24-ounce breakfast steaks – are served to big eaters around the clock in this wonderful, farm-tool-decorated diner. The menu is rooted in all-American meat and potatoes fare, although the homemade desserts will please anyone with a sweet tooth.

Hansa House Smorgasbord, $-$$; 1840 S. *Harbor Boulevard; tel.* 714 750 2411; *credit cards,* AE, DS, MC, V.

Only extremely fussy eaters will be hard pushed to find something to fill their plates – and their stomachs – from this sizeable, value-for-money buffet table, be it for breakfast, lunch or dinner.

LAGUNA BEACH

Bennie the Bum's Diner, $; 238 *Laguna Avenue; tel.* 714 497 4786; *credit cards, none.*

An always-open retro-diner that is well worth a call if you've ever wondered how it might feel to quaff a burger or guzzle a frothy milkshake surrounded by 1950s Americana.

The Cottage, $-$$; 308 N. *Pacific Coast Highway; tel.* 714 494 3023; *credit cards, none.*

No-nonsense American and Californian range of vegetarian dishes alongside the bounteous steaks and ribs, served with flair in an atmospheric turn-of-the-century building.

LA JOLLA

Fisherman's Grille, $$; 7825 *Fay Avenue; tel.* 619 456 3733; *lunch and dinner only; credit cards,* AE, DC, MC, V.

From oysters to mesquite-grilled mahi-mahi, this a choice spot for well-prepared, well-priced seafood. The menu also includes a long list of salads, sandwiches and pasta dishes.

George's at the Cove, $$-$$$; 1250 *Prospect Street; tel.* 619 454 4244; *lunch and dinner only; credit cards,* AE, MC, V.

Highly-rated among local gastronomes for its mouth-watering California-style pastas and grilled-to-perfection seafood drawn from the oceans of the world. The view, overlooking the fabulous contours of La Jolla Cove, is as exceptional as the food.

Soup Exchange, $; 777 *Fay Ave; tel.* 619 697 8561; *lunch and dinner only; credit cards,* MC, V.

A variety of fresh salads and homemade soups is available at this cheap and cheerful eatery, accompanied by servings of muffins, yogurt and fruit.

The Spot, $-$$; 1005 *Prospect Street; tel.* 619 459 0800; *lunch and dinner only; credit cards,* AE, DC, DS, MC, V.

A reasonably inexpensive place to indulge in amply-portioned American favorites such as steaks and barbecued ribs, or to munch your way through thick-crust pizzas served with a choice of 12 toppings. In the evening, develop your appetite in the popular upper-level cocktail bar.

NEWPORT BEACH

The Cannery, $-$$; 3010 *Lafayette Avenue; tel.* 714 675 5777; *credit cards,* AE, DC, MC, V.

In the 1930s, this place really was a seafood factory, packing thousands of tons of mackerel and swordfish into tins each year. As you'd expect, the seafood selections are the menu's main draws – the lobster and abalone being especially good – but there is also a fair variety of steak and pasta dishes.

The Crab Cooker, $-$$; 2200 *Newport Boulevard; tel.* 714 673 0100; *credit cards, none.*

Crabs, scallops, oysters and lobsters, and a variety of fish, are all on offer at this unpretentious spot, where the sizzling seafood is served on paper plates and eaten with plastic knives and forks.

Ruby's, $; 1 *Balboa Pier; tel.* 714 675 RUBY; *credit cards,* AE, MC, V.

It would be odd to come to Newport Beach and not pay a call on Ruby's, a 1950s-style diner perched at the end of the Balboa Pier. The setting is more of an attraction than the food, however, which is predominantly an edible though unexciting mix of burgers and sandwiches.

San Francisco: *introduction*

A complete antithesis of the sprawling America metropolis, San Francisco's 700,000 inhabitants live in tight-knit but strongly contrasting neighborhoods set across a small peninsula in one of the country's most desirable natural settings. Watching fog shroud the Golden Gate Bridge or seeing the Transamerica Pyramid rise in extraordinary contrast behind houses of an earlier era are not isolated incidents but everyday occurrences in this city where beauty comes close to being taken for granted. Small wonder then, that even the travel writers most hopelessly addicted to hyperbole run out of superlatives when trying to describe San Francisco: in short, it's a place that's hard to fault – and sometimes even harder to believe.

A delightfully self-possessed city and the only urban area in California where having a car is a liability, San Francisco also has a past of distinction. The gold-rush helped make it a major Pacific port, and a few decades later the outrageously rich Big Four rail barons controlled the fate of the whole state from million-dollar mansions on the city's Nob Hill. Like much of San Francisco, the Nob Hill houses were destroyed by a calamitous earthquake and fire in 1906, but an incredible amount of the city's history survives forcefully into the present, be it the vibrant ethnic enclave of Chinatown, a result of one of the grimmer episodes in California's back pages, or the magnificent leftovers of the 1915 Panama-Pacific Exposition, such as the breathtaking Palace of Fine Arts, which signalled the city's recovery from the 1906 disaster.

Since then, San Francisco has been the birthplace of beatniks, hippies, and gay and lesbian liberation: social explosions right in step with San Francisco's spirit of liberalism and tolerance, but never threatening to upset the equilibrium of what could well be America's most harmonious community.

USING THIS SECTION

So compact and close together are San Francisco's various districts, and so rich are they in points of interest, San Francisco is ideally discovered on foot.

• *Survivors of the 1906 earthquake and fire.*

For this reason, I have interpreted the whole city in terms of five different walks, each with a theme, and each introducing key areas of the city.

As with all the itineraries in this guide, there is no compulsion to follow them from beginning to end; and indeed, you don't have to follow them at all. The information in each of the five walks can just as well be absorbed in an armchair to get to grips with the city in its various different aspects; and, of course, the hotel and restaurant recommendations at the end of this section can be consulted as and when needed.

Although anyone who runs short of breath trudging up the city's hills may think otherwise, the ups and downs of San Francisco are an essential part of its character, rewarding all who climb them with stunning views at every peak.

My five walks take in all the city's major sights while exploring its most distinct and interesting districts, also focusing on **history**, **architecture** and **shops**, and imbibing the contemporary flavor.

Each route can easily be covered in half a day, but I suggest giving a full day to a leisurely pursuit of each one – which will also allow plenty of time to recover after scaling the stiffer gradients.

Ideally, the walks should be combined with putting our restaurant recommendations to the test. San Francisco has more dining places than New York and, whether it's a dim sum lunch in Chinatown, a six-course Italian dinner in the North Beach, or a burger in a surrealistically-decorated nightclubbers' hang out on Haight Street, eating is an essential aspect of this city's life, a subject close to San Franciscan hearts. The restaurant recommendations are on pages 135-137.

ARRIVING

Transportation links are generally quick and reliable from San Francisco's airport (tel. 415 761 0800), which is 13 miles south of the city. Numerous privately-run minibuses, such as Express Airport Shuttle (tel. 800 675 1115) and Super Shuttle (tel. 415 558 8500) collect passengers from the traffic island directly outside the terminal; fares are $9-14. Alternatively, the SFO Airporter (tel. 415 673 2433) coach runs every 20 minutes between 6 am and 11.10 pm from the airport to the hotels around Union Square; the fare is $7. A cheaper, slower alternative are Routes 7F and 7B of the SamTrans bus service (tel. 800 660 4BUS) although baggage is limited to one small item. Taking a taxi into the city will cost around $30.

If you come to San Francisco by train (tel. 800 872 7245), you'll find yourself across the bay in Oakland, where free shuttle buses meet the trains and carry passengers to the city's Transbay Terminal, 425 Mission Street. Greyhound buses (tel. 415 558 6789) also finish their journeys at the Transbay Terminal.

PUBLIC TRANSPORTATION

Cable cars are an enduring symbol of San Francisco but these days are primarily run as a tourist attraction, being limited to two routes: one between Downtown and Fisherman's Wharf, the other between the Financial District and Nob Hill. Tickets cost $3 and can be bought from self-service machines. Much more widespread are the buses run by MUNI (tel. 415 673 MUNI) on routes displayed at most bus stops and in local phone books. Single journey fares are $1.25 (pay the driver with exact fare) with free transfers valid for two changes of route within 90 minutes. A MUNI Passport might save money; valid on all MUNI services for one or three days, these cost $6 or $10 respectively. The Bay Area Rapid Transit (BART) system is an underground train system chiefly of use for crossing the bay to Berkeley and Oakland: fares range from 80c to $3 according to distance travelled; tickets can be bought from machines at BART stations.

• *Quick route to Fisherman's Wharf.*

ACCOMMODATION GUIDELINES

Not only eating, but sleeping, is rich with possibilities in San Francisco. The main hotel areas are close to Union Square and Fisherman's Wharf, but I prefer to avoid these congested areas in favor of the more residential neighborhoods, which have greater character. If money is no object, the luxury hotels of Nob Hill should be your goal. For style and attentive service at a lower price, the small "boutique hotels," which tend to found between Nob Hill and Downtown, are a sound choice.

The city's most atmospheric places to stay, however, are the scores of rambling Victorian houses which have have been refurbished and converted into bed-and-breakfast inns. My suggestions, on pages 132-135, cover a broad selection of what is available. The **Visitor Information Center**, at Hallidie Plaza at the junction of Powell and Market Streets, can provide further ideas with their lodgings guide, a free brochure with listings and prices.

NEIGHBORHOODS TO AVOID

A relatively safe place with few of the social problems of other major American cities, San Francisco does nonetheless have its unpleasant sections. Avoid the Tenderloin area, west of Union Square, which has street prostitutes and seedy bars, and expect homeless people around the plazas of the adjoining Civic Center area. Overall you will find San Francisco is among the world's most user-friendly cities. What's more, with the exception of the contrived attractions of Fisherman's Wharf, it is not a place that falls over itself to please visitors – which, of course, should please them all the more.

The Financial District and Chinatown

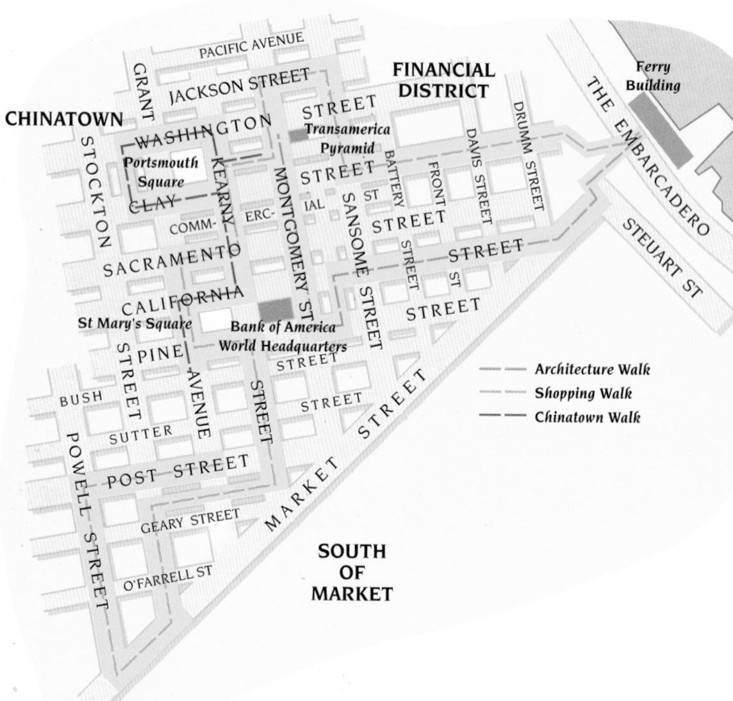

Nowhere are the vivid contrasts of San Francisco's tight-knit neighborhoods better demonstrated than close to the eastern waterfront where the sleek, vertical towers of international high-finance cast their shadows across the painted balconies, food stands and century-old temples lining the bustling streets of Chinatown.

I suggest three walks in these districts, which cover an area of barely a square mile. The first joins the city's power-dressed power-brokers and discovers the best (and the worst) of the city's commercial architecture; the second explores the sights, sounds and smells of the city's longest-established ethnic area; and the third is a shopping expedition that draws on the area's diversity, passing from Chinatown herbalists to the high fashion department stores of Union Square.

For ease of description, the walks are described as if proceeding in one direction only, but you can use the maps to follow them in any direction.

ARCHITECTURE WALK

Start Ferry Building – see map. A midget when compared to the Financial District towers a few minutes' walk away, the 235-ft **Ferry Building** – modelled on the Giralda in Seville – became the city's tallest building on its completion in 1903, and also one of the busiest. The major entry point to the city prior to the 1937 opening of the Bay Bridge, up to 50 million people passed through the Ferry Building annually. Save for its pretty appearance and its historical significance, however, the Ferry Building holds little interest. Within its extended arcaded façade are the offices of the **World Trade Center,**

while its dock sees just a few ferries a day, carrying nostalgic day-trippers to and from Marin County. Directly opposite the Ferry Building, the much more recent Embarcadero Center is approached by crossing Justin Herman Plaza, a concrete expanse softened by waterfalls, buskers, skateboarders and alfresco diners. The attractions of the Embarcadero are described in the Shopping Walk, below.

The Embarcadero Center stands on the junction of Market and California streets: walk up the latter into the heart of the **Financial District**. The city's densest grouping of modern skyscrapers are gathered here, loved and loathed in varying degrees and collectively a symbol of what, in the 1980s, concerned San Franciscans saw as the "Manhattanization" of the city. For many, the chief esthetic offender is 101 California Street, a Philip Johnson-designed semi-cylindrical tower, the harsh effect of which is only partly softened by the potted vegetation in its sunny atrium. By contrast, the **Museum of Money of the American West**, in the basement of the Bank of California, 400 California Street, provides an entertaining effort to place trans-global

• *The Ferry Building, behind the Embarcadero Center.*

wheelings and dealings in a Californian historical context: gold nuggets of all shapes and sizes and early currency fill the display cases. Also on show are a pair of duelling pistols, fired in anger during a famed dispute between two rival political figures in 1859.

At 465 California Street, the **Merchant Exchange Building** was designed by the noted Willis Polk and completed in 1903. At that time, this area formed the San Francisco waterfront (when the city was a leader in Pacific sea trade) and a look-out posted on the roof of the Merchant Exchange would announce approaching ships to the traders and businessmen massed below in the building's Grain Exchange Hall, now occupied by First Interstate Bank and entered by way of a grandly pillared lobby. Decorating the hall are immense and impressive marine paintings by Irish-born William Coulter; less appealing model ships grace the entrance hall.

Next door, the 1969 Bank of America Building is an imposing but not immediately likeable 52-storys of dark red carnelian marble, with a large slab of sculptured dark marble standing in its plaza, which looks uncannily like a giant tortoise shell.

Next make a swift detour along Leidesdorff Street to the **Pacific Stock Exchange**, 301 Pine Street. Finished in 1930, the Stock Exchange's ambitious but not entirely successful exterior mating of classical and modern motifs has been a feature of the Financial District for longer than most people realize.

Turn the corner to walk north on Montgomery Street, the Financial District's major north-south artery. On the south side of the junction with California Street stands the elegant 1922 **Security Pacific Bank Building** (currently being renovated). On the north side, the Wells Fargo Bank allocates a generous portion of its ground floor to the **Wells Fargo Museum**, charting the company's rise from carrying mail across pioneer-period California to becoming one of the nation's bastions of high finance. Besides a large assortment of postage stamps, gold-scales and coins, there is a simulated stagecoach ride and a tribute to the 19thC poet-bandit, Black Bart, said to have robbed so much from Wells Fargo stagecoaches that the company paid him to retire.

Further north along Montgomery Street, it is hard to resist being drawn to what, on its opening in 1972, became the city's best-known modern landmark: the 853-ft **Transamerica Pyramid**, by the junction with Clay Street. The Pyramid is far more interesting from the outside than the inside, but so you can say you've done it, take the elevator to the 27th floor observation level and make the most of the disappointingly restricted city views.

CHINATOWN WALK

Start Junction of Bush Street and Grant Avenue. The jade-colored dragon-topped Chinatown Gate, a gift from the Taiwanese government in 1970, at the junction of Bush Street and Grant Avenue, makes an inauspicious entry point to Chinatown: its manufactured neatness is at odds with the spontaneous street life of a compact 20-block area housing an incredible 40,000 people – the largest Asian community outside Asia.

Adjust your walking pace to suit the throng along **Grant Street**, Chinatown's showcase street with numerous intriguing shops (see the Shopping Walk, below) and continue to the corner with California Street, where the **Old St. Mary's Church** has stood since 1854. Though the church's interior is dull, look up at the clock tower and its inscription reading **Son Observe the Time and Fly from Evil**, a message aimed at customers arriving to use the numerous brothels in the area a century ago. The church survived the earthquake of 1906 but many of the brothels were destroyed, making room for the landscaped space that is now **St. Mary's Square**, where a stainless-steel statue of Sun Yat-Sen – founder of the Republic of China – sits on a granite pedestal, helping to disguise the park's function as the roof of an underground car-park.

Packing its exhibits into a single small room, the absorbing **Chinese Historical Society of America**, 650 Commercial Street, charts the massive influx of Chinese men into California during the gold-rush, their subsequent contribution to the building of the state – and the Exclusion Act of 1882 which prohibited further migration, causing the long-term separation of families and the ethnic hostility that led to the founding of self-contained Chinatown districts in many Californian towns.

Continuing north, step off Clay Street into **Waverly Place**, a tiny alley known as "the Street of Painted Balconies," for reasons which are immediately obvious. Waverly Place also holds several **temples**. The temples occupy the top floors of several buildings and visitors who can clamber up enough stairs are welcome to look around them (a donation is appreciated). Temple opening hours are irregular but, with luck, the Tin How Temple, at number 125, founded in 1852, will reward a call with a chance to peek into its incense-charged inner sanctum.

From Waverly Place, walk down the hill to **Portsmouth Square**, named after the ship which brought Commander John Montgomery ashore in 1846 to wave the Stars and Stripes for the first time in San Francisco. Two years later, Sam Brannan stood here proclaiming the discovery of Californian gold; 30 years after that, Robert Louis Stevenson used the square as an open-air writing room – he is commemorated here by a sculptured ship on a granite plinth. The square is predominantly the domain of elderly Chinese engrossed in chess matches or going through the slow-motion routines of tai chi. Overlooking the square, the high-rise Holiday Inn holds the **Chinese Cultural Center**, where some strong temporary exhibitions are staged. On the north side of the square, **Buddha's Universal Church** – serving the city's growing Zen Buddhist community – was completed in the early 1960s after eight years of largely volunteer labor. The many bazaars held to raise money for its construction fuelled a myth that the church was funded on the proceeds of fortune cookie sales. (A fortune cookie is a biscuit containing a piece of paper carrying a prediction of your future.) The terazzo floor, polished woods and top-floor lotus garden can only be seen on guided tours (Sun at 1 pm and 3 pm).

SHOPPING WALK

Start Embarcadero Center, at the junction of Market and California Streets. Facing the historic Ferry Building (described in the Architecture Walk, above), the **Embarcadero Center** arose during the 1970s and 1980s, a combination of high-rise office towers and open-air walkways that wind through three tiers of diverse shops and restaurants. Better for browsing and snacking than actually buying anything, the Embarcadero's shops are the kind found in most Californian shopping malls. They include a sizeable branch of **B. Dalton Bookseller**; **The Nature Center**, with its intriguing, ecologically-friendly toys and gadgets; **The Gap** clothing store, with California-style casual wear; and **See's Candies**, with a selection of dreamy chocolates in fancy wrappings.

Walk from the Embarcadero Center through the Financial District to **Jackson Square**, just north of the Transamerica Pyramid. Jackson Square is a block of Victorian buildings, most dating from the 1850s, which survived the earthquake and fire of 1906. Along Jackson Street, several of the buildings form an "antiques row" of shops specializing in high-quality 17thC to 19thC European furniture, porcelain, ceramics, carpets and tapestries. Also in the Jackson Square area are a number of wholesale fabric, furniture and architectural supply centers – and **William Stout Architectural Books**, 804 Montgomery Street, which has a formidable stock of new and used tomes relating to building and design.

The subdued atmosphere that prevails in the antiques area is far removed from Chinatown's vibrant Grant Avenue, a few blocks east. It is widely acknowledged that the Grant Avenue shops are aimed at tourists rather than Chinese, but that doesn't diminish the fun and exhilaration of exploring them. The **Canton Bazaar**, number 616, and the **China Trade Center**, number 838, are bustling emporiums where wood and jade carvings, vases, pottery, baskets, silk lingerie, and assorted inexpensive souvenirs are touted with glee (and where you'll find the cheapest postcards in San Francisco). Ingenious Chinese toys, such as puzzle boxes and finger traps, are the speciality of **Gin Lang Arts**, number 627. The most colorful collections of windsocks, silk dragons, and other types of kite – which, if you're not planning to fly them, make excellent decorations – are found at the **Chinatown Kite Shop**, number 717. Anyone bemoaning the lack of quality tea in the U.S. won't want to leave the **Ten Ren Tea Company**, number 949, which imports and sells many fine blends – and often has free samples steaming on the counter. If the Chinatown energy saps your strength, seek a pick-me-up from the rows of traditional Chinese herbal remedies lining the shelves of **Yau Hing Co**, number 831.

Leaving Chinatown, the **Crocker Galleria**, off Montgomery Street, allows the Financial District's stressed executives to indulge in soothing bouts of consumption in 50 up-market shops. The Galleria's walkways are lined by tempting food stands and wind up to rooftop gardens, but the shops themselves are a conservative and uninspiring bunch. Exit the Galleria onto Post Street and you soon reach the two-block Maiden Lane, lined by stylish boutiques and imitation gas lamps. **Chanel**, number 155, has three floors laden with the French company's finest products, and **Orientations**, number 34, stocks exquisite Far Eastern furnishings and ornaments. More eye-catching, however, is the **Circle**

• *Chinatown's ubiquitous dragon motifs.*

Gallery, number 140, a contemporary art showcase occupying a 1949 building designed by Frank Lloyd Wright, for whom it served as a model for the subsequent Guggenheim Museum in New York; the artworks are viewed from a spiral walkway.

Maiden Lane's western exit leads on to Stockton Street, directly opposite Union Square and a cluster of distinguished department stores. From the corner of Stockton and Geary Streets **I. Magnin & Co** has catered for the sartorial needs of San Franciscan high society from since 1896: the luxurious interior of the 10-story store is a result of a 1940s refit and includes a ladies' powder room furnished more expensively than many people's homes. **Neiman-Marcus**, 150 Stockton Street, has more quality clothing and household goods, although the merchandise takes second place to the architecture – a stern but amusing postmodern work by Philip Johnson which incorporates the delightful stained-glass rotunda of the City of Paris, a store which occupied the site from 1908. Even if you don't intend buying anything there, call into **Nordstrom**, inside the $145-million **San Francisco Shopping Center** at 865 Market Street, and cruise between the eight floors –don't miss the Bugs Bunny ties and Roadrunner T-shirts on sale in the center's Warner Brothers Store – on spiral escalators. Before leaving the area, take a look at **Gump's**, 250 Post Street, founded by two German brothers in 1861 and stocking a monumental collection of china, silver and crystal – and some world-class jades and pearls – all of it on offer at pulse-quickening prices.

JAPANTOWN

Few of northern California's 11,000-strong Japanese population actually lives in San Francisco's Japantown, an artificially created "ethnic area" of minor appeal. Many come to buy Japanese goods and food from the Japan Center, bordered by Post and Webster streets, however, and to soak in a traditional Japanese mineral bath at Kabuki Hot Spring, 1750 Geary Boulevard.

The North Beach and Telegraph Hill

As Chinatown spills northwards, its borders with the North Beach district become blurred. There's no diluting of the North Beach's strong Italian flavor, however: the area having been the base of the city's Italian community since the 1880s. My walk reveals the churches, cafes, bakeries and delis that have earned a niche in community folklore. It also explores some of the sites associated with 1950s North Beach when, attracted by cheap rents, cheap wine, and late-night discussions in the cafes, a bunch of disaffected writers and artists colonized the area, soon to be immortalized as the leading lights of the beat generation. The walk leaves the North Beach to climb into Telegraph Hill, a quiet residential area where secluded lanes and stairways hold intriguing buildings, and ends at the major city landmark of Coit Tower.

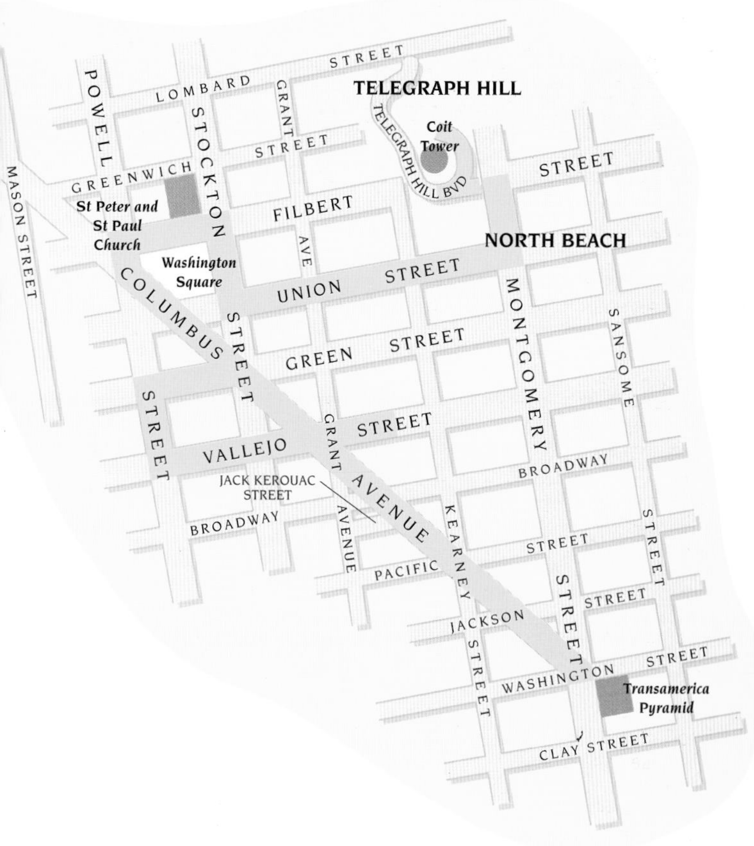

Start Close to Transamerica Pyramid, at the junction of Montgomery and Clay Streets. From the Financial District northwards, Columbus Avenue cuts a diagonal swath through the **North Beach**, intersecting the otherwise chessboard street pattern and creating sharply-angled junctions. There are some triangular-shaped buildings, too, such as the **Columbus Tower**, a classic flat-iron structure dating from 1905 that was bought and restored in the 1970s by film-director Francis Ford Coppola and currently mutating into a fashionable apartment building. As old as the Columbus Tower and just as well preserved, the saloon bar of the **San Francisco Brewing Company**, 155 Columbus Avenue, delights discerning beer drinkers with its own brews. Legend has it that champion boxer Jack Dempsey once worked here, helping drunken brawlers to find the street. Broadway meets Columbus Avenue to form San Francisco's busiest crossroads. The through-traffic has drawn restaurants to the area by the score, joining the long-established Italian cafes that waft a smell of fresh-brewed coffee across the pavement. Also here are a few video porn arcades and sleazy nude-dancing venues: reminders of the moment in 1964 when the silicone-implanted breasts of Carol Doda made their famous debut at Broadway's Condor Club.

Just south of Broadway, **City Lights**, 261 Columbus Avenue, was opened by local poet Lawrence Ferlinghetti in 1953, with the intention of using the profits to finance a small literary magazine. The first all-paperback bookshop in the U.S., City Lights achieved greater fame by publishing Allen Ginsberg's narrative poem, *Howl*, in 1955. The controversy which ensued brought worldwide attention to the underground cultural scene flourishing in the North Beach – what became known as the beats (derisively dubbed "beatniks" by a San Francisco newspaper columnist). The shop continues to carry the definitive stock of writings by and about the beats, plus a wide range of political and general titles on its tightly-packed shelves. Facing City Lights, **Vesuvio's Cafe** was, and still is, the definitive beat hang out, complete with satirical art and bizarre ornaments. The alley between the book shop and the cafe has been re-named **Jack Kerouac Street** to mark one of the beat generation's leading figures.

Continuing north along Columbus Avenue, the corner with Vallejo Street finds **Molinari's Deli**, purveyors of fine cheeses, meats (the salami in particular has many admirers) and pastas – any or all of which will be placed in a sandwich on request. Across the street, **St. Francis of Assisi Church** was founded in 1849, becoming the first Catholic church established in California since the Spanish missions **Caffè Trieste**, 609 Vallejo Street, is another local landmark for its espresso coffee and live opera on Saturday afternoons.

Turn on to Stockton Street for the **Eureka Savings Bank**, number 1435, on the upper level of which are the changing exhibitions of the **North Beach Museum**, drawn from the experiences of local residents and displaying many photos and objects donated by them. Also on Stockton Street (number 1362), the **Victoria Pastry Company** has been turning out wondrous Italian cakes and French pastries since 1914; admire the inventive architecture of the wedding cakes displayed in the window. Just north at 678 Green Street, the terracotta-decorated **Fugazi Hall** was financed by John Fugazi, founder of the Transamerica Corporation, and donated in 1912 to the North Beach's Italian community. The ground floor currently houses a long-running revue called Beach Blanket Babylon. A pocket-sized but much-loved patch of greenery, **Washington Square** has a statue of Benjamin Franklin at its center and the twin-spired Church of St. Peter and St.

SOMA

Its name an abbreviation of its location, "South of Market Street," SoMa had nothing but warehouses until a section of Folsom Street became a lively nightlife strip of restaurants, bars and nightclubs. With the continuing expansion of the Moscone Convention Center, which opened here in 1981, and the excellent Museum of Modern Art relocating to a site on Third Street in 1995, there is every indication that SoMa will become increasingly interesting.

• *Telegraph Hill and Coit Tower.*

Paul on its northern side. The 1924 church, where Marilyn Monroe married Joe di Maggio, reflects the ethnic balance of the community by saying Mass in Cantonese, Italian and English. The park is in constant use by practitioners of tai chi and each weekend sees dozens of artists displaying their wares.

Grant Avenue north of Broadway is lined by numerous one-of-a-kind shops capturing the eclectic spirit of the North Beach. None is better for a lengthy rummage than **The Schlock Shop**, number 1420, which lives up to its name with an enormous stock of second-hand clothes, ornaments, bric-a-brac – and much more that defies description.

Telegraph Hill

Further north along Grant Street, the noise and commotion that characterizes the North Beach gives way to the sedate **Telegraph Hill** district, a well-to-do residential area of old and new houses set across a steep hillside. Rising steeply from Montgomery Street the **Filbert Steps** pass the well-tended gardens of equally well-tended 19thC cottages on a stiff climb to Telegraph Hill's major landmark, **Coit Tower**.

When Lillie Hitchcock Coit died in 1929, she left $100,000 for a memorial to the city's volunteer firemen. The result – uncharitably said to be a fire-hose nozzle – was Coit Tower, completed in 1934. The views from the 210-foot-high observation level are spectacular but equally interesting are the 16 murals decorating the tower's ground floor, a Depression-era Public Works Project. The apparently leftist nature of some of the murals – depicting laborers in heroic poses and some well-known left-wingers of the time – delayed the tower's opening on the charge that it was disseminating communist propaganda.

ALCATRAZ ISLAND

From the top of Coit Tower, the island of Alcatraz and the buildings of its infamous prison which incarcerated America's Most Dangerous between 1933 and 1963 are (fog permitting) clearly visible in the bay. Tours of the former prison depart several times daily from Pier 41 at Fisherman's Wharf (for details; tel. 800 BAY CRUISE).

Nob Hill and Russian Hill

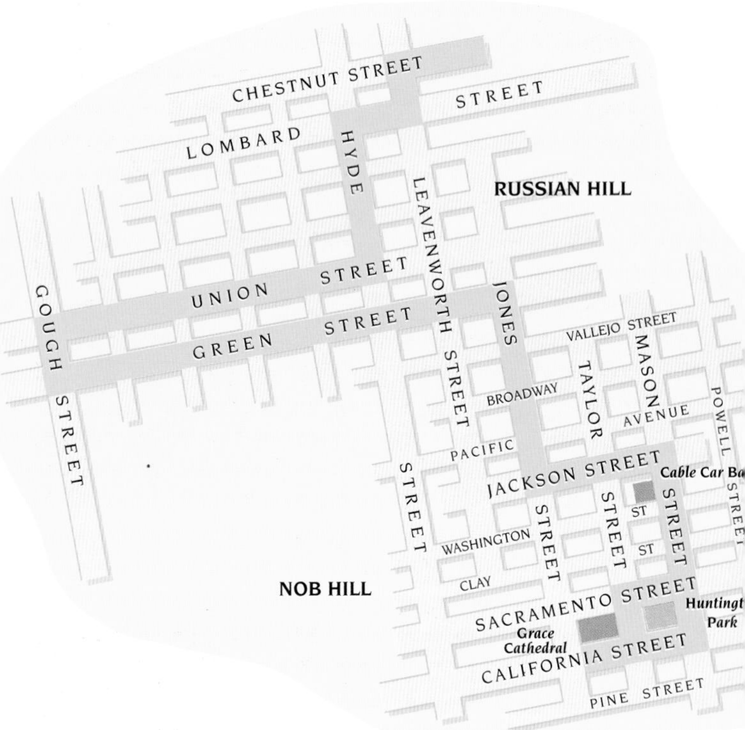

Just west of and high above Chinatown, Nob Hill became accessible with the invention of the cable car in 1873 and it was selected by the Big Four (railway magnates Charles Crocker, Mark Hopkins, Collis P. Huntington and Leland Stanford), and several of the silver barons of the Comstock Lode, as the site of the most expensive homes ever seen in California. The 1906 earthquake and fire finished off the millionaires' mansions but Nob Hill is still the city's most prestigious address, with a cathedral, a park, and several very elegant hotels occupying the spots where the great houses once stood.

This route starts from Grace Cathedral at the crest of Nob Hill, tours the adjacent buildings of interest and descends to the cable car barn – a museum devoted to the city's most romanticized form of transportation. From here, the walk (which may be combined with a cable car ride) leads north into Russian Hill, passing an excellent collection of San Francisco's varied residential architectural styles, and finishes at the very chic shops that fill the quaint Victorian buildings of Union Street.

Start Junction of California Street and Jones Street. The building of **Grace Cathedral** began in 1910 when a corner-stone was laid on the former site of the Crocker mansion. The construction, to a design based on Paris's Notre-Dame, was not completed until 1964, however. Though a pleasing neo-Gothic pile, the cathedral has few notable fea-

• *Mark Hopkins Hotel, seen from Huntington Park.*

tures save for its stained-glass windows depicting Californian history, a pair of gilded bronze doors from a Lorenzo Ghiberti cast, and the 15thC French altarpiece and Flemish reredos found inside the Chapel of Grace (only open for services). A few strides from the cathederal, the small but restful **Huntington Park** occupies the former plot of the Huntington mansion. Overlooking the park are stylish high-rise apartment blocks, luxury hotels and – directly across Cussman Street – the brownstone mansion built by silver-baron James C. Flood and the sole Nob Hill survivor of the 1906 fire. Since 1911, the Flood Mansion has belonged to the **Pacific Union Club**, an ultra-exclusive male-only haunt for California's very seriously rich.

The Pacific Union Club is strictly off-limits to non-members, but a couple of the neighboring hotels can happily be explored. At 950 Mason Street, the **Fairmont Hotel** was founded in 1902 by the daughter of another Comstock Lode silver mine beneficiary, James G. "Bonanza Jim" Fair. Walk through the grand lobby and sink into a comfy armchair to admire the ground floor's wealth of Beaux Arts features, then ride the tower's glass-sided elevator for dizzying views of the city.

Directly across California Street, the **Mark Hopkins Hotel** opened in 1926 on the site of the Hopkins mansion. A noted high-society rendezvous, the hotel has often hosted U.S. presidents and in 1945 staged the meetings that led to the founding of the United Nations. The equally high-class but much less ostentatious **Huntington Hotel**, 905 California Street, was raised on the site of Leland Stanford's mansion. With few showy features to encourage sightseers, this hotel finds favor with those who like to enjoy their wealth discreetly.

Descend from the crest of Nob Hill to the **Cable Car Barn** at the corner of Washington and Mason Streets. Nowadays the cable cars are more of a tourist attraction than a viable means of getting around, but from 1873 to 1982 they were an essential part of the San Francisco public transportation system. Exhibits at the barn explain the development and the workings of the system: on the lower level, the cable-winding gear can be seen (and heard) in operation, pulling the 11 miles of steel cable that lie beneath the city's streets.

Russian Hill

After viewing the barn, conserve your strength by hopping aboard a north-bound cable car on the Powell-Hyde Line to climb the steep streets of **Russian Hill**. Many fine examples of the architectural styles that have shaped San Francisco are scattered throughout this district, and several contrasting buildings are grouped together on the 1000 block of Green Street. The English Tudor look of **number 1088**, the Beaux Arts villa at **number 1055**, and the South-Western pueblo-style house at **number 1030**, being just three in close proximity. The oddest house on Green Street is the 1859 **Feusier Octagon House**, number 1067, partly hidden behind a large hedge: its eight sides are believed to bring luck and health to the occupants. Six blocks east at **2645 Gough Street** stands another octagonal house, built in 1861 and now owned by the Colonial Dames of America – an historical organization which opens the house for tours (second and fourth Thurs of each month).

Immediately north of Green Street, **Union Street** is the showpiece thoroughfare of Russian Hill, lined by the boutiques, clothing stores and restaurants where the predominantly well-heeled and fashion-conscious residents like to buy expensive ornaments for their homes, to dress themselves in European-designer clothes, and be seen dining on pricey French and Italian food. Many of the businesses occupy carefully-preserved buildings – decorated by wrought-iron work and imitation gaslamps – which date from the late 1800s, when the area was dairy farmland and nicknamed Cow Hollow. **Number 2040 Union Street** was the three-story home of one early dairymen, James Cudworth. At **number 1980** are the twin houses – identical bungalows joined by a common wall – which Cudworth built as wedding presents to his two daughters.

Browsing the Union Street speciality shops captures the chic mood of contemporary Russian Hill. Those worth dropping into include **Paris 1925**, number 1954, for well-crafted art deco ornaments and accessories; **Images of the North**, number 1782, with arts and crafts of the Inuit people and other native American cultures of the far north; **Sanuk**, number 1810, which features south-east Asian arts and artifacts; and the **Union Street Music Box Co**, number 2201, with hundreds of intricate antique music boxes.

Three blocks north, the section of **Lombard Street** between **Hyde** and **Leavenworth Streets** is usually marked by camera-pointing tourists aiming their lenses at what is famosly known as the "crookedest street in San Francisco." The steepness of the gradient made the street impassable for vehicles until a series of gardens was installed in the 1920s, enabling traffic to make the descent in corkscrewing fashion. The intention to raise the value of the street's properties backfired as publicity spread. The procession of cars weaving downwards, observing the 5mph speed limit, is seemingly endless. Walk down Lombard Street by its staircase pavement and cross into Chestnut Street for the **San Francisco Art Institute**, number 800. The West Coast's oldest art school, the Institute was founded in 1897 and moved into these vaguely monastical-style buildings in the 1920s. Inside are a tremendous Diego Rivera mural, several galleries with noted temporary exhibitions, and a cafe with splendid views. The tower, incidentally, is said to be haunted by the creative spirits of former students who never realized their full potential.

CIVIC CENTER

The beautiful Beaux Arts buildings of the Civic Center were raised in the early decades of the 20thC as part of a grand plan to reshape San Francisco in the image of the great cities of Europe. The plan was thwarted by profit-hungry property speculators, however, and only this tight grouping of public buildings gives an indication of what might have been. None is more imposing than the 1915 City Hall, topped by a dome modelled on St. Peter's in Rome and its entrance dominated by a flowing baroque staircase. The Civic Center is safe to explore on foot, although many of the city's homeless congregate on its grassy plazas, and just north lies the seedy Tenderloin area.

The Northern Waterfront

• *Ghirardelli: best chocolate in the city.*

On the city's northern waterfront, Fisherman's Wharf is the only area of San Francisco designed with tourists in mind. A declining fishing trade caused many of the piers and wharves here to fall into disrepair and they were swiftly transformed into the rows of souvenir shops and amusement centers seen today. Crowded night and day, Fisherman's Wharf is nonetheless where I've begun this walk, partly because it is very easy to reach on public transportation and also because it does have redeeming qualities.

The walk moves west to visit restored ships and the excellent small museums of the Fort Mason Center, continuing to the strangest sight in the city – the Palace of Fine Arts. The distance covered is about two miles, but walkers with stamina can press ahead for another two, reaching the Golden Gate Bridge.

Start Pier 39, opposite Beach Street's junction with the Embarcadero Center. Holding scores of souvenir shops but much less tacky than might be expected, the split-level **Pier 39** was built of recycled timber in the late 1970s above an abandoned 1905 cargo pier. The views of the city from the pier's upper level are impressive, and the **Eagle Cafe** has been serving the cheapest meal in Fisherman's Wharf's for years. **The San Francisco Experience**, at the pier's entrance, is an entertaining multi-media account of San Francisco's history – though stronger on special effects than factual accuracy. Lining Jefferson Street are out-and-out tourist attractions such as the **Wax Museum**, number 145, **Ripley's Believe or Not**, number 175, and the **Guinness Museum of World Records**, at 235. All of these do a roaring trade, as does the **Boudin Sourdough French Bread Factory**, number 156, which has bona fide local roots, being a descendant of Isadore Boudin's original sourdough bread factory which opened in 1849 and produced the crusty, no-yeast loaves which became linked with the city.

Between Jefferson and Beach streets, a variety of browsable shops and galleries fill the **Cannery**, 2801 Leavenworth Street, once a fruit-canning center. Another major conversion created **Ghirardelli Square**, 9800 N. Point Street, where interesting speciality stores – such as Folk Art International and the Xanadu Gallery – are secreted through the red-rick buildings of a chocolate factory that operated here from 1893. (Now produced across the bay, Ghirardelli chocolate can be sampled on the lower level.)

On the bay side of Jefferson Street on Pier 45, the **USS Pampanito**, a submarine which saw action in the Pacific during the Second World War, can be climbed aboard and explored, and is the first of the Maritime National Historic Park System's collection of historical vessels. Several more in varying stages of restoration are docked at Hyde Street Pier. They include the resplendent **Balclutha**, a Scottish-built three-masted square-rigged sailing ship launched in 1886, which rounded Cape Horn regularly before ending its days transporting Alaskan salmon along the American west coast; and the paddle-wheeled **Eureka**, dating from 1890, which had a less arduous life moving cars and people across the bay to Sausalito – a large collection of period-autos fills its car decks. More memories of San Franciscan seafaring are stored at the **National Maritime Museum**, facing the north end of Polk Street, although the Streamline Moderne style of the 1939 building – imitating an ocean liner – is more striking than the exhibits.

From the Maritime Museum, follow the waterfront path that winds around the foot of a tall bluff beneath **Fort Mason**, part of a Civil War-era military complex, and past the Jeremiah O'Brien, a 1940s "Liberty Ship" and a tourable monument to the efforts of the U.S. Merchant Marine Corp who carried supplies to needy nations during the Second World War. Just beyond lie the museums, arts centers and environmental offices that fill the former ware-

• *Lombard Street: gardener's delight, driver's nightmare.*

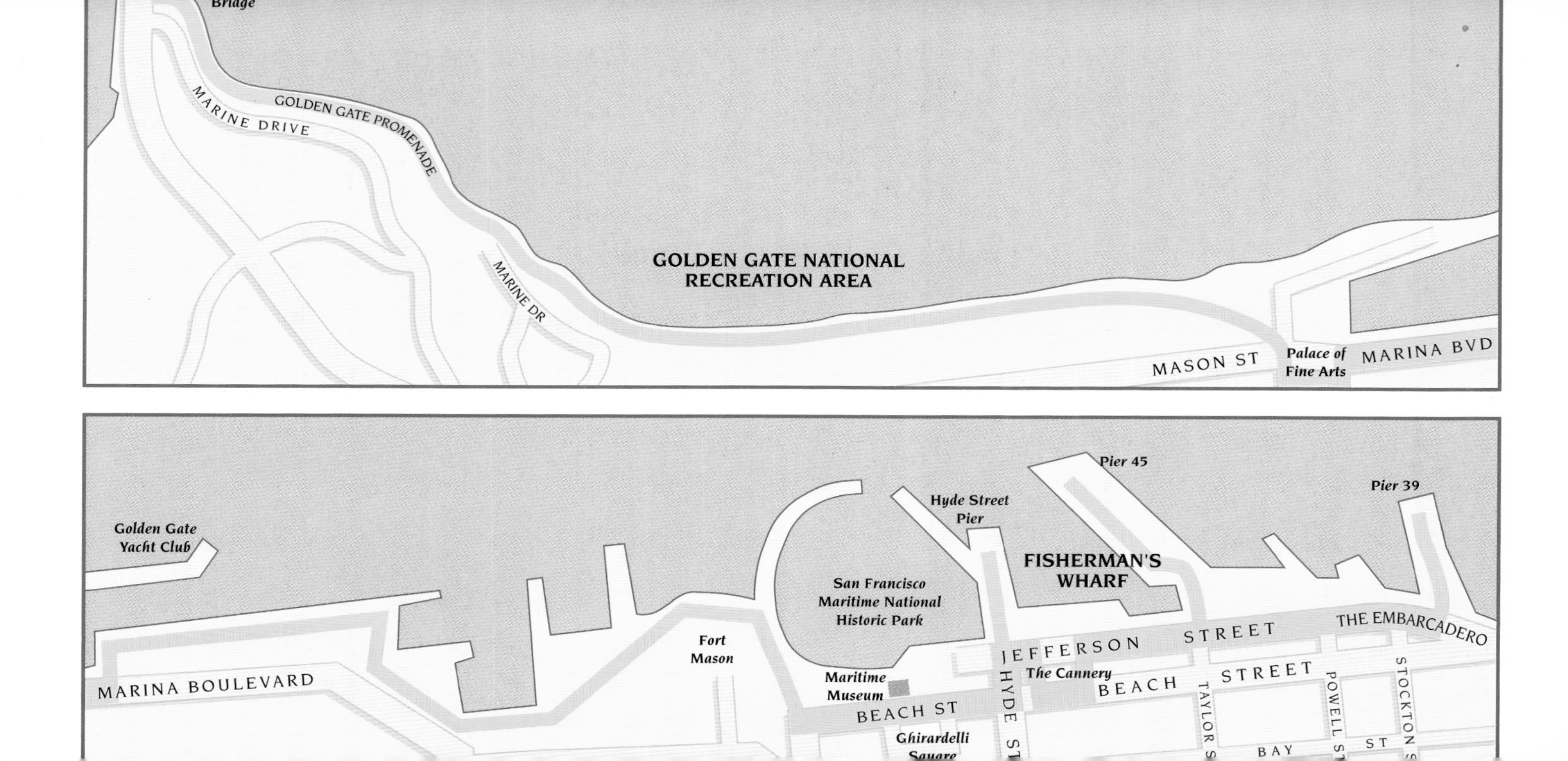

Bridge
MARINE DRIVE
GOLDEN GATE PROMENADE
MARINE DR
GOLDEN GATE NATIONAL RECREATION AREA
MASON ST
Palace of Fine Arts
MARINA BVD
Golden Gate Yacht Club
MARINA BOULEVARD
Fort Mason
San Francisco Maritime National Historic Park
Maritime Museum
BEACH ST
Ghirardelli
Hyde Street Pier
Pier 45
FISHERMAN'S WHARF
JEFFERSON STREET
HYDE ST
The Cannery
BEACH STREET
TAYLOR S
Pier 39
THE EMBARCADERO
POWELL ST
STOCKTON S
BAY ST

• *Palace of Fine Arts.*

houses of **Fort Mason Center**. Highlights include the **Craft & Folk Art Museum** (Building A), and its temporary displays of handicrafts from around the world; the **Museo Italio Americano** (Building B), focusing on the works of San Franciscan artists of Italian descent, and the outstanding **Mexican Museum** (Building D) – presently seeking a larger home for its many thousands of objects from the rich cultures of Mexico. The **Friends of San Francisco Public Library** (Building A) fills a room filled with discarded library stock and is a great spot to find bargain books.

Back at the waterfront are the city's major yacht clubs and, half-a-mile east, close to the junction of Marina Boulevard and Baker Street, the remarkable **Palace of Fine Arts**. Never a completed building, the Palace of Fine Arts was constructed as a series of Beaux Arts classical ruins for the Panama Pacific Exposition, held in San Francisco in 1915. With demolition prevented by public demand and by private money, the palace today retains a slightly spooky presence, the pained expressions of its sculptured figures intended to suggest the melancholy of life without art. Beside the palace, the **Exploratorium** is more upbeat: an immense gathering of hands-on scientific exhibits which will inform and amuse minds of all ages for hours on end.

If a blustery 2-mile hike along the coast appeals, continue west following the Golden Gate Promenade, along a stretch of barely-developed coastline that concludes beneath the **Golden Gate Bridge** at **Fort Point**, a 19thC military installation that never fired a shot in anger. A few rooms within the fortress's 15-ft-thick walls serve as a museum and guides clad as Civil War soldiers lead guided tours. Listen out for the fort's canons: they are fired twice daily.

GOLDEN GATE BRIDGE

Completed in 1937 and named for the bay it crosses rather than its color (which is rust-red, designed for maximum visibility in fog), the Golden Gate Bridge links the city to Marin County and – until the opening of the Transamerica Pyramid – was San Francisco's most familiar landmark. Just over a mile across, the bridge can be traversed on foot and by bike (expect high winds) as well as by car. The bridge is a fabulous feat of engineering – but don't expect great things from the Visitor Center near the entrance, which is packed with dismal souvenirs.

Haight-Ashbury and Golden Gate Park

In the geographical heart of San Francisco, the streets of Haight-Ashbury are lined with large and graceful Victorian homes originally occupied by middle-income families. By the 1960s, these had become low-rent apartment houses that attracted many young people – the start of what was, by 1967, being described as "the vibrant epicenter of America's hippie movement." Although the evidence of Haight-Ashbury's pivotal role in the counterculture remains, today the area is in the throes of upward mobility. The houses are more likely to be luxurious bed-and-breakfast inns than communal pads, while Haight Street's remarkable collection of vintage clothing stores draws shoppers from far and wide.

The walk described here is a simple one along Haight Street, taking in the most stately of the Victorians and the most interesting of the shops, before continuing into Golden Gate Park: one of the world's largest urban parks and filling the three miles between Haight-Ashbury and the ocean, dotted by lovingly tended gardens and the locations of two exceptional museums.

Start Junction of Haight and Baker streets. Sharply rising stairways and paths penetrate the jungle-like foliage of Buena Vista Park, where redwoods,

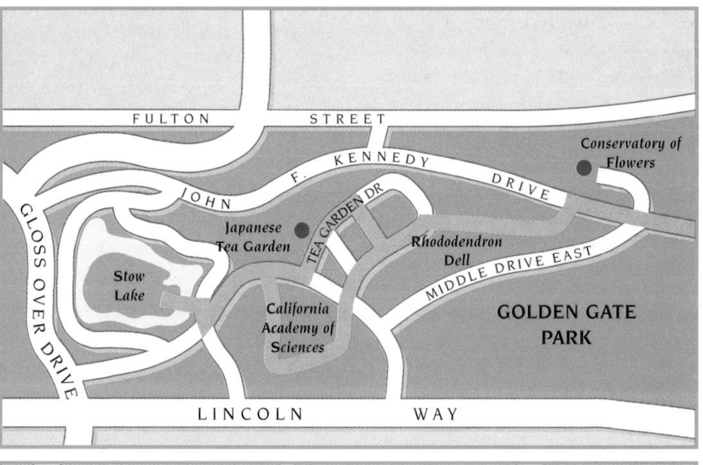

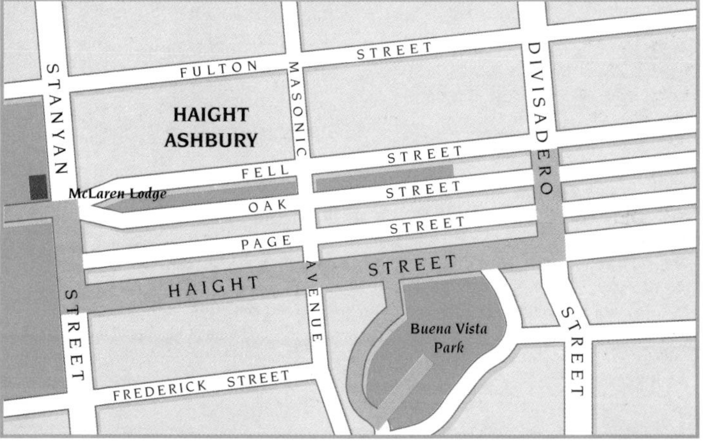

• *Spreckels Mansion.*

oaks, eucalyptus and pine trees (grown from seedlings planted in the 1880s) are entangled across a hillside. The ascent is eventually rewarded with excellent views across the city. Facing the park are several of the city's most ornate Victorian houses. Fanciest by far, the 1895 **Spencer House**, 1080 Haight Street, has a remarkable three-story corner-turret rising from its square base to become octagonal before culminating in a conical roof. Also worth a look, the **Spreckels Mansion**, 737 Buena Vista W., was built in 1897 for a sugar mogul and was utilized during later periods by writers Jack London and Ambrose Pierce, and by the legendary San Francisco rock group, the Grateful Dead. Far less architecturally distinguished, the oldest house in San Francisco stands inconspicuously three blocks away at 329 Divisadero Street, built in 1850. It is worth detouring back if you have time.

Walk west along **Haight Street** and you pass the ultra-hip cafes and eccentric vintage clothing shops that form the core of today's Haight-Ashbury. The best places to hunt down vintage, bizarre, or just unusual and cheap, men and women's apparel include **Aardvark's Odd Ark**, number 1501, which has a very large stash; **Held Over Too**, number 1537, strong on 1950s sartorial favorites; **Dharma**, number 1600, specializing in Third World clothing; and **Spellbound**, at number 1670, with glad-rags from the 1890s to the 1920s.

Haight Street is also a happy hunting ground for books on the psychedelic Sixties: browse among the local history shelves at **The Booksmith,** number 1644, a new title stockist, or through the vast second-hand stocks of **Forever After**, number 1475. For a real blast of the past, visit **Pipe Dreams**, number 1376, purveyors of giant-sized rolling papers, water pipes and other paraphernalia designed to heighten smoking pleasure.

Golden Gate Park

The northern end of Haight Street runs into Stanyan Street, beyond which lies the 1,000-acre Golden Gate Park. To the right as you enter the park, the sandstone **McLaren Lodge** was the home of the park's first superintendent and earliest guiding light, John McLaren. Scottish-born McLaren fought sand dunes and city bureaucrats to create the park according to his vision and lived here from 1896 until his death in 1943. The building now serves as the park's administrative offices and supplies park maps and information. Continue along John F. Kennedy Drive and the **Conservatory of Flowers** appears on the right fronted by lush, floral gardens. This is the oldest building in the park, built in 1878 to a design borrowed from London's Kew Gardens. Slightly further ahead, on the left side of John F. Kennedy Drive, the **Rhododendron Dell** is the first of the park's many secluded gardens and groves and the only place in the park where you'll find a likeness of John McLaren: a statue here depicts him holding a pine cone. Weave along the narrow lanes through the 20-acre dell and emerge close to

> **ALAMO SQUARE**
> Half a mile from the start of this walk, the east side of Alamo Square is formed by the 700 block of Steiner Street and the "painted ladies" – a row of six superbly maintained houses erected by developer Matthew Kavanaugh in the 1890s. With the modern skyline of the Financial District behind them, the painted ladies are among the most photographed private residences in the city.

MISSION DOLORES
Sixth of the 21 Spanish missions founded in California, Mission Dolores was completed in 1791 and stands at 320 Dolores Street in the heart of San Francisco's predominantly Spanish-speaking Mission District. Within the thick adobe walls, which helped the building survive the 1906 earthquake intact, a small museum stores remnants from the earliest days and the intimate chapel is rich in atmosphere. The 1913 Basilica next door, which now serves the spiritual needs of the local community, has a grander façade but a much less interesting interior.

the **Music Concourse**, scene of the California Midwinter Fair of 1894, intended to restore confidence after the previous years' economic slump.

On the north side of the concourse, the M.H. de Young Memorial Museum had its origins in the Midwinter Fair and, due to the efforts of Michael de Young, publisher of the *San Francisco Chronicle*, gradually evolved into a respected art collection. Some major European names are represented, but the museum's strength lies in its gathering of American arts and handicrafts from colonial times to the 20thC, taking in the folk art of religious communities such as the Shakers, the artists of the

• *The Conservatory, Golden Gate Park.*

American West such as Frank Remington, and the 1910s Arts and Crafts movement. In 1966, the museum acquired Avery Brundage's acclaimed collection of Asian art, now housed in a wing of the main building. Only a fraction of the immense collection can be displayed at one time, but few people will be disappointed. Beside the museum you will find another survivor of the 1894 Midwinter Fair, the **Japanese Tea Garden**. An elegant conglomeration of winding pathways, azaleas, cherry trees and carp-filled ponds, the garden has a bronze Buddha, cast in Japan in 1790, at its center. A San Franciscan-Japanese, Makota Hagiwara, created the garden and maintained it until he was interned during the Second World War. Tea and cookies – despite the claims of Chinatown bakers, the fortune cookie was invented here in 1909 by Hagiwara – are served at the garden's **refreshments hut.**

Directly west of the Japanese Tea Garden, the tree-covered **Strawberry Hill** rises in the center of Stow Lake. Several paths wind their way to the hill's 400-foot crest. If the climb doesn't appeal, continue instead through the Friend's Gate into the **Strybing Arboretum and Botanical Gardens**, where a series of specially-designed plots have much to please the eye and, with the herbs of the **Garden of Fragrance**, also the nose.

The buildings on the concourse's south side belong to the **California Academy of Sciences**, a privately run institution founded in 1853 which moved here in 1916. Devoted to natural history and the natural sciences, the academy is often packed with school groups. Highlights include simulations of the earthquakes which rocked San Francisco in 1865 and 1906, and the excellent Steinhart Aquarium, filled with 14,000 creatures of the deep.

Two more miles of Golden Gate Park lie to the west, mostly taken up with sports facilities – archery, angling, riding, and even a nine-hole golf course. Anyone on a Sixties pilgrimage, however, will want to gaze over the **Polo Field**, scene of many mythologized rock concerts and communal LSD trips during the halcyon days of hippiedom. In 1991, 200,000 people gathered here for a free concert to mark the sudden death of seminal rock promoter Bill Graham.

RECOMMENDED HOTELS

Abigail Hotel, $$; 246 Mc*Allister Street; tel.* 800 553 5575; *credit cards,* AE, DC, MC, V.

From 1926, the Abigail specialized in hosting theater companies on tour. Though clean, compact and tidy, it still exudes a lived-in atmosphere – and the moose heads that gaze across the lobby add an interesting touch of eccentricity. The price includes breakfast.

Alamo Square Inn, $$-$$$$; 719 *Scott Street; tel.* 415 992 2055; *credit cards,* AE, MC, V.

Fabulously-sited on an attractive square between Haight-Ashbury and Pacific Heights, this rambling Queen Anne house has 13 guest rooms, each furnished in a very different style: from the ultra-modern, equipped with jacuzzi and CD-player; to the more traditional four-poster beds and claw-foot bathtubs. An appetizing breakfast is served around a large communal table and wine for guests' use is placed in the lounge each evening.

Alexander Inn, $$; 415 O'*Farrel Street; tel.* 800 253 9263; *credit cards,* AE, DC, MC, V.

A cozy Downtown niche, with sturdy dark-wood fixtures and vases of flowers in every corner; complimentary fresh-baked pastries each morning.

Amsterdam Hotel, $$-$$$; 749 *Taylor Street; tel.* 415 673 3277; *credit cards,* AE, MC, V.

A stylishly appointed and attractively-priced bed-and-breakfast option in Nob Hill, with spacious, tastefully furnished rooms and San Francisco fogs permitting – breakfast served on a sunny patio.

Cartwright Hotel, $$$–$$$$; 524 *Sutter Street; tel.* 800 227 3844; *credit cards,* AE, DC, DS, MC, V.

Some rooms can be cramped at this centrally-placed hotel, but the individual antique furnishings in each add a touch of character; complimentary afternoon tea and cakes are offered in the book-lined study.

Diva, $$$; 440 *Geary Street; tel.* 800 533 1900; *credit cards,* AE, DC, MC, V.

To the delight of visiting design buffs, the Diva has a sleek, high-tech look that sets it well apart from most San Franciscan accommodation. A video player is a feature of every room, and the hotel holds a large collection of tapes for hire. Behind the futuristic chrome fittings, however, the staff are refreshingly human.

The Fairmont Hotel & Tower, $$$$; 950 *Mason Street; tel.* 415 772 5000; *credit cards,* AE, CB, DC, MC, V.

For 80 years, the highest of high society has been passing through the opulent marble lobby of the Fairmont, a landmark of the exclusive Nob Hill district since 1907. Indeed, once inside you need hardly venture out: the hotel has its own top-notch shops and several highly-rated restaurants. Many of the finely-furnished rooms have wonderful views across San Francisco.

Hotel Bedford, $$$–$$$$; 761 *Post Street; tel.* 800 227 5642; *credit cards,* AE, DC, DS, MC, V.

Every room at the Bedford has a minibar and a VCR; the higher rates are for smallish but comfortable suites and the higher floors offer lovely views across the city. Also offers a complimentary wine hour and a free morning shuttle bus to the Financial District.

Hotel Union Square, $$$-$$$$; 114 *Powell Street; tel.* 800 553 1900; *credit cards,* AE, CB, DC, MC, V.

Cable cars rumble romantically along the street past this thoroughly renovated hotel – a former hang-out of author Dashiell Hammett, who is said to have written *The Maltese Falcon* here. Thoughtful decoration and design touches, such as exposed-brick walls, add to the sense of relaxation. Come morning, complimentary morning croissants and herbal teas are served.

Hotel Juliana, $$$-$$$$; 590 *Bush Street; tel.* 800 382 8800; *credit cards,* AE, CB, DC, MC, V.

Muted pastel colors enhance the appeal of the smallish rooms in this completely renovated 1903 building two blocks from Union Square. Complimentary wine is served each evening in the lobby, and a light breakfast is also included in the price.

Inn at the Opera, $$$–$$$$; 333 *Fulton Street; tel.* 800 423 9610; *credit cards,* AE, CB, DC, MC, V.

If you're in San Francisco for the opera or ballet, this thoughtfully furnished hotel is the perfect place to stay. In the morning you may be sharing the substantial breakfast buffet with the performers who earned your applause the night before.

Kensington Park, $$$; 450 *Post Street; tel.* 800 553 1900; *credit cards,* AE, CB, DC, MC, V.

One of the growing band of the city's so-called "boutique hotels," small establishments that pride themselves on attention to detail and outstanding personal service. The compact rooms are tastefully furnished and each evening a pianist wistfully tinkles the ivories in the lobby as guests enjoy complimentary wine and snacks.

The King George, $$$; 334 *Mason Street; tel.* 800 288 6005; *credit cards,* AE, CB, DC, MC, V.

Pleasantly, if unspectacularly, furnished rooms in a useful Downtown location. The warm and friendly atmosphere is a plus, as is the (supposedly) English-style Bread & Honey Tearoom – which offers a very decent cup of afternoon tea, and cakes and pastries.

Mark Hopkins Hotel, $$$$; 1 *Nob Hill; tel.* 800 327 0200; *credit cards,* AE, CB, DC, MC, V.

It is expensive to stay in this Nob Hill landmark hotel, but the price brings views across San Francisco Bay that have thrilled guests since 1927, plus all the benefits of a recent $10 million facelift. Choose between the "traditional" and "contemporary" rooms – or blow a lifetime's savings on a top-floor suite, which comes equipped with a grand piano.

The Miyako, $$$$; 1625 *Post Street; tel.* 415 922 3200; *credit cards,* AE, DC, DS, MC, V.

A luxurious Japantown retreat which

skilfully combines Western and Japanese ideas. All rooms have sliding shoji screens and marble bathrooms with furo tubs (and a sachet of genuine Japanese mineral water for a relaxing soak). The more traditional Japanese rooms feature tatami mats and futons.

The Pickwick, $$-$$$; 85 *Fifth Street; tel.* 415 421 7500; *credit cards*, AE, CB, DC, MC, V.

Though it lacks the warmth and character of other city districts, the SoMa (South-of-Market-Street) area is a viable base – all the more so if you stay at this sound-value, comfortable hotel which often cuts its regular rates.

The Raphael, $$$; 386 *Geary Street; tel.* 415 986 2000; *credit cards*, AE, DC, MC, V.

Well-furnished though slightly poky rooms and a prime Downtown location earn the Raphael plenty of admirers, but the bustle around the lobby tends to leave guests feeling rather anonymous.

The Red Victorian, $$-$$$; 1665 *Haight Street; tel.* 415 864 1978; *credit cards*, AE, MC, V.

A truly New Age bed-and-breakfast experience, this 1904 house on hippie-flavored Haight Street is equipped with everything for a serene California-style stay: the color scheme is rainbow-hued; there is a meditation room, resident masseurs, and a very health-conscious breakfast each morning.

San Remo Hotel, $$; 2237 *Mason Street; tel.* 415 776 8688; *credit cards*, MC, V.

A lovingly restored 1906 Italianate villa that is strong on atmosphere and charm but very quiet considering how many rooms are clustered close together off a central atrium. Rooms have sinks rather than private bathrooms but the building has ample W.C. shower facilities. The location is convenient: a residential street between the North Beach and Fisherman's Wharf.

Sheehan, $$; 620 *Sutter Street; tel.* 800 848 1529; *credit cards*, AE, DC, MC, V.

For many years the city's YWCA, the Sheehan has lately transformed itself into a pleasantly furnished, good-value hotel. An olympic-sized swimming-pool and a gymnasium are further draws for fitness-conscious guests.

Stanyan Park Hotel, $$$; 750 *Stanyan Street; tel.* 415 751 1000; *credit cards*, AE, CB, DC, MC, V.

A fine-looking Edwardian hotel facing Golden Gate Park. The extremely friendly staff help evoke an ambience closer to a small bed-and-breakfast inn than a 36-room hotel. A complimentary selection of rolls, muffins and fruit is laid out each morning in the spacious dining room.

Sutter Larkin Hotel, $; 1048 *Larkin Street; tel.* 415 474 6820; *credit cards*, MC, V.

A safe but decidedly downmarket hotel that offers very simple rooms, with or without bathrooms, at the cheapest rates in town; but in a location close to the seedy Tenderloin area.

Tuscan Inn, $$$$; 425 *North Point; tel.* 800 648 4626; *credit cards*, AE, CB, DC, DS, MC, V.

A touch of elegance among the predominantly run-of-the-mill Fisherman's Wharf area hotels, this modern facility has pleasantly bright and tidily-furnished rooms, and a cozy lobby where complimentary drinks can be consumed beside the fireplace. Also in the lobby is a display of the historical oddments unearthed during the hotel's construction.

Washington Square Inn, $$-$$$$; 1660 *Stockton Street; tel.* 800 388 0200; *credit cards*, MC, V.

Situated in the heart of enjoyable North Beach, this is one of the city's best-located bed-and-breakfast inns. The rooms – the cheaper ones have no bathrooms – are decorated with French antiques and are remarkably effective at evoking the tranquil mood of rural France. Besides breakfast, the rate includes afternoon tea and scones, and evening wine and cheese.

BUDGET ACCOMMODATION

Many of the recommendations on the preceding pages are inexpensive; here is a selection of hostel or other exceptionally cheap accommodation:

Central YMCA, 220 *Golden Gate Avenue; tel.* 415 885 0460.

European Guest House, 761 *Minna Street; tel.* 415 861 6634.

Globetrotters Inn, 225 *Ellis Street; tel.* 415 346 5786.

International Guest House, 2976 *23rd Street; tel.* 415 641 1411.

San Francisco International Hostel, *Building* 24, *Fort Mason; tel.* 415 771 7277.

18th Street Guest House, 3930 *Eighteenth Street; tel.* 415 255 0644.

RECOMMENDED RESTAURANTS

Ananda Fuara,$; 1298 *Market Street; tel.* 415 621 1994; *credit cards, none.*

A small but tempting selection of vegetarian dishes: try the chef's special: the "Neatloaf."

Asuka Brasserie, $$-$$$; *in the Miyako Hotel,* 1625 *Post Street; tel.* 800 533 4567; *cards,* AE, DC, DS, MC, V.

Traditional Japanese cookery combined with Californian culinary inventiveness to produce sensational, artfully presented meals – be it sashimi or burnt bananas with chili, chocolate and coconut – in a relaxing Japantown setting. If the high prices for lunch and dinner are beyond your means, drop by for a protein-packed Japanese breakfast.

Blue Light Cafe, $-$$; 1979 *Union Street; tel.* 415 922 5510; *dinner only; credit cards,* MC, V.

The fiery cuisine of the American South West – ranging from mesquite-grilled fish to ultra-spicy barbecued ribs – enthusiastically consumed by a predominantly young and image-conscious Pacific Heights crowd.

Bohemian Cigar Store, $; 566 *Columbus Ave; tel.* 415 362 0536; *closed Mon; credit cards, none.*

A delightful, typically North Beach cafe, and a perfect place in which to watch the crowds milling by while sipping an espresso coffee or snacking on a tasty sandwich.

The Buena Vista, $; 2765 *Hyde Street; tel.* 415 474 5044; *credit cards, none.*

In a plum position overlooking Fisherman's Wharf with better – and better-value – food than many of its neighborhood rivals, the Buena Vista's speedy and chatty waitresses bring American breakfasts, lunches and dinners to the tables and encourage diners to sample an Irish coffee – claimed to have made its American debut here in 1952.

Caffè Trieste, $; 601 *Vallejo Street; tel.* 415 392 6739; *credit cards, none.*

From the beatniks of the 1950s to the New Agers of the 1990s, this place has drawn North Beach writers, poets, intellectuals, visionaries and pseuds for endless cups of espresso coffee and hours of animated conversation. Light soups, salads and sandwiches are also on offer, and on Saturday afternoons, the owner's family plays music and sings for the customers.

Calzone's, $$; 430 *Columbus Ave; tel.* 415 397 3600; *lunch and dinner only; credit cards,* AE, MC, V.

Enterprising mixture of traditional Italian cooking and California cuisine which features wood-fired pizzas with a variety of inventive, exotic toppings, and an assortment of deliciously fresh pasta dishes.

Cha Cha Cha, $; 1805 *Haight Street; tel.* 415 386 5758; *lunch and dinner only; credit cards, none.*

An enticing array of simple Cuban and other Caribbean favourites, such as black-bean soup and gigantic rolls stuffed with pork and vegetables. This tropically-decorated diner on lively Haight Street makes an ideal place for an eat-and-run snack or for lingering over a fuller meal.

Crown Room, $$; *at the* Fairmont Hotel, 950 Mason Street; *tel.* 415 772 5131; *lunch and dinner only; credit cards,* AE, CB, DC, MC, V.

Piled high with meat, fish and vegetables, there is something of almost everything at the groaning buffet table, but the real attraction is this 24th-floor restaurant's panoramic view of the city.

Eagle Cafe, $; Pier 39, Fisherman's Wharf; *tel.* 415 433 3689; *breakfast and lunch only; credit cards, none.*

When Fisherman's Wharf transformed itself from a working dock-side area into a tourist attraction, the Eagle Cafe – long a mainstay of local life – was shifted by crane to this new location. Though surrounded by souvenir shops, it still dishes up the cheapest – if somewhat limited – breakfasts in the vicinity. The clientele are crusty locals and tourists who can't believe their luck at finding such a place.

The Elite Cafe, $-$$; 2049 Filmore Street; *tel.* 415 346 8668; *dinner only, brunch on* Sun; *credit cards,* AE. MC, V.

A large bowl of creole gumbo or seafood chowder could well be a match for most appetites, but they are just starters at this specialist cajun/creole restaurant, where main courses include delights such as baked eggplant stuffed with crab and gourmet-class red beans and rice. Should the spiciness be too much, turn to the strong selection of Californian wines.

Fior d'Italia, $$; 601 Union Street; *tel.* 415 986 1886; *credit cards,* AE, CB, DC, DS, MC, V.

Claims to be the oldest Italian restaurant in the U.S. and divides its dining sections into a window-side area near the bar and a more formal main dining room, patrolled by suited waiters. Top picks are the fresh pastas and the veal dishes.

Fog City Diner, $-$$; 1300 Battery Street; *tel.* 415 982 2000; *lunch and dinner only; credit cards,* MC, V.

A very popular eatery, shaped like a railway carriage and decked out in chrome and neon to evoke the 1950s, but offering a very 1990s brand of Californian cuisine, with a host of innovatory appetizers and main courses based on regional American cooking.

Gaylords, $$; 1 Embarcadero Center; *tel.* 415 397 7775; *lunch and dinner only* Mon-Sat, *dinner only* Sun; *credit cards,* AE, CB, DC, MC, V.

One of a large chain of dependable restaurants (there's another at Ghirardelli Square in Fisherman's Wharf) specializing in northern Indian cuisine, particularly tandoori dishes. There is a range of vegetarian dishes, too, and a lunchtime buffet which promises excellent value for anyone with a large appetite.

Green's, $$-$$$; Building A, Fort Mason; *tel.* 415 771 6222; *lunch and dinner only, closed* Mon; *credit cards,* MC, V.

Green's ingredients come from the organic farm of a Buddhist retreat across the bay in Marin County – the bread is baked at the Tassajara Buddhist retreat on the Central Coast – and are moulded into gourmet-standard vegetarian meals ranging from pizza, with toppings such as sautéed spinach and feta cheese, to black bean chili. Fridays and Saturdays see a fixed-price five-course dinner that should delight even devoted carnivores. The outstanding food is matched by outstanding views of the Golden Gate Bridge.

Hamburger Mary's, $; 1582 Folsom Street; *tel.* 415 626 5767; *credit cards,* AE, DC, MC, V.

Mary's hamburgers are admired all over the city and many come to munch them while mingling with the sometimes outlandish local clientele. Besides burgers, there are soups, fish dishes and salads.

Hang Ah Tea Room, $; 1 Hang Ah Street; *tel.* 415 982 5686; *credit cards, none.*

This small Chinatown cafe draws a regular local crowd to its wonderful selection of inexpensive dim sum; in the evening, there is broader choice of more substantial meals.

Indonesia Restaurant & Cafeteria, $; 678–680 Post Street; *tel.* 415 474

4026; *credit cards*, AE, MC; *closed* Mon.

Fish cake wrapped in banana leaf is just one item from a long list of health-conscious Indonesian dishes served at unbeatable prices in this usually costly downtown area.

John's Grill, $–$$; 63 *Ellis Street; tel.* 415 986 1133; *credit cards*, AE, MC, V; *dinner only on* Sun.

While making the most of its mention in Dashiell Hammett's *The Maltese Falcon* and displaying photos of celebrities who've dined here since the restaurant's 1908 opening, John's Grill also finds time to serve some exceptionally good steak, seafood and pasta.

Judy's Cafe, $; 2268 *Chestnut Street; tel.* 415 922 4588; *credit cards, none.*

The well-heeled thirtysomethings of the Marina District can be found here at weekends, lingering over fresh fruit and bran-cake breakfasts. Less fussy eaters show up at anytime to quaff giant-sized omelettes or sandwiches. Even if you're not hungry, stop here for a coffee and to eavesdrop on local gossip.

La Follie, $$$; 2316 *Polk Street; tel.* 415 776 5577; *dinner only, closed Sun; credit cards*, AE, MC, V.

Only fresh, locally-produced ingredients go into the outstanding French food created here in a relaxed and informal atmosphere. If you find yourself dithering over the menu, opt for the five-course dinner designed to reveal the chef's special (artistic as well as culinary) talents. Reservations are recommended.

Lori's Diner, $; 336 *Mason Street; tel.* 415 392 8646; *credit cards, none.*

This 1950s–style diner is a great place for breakfast at any time of the day or night, and also serves a variety of sandwiches, hot dogs, burgers and frothy milkshakes.

Max's Diner, $-$$; 311 *Third Street; tel.* 415 546 6297; *lunch and dinner only; credit cards*, AE, MC, V.

Lunching office workers and just-woken-up nightclub folk pack this traditional-style diner – located in SoMa, just outside the usual tourist areas – for large helpings of traditional American fare, such as meatloaf, turkey sandwiches, burgers, onion rings, and a fine selection of salads.

The New San Remo Restaurant, $-$$; 2237 *Mason Street; tel.* 415 673 9090; *dinner only; credit cards*, AE, MC, V.

Northern Italian cooking that is best sampled through the fixed-price five-course dinners, usually featuring two specials of the day.

North Beach Pizza, $; 1310 *Grant Street; tel.* 415 433 2444; *lunch and dinner only; credit cards*, AE, DC, MC, V.

There is nearly always a line for a table here, where excellent pizzas with a wide variety of toppings – and a chance to sit and watch the crowds go by – make a perfect start or finish to an evening spent exploring the North Beach.

Perry's, $-$$; 1944 *Union Street; tel.* 415 922 9022; *credit cards*, AE, DC, MC, V.

The elegant dark-wood interior of Perry's is a fabled meeting place for the unattached of stylish Pacific Heights, though plenty of customers come here thinking only of food – large and succulent portions of well-cooked American fare are served throughout the day.

Pork Store Cafe, $; 1451 *Haight Street; tel.* 415 864 6981; *credit cards, none.*

Dependable Haight-Ashbury retreat for classic American breakfasts – including pancakes and grits – and lunchtime fare that includes soups, sandwiches and some very juicy burgers.

Sam Woh, $; 813 *Washington Street; tel.* 415 982 0569; *closed Sun; credit cards, none.*

A Chinatown institution for many years, the Sam Woh's kitchen occupies the entire ground floor. Upstairs diners attack filling, low-cost food at shared tables: great value and great atmosphere; but not a place for a quiet meal.

Northern California

Marin County and the Russian River Valley

120 miles (round trip); map Kummerley + Frey California-Nevada

I have described this route as if your starting point will be San Francisco, but as with all the routes and tours in this guide, you can join it at any point and follow it clockwise or counterclockwise.

The tour is designed to give a lasting impression of natural California without taking you more than a two-hour drive from San Francisco. As such, it is ideal for anyone based in the city with only a few days to spare, but also links neatly with the explorations of the Mendocino Coast (number 2), and of the Napa and Sonoma valleys (numbers 6 and 7).

Visible across the Golden Gate from San Francisco, the first stop is the rugged Marin Headlands, penetrated by easy (and hard) hiking trails and a couple of roads. I suggest that you allocate half your first day to exploring the headlands; the second half should be used to cross eastwards to the enticing bayside town of Sausalito – pick one of its romantic hillside hotels to pass the night.

Awake in Sausalito to admire the sight of San Francisco emerging from the morning fog, and then weave inland through the folds of the Marin hills, and insular villages such as Mill Valley, before rising into Mount Tamalpais State Park for some spectacular scenery and views.

Then, descend to the coast, and choose one of the tiny Point Reyes area settlements for your second night. Next day, make a leisurely tour of the Point Reyes National Seashore, a geologically bizarre area where the impact of the San Andreas Fault is clearly visible. Leave the coast by forested backroads and spend your third night at Guerneville, the largest and busiest of the quintessentially country communities of the Russian River Valley, which cater to the frustrated outdoorsman in every city-dwelling Californian male.

From Guerneville, it is simple to strike east to the Sonoma Valley, or back to the coast to continue north. If you're returning to San Francisco, I recommend that you do so via the hillside communities of Fairfax and San Anselmo, and have a final meal at the peninsula town of Tiburon.

On this tour, accommodation and eating are – enchantingly, I feel – subject to local eccentricities, especially so in the pint-sized settlements around Point Reyes, where dairy farmers are becoming adept bed-and-breakfast hosts and almost every eatery features local oysters. Avoid crowds and hiked-up prices by taking this tour in midweek; and do so outside winter, when gales and constant fogs heighten the natural drama but don't make for comfortable touring.

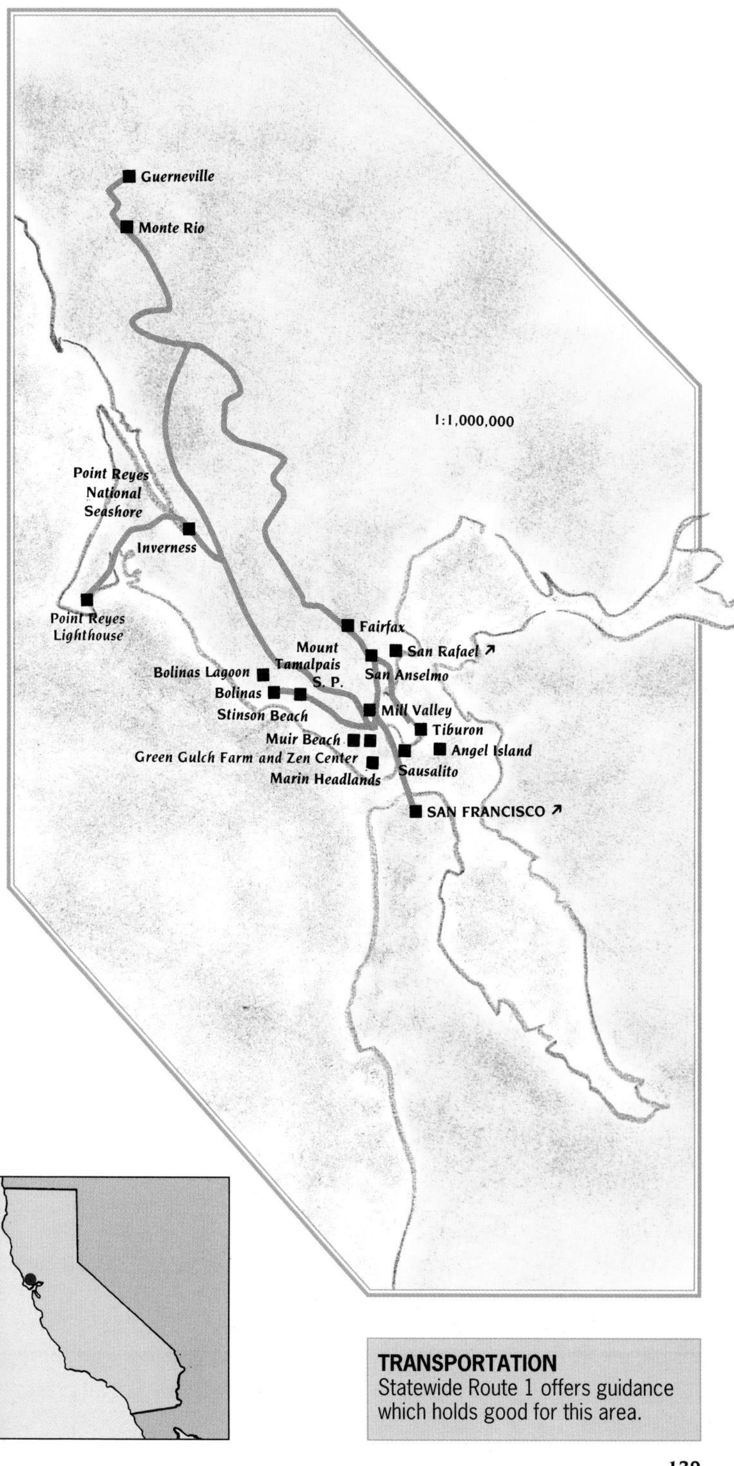

TRANSPORTATION
Statewide Route 1 offers guidance which holds good for this area.

SIGHTS & PLACES OF INTEREST

BOLINAS LAGOON
A lengthy sand spit curls westwards off Stinson Beach (see page 144), sheltering Bolinas Lagoon, the calm waters of which are as attractive to species of waterfowl and migratory birds as the beach is to human swimmers and surfers. Facing the lagoon beside Hwy-1, the **Audubon Canyon Ranch** research center occupies a redwood-lined valley that provides a protected nesting place for egrets and great blue herons, among other species. During the mid-March to July nesting season, the ranch office (closed Mon) dispenses free literature and is the start of a trail to an observation platform – from which the birds can be discreetly watched.

FAIRFAX
Mountain bike enthusiasts might feel the urge to make a pilgrimage to Fairfax, just west of San Anselmo on Francis Drake Boulevard. An uninteresting community, it is nonetheless where the rugged all-terrain bike evolved during the mid-1970s when a group of locals began customizing regular bikes for races on the local slopes.

The popularity of the mountain bike, and the several hundred miles of bike routes which now lace the Fairfax area, have led to tight controls on cyclists' speed (15mph is the limit) and on-the-spot fines – imposed by patrolling park rangers – for deviating from designated cycle routes. Should you want to join the two-wheel crowd, mountain bikes can be hired in Fairfax from the Sunshine Bicycle Center, 737 Center Boulevard (tel. 415 459 3334).

DETOUR – **BOLINAS**
Horseshoe Hill Road, off Hwy-1, follows the western side of Bolinas Lagoon, eventually reaching the tiny settlement of Bolinas. Afraid of being trampled beneath a tourist stampede, the writers, artists and craftspeople who live in Bolinas are known to tear down signs marking the route to their ramshackle – and very Californian – village. Bolinas is worth a quick look but the main reason for making the detour is to spend an hour or two at low tide observing the domestic arrangements of marine life in the pools of the Duxbury Reef Marine Reserve, a mile west.

HORSE TREKKING
Ranging from half-day to three-day treks, horseback journeys into the Austin Creek State Recreation Area, a 4,000-acre hilly wilderness area north of Armstrong Redwoods State Reserve, are arranged by Armstrong Woods Pack Station (tel. 707 887 2939).

GUERNEVILLE ✕
Full of rustic charm and set in the verdant valley of the Russian River, Guerneville (pronounced GURN-ville) began life as a logging center (once unceremoniously known as Stumptown) but for decades has been doing a brisker business as a recreational center, attracting San Franciscans to weekends of fishing, canoeing and kayaking. If this appeals, you'll find rental outlets for fishing tackle, boats and bikes spread along River Road.

Two miles north of the town, foot trails lead through the dark, damp groves of **Armstrong Redwoods State Reserve**, where an impressive batch of redwoods are staging a comeback after years of being scythed down for profit.

Besides a fair number of Victorian houses providing bed-and-breakfast accommodation and several enjoyable cafes, Guerneville itself doesn't have much to draw attention from the natural attractions in its vicinity. If a few glasses of sparkling wine hold more appeal than messing about on a river or looking at trees, call to the **Korbel Champagne Cellars**, 13250 River Road (tel. 707 887 2294), which has been producing to much acclaim since 1882 and is open daily for tours and tastings.

INVERNESS
Named in 1889 by an immigrant who recognized the landscapes around Tomales Bay as similar to the highlands of his native Scotland, tiny Inverness is on Sir Francis Drake Boulevard, the main approach road to Point Reyes National Seashore, and has a couple of likely places to stay overnight.

RECOMMENDED HOTELS

GUERNEVILLE

Creekside Inn & Resort, $$; 16180 *Neeley Road; tel.* 707 869 3623; *credit cards,* MC, V.

A place that makes the most of Guerneville's rural setting while offering outstanding value for money. Inside the main building, the homey rooms are simply but adequately fitted out. Spread across the 3-acre, redwood-studded grounds, the kitchen-equipped cabins are a better option for families or several people sharing.

The Estate Inn, $$$-$$$$; 13555 *Hwy-116; tel.* 707 869 9093; *credit cards,* AE, DC, MC, V.

In the 1920s, what is now the Estate Inn was among Guerneville's most elegant mansions. As a bed-and-breakfast inn, the accent is still on refinement, with tasteful decoration throughout and owners who pride themselves on offering attentive, personal service – including little extras such as leaving chocolates on your pillow. Several of the ten rooms are equipped with jacuzzis and in the grounds you'll find an open-air swimming-pool bordered by a redwood grove.

INVERNESS

Blackthorne Inn, $$$-$$$$; 266 *Vallejo Avenue; tel.* 415 663 8621; *credit cards,* MC, V.

What began as a wooden cabin has grown into a rambling, architecturally eccentric dwelling with strangely-angled turrets and protuberances of all kinds at ground level, and something resembling a lookout tower comprising the top floor. The five guest rooms are as diverse as the house. As you might expect, the eight-sided lookout tower (called the "Eagles' Nest") has the best views. A minimum two-night stay at weekends.

Golden Hinde Inn & Marina, $$-$$$$; 12938 *Sir Francis Drake Boulevard; tel.* 800 443 7575; *credit cards,* CB, DC, MC, V.

There are plenty of endearingly tacky reminders of the region's links with Francis Drake at this otherwise fairly standard, but promisingly-located, hotel. Some rooms have fireplaces – a welcome sight when chilly fogs envelop the coast – and a few are fitted with kitchens.

SAUSALITO

Alta Mira, $$-$$$; 125 *Bulkley Street; tel.* 415 332 1350; *credit cards,* AE, CB, DC, MC, V.

Reasonably-priced by the costly standards of Sausalito and reached by a staircase hewn into the hillside that climbs sharply above the town center. The least expensive rooms are in the Victorian main building and most have a sensational outlook across San Francisco Bay. The charge rises for the fully-equipped cottages spread across the neatly landscaped grounds.

Casa Madrona, $$$-$$$$; 801 *Bridgeway; tel.* 800 288 0502; *credit cards,* MC, V.

The most up-market of Sausalito's evocative hillside hotels, the Casa Madrona rooms are split between the wood-framed 19thC main building and a more recent annex. Each is individually decorated with flair to a particular theme. The price includes a light breakfast and evening wine and cheese.

TIBURON

Tiburon Lodge & Conference Center, $$-$$$$; 1651 *Tiburon Boulevard; tel.* 800 TIBURON; *credit cards,* AE, CB, DC, MC, V.

A short walk from the town center, the lodge does a valiant job of combining Tiburon's appealing rusticity with the comforts and facilities demanded by the business traveller. For casual visitors, there can be some very attractive midweek rates – but not during public holidays or major conferences.

BUDGET ACCOMMODATION

MARIN HEADLANDS

Golden Gate AYH Hostel, *off Bunker Road (tel.* 415 331 2777).

POINT REYES

Point Reyes AYH Hostel, *off Limantour Road, near Point Reyes Station (tel.* 415 663 8811).

DETOUR – **GREEN GULCH FARM AND ZEN CENTER**
Trails through the canyons inland from Muir Beach reach the Green Gulch Farm and Zen Center. The organic farm here supplies San Francisco's premier vegetarian restaurant, Green's, while the center's meditation classes are open to the public on Sunday mornings – a truly Californian way to pass a few hours: for details, tel. 415 383 3134.

MARIN HEADLANDS

Tall cliffs lashed by ocean waves and broad stretches of chaparral – carpeted each spring by colorful wildflowers – form the Marin Headlands, a strikingly undeveloped area that faces San Francisco from the north side of the Golden Gate.

Only a couple of roads cross the headlands, branching off the combined Hwy-101/Hwy-1 soon after it crosses the Golden Gate Bridge from the city. Take the Alexander Avenue exit to enter the headlands (part of the Golden Gate National Recreation Area) and call first at the Marin Headlands Visitor Center for maps and information. The center stands close to **Rodeo Beach**, a slim sand spit dividing the raging ocean (swimming rarely permitted) from an uncannily still lagoon that teems with birdlife – and bird watchers, armed with checklists. Above the lagoon, the **California Marine Mammal Center** nurses injured seals and sea lions back to health: those who are fit enough can be observed frolicking in their pens in anticipation of their return to the ocean. The center also carries displays and exhibits on California's coastal ecology.

High above the Golden Gate, the southerly portion of the headlands holds several disused gun placements, intended to defend San Francisco in hostilities from the Civil War to the Second World War, and a 1950s ballistic missile bunker aimed at foes further afield. The military sites are open occasionally for tours (for details, call 415 556 0693).

A spot of more enduring interest lies further south at Point Bonita, where a spectacular half mile trail – which negotiates a tunnel, gouged from the rock by hand in 1877, and a wooden bridge – runs to **Point Bonita Lighthouse** (open on weekends; closed during winter), built in 1855 and one of the West Coast's earliest beacons.

Even if the Marin Headlands doesn't sound remotely appealing, be assured that there is no better place for taking a photograph of San Francisco artily framed by the towers of the Golden Gate Bridge.

MILL VALLEY ×

On the redwood-studded eastern slopes of Mount Tamalpais, the enchantingly pretty Mill Valley has logging origins and a present-day mellowness engendered by its comfortably-off but liberally-inclined community of San Francisco commuters. In summer, hikers fortify themselves at the amiable little cafes around Lytton Square, in the heart of the village, before tackling a 7-mile trail – the Dipsea Trail – that climbs a ridge of Mount Tamalpais prior to descending to Stinson Beach. Since 1905, the "Dipsea Race" has been contested over this course annually, usually during June.

Mill Valley is also artistic enough to have its own film festival each fall, featuring independent and avant-garde productions.

MONTE RIO

Monte Rio was a popular resort town in the 19thC, but might have faded from the map altogether were it not for the 2,700-acre **Bohemian Grove**, owned by the Bohemian Club, that keeps many locals in work. Founded by left-leaning San Francisco newspapermen in 1872, the Bohemian Club has since evolved into a secretive lodge for the nation's richest and most powerful men. The club's week-long Bohemian Days, each July, sees stretch limos and helicopters bearing the dignitaries who arrive for several days of (allegedly) nefarious activities, screened from ordinary folk by high walls, high-tech security systems, and conspicuously muscular bodyguards.

MOUNT TAMALPAIS STATE PARK

To enjoy the best views in Marin County, take the aptly-named Panoramic Highway from Stinson Beach. It winds through the redwood-filled canyons of Mount Tamalpais State Park to emerge on to sunny ridges. From the upper elevations you will be able to take in a remarkable panorama of San Francisco, the Bay Area, and a large chunk of northern California spread out beyond. The coastal features are sometimes obscured by a dramatic white blanket of fog.

Forty-two miles of hiking trails penetrate the park (get a map from Park Headquarters, beside the highway). However, you only need make a short – though steep – walk from a car-park to reach the park's highest point: Mount Tamalpais' 2,571-ft East Peak. A little more leg work will take you to the Mountain Theater, an amphitheater gouged from natural rock in the 1930s, where up to 3,750 people gather for concerts and performing arts shows each spring.

San Franciscans began visiting the mountain in force during the 1880s, after it was made accessible by "the crookedest railway in the world" winding up from Mill Valley. At that time, Mount Tamalpais was privately owned; but in the early 1900s, William Kent, an ecologically-concerned congressman, donated it to the state. Kent insisted that the park's outstanding patch of redwoods be named after California's foremost conservationist, John Muir. The result was – and is – the **Muir Woods National Monument**, reached by several mile-long rabbit-patrolled trails off Panoramic Highway (and off Muir Woods Road, north of Muir Beach). There are taller and older redwoods further north, but the trees, some rising above 250 feet, in this cool, lush grove, provide an excellent introduction to the wonders of California's forests.

MUIR BEACH ×

Nestled in a semi-circular cove beside Hwy-1, Muir Beach is the first coastal settlement north of San Francisco. In sunny weather, the village's slender stretch of sand (swimming prohibited) makes a likely picnic spot. On a rainy day, time is better spent exploring the eccentricities of the Pelican Inn, 10 Pacific Way, a replica 16thC English pub inspired by Francis Drake's landing here (or hereabouts: the actual site is much disputed) in 1579. As you leave Muir Beach headed north, keep an eye out for the signpost indicating Muir Beach Overlook, a spot with views over many miles of this superb coastline.

• *Golden Gate Bridge from the Marin Headlands.*

POINT REYES NATIONAL SEASHORE ×

Even by the standards of the northern Californian coast, the landscapes of Point Reyes National Seashore are extraordinary. The triangular-shaped area embraces sand dunes, beaches and marshlands, and reaches inland to the rolling hillsides that provide prime dairy farming territory. Point Reyes also has the white cliffs which, legend has it, inspired Francis Drake to name the area Nova Albion (or "New England") at the time of his landing in the1500s.

Turn off Hwy-1 at Olema, one of a handful of tiny settlements that provide access to the national seashore area, for the **Bear Valley Visitors Center**, which puts the landscape into a historical and geological context. Try not to panic when you discover that the whole region sits atop the San Andreas Fault – one of the major seismic fault lines underneath California – and was the epicenter of the 1906 earthquake that flattened much of San Francisco. Outside the center, the Earthquake Trail reveals evidence of the 1906 quake, which caused the Point Reyes area to jump 16 feet northwards in one second. Another trail here leads to Kule Loklo, an impressive re-created Miwok Indian village built with traditional tools to a traditional plan.

To penetrate further the national seashore area, continue north to join Sir

Francis Drake Boulevard which passes through Inverness and navigates the western edge of placid Tomales Bay. Often bathed in sunshine when the southerly section of the Seashore area is shrouded in fog, **Tomales Bay State Park** has several bay-side beaches ripe for enjoying a picnic while watching the small vessels which harvest oysters on the bay.

Sir Francis Drake Boulevard continues between marshes and sand dunes into the southerly section of the National Seashore area, a region blighted by frequent fogs and enduring the coolest summer temperatures anywhere in the continental U.S. Marked by the **Point Reyes Lighthouse**, hopefully casting its beam into the gloom since the 1870s, the Seashore's south-western tip is a noted vantage point for spotting California gray whales during their December to June migration.

SAN ANSELMO

A smug residential town enviously sited in the Marin hills, San Anselmo makes a pitch for the disposable income of San Franciscans by styling itself the "antiques capital of Northern California." An enormous number of antiques, book, and other speciality shops, are indeed clustered together in its diminutive center. While bargains are thin on the ground, browsing here could easily fill half a day. A note of minor historical interest is provided by the San Francisco Theological Seminary, located above the town, where graduates of the Presbyterian Church have been trained since 1892.

SAN RAFAEL

See California Overall: 1.

SAUSALITO 🛏 ✕

Beside a sheltered portion of San Francisco Bay and rising sharply across a hillside, Sausalito enjoys a superb natural setting, wonderful views and a spectacular history. A 19thC whaling port, the town became a Prohibition-era site of saloons and brothels, and in the 1940s acquired a ship-building industry that split the community between the scruffy bayside "Wharf rats" and the "hill snobs" living in the smart houses above.

Along the way, the town also acquired a reputation as a stamping ground of artists and non-conformists, elements still present today and evinced by numerous art galleries, although it soon becomes clear that Sausalito is a popular excursion from San Francisco (regular ferries cross from the city's Fisherman's Wharf). Spend a night here, however, mingling with the locals who pass their evenings in the bayside bars and restaurants after the day-trippers have departed, and a calmer, deliciously seductive, Sausalito emerges. However long you stay in Sausalito, try to find time for the **San Francisco Bay and Delta Model**, 2100 Bridgeway, housed in a huge hangar a mile or so north of the town center. An extraordinary creation covering an area as big as an American football field, the model was built to study the effects of tides and water-flow patterns in the Bay Area; a short film and a set of interactive exhibits help explain its workings.

STINSON BEACH

An appealing swath of sands overlooked by Mount Tamalpais, Stinson Beach is one of the few places north of San Francisco where swimming is permitted (May to mid-Sep only). The water is cold, though, and many locals don wet-suits before taking a dip. The beach and the adjoining village make a pleasant picnic and walking spot, and several hiking trails wind inland into Mount Tamalpais State Park (page 142).

FERRY TRIP TO ANGEL ISLAND

The 740-acre Angel Island was occupied by the Spanish in 1775 and, during U.S. administration, saw use as a Civil War military base, as an immigrants' processing center, and as an internment camp for Japanese-Americans during the Second War. Now a state park with several of its ageing structures viewable on ranger-guided tours (usually weekends only), Angel Island is ringed by paved foot trails and cycle paths and makes a great day trip.

Ferries to Angel Island leave Tiburon daily in summer, weekends only during the rest of the year. For details; tel. 415 435 2131.

TIBURON 🛏 ✕

A century ago, the town of Tiburon was a busy rail terminus and shipping port. Such times are hard to picture in what is now a small and likeable town providing expensive rustic housing for San Francisco commuters and a refuge for intrepid tourists who find Sausalito overcrowded. Tiburon's appeal centers on the cafes and restaurants grouped along the bay side – and on the shops of Ark Row, their contents, from the wacky to the tacky, filling the insides of 19thC houseboats.

RECOMMENDED RESTAURANTS

GUERNEVILLE

Little Bavaria, $$; 17123 *Hwy*-116; *tel.* 707 869 0121; *lunch and dinner* Thurs-Sun, *dinner only* Mon-Wed; *credit cards,* MC, V.

A craving for German sausage and sauerkraut is one reason to stop by this deservedly popular restaurant, which has an even more popular beer garden. Another is to sample the interesting combination of local fare – be it beef, pork, seafood, or vegetables – and traditional Bavarian cooking.

MILL VALLEY

Cactus Cafe, $; 393 *Miller Avenue; tel.* 415 388 8226; *credit cards, none.*

Delicious and devilishly inexpensive Mexican food served in a small and frequently busy eatery.

Mountain Home Inn, $-$$; 810 *Panoramic Highway; tel.* 415 381 9000; *closed* Mon, *no breakfast on weekdays, dinner only on* Sun; *credit cards,* MC, V.

Enjoying unparalleled views across the Muir Woods National Monument from the road between Mill Valley and Stinson Beach, this restaurant was established in 1912. Though it has now grown into an hotel, it still provides wholesome American breakfasts and lunch fare ideally consumed on the top-floor patio. Dinner is a slightly more formal affair.

MUIR BEACH

Pelican Inn, $; 10 *Pacific Way; tel.* 415 383 6000; *lunch and dinner only, closed* Mon; *credit cards,* MC, V.

An English 16thC Tudor-style pub built in 1979 to further Francis Drake's claims on California. Serves an undistinguished range of British beers and lagers but has a fireplace that provides a cozy nook when coastal fogs draw in. The standard of the food – stews, burgers, pies and more – is a cut above what you might find in a real English pub.

POINT REYES

Station House Cafe, $; 11180 *Hwy*-1; *tel.* 415 663 1515; *cards,* AE, MC, V.

Serves breakfast, lunch and dinner to a devoted local clientele. Besides offering American diner perennials such as omelettes, burgers and sandwiches, it does some grand things with freshly-caught seafood at a price to please.

SAUSALITO

Lighthouse Coffee Shop, $; 1311 *Bridgeway; tel.*415 331 3034; *cards, none.*

Hole-in-the-wall locals' favorite offering, beside the usual salads and omelettes, Danish specialities such as open sandwiches.

no name bar, $; 757 *Bridgeway; tel.* 415 332 0390; *credit cards, none.*

Primarily an evening drinking place, but order whatever food is on offer and devour it along with a mug of freshly brewed coffee in what has been the domain of Sausalito's bohemians since the 1950s. Expect intense chess matches, poetry readings, jazz, and off-beat banter. So-called because it really doesn't have a name, just a sign reading "bar".

Scoma's, $-$$; 588 *Bridgeway; tel.* 415 332 9551; *lunch and dinner, dinner only on* Tues; *credit cards,* AE, CB, DC, MC, V.

The local branch of a dependable seafood restaurant chain and a decent place for a mid-priced meal, but expect the views across San Francisco Bay to be as memorable as the food.

TIBURON

Sam's Anchor Cafe, $-$$; 27 *Main Street; tel.* 415 435 4527; *credit cards,* AE, DC, MC, V.

The pick of Tiburon's dozens of bayside restaurants, serving breakfast, lunch and dinner (though actual opening hours are somewhat erratic).

Northern California

Mendocino and Humboldt Coast

250 miles one way; map Travel Vision *California-Nevada*

Easily joined from California Overall: 1, this trip (three days to cover it all) features two of the things California does best: rugged coastline and enormous trees. I've selected highlights along the route to provide a handsome selection of both. Like California Overall: 1, this tour works best during summer, when the area's heavy rainfall gives way – hopefully – to clear, sunny skies.

If you begin the tour from the south, choose Mendocino or Fort Bragg as your first night's stop. Though these neighbouring coastal towns both merit a visit, they are markedly different. For its looks, Mendocino is unquestionably the more appealing, although its 19thC wooden architecture attracts off-putting numbers of tourists. Fort Bragg, by contrast, is a hard-working lumber town with less charm – but also far lower prices – than Mendocino. If money's tight, I suggest you explore Mendocino by day and spend the evening in Fort Bragg.

Continuing north, the near-impenetrable mountains of the Lost Coast cause Hwy-1 to swing inland to join Hwy-101 and in doing so briefly combine with California Overall: 1. A road does cross the Lost Coast, though, and I recommend the area as a detour from Eureka (one which could also be undertaken as an alternative route on the way to Eureka), a town of limited appeal but a useful base for your second night.

Beyond Eureka, the tour concentrates on the Redwood National Park, which is in fact a collection of state parks spread across 100,000 acres of California's extreme north-west. If you've already visited the sky-scraping trees at Humboldt Redwoods State Park (see California Overall: 1), you may not see the point in viewing still more. You need to travel this far north, however, to find the densest redwood groves and to see the tree tops moodily shrouded in coastal fog. From the highway, many foot trails weave through the redwood groves, often emerging on to seldom visited pockets of beach.

After the redwoods and a third night spent at Crescent City, all you can do (other than continuing into Oregon) is to head back the way you came. One option on the return leg is to veer inland from Arcata along Hwy-299 to link with Local Explorations: 3 and/or California Overall: 3.

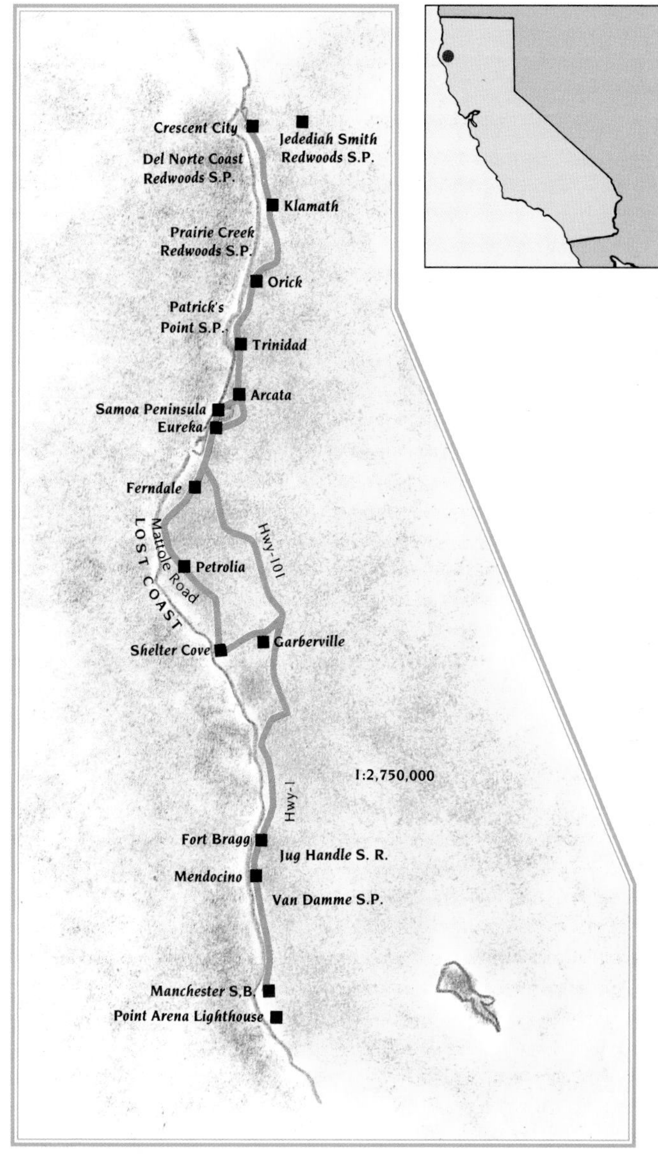

TRANSPORTATION
Four daily Greyhound buses in either direction traverse Hwy-101 between San Francisco and Eureka. Mendocino Transit Authority (tel. 707 884 3723) operates a few daily bus services in the Mendocino/Fort Bragg area. Other connections are possible with the Falcon bus; see California Overall: 1.

Most of the Redwood National Park is extremely difficult to reach without private transportation, although there are two Greyhound services daily in either direction between Eureka and Crescent City which make stops at Klamath and Orick. Additionally, the local Del Norte bus service (tel. 707 464 2807) links Crescent City and Klamath.

SIGHTS & PLACES OF INTEREST

ARCATA

See California Overall: 1.

CRESCENT CITY 🛏 ×

Named for the crescent-shaped bay on which it sits, Crescent City was founded in 1853 as a lumber port and just over a century later was almost totally destroyed by the tidal wave which followed an Alaskan earthquake. The rebuilt Crescent City is an unprepossessing place, dominated by the motels and quick-eateries aimed at visitors headed for the nearby redwood groves.

The **Del Norte Historical Society Museum**, 577 H Street, gathers remnants from the town's past and stores them in its former jail. A more intriguing destination is the 1856 **Battery Point Lighthouse**, reachable by footpath only at low tide. Inside the restored lighthouse, a tiny museum holds assorted nautical knick-knacks and a studious account of lenses.

DEL NORTE COAST REDWOODS STATE PARK

At the 6,000-acre Del Norte Coast Redwoods State Park, where the towering redwood trees are liable to be shrouded in damp fog even at the height of summer, the evocatively-named **Damnation Creek Trail** (accessed from Hwy-101) runs for 2½ miles along the route of an ancient Yurok Indian track and rises steeply as it passes through groves of old-growth redwoods before emerging on to a small, secluded beach.

Slightly further north, simpler trails penetrate the sections of the park

DETOUR – **THE SAMOA PENINSULA**

A short drive from Eureka along Hwy-255 reaches the Samoa Peninsula, a slender strip of sand dunes and not much else which shelters Humboldt Bay from the worst furies of the Pacific. Here, the **Samoa Cookhouse** satiated the gargantuan appetites of lumber workers from the 1880s. Still a functioning diner, the cookhouse also has a room of photos and ageing cutlery to mark its place in local folklore; see Recommended Restaurants, page 153.

DETOUR – **FERNDALE AND THE LOST COAST**

An immaculately preserved Victorian village originally settled by Scandinavian dairy farmers, **Ferndale**, on Hwy-1 18 miles south of Eureka, grew fat on the proceeds of butter production and acquired (and retains) many picture-postcard Queen Anne homes, the grandest of which were nicknamed "butter palaces." Besides the wonderfully elaborate old wooden homes, the village keeps a mighty stash of antiques and period furnishings from the thriving days of yore at the **Ferndale Museum**, 515 Shaw Avenue.

Continue south from Ferndale along Mattole Road and you enter the **Lost Coast**, where a handful of tiny communities sit beside – or at the end of – bumpy, gravel roads and count themselves lucky to see more than a dozen visitors a day.

The story might have been different. One Lost Coast hamlet, **Petrolia**, grew up in the 1860s around California's first oil well but any prospect of a Los Angeles-like evolution was ended by the area's remoteness and rough terrain.

Further south, **Shelter Cove** sits on a sandy bay beneath tall granite headlands and holds supply shops for those planning an assault on the nearby **Sinkyone Wilderness State Park**. Not named in jest, only well-equipped hikers should think about tackling the park's longer trails. If the weather is amenable, however, call at the visitors' center and spend a few hours exploring the park's less arduous sections – the rewards are unparalleled views of mountain peaks and glistening ocean.

The Lost Coast can be entered or left from the south, using Old Briceland Road or Thorne Road, both off Hwy-101 near Garberville.

RECOMMENDED HOTELS

CRESCENT CITY

Curly Redwood Lodge, $-$$; 701 *Redwood Highway; tel.* 707 464 2137; *credit cards,* AE, CB, DC, MC, V.

Crescent City has many motels but only this one claims to be built from a single redwood tree. The rooms are simple but spacious and free coffee is brewed in the lobby.

Northwood Inn, $-$$; 65 *Hwy*-101; *tel.* 707 464 9771; *credit cards,* AE, CB, DC, MC, V.

Facing the harbor and probably the town's best-equipped motel, the fairly-priced Northwood Inn is part of the Best Western chain and, besides dependable rooms, has a launderette for guests' use.

EUREKA

An Elegant Victorian Mansion, $$-$$$; 1406 C *Street; tel.* 707 444 3144; *credit cards,* MC, V.

Entirely what its name suggests, though this 1880s house plays up the historical theme by having a uniformed butler on hand to welcome guests and suggest a game of croquet on the lawn. Antiques fill every nook and cranny and the rooms are decorated with portraits of the original owner's family.

Matador Motel, $$; 129 *Fourth Street; tel.* 800 824 6630; *credit cards,* AE, DC, DS, MC, V.

Usefully located in the heart of Eureka's increasingly fashionable waterside area and boasting fair-sized rooms with coffee-makers; some of the costlier rooms are equipped with saunas.

FORT BRAGG

The Grey Whale Inn, $$–$$$; 615 N. *Main Street; tel.* 800 382 7244; *credit cards,* AE, MC, V.

What was once the town's hospital now provides 14 variously-sized rooms – ranging from compact to enormous – and wide corridors now lined by local artworks and historical memorabilia. A self-service breakfast of fruit, muffins and a hot dish is included.

MENDOCINO

Joshua Grindle Inn, $$$-$$$$; 44800 *Little Lake Road; tel.* 707 937 4143; *credit cards,* AE, MC, V.

A compact Victorian farmhouse offering bed-and-breakfast accommodation in the 19thC main house and in the recently-built pseudo-water tower in the back garden. In most of the ten rooms, you'll find fireplaces and four-poster beds.

MacCallum House, $$-$$$$; 45020 *Albion Street; tel.* 707 937 0289; *credit cards,* MC, V.

Dating from 1882, the oldest of Mendocino's many bed-and-breakfast inns and one which offers an interesting selection of variously-priced rooms in the main house and in adjoining cottages. Personal favorites are the attic rooms, which lack private bathrooms but boast wonderful views over the town's sloping rooftops.

Stanford Inn by the Sea, $$$$; *junction of* Hwy-1 *and Compteche Ukiah Road; tel.* 707 937 5615; *credit cards,* AE, CB, DC, MC, V.

A luxurious yet homey bed-and-breakfast retreat just south of Mendocino, set on a rolling hillside above the creek where the Big River flows into the ocean. The rooms are designed for stunning views, and stoves or wood-burning fireplaces and video players are found in each.

TRINIDAD

Trinidad bed-and-breakfast, $$$; 560 *Edwards Street; tel.* 707 677 0840; *credit cards,* DC, MC, V.

Only early bookings are likely to secure one of the four rooms at this quaint cottage where the views stretch across Trinidad's bay and continue – weather permitting – far along the coast. The hosts keep up a supply of hot cider to ward off fog-induced chills.

BUDGET ACCOMMODATION

Redwood AYH Hostel; 14480 Hwy-101, *near Klamath; tel.* 707 482 8265.

• *Gingerbread Mansion, Ferndale.*

where logging took place from the 1920s. The redwoods you'll find here – along the **Memorial Grove** and **Hobbs-Wood trails** – are younger, second-growth trees steadily reclaiming the forest: abandoned trestles and odd bits of machinery remain from the logging days.

EUREKA 🛏 ✕

The largest town on the north coast, Eureka is not especially appealing save for its stock of over a hundred preserved Victorian homes. The pick of the bunch is the 1885 **Carson Mansion**, 143 M Street, a rococo riot of painted window-frames, turrets and towers, which you should see even if you bypass the rest.

Eureka's once rough-and-ready water-front district is in the throes of change, with trendy galleries, boutiques and restaurants appearing in its century-old warehouses – rich territory for a souvenir hunt. Close by, the **Clarke Memorial Museum**, 240 E Street, boasts an absorbing display of basketry from the Native American tribes of the Pacific North West alongside the usual pioneer-era knick-knacks.

On the town's southern edge, **Fort Humboldt State Historic Park** preserves the remains of Fort Humboldt, erected in 1853 to deter Native American incursions into white homesteads and these days serving as a routine museum carrying displays on the fort's military links and the local lumber trade.

DETOUR – **POINT ARENA LIGHTHOUSE**

The heaving ocean and the rocky, foggy northern California coast have given mariners more than a few nightmares over the years. Pay a call on the museum of the 1908 **Point Arena Lighthouse** – at the southern end of Manchester State Beach and reached by Lighthouse Road off Hwy-1 – and you'll discover the sad stories of a few of the many ships and crews which have perished off local shores.

FORT BRAGG 🛏 ✕

In Fort Bragg, born as an army fort in 1855 but raised on the lumber industry, anyone mourning the decline of California's once-mighty redwood forests might be nonplussed by the uncritical accounts of the wood-cutting trade outlined in the town's small **Guest House Museum**, 343 N. Main Street, which occupies the 1892 home of the brother of one of the industry's bosses.

There is better stuff elsewhere: **Noyo Harbour**, the town's coastal section, sports a picturesque small-craft fishing fleet and hosts mouth-watering salmon barbecues at the slightest excuse. And on the town's southern boundary, the lovely **Mendocino Botanical Gardens** smother 47 acres of windy headlands with a selection of colorful and aromatic wildflowers, viewable and sniffable on self-guided trails.

Fort Bragg is also the western terminus of the **Skunk Train**, which travels inland to Willits – see California Overall: 1– from the depot behind the Guest House.

JEDEDIAH SMITH REDWOODS STATE PARK

When summer fogs cloak the coast, it's a fair bet that Jedediah Smith Redwoods State Park – sited just a few miles inland – will be bathed in sunshine, which is just one of many good reasons for making the effort to visit the northernmost section of Redwood National Park.

Like the salmon-stuffed Smith River which runs through it, the park is named after the man who, in 1827, made the first recorded crossing of the Sierra Nevada mountains. Smith's spirit of adventure is not something shared by the visitors who make no greater incursion into the park's 9,500 acres than the Stout Trail, a simple route to the underwhelming **Stout Tree**, the fame of which is based solely on the 21-ft diameter which makes it the plumpest coastal redwood.

Press deeper into the park, however, and nature reveals itself more impressively with primeval groves of redwood and fern, carpets of wildflowers, and a proliferation of wildlife: racoons and chipmunks are two-a-cent and, with luck, deer and bears may shyly reveal themselves. On the river, look out for beavers and otters busily rearranging nature's waterside architecture.

JUG HANDLE STATE RESERVE

California is packed with geological surprises but seldom is the impact of underground energies as visible or as easy to examine as it is at Jug Handle State Park, where a series of 100-ft rock terraces has been driven – at 100,000-year intervals – up from the ocean by the action of plate tectonics. Once the terraces surface, they are shaped by wave erosion and steadily rise higher, acquiring vegetation as they do so.

Half a million years of evolution can be assessed in an hour or so by following the **Ecological Staircase Trail**, which climbs the terraces. As you ascend, look out for the stunted cypress and pine trees forming the peculiar **Mendocino Pygmy Forest** on the third level.

KLAMATH

Hugging the Klamath River, a splendid sight flowing into the ocean, the village of Klamath is undistinguished except as a source of food and supplies, and as the home of **Trees of Mystery**: a pricey and slightly bizarre tourist attraction which displays a collection of twisted and deformed redwoods and others which have been sculpted by chainsaws into oversized recreations of figures from American history and folklore.

MANCHESTER STATE BEACH

Anyone who thinks that the San Andreas fault brings nothing but devas-

• *Guest House Museum, Fort Bragg.*

tation to California should come here. (Watch for the signposts as you pass through the Hwy-1 hamlet of Manchester.) California's rift of geological instability, in moving from the mainland out beneath the ocean, has created a broad and windswept beach of wild beauty. Walk among the dunes and driftwood with the breeze in your hair and you'll experience California's northern coast in its rawest and most invigorating form.

MENDOCINO 🛏 ✕

The prettiest town on the northern coast, Mendocino nestles on a bluff and is packed with characterful wooden buildings dating from its 19thC settlement by New England loggers. As the lumber trade declined during the 1950s and 1960s, Mendocino's picturesque perfection (now maintained by strict building codes) encouraged an influx of San Franciscan artists, their influence still apparent in the town's large number of art galleries. The bedrock of the local economy today, however, is the tourists who fill the town and its numerous bed-and-breakfast inns throughout the summer.

The **Kelley House Museum**, 45007 Albion Street, gives a flavor of 19thC Mendocino life, and is the departure point for guided walking tours which explore the town each summer Saturday (tel. 707 937 5791).

Fret not if you miss the tour, the town's Victorian architectural highlights are easily found and include Main Street's Gothic-style Presbyterian Church, the 1854 **Ford House** – Mendocino's oldest home – and the 1866 **Masonic Temple** (its lower floor now a bank), the steeple of which – complete with masonic symbols – rises above the corner of Lansing and Ukiah Streets.

If the weather's fine, set out on the interlinked foot trails crossing **Mendocino Headlands State Park** (for which the Ford House serves as a visitor center). Set across the undeveloped portion of Mendocino's coastal bluff, the park encompasses dramatic cliff tops and gives views of oddly-shaped rock stacks, formed by years of wave and wind erosion.

ORICK

Little more than a bend in the road, Orick marks the southern entrance to Redwood National Park and is the location of the **Redwood Visitor Center**, an essential stop for information on the park, and the maps and descriptions of its countless foot trails.

Of several trails in the Orick area, don't miss the aptly-named **Tall Trees Trail**, which leads to a grove holding the tallest redwood of the lot: the 368-ft Howard Libby Redwood. It's necessary to take the statistics at face value; from the ground the tree looks no more enormous than its neighbours.

PATRICK'S POINT STATE PARK

The high bluffs of Patrick's Point State Park provide excellent vantage points for watching the migration of California gray whales. Should the whales not be passing by, content yourself with watching the park's resident sea lions and exploring its tide pools. Find time, too, for the park's museum which goes some way to explaining why the Yurok Indian tribe chose this spot as their summer base and why they accorded it great spiritual importance.

PETROLIA

See Detour – Ferndale and the Lost Coast, page 148.

PRAIRIE CREEK REDWOODS STATE PARK

Trails weave through towering redwood groves to a scintillating 11-mile-long section of isolated coast called **Gold Bluffs Beach**. The park's inland sections are kept lush and fertile by heavy winter rainfall and the landscapes reach their peak at **Fern Canyon**, a moss-covered floor enclosed by 60-ft high walls of fern reached from the main coastal trail.

What really separates the park from others in the area, however, is the herd of Roosevelt elk which inhabits the grasslands lying between the redwood groves and the ocean. Stocky and lugubrious creatures, some of the elk graze within viewing distance of Hwy-101 and many more can be seen studiously ignoring the humans who walk the coastal trails.

SHELTER COVE and SINKYONE WILDERNESS STATE PARK

See Detour – Ferndale and the Lost Coast, page 148.

TRINIDAD

Spare a thought for Trinidad in the few minutes it takes to drive through. During the 1850s, machinery destined for the inland gold mines came ashore here and later, as the gold-rush subsided, the town continued to thrive as a whaling port. These days, Trinidad has little except an unsullied shoreline and one of the few bed-and-breakfast options on this section of the northern coast.

VAN DAMME STATE PARK

Divers plunge into the cold waters off the coastal section of Van Damme State Park in pursuit of abalone – an edible, rock-clinging mollusc. More interesting to the spectator is the park's inland trail to the **Pygmy Forest**: acres of mature cypress and pine trees rising no higher than a few feet, their growth limited by the soil's high acidity and lack of nutrients.

RECOMMENDED RESTAURANTS

CRESCENT CITY

Harbor View Grotto, $; 155 *Citizen's Dock Road; tel.* 707 464 3815; *credit cards, none.*

Crescent City does not rate highly for landscape views although the outlook across its harbor at this cozy seafood restaurant does much to please, as do the generous lunches or dinners chosen from a lengthy menu.

EUREKA

Hotel Carter, $$; 301 L *Street; tel.* 707 444 8062; *credit cards,* AE, CB, DC, DS, MC, V.

Fine dining by candle-light featuring exceptionally well-prepared meals based on fresh, locally available ingredients; the fish dishes are always worth trying.

Samoa Cookhouse, $; *Samoa Road; tel.* 707 442 1659; *credit cards,* MC, V.

A one-time lumber-workers' canteen now serving the public with the tree-fellers' favorites – plenty of red meat, piles of steaming vegetables, and generous helpings of apple pie, served at bench tables.

FORT BRAGG

Egghead Omelettes of Oz, $; 326 N. *Main Street; tel.* 707 964 5005; *credit cards, none; breakfast and lunch only.*

California leads the U.S. in the field of creative omelette fillings and here you'll find one of the best selections in the state – anything from piles of fresh vegetables to seafood being added to the three-egg mixture.

North Coast Brewing Co, $–$$; 444 N. *Main Street; tel.* 707 964 BREW; *credit cards,* DS, MC, V.

Popular for its acclaimed home-brewed beers and also offering a winning selection of lunches and dinners. The options include fish and chips, Cajun-style black beans and rice, and several pasta dishes.

MENDOCINO

Bay View Cafe, $-$$; 45040 *Main Street; tel.* 707 937 4197; *credit cards,* MC, V.

By avoiding the peak eating times, you should be able to claim an ocean view table here and enjoy the sight of the Pacific crashing against the shoreline as you tuck into your selection. Whether for breakfast, lunch or dinner, the daily specials are usually the best choices from an impressively diverse menu.

Cafe Beaujolais, $-$$$; 961 *Ukiah Street; tel.* 707 937 5614; *credit cards, none; closed Tues, Wed.*

The reputation of Cafe Beaujolais for providing essentially simple but excellently-prepared food – be it for breakfast, lunch or dinner (when reservations are recommended) – extends far beyond Mendocino and is fully justified; a meal in this lovely old house will be a memorable one.

Mendocino Cafe,$; 10451 *Lansing Street; tel.* 707 937 2422; *credit cards,* MC, V.

This informal locals' rendezvous – sit inside among the artworks or outside on the breezy patio – creates intriguing dishes fusing elements of Thai, Mexican and American cookery. The results are seldom other than tasty and always fair on the purse.

Trinity Lake

150 miles (round trip); map Kummerley + Frey California-Nevada

Looping off Hwy-299 between Arcata (see California Overall: 1) and Redding (see California Overall: 3), this short tour (one night) unearths some forgotten pioneer-period history and provides opportunities for fresh-air pursuits. It is a circumnavigation of one of northern California's numerous artificial lakes, created to redirect water to the Central Valley farmlands and to quench the ever-increasing thirst of Los Angeles.

In this landscape of cobalt-blue waters, scented pine forests and snow-capped distant mountains, local opposition to human meddling with nature is still apparent although it has been the revenue from increased tourism – fishing, boating and water-skiing lure thousands of vacationers – which has kept alive many of the tiny, isolated communities which the tour passes through.

As a base, I've chosen the comparatively large town (population 3,500) of Weaverville. Like other settlements in the area, Weaverville got started in the mid-1800s with the local discovery of gold. Unlike its neighbors, though, Weaverville has a glorious stock of its century-old buildings still intact. Other 19thC hamlets – French Gulch is a prime example and also an alternative accommodation option – comprise no more than a few buildings lining the roadside.

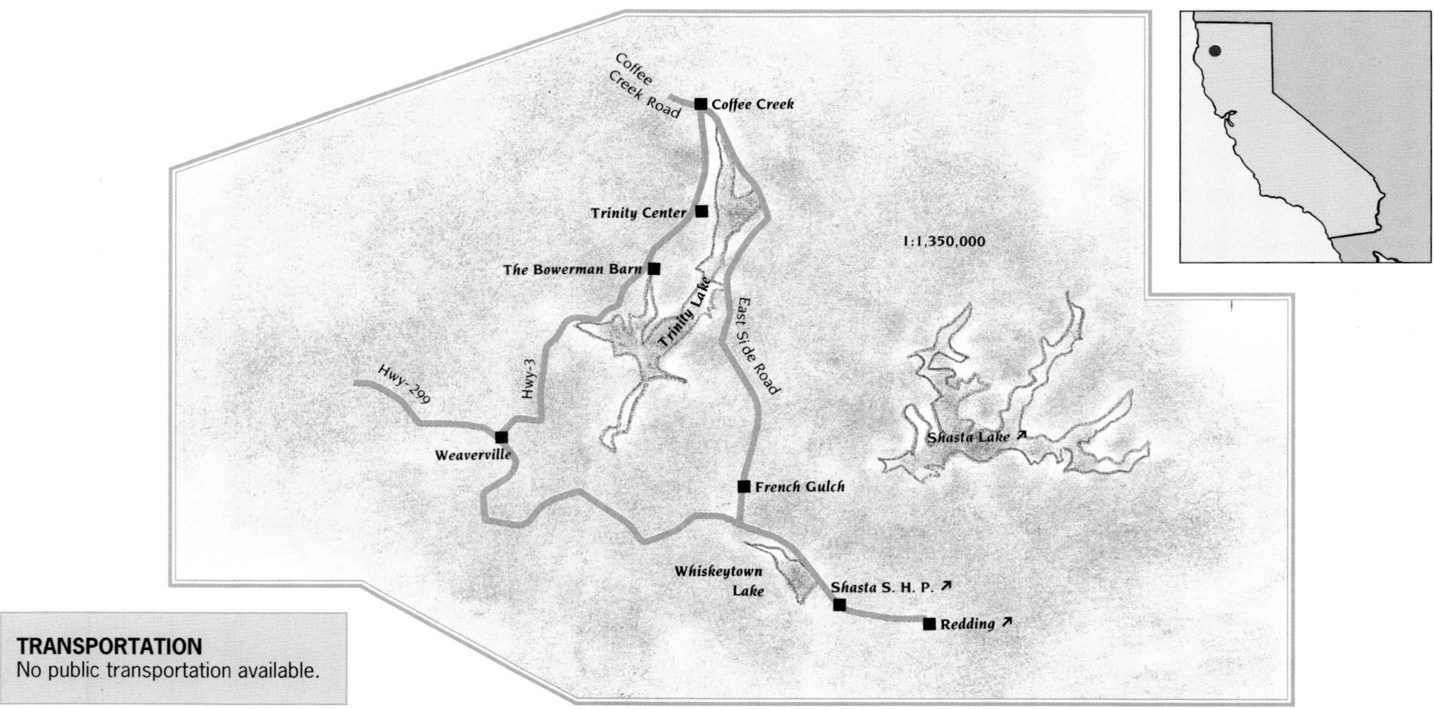

TRANSPORTATION
No public transportation available.

SIGHTS & PLACES OF INTEREST

THE BOWERMAN BARN

Old barns might not be what you came to California to see, but turn off Hwy-3 near the hamlet of Covington Mill and you'll come to the restored Bowerman Barn – a 19thC example of the genre which has earned a place on the U.S.'s prestigious National Register of Historic Places for its hand-laid stone base and pine walls held in place by hand-forged square nails.

COFFEE CREEK ✕

Marking the north point of the tour and providing a beckoning lunch stop in the form of the Forest Deli (see Recommended Restaurants, page 157), Coffee Creek is a minuscule hamlet where mining continued into the 1950s. Ten miles along Coffee Creek Road, a small lake at the **Coffee Creek Trout Farm** provides easy pickings for novice anglers.

FRENCH GULCH ✕

Seemingly undisturbed by development since its 1849 settlement, French Gulch is still highly redolent of a 19thC gold-mining community and even keeps alive the two mainstays of early backwoods California – the **French Gulch Hotel** (see Recommended Hotels, below), originally a brothel, and **St. Rose's Church** – in fine states of preservation along Main Street.

REDDING

See California Overall: 3.

SHASTA STATE HISTORIC PARK

See California Overall: 3.

TRINITY CENTER

The damming of the Trinity River (see Trinity Lake, below) caused Trinity Center to be unceremoniously shifted from its original location to a new one on the shores of Trinity Lake, where it became a base for watery activities – boating, fishing, jet-skiing – all of which and more are available from numerous outlets around the town's marina. Bizarre as it may sound, Trinity Center also keeps what must be California's finest selection of barbed wire, many different types of which form the core of the local ranching exhibits dutifully assembled at **Scotts Museum**, on Airport Road.

TRINITY LAKE

Only cartographers call Trinity Lake – created by the damming of the Trinity River – by its official name of Clair Engle Lake, adopted to commemorate the state senator who oversaw the dam's construction during the 1960s. Keeping the name suggested by the river is one way locals express their anger over the project, particularly those who owned the land, or had links with the two gold-rush-era villages which now lie at the bottom of the reservoir that the dam created.

Controversies aside, the lake sits

RECOMMENDED HOTELS

FRENCH GULCH

French Gulch Hotel, $-$$; 14138 *Main Street; tel.* 916 359 2114; *credit cards,* MC, V.

A 19thC gold-rush hotel that once saw service as a brothel, now completely renovated without losing any of its historic atmosphere. Only seven rooms, so book well ahead during the peak summer months.

WEAVERVILLE

Motel Trinity, $-$$; 1112 *Main Street; tel.* 916 623 2129; *credit cards,* AE, CB, DC, MC.

One of several fairly inexpensive motels along Weaverville's Main Street, with a swimming-pool, outdoor hot tub, and coffee provided in the rooms – plus all the usual facilities.

Weaverville Victorian Inn, $$-$$$; 1709 *Main Street; tel.* 916 623 4432; *credit cards,* MC, V.

A recently built hotel but one designed and furnished in fetching Victorian style. The more costly rooms boast private hot tubs. An eat-and-go complimentary breakfast of coffee and doughnuts is served in the lobby.

placidly at the foot of the rugged, glaciated peaks of the **Trinity Alps**, around which 400 miles of long, isolated hiking trails traverse forests, meadows and canyons. Hiking here is arduous and spectacular, and can also be dangerous: never venture into the wilds without proper clothes, equipment and preparation, which includes listening to the latest weather forecast and acquiring the latest information from the Ranger Station at Trinity Center, tel. 916 246 5338.

WEAVERVILLE 🛏 ✕

The only community of distinction and size (its population reaching four figures) on this tour, Weaverville flourished as a gold-mining center during the 1850s and has more than a hundred buildings from that time clustered within the small but grandly-titled **Weaverville National Historic District**.

During the 19thC, Weaverville's 2,500-strong Chinese community (Chinese labor was a common element in gold-rush towns) contributed to the construction of the **Joss House**, a Taoist temple dating from 1874 and decorated with handmade tapestries and ornaments set around an ancient Chinese altar. Now the centerpiece of **Joss House State Historic Park**, Main and Oregon Streets, the temple can be entered on half-hourly guided tours but is closed on Tuesdays and Wednesdays.

Across Main Street from the park, the **J.J. Jackson Memorial Museum** dwells on broader aspects of Weaverville's early days: an entertaining clutter of paraphernalia includes a steam-driven stamp mill and several jail cells still bearing their 19thC graffiti.

Should the museum's exhibits bring on a bout of gold fever, visitors can purchase gold-panning utensils at the museum and try their luck on the local rivers. The mineral riches which were once easy to find are long gone, however. A few hours' panning is unlikely to produce anything except backache.

WHISKEYTOWN LAKE

Locals decant to Whiskeytown Lake when they fancy a spot of swimming, skin-diving, fishing, hunting, or simply sunbathing – although sunshine can be a rare commodity in these parts. The lake has pleasant, sandy banks. The usual complement of fishing and boating equipment hire outlets line the lake, plenty of which will also rent out water- and jet-skis. For practical details, use the Visitor Information Center located on the lake's easterly corner, where Hwy-299 meets John Kennedy Drive.

RECOMMENDED RESTAURANTS

COFFEE CREEK

The Forest Deli, $; *junction of* Hwy-3 *and* Coffee Creek Road; *tel.* 916 266 3575; *credit cards, none.*

The concept of rustic dining comes into its own at this lovely place, where the wooden outdoor tables enable you to feast on ample portions of home-cooked country fare as the scent of cedar and maple trees fills your nostrils. Don't neglect the "old-fashioned" milk shakes, either.

FRENCH GULCH

French Gulch Hotel, $-$$; 14138 Main Street; *tel.* 916 359 2114; *credit cards,* MC, V.

Not only a great place to spend a night (see Recommended Hotels, page 156) but also a local legend for its generous dinners – large tureens of soup, piles of red meat, seafood and vegetables – consumed by chatty diners seated at benches.

WEAVERVILLE

The Brewery Restaurant, $; 401 Main Street; *tel.* 916 623 3000; *credit cards,* MC, V.

Serves hearty breakfast, lunch and dinner fare from no-nonsense country recipes, and also tempts with home-brewed beer.

The Mustard Seed, $; 252 Main Street; *tel.* 916 623 2922; *credit cards, none; breakfast and lunch only.*

A locals' favorite for its waffles, omelettes, sandwiches and quiches made with freshest ingredients. Occupying a lovely wooden building, The Mustard Seed also has patio dining – perfect for observing the goings-on along the small town's major thoroughfare while you eat.

Northern California

Lassen Volcanic National Park and Lava Beds National Monument

360 miles (round trip); map Kummerley + Frey California-Nevada

Joined from California Overall: 3, this tour covers the north-eastern corner of California, where the population is thin and local news is made by record-breaking salmon catches. In 1915, however, it was a volcanic eruption that captured the headlines, and Lassen Volcanic National Park – the scene of the eruption and centerpiece of this exploration – is laced by busy fumeroles, hot springs and bubbling mud pits.

An early booking might enable you to spend a night inside the park, but I've chosen Susanville as a more likely overnight stop. Susanville compensates for its isolation with a small-town friendliness, and I've included the option of a day's detour from the town by foot or bicycle.

The remainder of the tour involves a lengthy drive through very remote areas. I won't hold it against you if you decide against undertaking this section: the scenery soon becomes monotonous and the sole reward is the lava caves of the Lava Beds National Monument. Fascinating though they are, you'll need to decide for yourself whether the caves will justify the journey. If you decide they do, your second night can be spent at any convenient town in California Overall: 3.

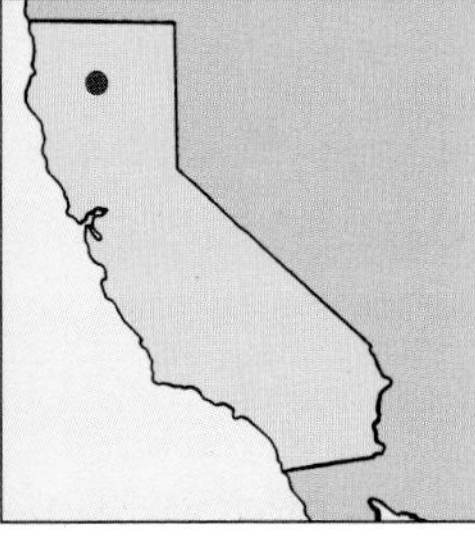

CYCLING AND HIKING – THE BIZZ JOHNSON TRAIL

Cycling or hiking part or all of the 25-mile Bizz Johnson Trail, between Susanville and Westwood, takes you through the lush Susan River Canyon along the route of the Fernley & Lassen Railroad, which operated from 1914 to 1956. The Lassen County Chamber of Commerce, 720 Main Street, in Susanville, has maps and bike-rental details.

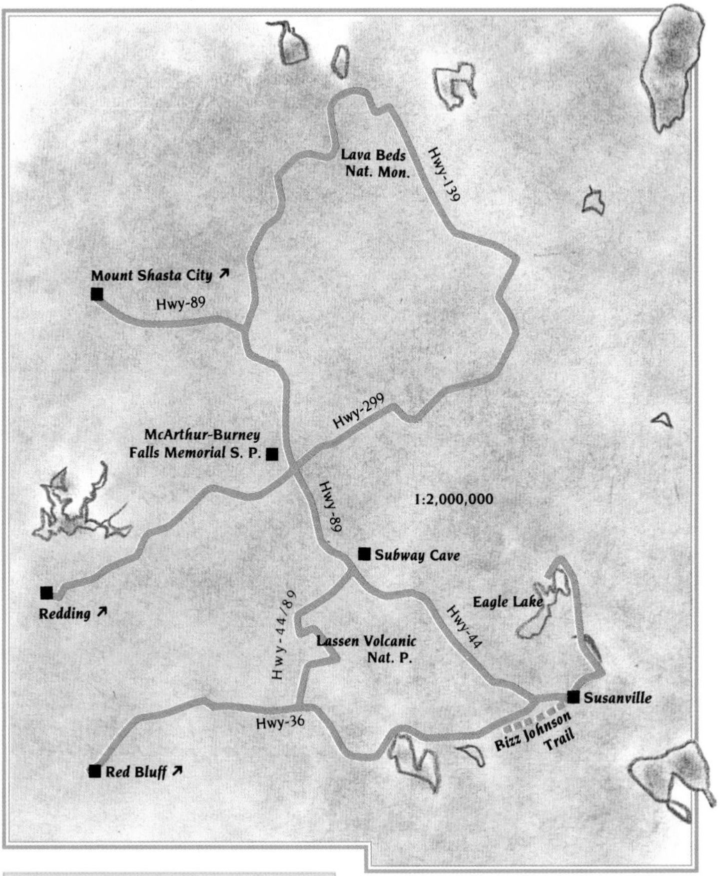

TRANSPORTATION

The only public transportation in the area is the once-daily (except Sunday) Mt. Lassen Motor Transit (tel. 916 529 2722) mail/passenger bus between Red Bluff and Susanville, which calls at Mineral, close to the entrance to Lassen Volcanic National Park.

WEATHER

This is a summer-only undertaking; even then, you should check the latest weather forecast before embarking on it. Conditions are particularly unpredictable at Lassen Volcanic National Park. For park weather, tel. 916 595 4444.

SIGHTS & PLACES OF INTEREST

LASSEN VOLCANIC NATIONAL PARK

California's only active volcano, Lassen Peak last gargled violently to life during 1915 when it spewed out five-ton boulders, smothered the surrounding countryside in a 20-ft-deep mud flow and threw a cloud of dust seven miles high. Unlikely to erupt again for many decades, Lassen Peak is the tallest of several peaks within Lassen Volcanic National Park, which fills a 165,000-sq mile caldera (a type of crater) created by the collapsing dome of a gigantic prehistoric volcano called Mount Tehama.

Even though the chances of another eruption may be slim, the sights (and smells) of Earth's primeval forces which are abundant throughout the park provide a lasting reminder that California's foundations are far from stable. Hwy-89 steers a 35-mile course through the park and the major points of geological interest are indicated by numbered markers corresponding to explanatory descriptions in the free leaflet distributed at the park entrance. Places not to be missed include **Bumpass Hell**, a seething landscape of hot springs and bubbling mud pits created as pressured gases (responsible for the all-pervasive bad-egg smell) come hissing to the surface through gaps in the lava, and the **Devastated Area**, where strands of young trees are slowly reclaiming a landscape razed of all vegetation by the mud flows and gases unleashed during the 1915 eruption. To the north of the Devastated Area, you'll spot the 400-ton boulder named the **Hot Rock** by locals who were pleased not to be underneath it when it landed here during Lassen's 1915 eruption; the gigantic rock remained warm to the touch for many years.

Lassen Peak itself can be reached by a 2½-mile zigzag trail, which makes the steep gradient comparatively easy going (beware, though, of altitude sickness). Allow at least five hours to go up, come down, and have time to savor the view of the park's volcanic phenomena from the peak's 10,475-ft summit.

DETOUR – **THE LASSEN BACKCOUNTRY**
A route into the northern backcountry of Lassen Volcanic National Park branches off Hwy-44 and concludes at Butte Lake. From the lake, the **Cinder Cone Nature Trail** makes for a rewarding, if potentially ankle-twisting, trek through loose rock, passing the aptly-named **Fantastic Lava Beds and Painted Dunes** – multi-colored lava flows created over a 2,000-year period, on the way to the top of 6,907-ft high Cinder Cone.

DRIVING DETOUR – **EAGLE LAKE**
Camping grounds and marinas dot the shoreline of Eagle Lake, 30 miles north of Susanville along Hwy-139 and an enjoyable half-day spin. The largest natural lake entirely within California and one plentifully supplied with unusually plump trout, Lake Eagle is predictably popular with anglers. Linger long enough by the lakeside and you may be treated to the sight of bald eagles, pelicans or ospreys swooping to claim their share of the lake's fish stocks.

LAVA BEDS NATIONAL MONUMENT

Cinder cones, craters and other debris of a thousand years of volcanic activity litter the Modoc Plateau which forms California's sparsely-inhabited northeastern corner. It is amid these bleak scenes that the Lava Beds National Monument sits, uniquely possessed of hundreds of lava tubes: cylindrical caves created just a few feet below ground level by cooling molten magma.

Nineteen of the lava caves are open for self-guided exploration but an essential first stop is the **Visitor Center**, at the monument's southern entrance, for the all-important flashlights (which can be borrowed here) and the electrically-lit **Mushpot Cave**, in which explanatory texts and displays describe the caves' creation. Despite being dark and cold, the caves are relatively easy to explore. For maximum safety, however, you might prefer to see them in the company of a park ranger on the **guided tours** conducted daily (except Wednesday) during the summer.

Native Americans were aware of the lava beds area long before Europeans set foot in California. Petroglyphs – prehistoric Native American rock paintings – can be seen inside many caves; the best collection decorates **Big Painted Cave**. Furthermore, the area known as **Captain Jack's Stronghold** was where 52 Modoc Indians held off a thousand U.S. soldiers for five months from November 1872, turning the natural terrain into a fortress in their struggle against forced relocation. Eventually removed after a two-day mortar bombardment, the Modocs' chief, Kentipoos (known to whites as Captain Jack), along with three other leaders, was tried and executed.

MCARTHUR-BURNEY FALLS MEMORIAL STATE PARK

Visiting in the 1800s, Theodore Roosevelt described the 129-ft waterfall at the heart of McArthur-Burney Falls Memorial State Park as the "eighth wonder of the world." His comment may have been an exaggeration, but this daily cascade of 1,900 million gallons of water is certainly an impressive one.

MOUNT SHASTA CITY

See California Overall: 3.

RED BLUFF

See California Overall: 3.

REDDING

See California Overall: 3.

SUBWAY CAVE

If you're not going all the way to Lava Beds National Monument, you'll get a taste of what you'll be missing with Subway Cave, a mile-long lava tube formed as molten lava cooled just beneath the earth's surface. A short trail from the car-park leads to the cave's entrance.

SUSANVILLE 🛏 ✕

Isaac Roop named this town, founded 1854, after his daughter. It sat at the heart of what Roop declared the Territory of Nataqua, a region independent of the state of California. Roop's breakaway was not recognized by the federal government, and eventually led to the bloodless Sagebrush War of 1863, waged between California and Nevada over ownership of the area – a period when Roop labelled his Susanville home Fort Defiance. Susanville these days is primarily a place to eat, sleep and stock up on provisions for trips into remoter areas, but finds space to document the 19thC disputes inside the **Lassen Historical Museum**, 75 N. Weatherlow Street.

RECOMMENDED HOTELS

LASSEN VOLCANIC NATIONAL PARK

Drakesbad Guest Ranch, $$-$$$; *tel.* 916 529 1512; *credit cards*, MC, V.

The only accommodation, other than camping, within Lassen Volcanic National Park, the Drakesbad Guest Ranch is a great place to enjoy the area's severe scenery in comparative comfort. The ranch has a naturally-heated swimming-pool, and is a departure point for horse treks.

SUSANVILLE

Super Budget Motel, $; 2975 *Johnstonville Road; tel.* 916 257 2782; *credit cards*, AE, DC, DS, MC, V.

On the whole, there's little to choose between Susanville's numerous motels, though this one usually has the most competitive rates.

RECOMMENDED RESTAURANTS

SUSANVILLE

Josefina's, $; 1960 *Main Street; tel.* 916 257 9262; *credit cards*, MC, V.

No one could pretend that Susanville is a happy hunting ground for gourmets, but the Mexican food served here in large amounts at fair prices seldom fails to please.

Walker's Coffee Shop, $; 1600 *Main Street; tel.* 916 253 3212; *credit cards, none.*

If you ever wondered what there might be to gossip about in a small Californian town, dwell over a high-cholesterol breakfast in this popular eatery and listen to the locals.

Northern California

Truckee and South Lake Tahoe

60 miles (one way); map Kummerley + Frey *California-Nevada*

Some 6,000 feet above sea level at the northern limit of the Sierra Nevada mountains, Lake Tahoe will take your breath away literally as well as metaphorically. The clear blue waters of the world's second-largest alpine lake – 22 miles long, 12 miles wide – are ringed by green, fir-tree cloaked slopes which rise sharply to magnificently moody peaks of gray granite.

This is essentially a summer journey, when the sunshine-filled days find Lake Tahoe and its surroundings bathed in a warm and sensuous natural glow. During winter, powdery snow covers the steep mountain sides and the area transforms itself into one of the U.S.'s major ski resorts – and one where skiers enjoy fantastic views.

While the so-called Rim of the Lake Road (actually an 80-mile route which uses several different highways) makes a complete circumnavigation of the lake easy, I have deliberately resisted this temptation when planning the tour. Such a trip actually turns up far fewer roadside highlights than might be expected. A better course is to concentrate on – as I have done – a shorter section of the lakeside route, being ready to spend time out of your car savoring the settlements such as Tahoe City and magnificent glacier-sculpted sights such as Emerald Bay.

Save for a couple of detours and short hops across the state border, the tour keeps to the California side of the lake. However, almost half of Lake Tahoe's shoreline lies in Nevada, where gambling is legal and where roulette wheels, card tables and slot machines bring more visitors than do the lakeside vistas.

Like all our tours, this one can be enjoyed traveling in either direction; indeed, you don't have to "do the route" – you can simply visit the various places of interest as and how you please. If you have three nights to spare, and want to make the full expedition, I suggest you include Kings Beach on the lake's north shore in addition to Tahoe City; both towns have direct roads to Truckee (where the tour connects with California Overall: 2). South Lake Tahoe is where you should spend your first or last night; though sprawling and largely unattractive, the large range of accommodation and eating options will be welcome and the town is well-placed for the Gold Country: Southern Mines (Local Explorations: 10) and the Eastern Sierra (Local Explorations: 11).

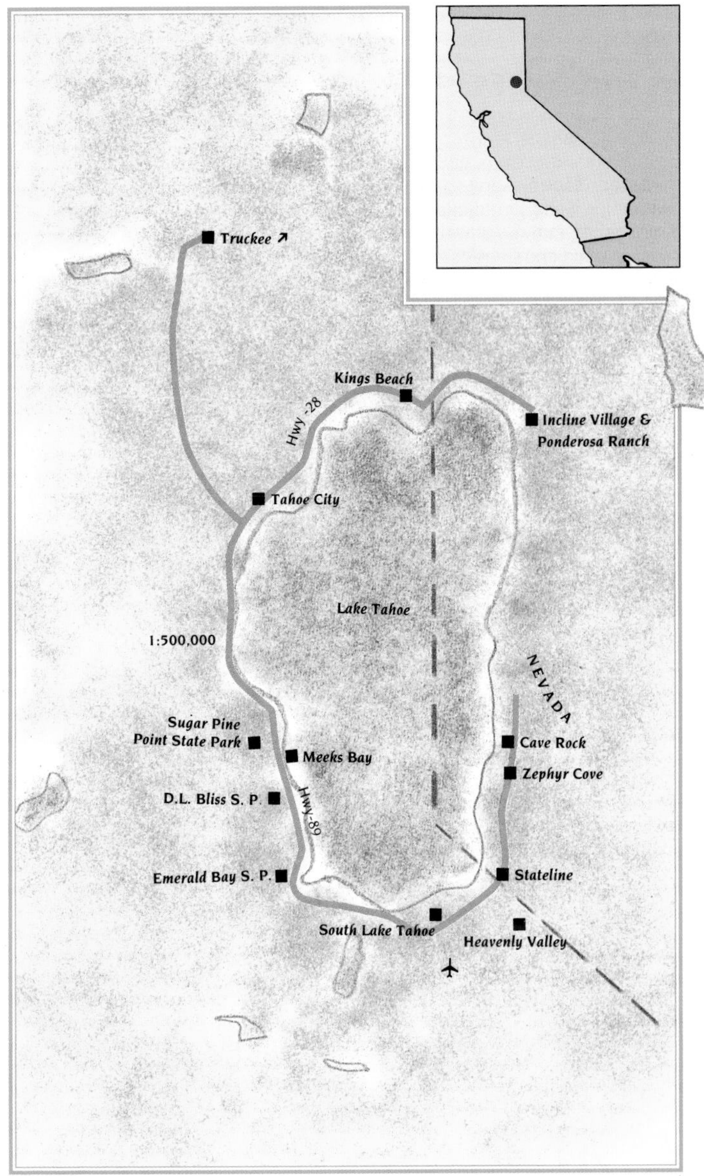

TRANSPORTATION

One daily train and several daily Greyhound buses link Sacramento with Truckee. From Truckee, however, there are no public transportation links to the Lake Tahoe communities. Greyhound buses from Sacramento also serve South Lake Tahoe and continue into the neighboring Nevada town of Stateline. Tahoe Regional Transport (tel. 916 581 6365) buses operate a limited number of services along the lake's western and northern shores; their routes are extended during summer to include Meeks Bay and Sugar Pine Point State Park.

SIGHTS & PLACES OF INTEREST

D.L. BLISS STATE PARK

Six miles of sandy shoreline bring hordes of summer vacationers to D.L. Bliss State Park, the premium strands of **Lester Beach** being favored for swimming, fishing, boating – and for simply sitting in the sun with the lake lapping around one's ankles.

The park also has a huge number of exceptionally smooth boulders: the **Balancing Rock**, a large hunk of granite naturally mounted on a pedestal, being the most spectacular. Another mighty slab of rock is the 600-ft high promontory, **Rubicon Point**, defining the park's northern perimeter. The point's summit can be reached by a steep but rewarding trail, which concludes with a splendid outlook across the blue lake and stands directly above its deepest section – a vertical drop of more than 1,000 feet.

With energy and a day to spare, gather picnic supplies and embark on the 4-mile trail leading south, a pleasant waterside amble which concludes at Vikingsholm, in Emerald Bay State Park (see below).

EMERALD BAY STATE PARK

The conifer-coated slopes of Emerald Bay State Park rise steeply above a secluded inlet, carved into a (supposedly) jewel-like shape by an Ice Age glacier. Hwy-89 passes through the park and beside a boulder-strewn roadside lookout point which provides an immensely photogenic view of Lake Tahoe and its only island – the rocky hump of **Fanette Island**, topped by a rustic stone structure known as the "tea house."

Thread your way down a mile-long trail from the lookout point and you'll reach **Vikingsholm** (open for guided tours; summer only), a 1920s version of a 9thC Nordic fortress. The summer residence of a rich heiress (who also owned Fanette Island's "tea house"), Vikingsholm's Swedish architect was instructed not to uproot a single tree in its construction and used traditional Scandinavian-style granite walls and part-earthen roofing to blend the building into the landscape. A castle half-buried in the forest, Vikingsholm and its 38 rooms are intriguing to visit.

DETOUR – PONDEROSA RANCH

Anyone weaned on Hollywood Westerns and the television cowboys of the 1950s and 1960s will need no encouragement to continue east from Kings Beach to the Nevada town of Incline Village. Here, the **Ponderosa Ranch** (open May–Oct) is a Western theme park built around the actual buildings used as the Cartwright family ranch in the series *Bonanza*. Other cowboy-connected attractions include a re-created saloon and a boardwalk-lined Main Street reverberating to the sound of staged shoot-outs.

BY CABLE CAR INTO THE MOUNTAINS

Twenty square miles of the 10,000-ft high slopes which rise behind South Lake Tahoe are consumed by **Heavenly Valley**, the country's largest alpine ski resort. Heavenly Valley relies for its summertime bread and butter on a cable car which – for a disconcertingly steep fee – brings camera-carrying tourists and diners to the Top of the Tram restaurant (see page 167), perched dizzily on a hillside 2,000 feet above lake level.

KINGS BEACH

The major town on Lake Tahoe's northern shore, Kings Beach has an enjoyably low-key seaside-resort mood and – while palm trees and surfers may be in short supply – warm summer days turn the lakeside sands of **Kings Beach State Recreation Area** into a surprisingly accurate imitation of a southern Californian beach scene.

MEEKS BAY

Judging by the scores of centuries-old arrowheads which have been found here, gracefully-curling Meeks Bay held as much appeal to Native Americans in the past as it does to vacationing families of the present who fill its rustic campsite. With a short stay in mind, aim for the picnic sites spread invitingly at intervals along the bay's mile-long beach.

SOUTH LAKE TAHOE 🛏 ✕

The beauty of the Lake Tahoe area is momentarily forgotten as you enter South Lake Tahoe: with 25,000 permanent residents it is a large settlement, sprawling for 8 miles along the lake and dominated by motels, quick-eat outlets and boat-rental offices. South Lake Tahoe makes a convenient touring base (and is ideal for anyone aiming to make their mark on the casinos of Stateline, see below) but otherwise deserves little of your time.

Be sure, however, to drop into the useful visitors' center, beside Hwy-89 on the town's western approaches, and take a look around the neighboring **Tallac Historic Estates** (open summer only), where several elegant 1920s houses are reassembled on a 75-acre site. Another worthwhile cultural stop is the **Lake Tahoe Historical Society Museum**, 3058 Hwy-50, which carries displays on the lake's formation and recounts the story of its human habitation.

LAKE TAHOE CRUISES

At some point when driving around Lake Tahoe it is inevitable that you will feel the urge to travel across it by boat. From South Lake Tahoe, a restored paddle steamer, the *Tahoe Queen*, sails to Emerald Bay and back, and at night hosts a dinner-dance cruise (tel. 800 23 TAHOE). Another paddle-steamer, the *M.S. Dixie*, plies between Zephyr Cove (on the Nevada side of the lake, a few miles north of Stateline) and Emerald Bay, and makes several other lake cruises. Also from Zephyr Cove, the *Woodwind* embarks on lazy sunset cruises (for details, tel. 702 588 3508).

STATELINE 🛏 ✕

Beginning where South Lake Tahoe meets the Nevada border, Stateline's half-mile strip of **casinos** provides a

RECOMMENDED HOTELS

KINGS BEACH

Falcon Motor Lodge, $$; 8258 N. *Lake Boulevard; tel.* 916 546 2583; *credit cards*, AE, CB, DC, MC, V.

Paying a few dollars above the standard rate at this small and cozy establishment brings a room with a lake view; all rooms have coffee-makers and fridges. The motel also has a modestly-sized private beach.

SOUTH LAKE TAHOE

Cedar Lodge, $-$$; *corner of* Cedar *and* Atlantic *Avenues; tel.* 916 544 6453; *credit cards*, MC, V.

Fairly priced and well-equipped, this motel is handy both for the casinos of Stateline and for central South Lake Tahoe.

Forest Inn, $$-$$$; 1101 *Park* Ave; *tel.* 916 541 6655; *credit cards*, AE, MC, V.

Set within 5 acres of landscaped grounds yet just a roulette-wheel's throw from the Nevada casinos. Most rooms at the Forest Inn are equipped with fridges and there are spas and saunas for guests' use; for several people sharing, the two-bed suites are as good a deal as you will find in the vicinity.

STATELINE

Harrah's, $$$-$$$$; Hwy-50; *tel.* 800 648 3773; *credit cards*, AE, CB, DC, MC, V.

If you have ever wondered what glitzy American casino-hotels are all about, this is the place to learn. Eighteen storys high, Harrah's windows look out on stunning lake and mountain views while inside there are shopping arcades, restaurants, bars – and gambling opportunities galore.

TAHOE CITY

River Ranch, $$; 2285 River Ranch *Road; tel.* 916 583 4264; *credit cards*, AE, MC, V.

A relaxing rustic retreat on the banks of the Tahoe River about three miles from the center of Tahoe City, the River Ranch is about as far from elbow-to-elbow motels as you can get: wake to the sound of birdsong in a room filled with antiques.

• *Lake Tahoe.*

DETOUR – **CAVE ROCK**
Two miles north of Stateline, two tunnels carry Hwy-50 through the 75-ft-thick Cave Rock. Park and walk to the picnic spot below the rock – formed by volcanic upheavals 5 million years ago – for tantalizing views across Lake Tahoe and a chance to ponder the Native American explanation for the rock's older tunnel (no mystery surrounds the more recent one, engineered in the early 1900s). Allegedly, when threatened by rising waters, the Washoe Indians who once lived here appealed to the Great Spirit for help; the Great Spirit responded by driving his lance through the rock, creating the tunnel which allowed the waters to drain away.

chance to win (or lose) a fortune at any time of the day or night, while the town's high-rise casino-hotels host extravagant cabaret shows of the kind much admired in Las Vegas. Other than gambling and nightlife, Stateline's appeal is limited to the absurdly low-priced buffet meals provided by casino restaurants – a ploy to lure people inside and keep them there, although even non-gamblers can turn up and eat their fill.

SUGAR PINE POINT STATE PARK
The waterside section of Sugar Pine Point State Park is dominated by the 1903 **Erhman Mansion**, resplendently sited on a knoll overlooking Lake Tahoe and built for a wealthy San Franciscan banker. By the 1920s, the mansion was a fashionable weekend retreat for Californian high society and

now earns a living as the park's visitor center. An eye-catching blend of timber and stone, the mansion – and its luxuriously-appointed interior – can be seen at close quarters on guided tours (summer only).

Heading inland, several effortless walking trails criss-cross the park's General Creek, passing a wealth of vibrant vegetation plus the remains of a 19thC "corduroy" road – a road built of tightly-packed logs held in place by mud.

TAHOE CITY 🛏 ✕

A city in name only, possessing just a few streets which will take no more than an hour to explore fully on foot, Tahoe City is one of the oldest Lake Tahoe settlements and was the site of a 1910 project to dam the lake's only outlet, the Tahoe River. Fanny Bridge, which carries Hwy-89 across the river, passes close to the old dam's picturesque outlet gates and the **Gatekeeper's Museum**, which carries displays on the damming project and on other elements of local history. More knick-knacks from early Tahoe City fill **Watson's Log Cabin**, 560 N. Lake Boulevard, a structure which began life as a honeymoon cottage for two pioneer-era settlers.

TRUCKEE

See California Overall: 2.

ZEPHYR COVE

See Lake Tahoe Cruises, page 165.

RECOMMENDED RESTAURANTS

SOUTH LAKE TAHOE

Fresh Ketch Lakeside Restaurant, $-$$; 2345 *Venice Drive*; *tel.* 916 541 5683; *credit cards*, AE, DC, MC, V..

Not surprisingly, seafood is the star attraction of this classy waterside eatery, with Long Island oysters featuring among the locally-caught delights from the deep.

Top of the Tram, $-$$; *Heavenly Valley*; *tel.* 916 544 6263; *credit cards*, AE, CB, DC, DS, MC, V.

The views from this 8,300-foot mountain-top perch may be stunning, but the food is only slightly less notable: a wide selection of sandwiches and salads for lunch, and pricey steak and seafood dinners; reachable by cable-car (see By Cable-car into the Mountains, page 000).

STATELINE

Harrah's Forest Buffet, $-$$; *Hwy*-50; *tel.* 702 588 6611; *credit cards*, AE, DC, MC, V.

Stateline's casino-restaurants provide exceptionally large amounts of buffet food at low prices; at Harrah's, not only will you find the town's best array of help-yourself fare but the best view too, from the hotel's 18th floor.

TAHOE CITY

Rosie's Cafe, $-$$; 571 N *Lake Boulevard*; *tel.* 916 583 8504; *credit cards, none*.

An eclectic mix of locals and tourists helps make Rosie's a lively spot for breakfast, lunch or dinner. For the quality of the food, the prices are hard to better and the menu includes many inventive creations – plus vegetarian dishes – alongside American staples such as burgers and fries.

Wolfdale's, $; 640 N *Lake Boulevard*; *tel.* 916 583 5700; *credit cards*, AE, DC, MC, V.

Clued-up gastronomes come from near and far to sample Wolfdale's enterprising mix of Californian and Japanese cuisines; the results are always interesting, though not always filling.

Northern California

The Napa Valley

100 miles (one way); map Kummerley + Frey California-Nevada

Access to this area, California's foremost wine region, is easy from my San Francisco-Lake Tahoe route (California Overall: 2); or from Healdsburg (California Overall: 1). Exploring it can also make an easy and interesting two- or three-day excursion from San Francisco.

Palm trees may be more synonymous with California than wine, but in these three short valleys (Napa, Sonoma and Russian River) some 50 miles north of San Francisco it is neat rows of vines which stretch for miles into the distance, bearing the grapes which have turned the state into a major wine producer.

The Napa Valley has wineries at every turn and most of them offer free tours and tastings. I have chosen a selection of them with the intention of highlighting the various types of wine which the state produces and to give a few insights into the practical aspects of wine-making. Have no fear if you are a newcomer to wine tasting: several wineries on the tour pride themselves on turning wine illiterates into comparative experts inside an hour.

Wine is unquestionably the valley's number one attraction: tens of thousands of visitors arrive in eager anticipation of it during the summer, when traffic jams regularly clog Hwy-29 – the main route through the valley. (The Silverado Trail, a parallel route a few miles east, usually provides a quieter alternative.) However, I have arranged the tour to include the valley's state parks, which combine beautiful scenery with reminders of the region's earliest white settlement, and the unusual geological phenomena resulting from the prehistoric eruptions of the now-dormant Mount St. Helena.

Unless pressed for time, I recommend that you make only a brief visit to the town of Napa and use the more charming St. Helena or Calistoga as one- or two-night bases, driving from them to the winery-dominated villages of Rutherford and Oakville in the valley's heart.

I have extended the route north of the valley to Lakeport, a quiet town sited close to Clear Lake, California's largest natural body of water and a delightfully relaxing place to come to rest.

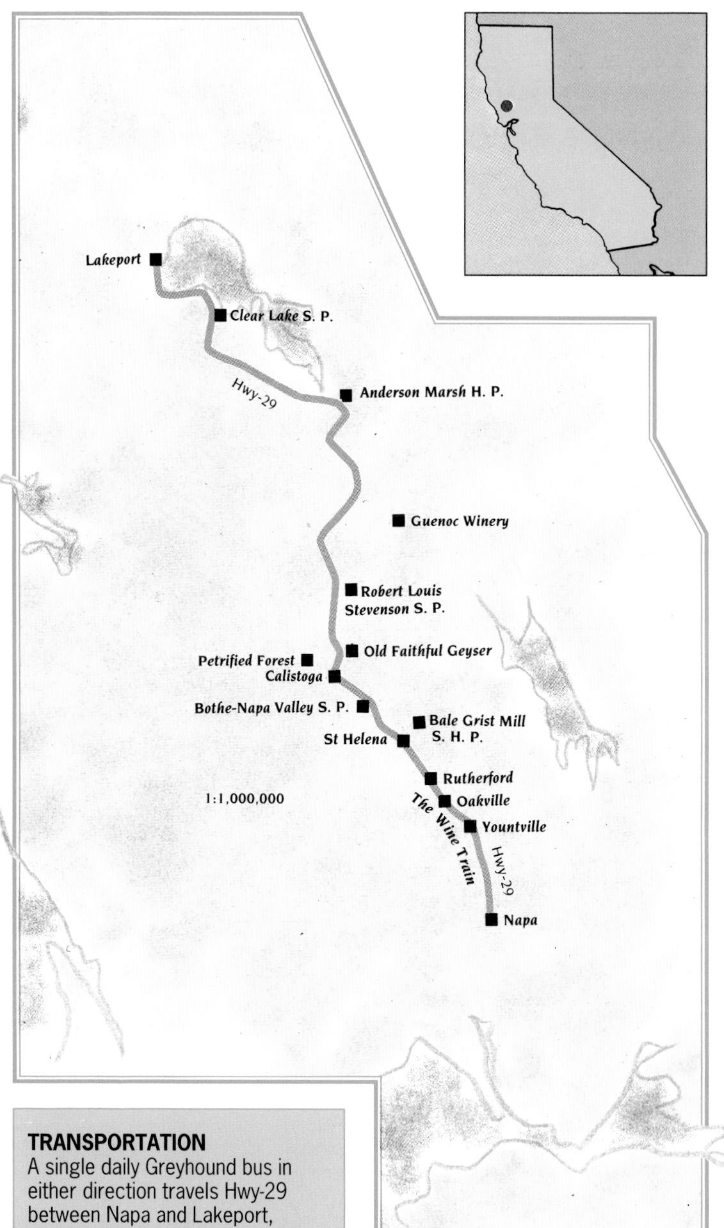

TRANSPORTATION
A single daily Greyhound bus in either direction travels Hwy-29 between Napa and Lakeport, stopping (sometimes only by request) at all the towns along the route. If you are travelling without a car, be reassured that renting a bicycle is a very pleasant and very popular way of touring the valley; see Touring the Napa Valley by Bicycle, page 172, for details.

SIGHTS & PLACES OF INTEREST

ANDERSON MARSH HISTORIC PARK

Archaeological finds at Anderson Marsh State Historic Park have revealed evidence of human settlement dating back 10,000 years. The area's oldest inhabitants are believed to have been hunter-gatherer groups who predated the area's better-known Pomo Indians by some 5,000 years. Displays at the site document the ancient finds, though much of the park is a wildlife refuge, bestowing protection on the scores of bird species – bald eagles among them – which thrive on the marshlands that denote the southern reaches of Clear Lake.

BALE GRIST MILL STATE HISTORIC PARK

One of the few prominent Englishmen in Mexican-era California was former ship's surgeon Edward Turner Bale, who lived in Monterey before marrying into a major land-owning family and acquiring a plot of land in the Napa Valley. It was here that he switched from practising medicine to turning the valley's grain harvest into flour, constructing the area's earliest water-powered grist mill to do so.

More than a hundred years after Bale's death, the restored mill's 36-ft-wide wheel is coaxed into three-and-a-half creaky revolutions per minute as park rangers and volunteers demonstrate its use and various long-neglected techniques of early Californian bread baking.

Passing a 19thC cemetery and the region's earliest church, the park's mile-long **History Trail** – which links with Bothe-Napa Valley State Park (see below) – also gives a hint of a bygone Napa Valley.

CALISTOGA'S SPAS

Calistoga's spa resorts are all pleasingly informal, and each offers a slightly different service, usually at very reasonable prices. Just a few dollars buys a dip in the mineral pools at Calistoga Hot Springs Spa, 1066 Washington Avenue (tel. 707 942 6269), or Golden Haven Spa, 1713 Lake Street (tel. 707 942 6793).

Fuller treatments – including mineral whirlpools and mud baths – are liable to cost upwards of $30: reliable practitioners include Nance's Hot Springs, 1614 Lincoln Avenue (tel. 707 942 6211), and Indian Springs, 1712 Lincoln Avenue (tel. 707 942 4913), built around Sam Brannan's original resort.

The more adventurous of Calistoga's spas utilize herbs, seaweed, eucalyptus steam- and Japanese-style enzyme-baths in their courses, and fill the air with the soothing strains of New Age music. If this appeals, try the International Spa, 1300 Washington Street (tel. 707 942 6122).

BOTHE-NAPA VALLEY STATE PARK

If you are feeling the effects of too much Napa Valley wine, pack a picnic, your sturdiest shoes and a swimming costume, and head for Bothe-Napa Valley State Park. Striking out across the park's grassy hillsides, studded by fir and pine trees and the easternmost groves of coastal redwoods, will soon clear the most hungover head. Afterwards, relax by swimming a few lengths of the park's public swimming-pool (open summer only).

CALISTOGA ✕

In 1859, wealthy San Francisco entrepreneur Sam Brannan followed the lead of Native Americans – who had been utilizing the health-improving qualities of the area's hot springs for generations – and opened a spa resort in the town he named Calistoga.

Although Brannan would later die penniless, the town he created quickly flourished as a health resort and is still synonymous with the improved mental and physical well-being which results from a combination of bathing in its mineral-rich waters, being smothered in its volcanic mud, and having one's bones kneaded by nimble-fingered masseurs.

Should your mind and body already be on an even keel, Calistoga's wineries might have more appeal than the town's spas. **Sterling Vineyards**, 1111 Dunaweal Lane (tel. 707 942 3344), is the only Californian winery

• *Oakville bounty - see page 173.*

visitable by way of a spectacular cable car ride. Its Mediterranean-style main building nestles on a hillside overlooking the valley. Also boasting better-than-usual landscaping is **Chateau Montelena**, 1429 Tubbs Lane (tel. 707 942 5105), where the 1973 Chardonnay which put California on the world wine map was produced, and where the winery's stone-built headquarters overlooks a lake and formal Chinese gardens.

After the spas and wineries, spare a thought for Calistoga's history by visiting the elaborate dioramas of the **Sharpsteen Museum**, 1311 Washington Street, which re-create critical moments in the town's past.

CLEAR LAKE STATE PARK

Enclosed by chaparral-covered slopes

DETOUR – **THE GUENOC WINERY**

In the 1880s, allegedly in pursuit of the quick divorce which Californian residency would permit, English actress Lillie Langtry purchased a country estate six miles east of Middletown (a crossroads community on Hwy-29 between Lakeport and Calistoga) along Butts Canyon Road, and imported a French vintner with the intention of founding a winery. While Langtry's wine-producing plans came to little, her former estate is now home to the Guenoc Winery, where the tales of Langtry's Californian exploits make an enjoyable accompaniment to sampling the estate's wines: tel. 707 987 2385.

• *On the road to Napa.*

THE WINE TRAIN

Uncharitably known locally as the "swine train" for the noise it makes rumbling through the valley, the restored 1915 Pullman cars of the Napa Valley Wine Train make a three-hour journey between Napa and St. Helena two to three times daily, serving expensive gourmet-standard food – and a selection of Napa Valley wines – for lunch or dinner (or for brunch at weekends). The return trip costs $29; meals are extra.

Tel. 800 427 4124.

indented with pockets of pine and fir trees, Clear Lake State Park gives access to two miles of Clear Lake's shoreline and is on the itinerary of every self-respecting Californian angler. Careful management of fish stocks keeps the lake teeming with large-mouth bass, catfish, perch and other favorites of the fisherman's frying pan. To gain an inkling of the lake's diverse fish population without reducing it, visit the aquarium inside the park's visitor center.

Besides fishing, the park provides a launch point for swimmers and water skiers during the summer and is well-endowed with picnic sites. Two park trails are also worth investigating: the short **Indian Trail** reveals the plants used for medicinal purposes by Pomo and Wappo Indians; the longer, steeper **Dorn Nature Trail** climbs through forests and meadows to give spectacular views of the lake and of Mt. Konocti, which rises behind. The boulder-strewn, 1,300-ft peak was formed, according to Native American legend, when two ancient chiefs held a stone-throwing battle.

TOURING THE NAPA VALLEY BY BICYCLE

Provided you stick largely to the quiet Silverado Trail, which parallels the busy Hwy-29, the Napa Valley can be pleasurably toured by bicycle. Depending on the machine, cycle rental costs $15-$25 a day, and is available from a number of outlets throughout the valley. These include Bryan's Napa Valley Cyclery, 4080 Byway East, Napa (tel. 707 255 3377); St. Helena Cyclery, 1156 Main Street, St. Helena (tel. 707 963 7736); and Calistoga Bike Rentals, 1227 Lincoln Boulevard, Calistoga (tel. 707 942 0421).

LAKEPORT ✕

With small-town charms aplenty, little Lakeport sits on the western edge of Clear Lake and does a brisk summer business catering to the needs of the tens of thousands of visitors who arrive to spend their vacations on and around the water. Several 19thC buildings stand intact along Lakeport's Main Street and one of them holds the **Lake County Museum**. If you need convincing of the importance of basketry in Native American culture or that the Pomo tribe, who settled around Clear Lake, were among the craft's leading exponents, a viewing of the museum's many excellent examples should be on your agenda.

NAPA 🛏 ✕

Sited on the Napa River, which provided a steamship link to San Francisco, the town of Napa was uniquely placed to benefit when the Napa Valley's wineries first got into gear during the mid-19thC. Despite lending its name to the country's major wine-producing area, Napa has few wineries of its own but does boast a plethora of extravagant Victorian architecture in its historic riverside quarter.

Many of the old buildings have been restored and converted into the antiques shops, quaint restaurants and bed-and-breakfast inns which service the town's plentiful wine tourists, but the commercial trappings should not deter you from a few hours' stroll. While here, drop into the distinctive Goodman Library Building, 1219 1st Street, where the **Napa County Historical Society** mounts displays and exhibitions on the origins and growth of the town.

OAKVILLE

Like nearby Rutherford (see page 174), the village of Oakville sits in a section of the valley where climate and soils are ideally suited to grape production. Consequently both tiny villages are completely dominated by more wineries than even seasoned oenologists can shake a stick at.

The 45-minute tours and tastings offered by the **Robert Mondavi Winery**, 7801 St. Helena Highway (tel. 707 963 9611) are unrivalled for revealing what California wines and wine-making are all about, and should be the first stop in the Napa Valley for the wine novice. The winery's mission-style buildings also feature a gallery displaying Californian artists' work. In summer, the strains of live classical music percolate through the expansive gardens.

The unexpected sight of a geodesic dome, which covers the workings and the visitor center, rises beside Hwy-29 to mark the reputable **De Moor Winery**, 7481 St. Helena Highway (tel. 707 944 2565). By contrast, **Silver Oak Cellars**, 915 Oakville Cross Road (tel. 707 944 8808), occupies a former dairy and devotes itself to producing Cabernet Sauvignon – to a high standard.

Sauvignon Blanc is the speciality of the small **Robert Pepi Winery**, 7585 St. Helena Highway (tel. 707 944 2807). Another modestly-sized but intriguing producer is **Villa Mt. Eden**, 620 Oakville Cross Road, first established in the 1880s, reopened in the 1970s and building its growing reputation on limited-production Chardonnay and Cabernet Sauvignon.

OLD FAITHFUL GEYSER

One manifestation of the geothermal activity around Calistoga is the Old Faithful Geyser, a mile north of the town, which has been sending a high-pressure jet of boiling water 60 feet skywards every 30 or 50 minutes (depending on local seismic activity) for many years. A small visitor center explains the fascinating process, although for anyone who has seen geysers elsewhere in the world, the admission fee will seem excessive.

DETOUR – **THE PETRIFIED FOREST**

When Mount St. Helena indulged in one of its periodic eruptions more than 6 million years ago, the tide of volcanic mud and ash which swept through the area uprooted a grove of gigantic coastal redwood trees. As chemicals in the ash reacted with wood fibers, the gigantic trees were turned into stone. To reach the Petrified Forest, as the trees are known, drive five miles west of Calistoga along Petrified Forest Road. Near the entrance, a small museum outlines the extraordinary events which created the fossilized trees, and a short foot-trail explores some of them at close quarters.

ROBERT LOUIS STEVENSON STATE PARK

In 1880, author Robert Louis Stevenson spent part of his honeymoon in a cabin of an abandoned silver mine on the site of what is now Robert Louis Stevenson State Park, spanning more than 3,000 undeveloped acres across the upper slopes of Mount St. Helena.

Facilities are few inside the park, although the reward for tackling the five-mile trail which leads to the summit of the long-dormant volcano is views reaching to San Francisco and – on clear days – as far north as snow-capped Mount Shasta and as far east as the Sierra Nevadas.

Fans of Stevenson's fiction might recognize the park from landscapes described in *The Silverado Squatters* – a story based on his stay here – while Mount St. Helena bears striking similarities to Spyglass Hill, the fictional mountain of Stevenson's *Treasure Island*.

THE VALLEY BY BALLOON
If you tire of looking at the Napa Valley through the bottom of a wine glass, try soaring above it in a helium-filled balloon. Several companies throughout the valley offer a few hours aloft for around $150 for four people. The price includes light snacks and champagne. Make reservations well in advance. Balloon companies are widely advertised throughout the valley and include: in Calistoga, **Once In A Lifetime** (tel. 707 942 6541); in Napa, **Balloons Above the Napa Valley** (tel. 707 253 2222); and in Yountville, **Above the West** (tel. 707 944 8638).

RUTHERFORD 🛏 ✕
It was the efforts of a Russian-born vintner working at Rutherford's **Beaulieu Winery**, 1960 St. Helena Highway (tel. 707 963 2411), which helped make Cabernet Sauvignon the grape most closely associated with California. Founded in 1900, Beaulieu stayed in business during Prohibition by manufacturing sacramental wine and is now among the valley's oldest continuously-producing wineries. Beaulieu's tours are rightly popular for lifting the lid on the wine-making process – and for their free tastings.

In 1887, Gustav Niebaum, a Finnish-born sea captain who had made a fortune through the Alaskan fur trade, purchased 1,000 Napa Valley acres and commissioned the building of the stone château which makes an imposing headquarters for the **Inglenook Vineyards**, 1991 St. Helena Highway (tel. 707 967 3362). Within the winery's cellars, a small exhibition traces the early days of valley wine production with a curious assortment of wine-glasses and goblets, before visitors

• *Opposite*: Napa Valley.

RECOMMENDED HOTELS

CALISTOGA

Brannan Cottage Inn, $$$; 109 *Wapoo Avenue; tel.* 707 942 4200; *credit cards*, MC, V.

Only three of the fourteen original cottages belonging to Sam Brannan's resort, which gave birth to Calistoga in the 1860s, remain and this is one of them, lovingly restored and offering six antique- and wicker-filled rooms for bed-and-breakfast accommodation.

Calistoga Inn, $-$$; 1250 *Lincoln Avenue; tel.* 707 942 4101; *credit cards*, MC, V.

Lack of TVs, telephones and private bathrooms conspires to keep the rates of the turn-of-the-century Calistoga Inn among the lowest in the Napa Valley. If you do not mind the lack of conveniences, a night at this atmospheric inn will be a delightful one: the rooms are modest but adequate and the price includes a breakfast of coffee, fruit juice and pastries.

See also Recommended Restaurants, *page* 176.

Mount View Hotel, $$-$$$$; 1457 *Lincoln Avenue; tel.* 707 942 6877; *credit cards*, AE, CB, DC, MC, V.

The guest wings of the Mount View Hotel, tastefully restored to its 1920s art deco appearance, lead off the main building to enclose an inviting swimming-pool and jacuzzi. The higher rates are for the decadently furnished suites; the regular rooms are plainer but offer exceptional value. All rates include a light breakfast.

NAPA

Churchill Manor, $$-$$$$; 485 *Brown Street; tel.* 707 253 7733; *credit cards*, AE, CB, DC, MC, V.

A three-story Colonial-Revival manor built in 1889 for a local banker, spacious Churchill Manor provides sumptuous bed-and-breakfast in a choice of ten diversely themed guest rooms, some of which have fireplaces and all of which have private bathrooms. Served in the sunny conservatory, breakfast features a healthy selection of fresh fruit and pastries.

John Muir Inn, $$-$$$; 1998 *Trower Avenue; tel.* 800 522 8999; *credit cards*, AE, DC, DS, MC, V.

A crisply efficient modern motel located just off Hwy-29, the John Muir Inn has spacious, well-furnished rooms equipped with cable TV and coffee-makers, while a swimming-pool beckons in the grounds.

RUTHERFORD
Rancho Caymus Inn, $$$-$$$$; 1140 *Rutherford Road; tel.* 707 963 1777; *credit cards,* MC, V.

Erected in 1985 with 26 rooms and mission-style architecture, Rancho Caymus Inn was the brainchild of a wealthy sculptress keen to create a showplace for local artists and craftspeople. Hand-crafted fixtures and fittings appear throughout and interesting artworks from Central America decorate the individually designed rooms.

ST. HELENA
The Ambrose Bierce House, $$$-$$$$; 1515 *Main Street; tel.* 707 963 3003; *credit cards, none.*

A turn-of-the-century literary figure famed for his caustic wit, Ambrose Bierce lived in this modest house for 13 years. Bierce paraphernalia, and markers to other luminaries of late-1800s Californian cultural life, fill what is now a compact bed-and-breakfast inn. Even if you arrive knowing nothing about Bierce, the host's enthusiasm for one of early California's more enigmatic characters will prove infectious.

El Bonita, $$–$$$; 195 *Main Street; tel.* 707 963 3216; *credit cards,* AE, MC, V.

Having the lowest rates in town means there is always a demand for rooms at this simple but smart art deco-style motel. Besides the standard rooms in the main building, six pricier rooms bordering the garden are equipped with kitchenettes and some newer additions have jacuzzis.

Harvest Inn, $$$-$$$$; 1 *Main Street; tel.* 800 950 8466; *credit cards,* AE, DC, MC, V.

A rambling and slightly impersonal modern hotel despite its English Tudor-style architecture and preponderance of antiques and fireplaces. Nonetheless, the inn is surrounded by fine scenery – a 14-acre vineyard, in fact – to encourage a relaxed stay.

are led into the tasting room.

One of the more recent wineries, **Grgich Hills Cellar**, 1829 St. Helena Highway (tel. 707 963 2784), opened in 1977, a year after its owner had cemented the reputation of modern Californian wines with the Chardonnay which won the prestigious Paris Tasting. Chardonnay is still the thing to sample here, although the estate-bottled Zinfandel also has its admirers.

ST. HELENA 🛏 ✕

Founded in the mid-19thC, St. Helena enjoys a prime position in the heart of the Napa Valley, surrounded by wineries and plentifully supplied with up-market restaurants, bed-and-breakfast inns, boutiques and gift shops aimed at the long-distance wine tourist and the week-ending San Franciscan. Most of the activity is along Main Street, illuminated at night by elegant street lamps of 1915 vintage.

Turn-of-the-century mining magnate William Bowers Bourn – who also financed the Californian mansion known to millions as the setting for TV's *Dynasty* – was responsible for the landmark stone building which houses St. Helena's **Christian Brothers-Greystone Cellars**, 2555 Main Street (tel. 707 967 3112). The Christian Brothers name is a trademark of a Catholic teaching order which produced altar and sacramental wines during the 19thC and who (though they no longer own this particular winery) are among the Napa Valley's major landowners. Tours, departing every half-hour, take in the winery's collection of historic wine-making equipment and a remarkable gathering of weird and wonderful corkscrews, before reaching the tasting room, where several tempting brandies might be found among the wines.

Close by, the **Charles Krug Winery**, 2800 Main Street (tel. 707 963 5057), has the distinction of being the oldest winery in the valley and the first to crush grapes with a press rather

RECOMMENDED RESTAURANTS

CALISTOGA

All Seasons Cafe, $-$$; *1400 Lincoln Avenue; tel.* 707 942 9111; *credit cards,* AE, DC, MC, V.

Great place to pick up nutritious picnic supplies or enjoy a delicate and tasty lunchtime pasta dish or sandwich. In the evening, the mood becomes more formal for a dinner menu which features interesting *nouvelle cuisine* offerings.

Calistoga Inn Restaurant, $-$$; *1250 Lincoln Avenue; tel.* 707 942 4101; *credit cards,* MC, V.

All the invention and flair of the best Californian cuisine goes into the appetizing lunches and dinners served at this informal and instantly likeable century-old inn. On sunny days, eat out on the rear patio. The drink choice spans top-notch Napa Valley wines and home-brewed lagers and ales.

LAKEPORT

Park Place, $; *50 3rd Street; tel.* 707 263 0444; *credit cards,* MC, V.

A lakeside location might be reason enough to eat here, but the wondrously-priced food – predominantly soups, salads, pastas and seafood dishes well-prepared each day from fresh local ingredients – is an even greater attraction.

NAPA

Jonesy's Famous Steakhouse, $-$$; *2044 Airport Road, at Napa County Airport; tel.* 707 255 2003; *credit cards,* AE, DC, DS, MC, V; *closed Monday.*

If California's obsession with healthy eating leaves you craving a big hunk of red meat, this long-established shrine to the carnivore is where to go: thick, juicy steaks are sizzled to perfection on an open grill.

Napa Valley Coffee Roasting Company, $; *948 Main Street; tel.* 707 224 2233; *credit cards, none.*

Rampant appetites will not be satiated here, but this pleasant if slightly cutesy cafe serves a variety of invigorating coffees and fresh-baked cakes and biscuits – within walls decorated by historic coffee-related bric-à-brac.

Table 29, $$-$$$; *4110 St. Helena Highway; tel.* 707 224 3300; *credit cards,* DC, MC, V.

than by foot. The valley's oldest continuously-operating winery, however, is **Beringer Vineyards**, 2000 Main Street (tel. 707 963 7115), going strong since 1876. The hugely ornate Rhineland-style mansion which the German émigrés Beringer brothers erected in 1883 is now the winery's visitors' center.

Teetotallers intrigued by wine but otherwise at a loose end in the area might find the **Napa Valley Wine Library**, 1492 Library Lane, a blessing: the continuously expanding stock currently numbers some 6,000 wine-related volumes. Anyone suitably interested can browse at their leisure.

One visitor to St. Helena who did not have wine on his mind was newly-married Scottish writer Robert Louis Stevenson, who passed through the town in 1880 with his bride Fanny Osbourne, on the way to a rustic honeymoon at what is now Robert Louis Stevenson State Park (see page 173). In an annex of the library, the **Silverado Museum** celebrates local Stevenson connections with a major horde: manuscripts, first editions, letters, paintings, photographs and much more.

YOUNTVILLE ×

In 1986, the economy of the pleasant village of Yountville was given a boost by the opening of **Domain Chandon**, California Drive (tel. 707 944 8844) by the top-bracket champagne and brandy producers, Moët et Chandon. Free tours describe the ultra-modern production process and a museum chronicles the long and illustrious history of champagne – but actually sampling the stuff costs $4 a glass.

Elsewhere in Yountville, the only place worthy of your time is the **Vintage 1870** complex, 6525 Washington Street, which fills a former 19thC winery and railway station with a collection of diverse retail outlets and eaterys. Even if you don't buy or eat anything, the cobbled pathways are ripe for a stroll.

The result of two celebrated California chefs moving closer to the source of their favorite ingredients, Table 29's lengthy menu is adjusted daily to highlight the best of Napa Valley's fruit, vegetables and wildlife.

RUTHERFORD

Auberge du Soleil, $$$; 180 *Rutherford Hill Road; tel.* 707 963 1211; *credit cards,* AE, MC, V.

Widely acknowledged as one of the Napa Valley's finest dining experiences, the fixed-price four-course dinners here – smart attire and reservations are essential – combine rural French and Californian cookery. Together with the excellent food come splendid views across the vineyards. Also serves a winning Sunday brunch.

ST. HELENA

St. Helena Coffee Shop, $; 61 *Main Street; tel.* 707 963 3235; *credit cards, none; breakfast and lunch only.*

Very plain but also, for anyone on a budget, a very welcome source of inexpensive, all-American hunger-busters – three-egg omelettes, substantial sandwiches, various burgers and plenty more.

Tra Vigne, $-$$; 1050 *Charter Oak Ave; tel.* 707 963 4444; *cards,* MC, V.

Contemporary Italian decoration and a popular wall-length bar make pleasing first impressions of this stylish and well-priced restaurant offering wood-fired pizzas, pasta dishes, and the meat and seafood specialities of northern Italy, all enlivened by Californian twists.

YOUNTVILLE

The Diner, $; 6476 *Washington Street; tel.* 707 944 2626; *credit cards, none; closed Mon.*

Tourists nonplussed by the pricey and pretentious restaurants in neighboring Napa are increasingly joining the locals who frequent this dependable, no-frills eatery. Generous breakfasts and lunches are drawn from a menu which combines standard American fare with numerous Mexican items and specialities; the dinner menu is essentially the same as earlier in the day, but with even larger portions.

<u>*Northern California*</u>

Sonoma Valley

30 miles (one way); map Kummerley + Frey California-Nevada

This tour is intended for anyone who already knows their Chenin Blanc from their Pinot Noir, and who might well find the popular wineries of the more famous Napa Valley (Local Explorations: 6) to be less enticing than the smaller, more specialized concerns which dot the Sonoma Valley, immediately west. In fact, it is a painless procedure to combine this tour with the Napa Valley tour. Alternatively, it can be joined from Santa Rosa (on California Overall: 1) and also makes an effortless excursion from San Francisco. To cover it all, one or two nights.

The aim is to provide a short but pleasurable trip, combining the sampling of some fine wines with the rural allure of a pair of expansive state parks and the former hillside ranch of writer Jack London, who fell in love with the Sonoma Valley during the early 1900s.

Included, too, is a detour to the state's oldest commercial winery. California's first wine was produced by its Spanish missions for sacramental use, using vine cuttings shipped from Europe. Although history records the mission wines as unfit for anything other than religious purposes, the news of the region's wine-friendly climate and soils spread, and many European vintners began migrating to the American west in the mid-19thC. One of the earliest among them was a Hungarian, Agoston Haraszthy, who opened a winery just outside the town of Sonoma in 1857 and is nowadays remembered as the "father" of Californian viniculture.

Small, green and instantly likeable, Sonoma is the perfect base for touring the valley. A lovely town to get to know during a few hours' stroll, Sonoma boasts the largest Mexican-era plaza in California and has an impressive historical pedigree. The town holds the state's most northerly Spanish mission and was where California briefly became an independent republic during the mid-1800s, prior to becoming a U.S. possession.

Travelling north from Sonoma on Hwy-12 brings you to the hamlets of Kenwood and Glen Ellen crouching on wooded hillsides, each with their share of wineries and each providing access to the woodlands and scrub-covered ridges which wall the valley.

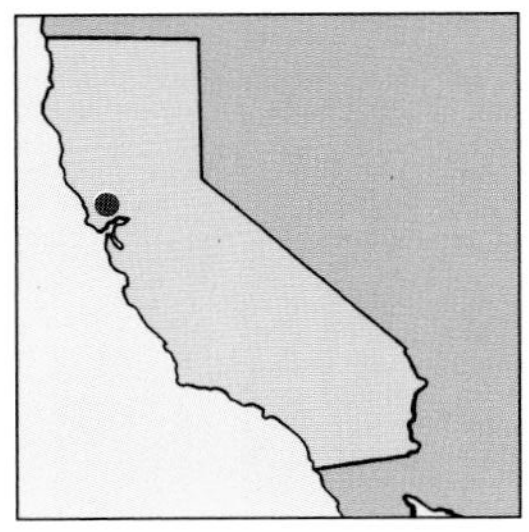

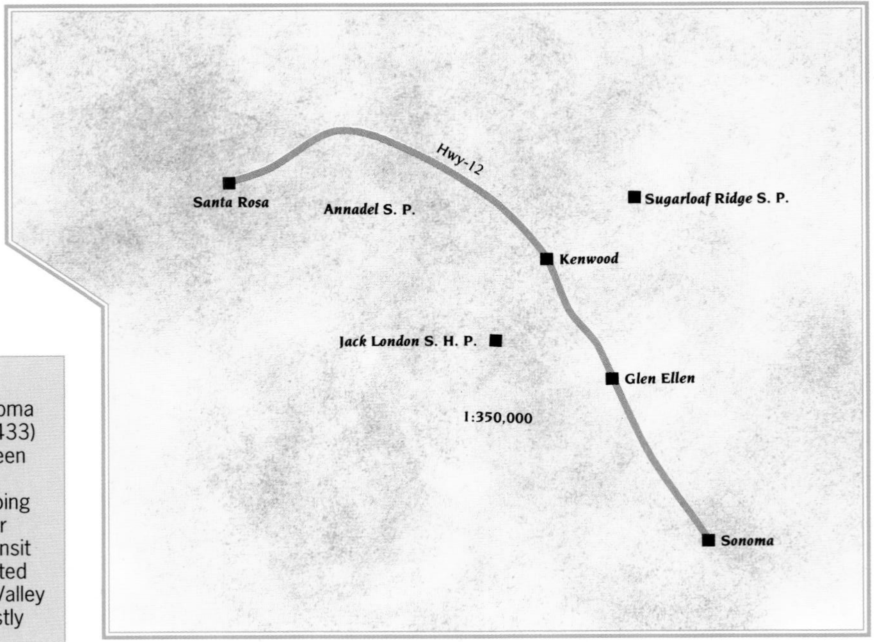

Santa Rosa
Annadel S. P.
Hwy-12
Sugarloaf Ridge S. P.
Kenwood
Jack London S. H. P.
Glen Ellen
1:350,000
Sonoma

TRANSPORTATION
Although infrequent, local Sonoma County buses (tel. 707 576 7433) serve the valley, running between Sonoma and Santa Rosa (see California Overall: 1) and stopping wherever requested along their Hwy-12 route.Golden Gate Transit (tel. 415 332 6600) has a limited service between the Sonoma Valley towns and San Francisco, mostly aimed at commuters.

SIGHTS & PLACES OF INTEREST

ANNADEL STATE PARK

Annadel State Park contains 5,000 acres of natural California in guises ranging from scrub-covered ridges and steep-sided canyons to woodlands of oak and fir separated by grassy meadows, carpeted in springtime by colorful wildflowers.

While 35 miles of hiking trails strike deep into the park, a walk from the carpark to the shores of Lake Ilsanjo will reveal some prime picnic sites. Birdwatchers should aim for Ledson Marsh, an ideal vantage point for observing some of the 130 species – from pileated woodpeckers to great blue herons – which have been sighted in the park.

GLEN ELLEN

A bucolic hamlet set on the wooded slopes beneath Jack London State Historic Park (see page 181), Glen Ellen has charm in abundance although specific places of interest are few. Anyone in the Sonoma Valley on a Jack London pilgrimage should make a beeline for the **Jack London Bookstore**, 14300 Arnold Drive, where you can plug any gaps in your collection of the author's books and also survey the store's ample stocks of London memorabilia.

On the hill road between Glen Ellen and Jack London State Park, the ter-

THE VALLEY'S PARKS ON HORSEBACK

Suitable for beginners and seasoned riders alike, horseback rides of one- or two-hours' duration are an exceptionally enjoyable way of touring Jack London State Historic Park and Sugarloaf Ridge State Park. For details, contact the Sonoma Cattle Company: tel. 707 996 8566.

RECOMMENDED HOTELS

GLEN ELLEN

Jack London Lodge, $$; 13740 *Arnold Grove; tel.* 707 938 8510; *credit cards,* MC, V.

Unelaborate but spacious rooms with private bathrooms and very appealing rates; close to the road leading to Jack London State Historic Park and next door to the popular and unpretentious local watering hole, the Jack London Saloon.

KENWOOD

Kenwood Inn, $$$$; 10400 *Sonoma Highway; tel.* 707 833 1293; *credit cards,* AE, MC, V.

Modelled on an Italian villa, the Kenwood Inn occupies a set of stone buildings – the walls and arched entrances decorated with hanging plants – and offers four luxuriously-appointed suites to satisfy the most demanding sybarite.

SONOMA

El Dorado Hotel, $$$-$$$$; 405 *1st Street* W.; *tel.* 707 996 3030; *credit cards,* AE, MC, V.

In one form or another, the El Dorado has been around since Sonoma's Mexican days. Given a total face-lift a few years ago, the hotel now strikes a balance between contemporary comfort and making the most of its history. Excellently placed, too, on Sonoma's plaza.

Sonoma Hotel, $$-$$$; 110 W. *Spain Street; tel.* 707 996 2996; *credit cards,* AE, DC, MC.

Also on the town's historic plaza, the Sonoma Hotel has been accommodating travellers since the early 1900s and many of the rooms in what is now an amply-sized bed-and-breakfast inn retain the mood of times past. Five of the 17 rooms have private bathrooms – in which clawfoot tubs are a popular feature – and breakfast is a lightweight affair of fruit, pastries and fruit juice.

Victorian Garden Inn, $$$–$$$$; 316 E. *Napa Street; tel.* 707 996 5339; *credit cards,* AE, MC, V.

Choose between the less costly rooms in the main building or venture through the effusive gardens to the decadent Wood Cutter's Cottage – a luxurious log cabin which comes complete with fireplace and extra-large clawfoot bathtub.

raced vineyards of the **Glen Ellen Winery** (tel. 707 935 3000), have produced noted Chardonnay and Cabernet Sauvignon. The winery holds daily tastings and conducts guided tours at weekends.

JACK LONDON STATE HISTORIC PARK

The title of Jack London's 1913 book, *Valley of the Moon*, bestowed a lasting nickname to the Sonoma Valley, even though the Oakland-born writer had mistranslated a Native American word when coining the phrase. Nonetheless, there was no doubting London's enthusiasm for the area when he bought 800 grassy acres of it – the site of what is now the Jack London State Historic Park – building an experimental farm and the 26-room Wolf House to house himself and his wife on what he named the Beauty Ranch.

Sadly, the farm and much of the Wolf House were destroyed by an arson attack shortly after completion, and London himself perished in 1916. Walking trails through the park reach the surprisingly substantial remains of the Wolf House, on what was London's pioneering farm, and the modest cottage where he and his wife lived after the Wolf House's destruction. London is buried in the park, too: his grave sited on a grassy knoll.

In the park's **House of Happy Walls**, built by London's widow, the writer's eventful life is documented with collections of letters, page proofs, numerous first editions and translations, and paraphernalia from London's socialist political campaigns in Oakland and his travels across the South Pacific.

KENWOOD ×

A cluster of wineries provides the bulk of the visitor interest in Kenwood. If you only have time to call on one, make it **Chateau St. Jean**, 8555 Sonoma Highway (tel. 707 833 4134), famed for its beautifully landscaped grounds as much as for its white wines. Among the village's other wineries, **Kenwood Vineyards**, 9592 Sonoma Highway (tel. 707 833 5891), was founded in 1906 by two Italian brothers who sold their produce door to door; meanwhile, two contemporary brothers, the Smothers Brothers comedy duo, are behind **Smothers Brothers Wines**, 9575 Sonoma Highway (tel. 707 833 1010).

The only alternative to sampling the produce of Kenwood's wineries is **Morton's Hot Springs**, a recreational complex with picnic facilities grown up around three swimming-pools fed by natural warm springs – a likely place for a day spent doing very little.

DETOUR - **BUENA VISTA WINERY**

Two miles outside Sonoma on the aptly-named Old Winery Road, the **Buena Vista Winery** (tel. 707 938 1266) was founded in 1857 by Agoston Haraszthy. A Hungarian count who arrived in the U.S. in 1840. Haraszthy tried wine-making in other parts of California before settling in Sonoma, attracted by the quality of the wines produced by General Vallejo. Haraszthy's commercial success is credited with stimulating the state's 19thC wine-producing boom. Always a flamboyant and controversial character, Haraszthy departed in the 1860s to grow sugar in Nicaragua, where he later died by drowning.

SONOMA ×

Sonoma's modest size belies its rich and colorful history. Site of the state's last and most northerly Spanish mission and a major center during California's Mexican era, Sonoma was also the site of the Bear Flag Revolt, which declared California an independent republic and pre-empted the switch to U.S. rule soon after.

Enclosed by many 19thC adobe buildings – all of them much restored and many converted to hotels, shops and restaurants – the center of Sonoma life is the tree-studded 8-acre plaza laid out in 1835 by General Mariano Vallejo, the founder of the town and a major California landowner in his time.

If local history seems unfathomably complex, visiting the buildings which make up the **Sonoma State Historic Park** (main entrance at 20 E. Spain Street, although there are no fixed boundaries) should make matters clearer. Within the park stand the remains of **Mission San Francisco Solano**, founded in 1823, the last and

• *Sonoma, the City Hall.*

most northerly of California's Spanish missions and the only one completed under Mexican rule. When its original church collapsed, Vallejo oversaw construction of the mission's adobe chapel, which still stands, as do the 1825 living quarters – Sonoma's oldest surviving structure.

Opposite the mission buildings, the two-story **Sonoma Barracks** date from the late 1830s and originally housed the modest garrison of Mexican soldiers posted to guard this northerly outpost. The Russian settlement at Fort Ross (see California Overall: 1) was a source of concern for the Mexicans, who owned California, but in 1846 an incursion by a ragged bunch of American fur-trappers prompted Vallejo's surrender and the proclamation of the independent Bear Flag Republic. William Bilde, who lead the fur-trappers and made the declaration of independence, was unaware that U.S. forces had landed at Monterey and taken California as a U.S. possession. Once he found out, the Big Bear Republic was ended. It had lasted just 25 days, and the makeshift bear flag (the root of California's present-day flag) flying above Sonoma's plaza was replaced by the stars and stripes of the U.S.

Also in the park, the former servants' quarters of Vallejo's Casa Grande home – the rest of the building was destroyed by fire in the 1860s – holds exhibitions on the Sonoma Valley's Native Americans.

Vallejo himself adapted to the architectural fancies of California's new rulers by building himself a New England-style house, named **Lachryma Montis**, in 1851. Stuffed with the general's furnishings and providing a cogent outline of his influence on the Sonoma region, the house stands half a mile north of the plaza at the junction of Spain and 3rd Streets.

Still more historic detail of Sonoma's rich heritage forms the temporary displays at the local historical society's **Depot Park Museum**, 270 1st W. Street, although if you have young minds to keep amused, a trip on the quarter-sized 1890s steam-train which journeys through the cleverly-constructed miniature landscapes of **Train Town**, 20264 Broadway, might be more suitable.

SUGARLOAF RIDGE STATE PARK

When the appeal of wineries weakens, leave Hwy-12 along Adobe Canyon Road and twist steadily upward to the entrance to Sugarloaf Ridge State

Park, where lush meadows and woodlands are walled by chaparral-covered ridges. The park's 25 miles of trails range from the simple **Creekside Nature Trail**, which follows a portion of Sonoma Creek – a dribble during summer but a torrent in the spring – to lengthier undertakings reaching the park's upper elevations and its highest point, the 2,700-ft summit of Bald Mountain.

If the prospect of venturing into the park's heartlands appeals but your feet have other ideas, horseback tours are an alternative way to experience its rural pleasures in comparative comfort: for details, see The Valley's Parks on Horseback, page 180.

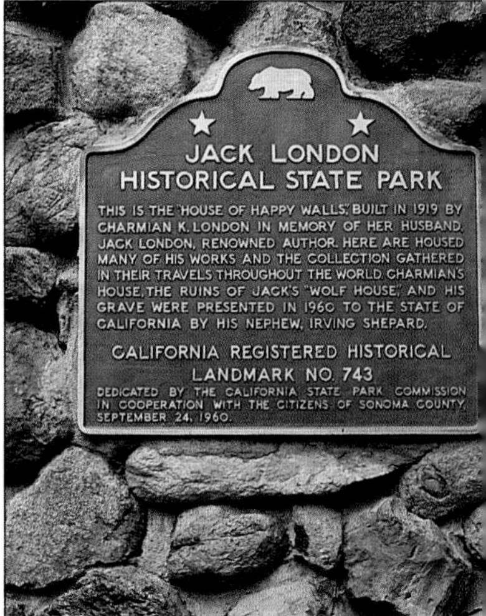

• *The House of Happy Walls, just inside Jack London State Historical Park.*

RECOMMENDED RESTAURANTS

GLEN ELLEN

Glen Ellen Square Deli, $; 13647 *Arnold Drive; tel.* 707 996 4400; *credit cards, none.*

A fine place for a quick, inexpensive lunch – load your tray from an array of cold pastas and salad ingredients, and pay for your meal by its weight – and eat at one of the four tables.

KENWOOD

Oreste's Golden Bear Restaurant, $$-$$$; 1717 *Adobe Canyon Road; tel.* 707 833 2327; *credit cards,* AE, DC, DS, MC, V.

Occupying a 35-acre plot on the way to Sugarloaf Ridge State Park, the effort needed to reach this splendid restaurant is well worthwhile (and a reservation is recommended). Choose from a stunning selection of northern Italian fare and eat in a leisurely fashion from a shady patio table, overlooking Sonoma Creek. Serves a generous Sunday brunch.

SONOMA

Big Three Cafe, $-$$; 18140 *Sonoma Highway; tel.* 707 938 9000; *credit cards,* AE, MC, V.

Part of the up-market Sonoma Mission Inn, this stylish but affordable diner produces inventively-filled burgers and exotically-topped wood-fired pizzas, along with a wide choice of gluttonous breakfasts and some fine pasta dishes at lunch and dinner.

East Side Oyster Bar & Grill, $–$$; 133 E. *Napa Street; tel.* 707 939 1266; *credit cards,* AE, CB, DC, MC, V.

For lunch or dinner, this stylish and busy restaurant offers a quality selection of seafood – be it New Orleans-style fried oyster or Giant California salmon – plus a few meat and vegetarian dishes. Dinner reservations are recommended.

Feed Store Cafe & Bakery, $; 529 *1st Street* W; *tel.* 707 938 2122; *credit cards, none.*

Drop in for a pick-me-up espresso coffee and a snack from the mouth-watering produce of the bakery; alternatively, linger longer over a full meal – a choice of omelettes, sandwiches and salads offered in a bright and cheerful setting.

Piatti, $$-$$$; 405 *1st Street* W; *tel.* 707 996 2351; *credit cards,* AE, MC, V.

The ground floor of the El Dorado Hotel (see page180) is taken up by this much-admired restaurant specializing in Italian regional fare. The pastas and pizzas are seldom short of excellent, while the grilled seafood is often exceptional. Whatever you order, be sure to leave space for one of the dreamy desserts.

Central California

San Francisco's East Bay and Peninsula Area

160 miles (one way); map Kummerley + Frey *California-Nevada*

Ideal as a two-day break from San Francisco or readily combined with a longer journey along the Central Coast (California Overall: 5), this tour explores the communities which face the city from the east side of San Francisco Bay and picks out the highlights – inland and coastal – of the peninsula at the head of which San Francisco sits.

Should you be approaching from the Central Coast, it is easy to split the tour into two parts, travelling along the peninsula to visit San Francisco before completing the East Bay portion of the route. As usual, the tour can be undertaken in either direction.

Though easily appreciated in little more than half a day, the two main communities of San Francisco's East Bay could hardly be more different. Berkeley has a world-famous university which warrants an hour or two's exploration, and the town's diverse restaurants – some serving excellent low-cost food, others pioneers of California Cuisine – make excellent lunch stops. Nearby, the more downbeat town of Oakland draws fewer tourists, even though the Oakland Museum is unrivalled as the premier historical collection hereabouts.

The freeway-dominated suburbia which covers the peninsula's neck is an unattractive introduction to San Jose, although the sprawling town's environs are studded by unusual sights and distinctive villages. If you have sufficient time on your first day, include a visit to another seat of learning: Stanford University.

Alternatively, you might leave Stanford until your second day and combine it with a leisurely exploration of Santa Cruz, a pleasurable coastal town which began life as a Spanish mission and where you should spend at least one of your two nights.

From Santa Cruz, it is easy to continue south along the Central Coast but I recommend that you complete the tour by following the coast northwards to Half Moon Bay. Set on a lovely strip of shoreline and with 19thC buildings in abundance, Half Moon Bay has all the history and small-town charm you could expect, and I guarantee that you will feel like spending your second night here. An early booking should secure an atmospheric lodging at one of the town's cozy bed-and-breakfast inns.

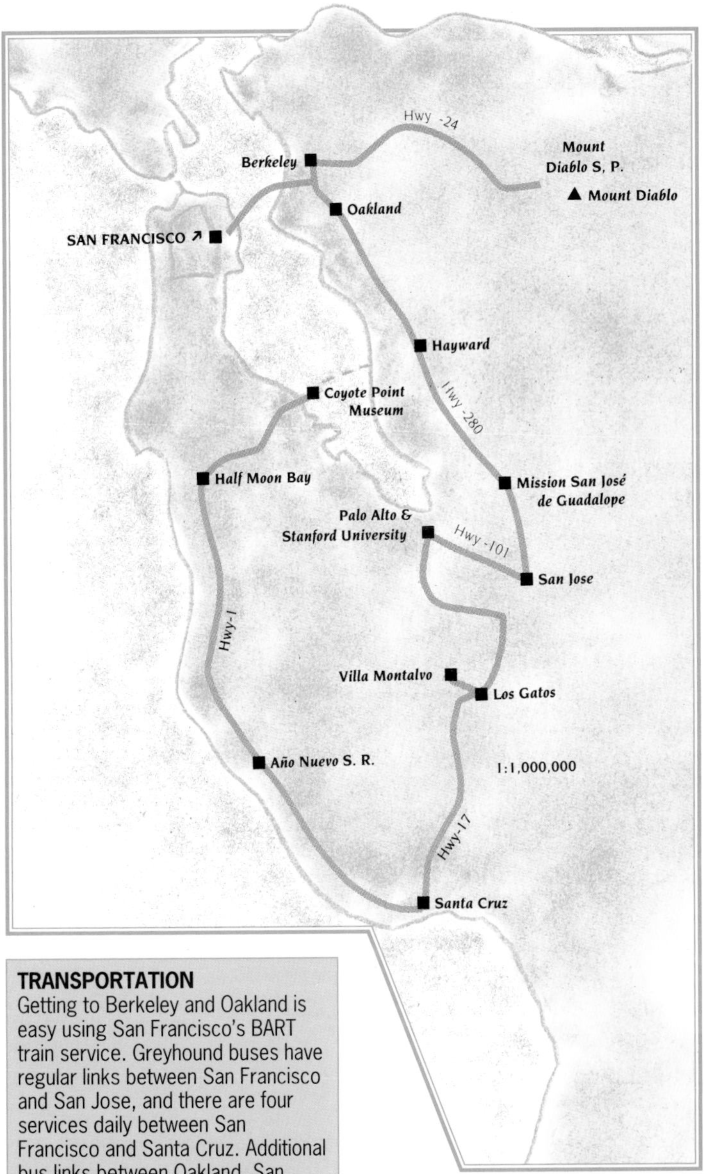

TRANSPORTATION

Getting to Berkeley and Oakland is easy using San Francisco's BART train service. Greyhound buses have regular links between San Francisco and San Jose, and there are four services daily between San Francisco and Santa Cruz. Additional bus links between Oakland, San Jose and Santa Cruz are provided by Peerless Stages (tel. 408 423 1800).The CalTrain is a state-of-the-art train link chiefly aimed at moving commuters between San Francisco, Palo Alto (for Stanford University) and San Jose (where a CalTrain bus continues to Santa Cruz), though services run throughout the day and also – albeit to a reduced timetable – on weekends.

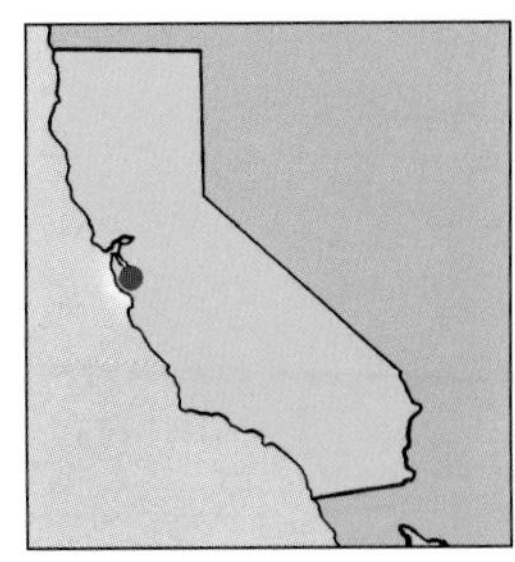

SIGHTS & PLACES OF INTEREST

ANO NUEVO STATE RESERVE

Between December and March, thousands of elephant seals – sea mammals weighing up to three tons – come ashore at Año Nuevo State Reserve to indulge in noisy mating rituals: the males demonstrate their strength before copulating vigorously with 50 or so females. Large crowds of humans go goggled-eyed at this unforgettable spectacle: to join them, reserve a place on the three-hour ranger-led tour; contact Mistix, tel. 800 444 7275.

BERKELEY ×

The idea of California as a hotbed of anarchy, radical ecology, religious cults, and a thousand and one other offbeat beliefs comes closer to being realized in Berkeley than in any other place in the state.

In the early 1960s, the Berkeley campus of the University of California was the birthplace of the Free Speech Movement, the stimulus for the vast anti-Vietnam War rallies which were rocking American society to its foundations by the end of the decade, and the town has been synonymous with People Power – in all its guises – ever since.

The campus and its 30,000 students dominate the town although Berkeley rebelliousness is by no means a student-only phenomenon. Many 1960s graduates are now among the left-leaning intellectuals and professionals who reside in comfortable homes in the surrounding hillsides, and Berkeley's local government is among the most liberal in the U.S.

Whatever your own attitudes may be, you would need to be a very wet blanket indeed not to get some fun out of a few hours in Berkeley, discovering for yourself why it's nicknamed "Berserkely." The **campus** should be your center of attention, but take time to explore the used bookshops and funky food stops along **Telegraph Avenue**, which leads from the university's main entrance.

The university has several worthwhile museums but a first stop – after passing along the makeshift student-run stalls along **Sproul Plaza** dispensing political and environmental literature – should be the elegant **Campanile**. Built in 1914 and modelled on the belltower of St. Mark's in Venice, the Campanile's tower can be ascended by elevator and the views stretch far across the campus and on to San Francisco Bay.

Among the university's historical collections, the **Bancroft Library** mounts changing exhibitions from its colossal stock of rare books and manuscripts, and permanently displays the nugget claimed to have started the state's gold-rush in 1846. The **Lowie Museum** displays selections from its enormous anthropological stash, though you should look in particular for the section devoted to Ishi. The lone survivor of a Native American tribe decimated by white settlers, Ishi lived in the university's anthropological department from 1911 until his death, after

DETOUR – **COYOTE POINT MUSEUM**

Travelling inland from Half Moon Bay along Hwy-92 to San Mateo not only carries you across a large rift caused by the San Andreas Fault, but leaves you within easy reach of Coyote Point. Here, the computers, dioramas and films of the **Coyote Point Museum** provide an exceptionally informative account of the natural life of San Francisco Bay.

DETOUR – **MOUNT DIABLO**

California's Native Americans and early Spanish explorers both ascribed supernatural powers to what the latter named **Mount Diablo**, or Devil's Mountain. On a sunny day at least, the mountain is a far from hellish place to be, the outlook from its 3,849-ft summit reaching far across northern California and south to the Sierra Nevadas.

To reach the mountain, leave Berkeley on Hwy-24 and then head south on I-680, shortly taking the turn-off for Danville and joining the Diablo Road for Mount Diablo State Park.

catching a cold, three years later.

Elsewhere in Berkeley, devotees of Californian cuisine might like to make the pilgrimage to the "**Gourmet Ghetto**" of Shattuck Avenue, where that particular culinary genre came into being during the 1970s – for eating suggestions, see Recommended Restaurants, page 19.

HALF MOON BAY 🛏 ✕

Born as a farming town and more recently protected from over-development by rustically-inclined refugees from suburbia staking out their own plot of Californian coastal heaven, Half Moon Bay is known throughout the state for its Halloween pumpkins,

DETOUR – **VILLA MONTALVO**

Head west from Los Gatos along Hwy-9 into Saratoga and watch for signs for Villa Montalvo. Complete with terraced gardens, arboretum and bird sanctuary, the 19-room villa was the former home of James D. Phelan, one-time U.S. senator and three times mayor of San Francisco. Since Phelan's death in 1930, the building has served as a home for the few writers and painters lucky enough to become the recipients of an arts endowment bequeathed by Phelan. Numerous cultural events take place in and around the villa's buildings – and the grounds make a great picnic setting.

• *Rodin at Stanford University, Palo Alto.*

grown in local fields and celebrated with a Pumpkin Festival every October. Rich-in-character Victorian buildings house the gift-shops, cafes and bakeries which line Half Moon Bay's streets, and peaceful swaths of beach lie on either side of the town.

HAYWARD

Now consumed by East Bay suburbia, in the mid-19thC Hayward enjoyed the wealth and prestige which stemmed from its role as a supply stop on the route to California's gold mines. Past glories are documented by the **Hayward Historical Society Museum**, 22701 Main Street. A look around the spacious interiors of the **McConaghy House**, 18701 Hesperian Boulevard, will demonstrate how rich townsfolk enjoyed life during the late 1800s.

LOS GATOS

Expensive hillside homes line the lanes of Los Gatos and the quaint Old Town section has dozens of pricey boutiques. The town is really best appreciated without stopping, although if you are in the mood, the science and nature displays of **Los Gatos Museum**, corner of Main and Tait streets, will pass an hour or so – as will bouncing along on the **Billy Jones Wildcat Railroad** in Oak Meadow Park, junction of University Avenue and Blossom Hill Road.

MISSION SAN JOSE DE GUADALOPE

Though it gave its name to the town of San Jose, Mission San José de Guadalope stands at 43300 Mission Boulevard on the eastern edge of the bland residential community of Fremont. Founded in 1797, the mission was the 14th in the Spanish-built chain across California and its intimate interior (greatly benefiting from a $5-million restoration in the 1980s) and small museum provide a taste of the trials and tribulations of the mission era.

RECOMMENDED HOTELS

HALF MOON BAY

Old Thyme Inn, $$-$$$; 779 *Main Street; tel.* 415 726 1616; *credit cards,* AE, MC, V.

An 1890s Queen Anne cottage now providing relaxing bed-and-breakfast accommodation in a choice of reposefully-painted rooms, all of them named after a particular spice. Actual spices, grown in the grounds, enliven the breakfast dishes.

Mill Rose Inn, $$$$; 615 *Mill Street; tel.* 415 726 9794; *credit cards,* AE, MC, V.

One of California's most elegant – and most highly priced – bed-and-breakfast establishments, the Mill Rose Inn has an English theme running through its elaborate decoration, and its rooms retain a tranquil mood despite being well-equipped with modern devices such as fridges and (optional) VCRs. Complimentary wine is served each evening.

SANTA CRUZ

Darling House, $$–$$$$; 314 *West Cliff Drive; tel.* 408 458 1958; *credit cards,* AE, DS, MC, V.

Set on a cliff top nicely distanced from the busy Broadwalk – though within an easy walk of it – the Darling House is a 1910 Craftsman mansion which retains many of its original features. At breakfast, you can enjoy the view of the ocean through the living/dining-room's picture window.

Dream Inn, $$$-$$$$; 175 *W. Cliff Drive; tel.* 408 426 4330; *credit cards,* AE, CB, DC, MC, V.

The rates at this only slightly-above average hotel may seem extortionate, but the view of the town's shoreline from your private balcony is what raises the tariff. Along with the sea view, rooms have fridges or minibars, and the hotel sports a heated swimming-pool and an open-air jacuzzi.

Sunset Inn, $$; 2424 *Mission Street; tel.* 408 423 3471; *credit cards,* AE, DC, MC, V.

For room size and facilities, this is one of the best-priced of Santa Cruz's many motels; a few of the rooms are equipped with kitchens.

OAKLAND

A major port and rail terminus, Oakland has long been the gritty counterpart to its liberal neighbor, Berkeley. Nonetheless, Oakland has much more to offer than Jack London Square, mainly for day-trippers, would suggest – it is a waterside shopping complex of minor appeal named after the locally-born writer.

The core of the town lies across I-88 (the elevated freeway which cuts through the town), where the grand 19thC homes of the **Old Oakland** area, between 7th and 10th Streets and Broadway and Jefferson Street, sit just north of a compact and energetic **Chinatown** district.

Continuing south, the **Oakland Museum**, corner of 10th and Oak Streets, has copious art and natural science exhibits but earns top marks for its extensive, candid and entertaining accounts of California's history, including a recreated beat generation coffee bar and genuine 1967 hippie paraphernalia. Nearby, the tree-shaded walkways fringing the expansive **Lake Merritt** are where Oaklanders walk their dogs or hire paddle boats for a leisurely afternoon afloat.

PALO ALTO AND STANFORD UNIVERSITY ✕

Except for a number of inexpensive eating places (see Recommended Restaurants, page 19), the sum of visitor interest in Palo Alto is the 8,000-acre campus of Stanford University, a privately-run body of learning founded by railway magnate Leland Stanford in 1885 and specializing in producing conservative-minded lawyers, doctors and scientists, some of whom have contributed to the inventions which reputedly bring the university $5 million a year in royalties.

Designed by Frederick Law Olmstead, a co-architect of New York's Central Park, a grand driveway leads into the university's mission-style Main Quad. A climb to the top of **Hoover Tower** – named after Herbert Hoover, one-time U.S. President and Stanford student – will reveal the far-flung nature of the sprawling campus and leave you in no doubt that further exploration is best undertaken with the aid of the free shuttle buses which leave from the Main Quad.

Works by Rodin in the **Cantor Sculpture Garden** and the Asian and Egyptian collections of the **Stanford University Museum of Art** are well worth seeing, but for anyone who knows nothing about particle physics but would like to, the graduate-guided tours of the **Stanford Linear Accelerator Center** (reservations: tel. 415 926 2204) – a device which fires electrons along a two-mile course – will be the undisputed campus highlight.

BUDGET ACCOMMODATION

Santa Cruz Youth Hostel; 511 *Broadway; tel.* 408 423 8304.

Point Montara Lighthouse Hostel; *near Montara on Hwy-1 4 miles N of Half Moon Bay; tel.* 415 428 7177.

SAN FRANCISCO

See pages 110-137.

SAN JOSE

The booming computer industry of the early 1980s turned San Jose into a sleek, charmless and smog-blighted community the center of which was colloquially named "Silicon Valley" (officially, it is the Santa Clara Valley), an area associated with pioneering electronics since the 1940s. Within San Jose's freeway-caged suburbia, however, are two of California's strangest sights.

No lesser thing than a recreated avenue from the ancient Egyptian town of Thebes serves as the driveway into **Rosicrucian Park**, 1342 Naglee Avenue, where the Rosicrucian Order maintain the **Egyptian Museum**, a world-class collection of amulets, mummies and other objects from Assyria, Babylon and Egypt.

An equally unlikely find is the **Winchester Mystery House**, 525 Winchester Boulevard. The house was financed by Sarah Winchester, heir to the Winchester rifle fortune, who believed herself haunted by the spirits of all those killed by Winchester weapons and certain to die if the house were ever completed. Consequently, construction work continued non-stop for 38 years until Sarah's death in 1921, and resulted in a 160-room house packed with stairways leading

• *Lake Merritt, Oakland.*

nowhere, dead-end corridors, and doors and windows which open on to blank walls. The house is a strange and absorbing place, though one with its atmosphere diluted by a high admission price and far too many commercial trappings.

SANTA CRUZ ×

Collared by redwood-coated hillsides and set above a sculptured bay, Santa Cruz is populated by a curious mix of retired folk, surfers and students, and each weekend accommodates hordes of inland suburbanites arriving to cruise the town's beach-side Boardwalk and revel in its tacky diversions.

The commercial heart of Santa Cruz is along Pacific Garden Mall, where many of the shops were rebuilt following the earthquake of 1989.

Half a mile west, at the coast, the **Boardwalk** was built in 1904, and marks Santa Cruz's determination to market itself as a tourist destination as its logging industry declined. It is a slice of local history which should not be missed regardless of your feelings for its vintage carousel, big dipper, shooting arcades, haunted house, dodgems and cotton candy, and hot dog stands.

Other worthwhile calls are the **Surfing Museum** (in the lighthouse on W. Cliff Drive), with modest but interesting displays tracing the evolution of the sport which began in Hawaii but took off in California following the invention of the lightweight surfboard in the 1950s, and the local history and ecology exhibits of the **City Museum of Natural History**, 1305 E. Cliff Drive.

Worry not if you miss the **Santa Cruz Mission**. Founded in 1791, the original mission was totally ruined by earthquakes, and only an uninteresting half-size replica of it can be seen at 126 High Street, alongside a gift shop storing a few of the original mission items.

On the approach to town, perhaps the only real mystery at the **Mystery Spot** is why thousands flock there year after year: within a redwood grove, carefully manipulated distortions of perspective fool the senses into believing gravity has gone haywire.

RECOMMENDED RESTAURANTS

BERKELEY

Blondie's Pizza, $; 2340 *Telegraph Avenue; tel.* 510 548 1129; *credit cards, none.*

Slices of chewy, greasy pizza served in an establishment which has become a local legend for its surly staff and for being packed with strange characters from morning to night.

The Blue Nile, $-$$; 2525 *Telegraph Avenue; tel.* 510 540 6777; *credit cards,* AE, MC, V.

The joys of Ethiopian food have yet to spread far and wide across California – possibly because Californians have yet to master eating with their fingers – but this restaurant has been providing excellent dishes from the east African country for years, and continues to do so at absurdly low prices.

Chez Panisse, $$-$$$; 1517 *Shattuck Avenue; tel.* 510 548 5525; *credit cards,* AE, MC, V.

Famed among gourmets as the birthplace of California cuisine but much more affordable and enjoyable than you might expect, thanks to the upstairs section where you will be able to sample top-notch creations at a fraction of the price charged in the main eating room downstairs.

HALF MOON BAY

Main Street Grill, $; 435 *Main Street; tel.* 726 5300; *credit cards,* MC, V; *breakfast and lunch only, closed* Wed.

A hearty way to start the day: a mouthwatering selection of fresh-baked muffins and "create-your-own" omelettes – select the fillings of your desire from a wide choice.

San Benito, $-$$; 356 *Main Street; tel.* 415 3425; *cards,* AE, DC, MC, V.

Fine place to stop for a well-prepared lunch, or to linger over a memorable dinner. The dishes bear the imprint of French and Italian cooking, while the varying menu makes the most of fresh ingredients and locally caught seafood.

PALO ALTO

The Good Earth, $; 185 *University Avenue; tel.* 415 321 9449; *credit cards,* AE, MC, V.

Somewhat spartan and lacking in atmosphere but offering a wide selection of dishes made from fresh, natural ingredients using traditional recipes; particularly useful for breakfast omelettes. Fresh fruit juices.

University Creamery, $; 209 *University Avenue; tel.* 415 323 7594; *credit cards, none.*

If you thought all-night diners had long since faded away, this is the place to rediscover the refreshing powers of the frothy milk shake and ketchup-coated burger consumed to the sound of a jumping jukebox.

SANTA CRUZ

Dolphin Restaurant, $–$$; *on the Wharf; tel.* 408 426 5830; *credit cards, none.*

Pricey and over-priced restaurants line Santa Cruz's Wharf, beside the Boadwalk, but not until you reach the very end will you come across the Dolphin Restaurant, which offers excellently-prepared food at reasonable cost in an enjoyable, low-key setting throughout the day.

Santa Cruz Brewing Co. & Front Street Pub, $; 516 *Front Street; tel.* 408 429 8838; *credit cards,* MC, V.

A California version of an English pub, offering several notable home-brewed beers and a dartboard together with generously-sized ploughman's lunches and plates of tasty fish and chips.

Saturn Cafe, $; 1230 *Mission Street; tel.* 408 429 8505; *credit cards, none.*

If you are not a vegetarian when you arrive at the Saturn, you might well be sufficiently impressed to reconstruct your dietary habits after consuming one of the mouth-watering meat-free dishes caringly prepared and served throughout the day.

Central California

The Monterey Peninsula Area

70 miles (one way); map Kummerley + Frey California-Nevada

This itinerary makes a natural three-day stopover while travelling the Northern Central Coast, and includes some of the more fascinating and varied of the region's communities. These lie within a short drive, or in some cases a bicycle ride, of one another, on, or close to, the Monterey Peninsula.

I suggest that you spend your first day in the town of Monterey in order to gain a real sense of California's Spanish and Mexican past. Some of the state's earliest official buildings were cited here and many still stand in an excellent historical park. The Spanish mission originally sited at Monterey mission was moved a few miles south to Carmel where it remains in a community otherwise famed for its dainty, half-timbered cottages – a rare sight indeed in the U.S.

You'll find it makes sense to allocate half your second day to Carmel and the other half to crossing the peninsula by its labyrinthine local roads to Pacific Grove, spread across the northern tip, a quiet residential community with fantastic ocean views that attracts more butterflies than tourists.

You can use the third day to travel east from the peninsula to the inland valleys, which are warm and sunny even when fogs chill the coast. Salinas, the largest valley town, is a reminder of California's role as one of the world's major agricultural producers, but has greater appeal as the birthplace of writer John Steinbeck. Nearby San Juan Bautista has a mission, and a State Historical Park that offers an interesting glimpse into the California of the late 1800s.

The accommodation suggestions span the whole range, from standard chain hotels to a converted dairy farm. As usual, cost, comfort and atmosphere are taken into account. This is a popular vacation area, so be prepared for prices which are higher than usual and try to book several months ahead. That said, one trick of mine that often works is to turn up on spec in the hope of being offered an otherwise unoccupied room at a knock-down rate.

Eating can be expensive, too, although the quality of the restaurants is high. Seafood is plentiful and fresh, while the preponderance of classy European cuisines is one reason why Californians – noted as discerning diners – have a special fondness for the peninsula area.

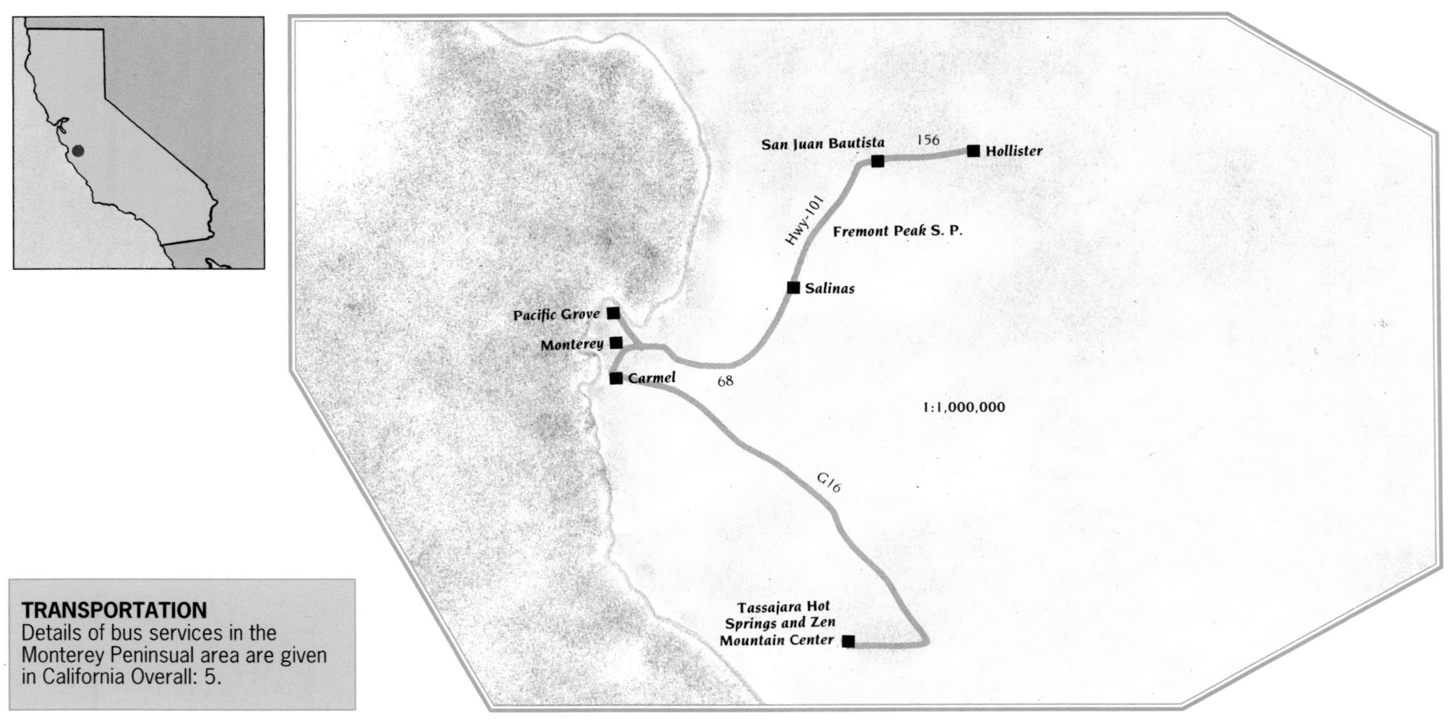

TRANSPORTATION
Details of bus services in the Monterey Peninsual area are given in California Overall: 5.

• *The mission at Carmel.*

SIGHTS & PLACES OF INTEREST

CARMEL 🛏 ×

Among California's most distinctive small communities, Carmel was originally settled by Spanish soldiers, but acquired its first rustic houses when a colony of bohemian writers, painters and academics began settling on pristine ocean-side plots in 1904. By the mid-1920s, the artistic community had run its course and architect Hugh Comstock began filling the town with whimsical wooden (in some cases wood and adobe) cottages to tickle the fancy of moneyed San Franciscans.

Today, Carmel is where the Californian concept of "quaint" finds its ultimate expression. Lines of almost-too-perfect gingerbread structures line short lanes and courtyards. To preserve the fairy-tale – but surprisingly charmless – atmosphere, Carmel's wealthy residents ban traffic lights, fast-food stands and the cutting down of trees, although there's no hesitation when it comes to embracing tourists: souvenir shops and art galleries are everywhere.

An antidote to the picture-postcard cottages is the **Tor House**, on Ocean Avenue, built from granite carried up from the beach (with the aid of horses) by its owner, Robinson Jeffers, who settled in Carmel in 1914. Jeffers' epic poetry made much of the area's commanding landscapes and forged his reputation as one of the leading writers of the American West. Tours of the Tor House (Fri and Sat only) are by reservation only; tel. 408 624 1813.

The high point of a visit to Carmel, however, is the **Carmel Mission**, 3080 Rio Rd. Resited here in 1771 following an unhappy year in Monterey, the mission was the second to be established in California and became the main base of Junípera Serra, the head of the Spanish expedition into California, until his death in 1784.

Undergoing a thorough restoration during the 1930s, the mission is a feast for the eye. The most striking part is the **stone church**, topped by a Moorish tower, with its vaulted interior decorated with oil paintings and wooden images of Christ. The museum sections carry comprehensive displays relating to mission life and the development of the mission chain across California, together with a re-creation of Serra's spartan living quarters and of California's first library: the shelves of which held Serra's 600-volume collection.

Besides some lovely gardens, the mission grounds contain the Indian cemetery, where you should seek out the marker to Old Gabriel, a fellow credited with living 150 years.

HOLLISTER

It may look like a sleepy farming town, but Hollister is at the junction of four of the state's six geological faultlines, bringing the local community more than their share of earthquakes. Fortunately, most quakes aren't severe, a fact borne out by the numerous Victorian buildings standing intact within the small but enjoyable **Old Town** area. Close by, at the junction of West and Anne streets, the **San Benito County Historical Museum** (open weekends only), explains more than anyone might want to know about the town's sheep-ranching origins.

One event of significance not covered in the museum occurred in 1947: the invasion of Hollister by leather-clad motor cyclists, which inspired the seminal 1953 biker film, *The Wild One.*

MONTEREY

Enjoying a pivotal role in early Californian history by dint of the natural harbor which made it a favored landing point, Monterey was settled by the Spanish from 1770, became capital of California through the Spanish and Mexican eras and, after U.S. acquisition, was the site of California's first state government in 1849.

Less glamorously, Monterey spent the first half of the 20thC as the world's largest sardine canning center. The former fish factories along **Cannery Row** are now occupied by lackluster trinket shops aimed at the town's 3 million yearly visitors. Adjoining Fisherman's Wharf, where ocean-going schooners once berthed, now holds seafood restaurants and snack bars.

More evocative of the past are the preserved and restored 19thC structures which form **Monterey State Historic Park** – actually a collection of (mostly) adobe structures dotted amid the banks, shops and supermarkets of downtown Monterey.

A map outlining the park's **Path of History** is widely available around the town, and can also be picked up at the **Coton Hall Museum**, between Jefferson and Madison Streets. The intriguing museum preserves the room and the furnishings which witnessed the drafting of California's first constitution in 1849 and keeps open the **Old Monterey Jail** (entrance at rear of the museum), which incarcerated ne'er-do-wells for more than a hundred years from 1854.

Other places of interest in Monterey are the small former rooming house at 530 Houston St., where Scottish writer Robert Louis Stevenson spent a few weeks in 1879 and which now stocks mementoes of his stay; and the Royal Presidio Chapel, 555 Church St., in use since 1795 and decorated with Native American and Mexican folk art.

Two modern additions to Monterey well worth a look are the **Maritime Museum and History Center**, opposite the Customs House close to Fisherman's Wharf, which details – with models, maps and endless nautical paraphernalia – Monterey's role as a seaport, and the wonderful **Monterey Bay Aquarium** at the western end of Cannery Row, a multi-million dollar facility displaying and describing the secrets of ocean ecology well enough to entertain and educate curious minds for hours.

PACIFIC GROVE

Up until 1969, the sale of alcohol was illegal in Pacific Grove, a reminder of the community's 19thC origins as a Methodist summer retreat and the God-

DETOUR - ZEN MOUNTAIN CENTER

Turn off Hwy-1 at Carmel and drive inland along Carmel Valley Road (G 16). After passing the pricey houses, ranches and golf courses that represent the wealthy residential overspill from the Monterey Peninsula, the road then climbs quickly into the hills between the Santa Lucia and the Sierra de Salinas mountains. Turn right on to Cachagua Road and right again on to Tassajara Road, both narrow, winding mountain roads, for **Tassajara Hot Springs**. The spa resort which opened here in 1904 is now the Zen Mountain Center, a Buddhist retreat. From May to September, visitors are permitted to bathe in the luxuriant springs: the serene setting and the minerals in the water co-operate to create a tremendous sense of well-being.

RECOMMENDED HOTELS

CARMEL

Carmel Village Inn, $$$-$$$$; *corner of* Ocean *Avenue and Junipero Street; tel.* 408 624 3864; *cards* AE, MC, V.

With rooms furnished in a peaceful French rural style overlooking award-winning gardens, the Village Inn is an exceptionally cozy and fairly-priced resting place in the center of Carmel. The suites are equipped with gas fires, fridges and kitchens. A morning paper is delivered to your door; a light breakfast is included in the price.

• *The Village Inn, Carmel.*

Mission Ranch, $$-$$$; 26270 *Delores Street; tel.* 408 624 6436; *credit cards,* AE, CB, DC, MC, V.

A 20-acre former dairy farm close to the Carmel Mission with a choice of fairly standard motel-like accommodation, rooms in the old farmhouse, or fully-renovated 1930s cottages equipped with kitchen facilities. The real reasons for staying here are the fair price and the unbeatable setting: a cypress-lined meadow overlooking the ocean.

MONTEREY

Casa Munras Garden Hotel, $$$-$$$$; 700 *Munras Avenue; tel.* 800 222 2446; *credit cards* AE, CB, DI, MC, V.

Standing apart from the numerous chain hotels which proliferate in and around Monterey, Casa Munras dates from 1824 and fully deserves its setting in the heart of the town's historic district. The hotel section is more recent, but is designed to blend in with the surroundings. Comfortable, airy rooms face the grounds, where you'll find a heated swimming-pool.

Old Monterey Inn, $$$-$$$$; 500 *Martin Street; tel.* 408 375 8284; *credit cards, none.*

Few Californian bed-and-breakfast inns come close to matching the care and concern for detail that has gone into the Old Monterey Inn. The Tudor-style house, erected in 1929 and shaded by towering oak trees, has ten rooms individually furnished, brightened with fresh flowers, and enjoying a view of the garden. Breakfast consists of croissants and muffins served around an oak bench table (or in your room); picnic baskets are prepared on request.

Stagecoach Motel, $$-$$$; 1111 *10th Street; tel.* 408 373 3632; *credit cards* AE, CB, D, MC, V.

Nothing pretentious here, just a well-run, friendly motel that provides accommodation in quiet surroundings. Free coffee is always on offer, and there is an outdoor pool, a sauna, and a coin-operated laundry for guests' use.

PACIFIC GROVE

Gosby House, $$$-$$$$; 643 *Lighthouse Avenue; tel.* 408 373 1287; *credit cards* AE, MC, V.

Bay windows, turrets, and a mass of intricate, decorative woodwork adorn this antique-filled 1887 Queen Anne house. A rambling property (half the fun is simply finding your way around), most of the 22 rooms are equipped with en-suite bathrooms. Its location, far from the tourist hordes of Monterey and Carmel, makes this am exceptional base for exploring the entire peninsula.

BUDGET ACCOMMODATION

MONTEREY

Monterey Peninsula Youth Hostel; *summer only, location changes yearly; tel.* 408 298 0670.

fearing nature of the wealthy and well-to-do folk who have colonized it since. The emphasis of this community on the north-west tip of the Monterey Peninsula is still very much on home life and, unlike neighboring Monterey and Carmel, Pacific Grove doesn't knock itself out to cater to tourists – commercial trappings are refreshingly few.

The main draws are several streets of Victorian houses – linked by the **Historic Trail** – and 3 miles of uplifting panoramas along the aptly-named Ocean View Boulevard.

Visit Pacific Grove between late October and March, though, and your attention will be diverted to the orange-and-black Monarch butterflies which migrate here from Alaska, often hanging in their thousands from branches. The background to the butterfly migration can be discovered in the **Museum of Natural History**, 165 Forest Ave.

Near the museum, Pacific Grove life revolves around the cluster of cafes and shops close to the junction of Lighthouse Avenue and Forest Avenue. A longer-lasting picture of Pacific Grove, however, is provided by a stroll along Ocean View Boulevard – a thoroughfare which fully merits its name and eventually leads to the diminutive **Point Pinos Lighthouse**, on Lighthouse Avenue, erected in 1855 and open on weekend afternoons for free tours.

RECOMMENDED RESTAURANTS

CARMEL

Clam Box, $$-$$$; *on* Mission Street *between* Fifth *and* Sixth *avenues; tel.* 408 624 8597; *dinner only; credit cards,* AE, MC, V.
For its wholesome seafood cooking and informal atmosphere, the Clam Box is patronized by locals as much as out-of-towners. Be warned: it is not a place for light nibbles. The substantial three-course dinners range from rock cod to an entire lobster and include all the trimmings. Service is quick and convivial.

Tuck Box, $; *corner of* Delores *and* Seventh *streets; tel.* 408 624 6365; *credit cards,* AE, MC, V.
Among Carmel's most photographed buildings, this tiny cottage restaurant offers tasty and well-prepared breakfasts and lunches, with a British rather than an American accent. Specialities include Welsh rarebit and shepherd's pie. Drop by in the afternoon and you'll find tea and scones on offer.

MONTEREY

Old Monterey Cafe, $–$$; 489 Alvarado Street; *tel.* 408 646 1021; *credit cards,* AE, CB, DC, MC, V; *breakfast and lunch only, closed* Tues.
A rightly popular downtown eatery epitomizing all that's good about inexpensive eating in California. The breakfast choice spans banana pancakes and four-egg omelettes with the freshest fruit juices; for lunch, changing seafood specials complement a selection of sandwiches and salads.

Whaling Station Inn, $$$; 763 Wave Street; *tel.* 408 373 3778; *dinner only; credit cards* AE, CB, DI, DS, MC, V.
The flickering candles in wrought-iron holders and the crisp creases in the table linen might at first suggest otherwise, but this is the most amenable of Monterey's up-market restaurants. The staff are attentive and the waiters eager to pass on tips for getting the best from the extensive menu, which runs from pasta dishes to mesquite-grilled seafood and steaks; house specialities include pheasant, and lamb with aubergine.

PACIFIC GROVE

The Old Bath House, $$$; 620 Ocean View Boulevard; *tel.* 408 375 5195; *dinner only; credit cards,* AE, CB, DC, MC, V.
Exquisite food and matching ocean views are found at this top-class establishment. The chef brings a Californian touch to dishes inspired by the regional fare of northern Italy and France, doing delicious things with duck, lamb and lobster, alongside a slightly less inventive assortment of steaks and other seafood. The desserts are a point of pride, the wine list is comprehensive, and the service spot-on. Reserve a table.

• *Point Pinos Lighthouse, Pacific Grove.*

SALINAS 🛏

Salinas sees comparatively few visitors, despite being just 18 miles inland from the busy Monterey Peninsula. It is first a farming community and those visitors who do show up are usually attracted by the town's links with author John Steinbeck, who was born here in 1902 and featured Salinas – and its agricultural workers – in many of his books.

It's taken time, but Salinas is finally waking up to the tourist interest – and money – that their only literary son might generate. A $35-million plot of shops and offices called **Steinbeck Square** is currently under construction on the 100 block of Main Street. Intended to include the up-market Steinbeck Hotel and the permanent base of the **Steinbeck Foundation** (currently mounting temporary exhibitions on the writer at 371 Main Street), Steinbeck Square marks the town's recognition of the man regarded "as popular as lettuce blight" in the town during his lifetime. For his part, Steinbeck said of Salinas: "They want no part of me except in a pine box."

Steinbeck was born in 1902 in an elegant house which still stands at 132 Central Avenue, known as **Steinbeck House,** and earns its living by hosting gourmet lunches. Free tours of the

DETOUR – THE 17-MILE DRIVE

This is a signposted route through the western side of the Monterey Peninsula between Carmel and Pacific Grove. Much of the route is private land (which explains the $5.75 toll). The views of craggy headlands and the gale-defying Lone Cypress Tree – and the district's multi-million-dollar homes – can be astounding. Maps of the drive are issued at the entry gates.

BICYCLE TOUR – SHORELINE BIKE PATH

A healthy, cheap, and equally attractive alternative to The 17-Mile Drive, is to rent a bike in Monterey and cycle the Shoreline Bike Path between Fisherman's Wharf and Lover's Point in Pacific Grove (a 6-mile round trip). With energy to spare, continue from Lover's Point to Point Pinos, a further 3 miles. Bay Bikes (tel. 408 646 9090) offer bike rental from outlets in Monterey, 640 Wave Street, and Carmel, on Lincoln Street between 5th and 6th Streets.

> DETOUR – **FREMONT PEAK STATE PARK**
> Drive 11 miles south from San Juan Bautista along San Juan Canyon Road and you ascend to the tree-studded ridges of Fremont Peak State Park, giving views across the Monterey Peninsula. At night, distanced from polluting cities, the sky here is exceptionally clear and the park's Fremont Peak Observatory hosts entertaining evening astronomical talks during the summer. For details tel. 408 623 4255.

house are available, however, for anyone who knocks on the door between 10 am and 11 am Tuesday to Friday or between 2.30 and 3.00 pm Monday to Thursday. Another worthwile call is to the John Steinbeck Public Library, 110 W. San Luis Street, which displays photographs, manuscripts, first editions, and plays taped interviews relating to the Nobel Prize-winning writer.

Still the big event in Salinas, however, is the California Rodeo: four days of bronco-taming, lasso throwing, campfire cooking, and more, which comes to town each July.

The rodeo takes place in a purpose-built stadium a few miles north of the town center beside Hwy-101. On the stadium's south side, the Rodeo Heritage Collection (for times, tel. 408 757 2951) stores a small but entertaining collection of memorabilia.

SAN JUAN BAUTISTA

The mission at San Juan Bautista, founded in 1797 partly to shield the Monterey Peninsula from Native American raiding parties, boasts the largest of all the Californian mission churches, completed in 1812. Though the church continues to serve the local community and the mission is generally well-preserved, of more abiding interest are the buildings of **San Juan Bautista State Historic Park**, facing the mission across the town's Spanish plaza.

• *Monarch butterflies.*

Central California

Sierra Nevada Foothills: Gold Country

110 miles (one way); map Kummerley + Frey California-Nevada

Winding along Hwy-49 through the rolling foothills of the Sierra Nevada mountains, this short tour – one night – passes through the small towns which have barely changed in appearance since the gold-rush days of the 1840s triggered their settlement. As usual, the journey can be undertaken in either direction. To the north, the tour links neatly with California Overall: 2 at Placerville; in the south at Mariposa, it leaves you perfectly placed to continue to (or to join the tour from) Yosemite National Park (Local Explorations: 13).

Unlike the larger, more modernized towns of the Northern Mines (explored in California Overall: 2), the communities of the Southern Mines lie far from freeways and the state's present-day population centers. In some, like Angels Camp (typical of the area's eccentricities, Angels Camp has a curious relationship with frogs) and Jamestown, the tourist appeal of wooden awnings and wooden sidewalks is milked to the maximum and gift shops and boutiques are everywhere. In others, such as Coulterville and Mokelumne Hill, things seem barely to have altered in a hundred years, and I feel nothing better epitomizes the true nature of the Gold Country than pushing through the swing-door entrance to the local saloon in one of these evocative towns.

The peaceful and verdant landscapes of the region – these days, many local livelihoods depend on the apple orchards which cover the hillsides – do little to suggest the violence of the frontier days, when some of these now placid towns had mines which produced millions of dollars' worth of gold and held single-male dominated populations where heavy drinking, brawling and vigilante hangings were commonplace.

Evidence to bring alive that period lies within the small but copiously-stocked historical museums, of which every town has one, and which, after the picture-postcard Old West architecture loses its novelty appeal, provide the region's main source of interest.

If you're making this journey, do it between April and October: outside these months, snowfalls are likely and many museums and visitor services are closed.

TRANSPORTATION
Greyhound buses from Sacramento call several times a day at Placerville, but there is no public transportation elsewhere on this tour.

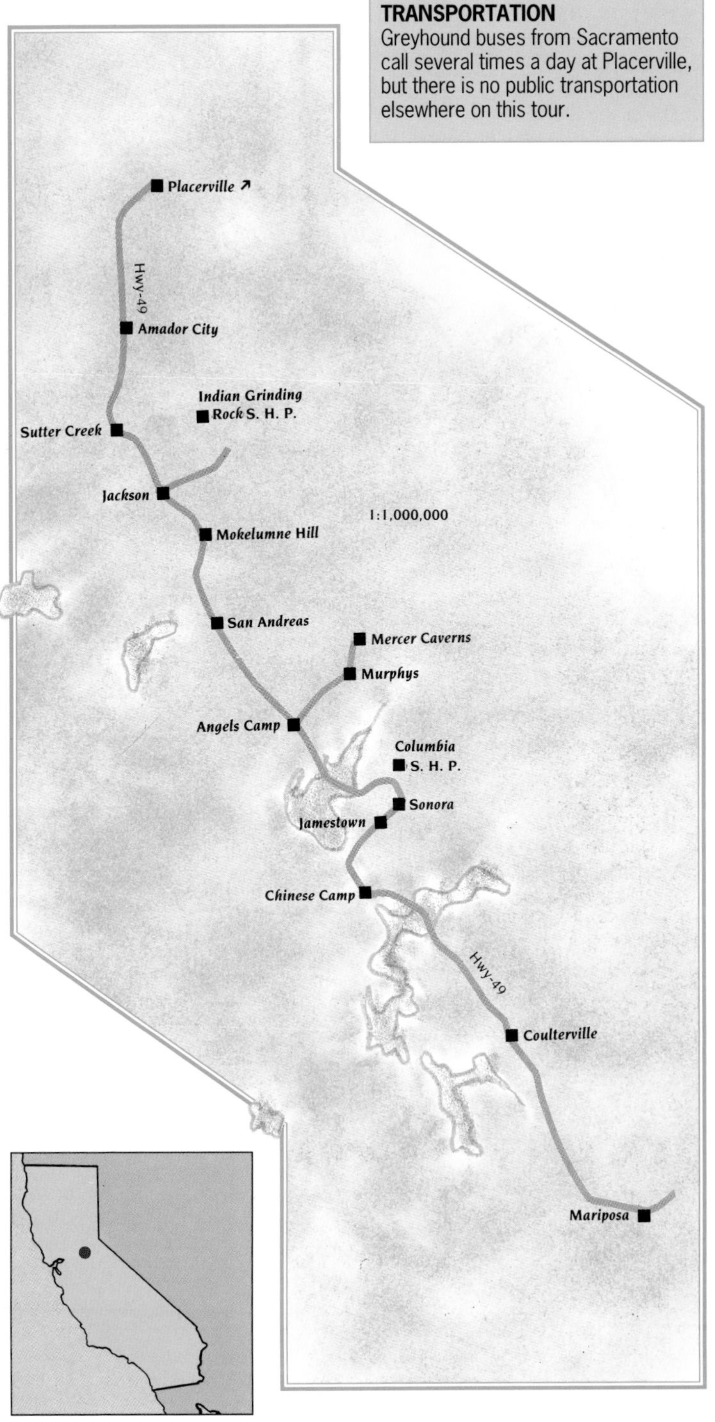

SIGHTS & PLACES OF INTEREST

AMADOR CITY
Blink and you'll miss it, but Amador City is officially a city – the smallest in California – with just a handful of houses, cafes, art and antique shops, and the stately **Imperial Hotel**, providing a few minutes' diversion as you pass through on Hwy-49.

ANGELS CAMP 🛏 ✕
One night in the 1860s, Mark Twain was relaxing in the bar of Angels Camp's Hotel Angels, 1227 Main Street, when he heard the miners' tale about jumping frogs which inspired his short story, *The Celebrated Jumping Frog of Calaveras County*, which later became the title of his first published collection.

How much truth there is in this tale – or indeed in Twain's story of a jumping frog competition – is open to debate, but since 1928 Angels Camp has had few qualms about cashing in on its literary links by staging (each May) a Jumping Frogs Jamboree, in which frogs compete over three measured hops for a $1,000 prize in front of hundreds of spectators.

While frog-related motifs are now found all over the town, Angels Camp was once a highly productive mining center, yielding 19 million dollars' worth of gold between 1886 and 1910. The fine points of local history are detailed in the **Angels Camp Museum**, 753 Main Street.

> DETOUR – **MURPHYS AND MERCER CAVERNS**
>
> Nine miles east of Angels Camp on Hwy-4, the mining village of Murphys was named after the two Irish brothers who founded it in 1848. Murphys's Main (and more or less only) Street holds the **Murphys Hotel**, which opened in 1856 and early on hosted luminaries such as writer Bret Harte, financier J.P. Morgan and future U.S. president, Ulysses S. Grant. The restaurant of the ramshackle hotel makes a useful lunch stop; afterwards poke your head around the tiny town's **Oldtimer's Museum**.
>
> With time to spare, make a three-mile detour from Murphys along Sheep Ranch Road for the nature-sculpted crystalline formations deep within **Mercer Caverns**, revealed on guided tours.

> DETOUR – **INDIAN GRINDING ROCK STATE HISTORIC PARK**
>
> Eight miles east of Jackson on Hwy-88, a large chunk of limestone is indented by thousands of chaw'se, or mortar cups, created by many generations of Miwok Indians using the rock to grind nuts. The rock stands in **Indian Grinding Rock State Historic Park**, where its use – and local Native American life – is described by the Museum Cultural Center.

CHINESE CAMP
Today, only crumbling ruins and a small visitors' center in the 1854 General Store mark the spot, but in 1851 a fifth of California's 250,000 Chinese gold-miners were living in Chinese Camp. California's Chinese migrants provided labor for the mines and later toiled on the transcontinental railway before being forced to band together in Chinatown districts by the racism which flared during the post-gold-rush depression, and which was compounded by the U.S.'s anti-immigration laws of the 1890s.

COLUMBIA STATE HISTORIC PARK
Thriving Columbia narrowly lost the vote to become California's state capital in 1854 and the defeat sealed its fate: as soon as its mines closed down, so too did the town. With Columbia State Historic Park, however, a re-created gold-rush town has grown up around the ruins of the original Columbia, complete with grizzled banjo players, a rowdy saloon, a fearsome dentist's surgery and stage-coaches cruising the dusty streets. Hangings and lynchings may be conspicuous by their absence, but impressive attention to detail makes the park an essential Gold Country stop.

COULTERVILLE
A town relatively untarnished by tourism, many of Coulterville's mining-era stone buildings remain in an unre-

• *Hanging around, Jamestown.*

stored condition along Main Street. One of them in a decent state of repair is the former Wells Fargo office, which is now occupied by the absorbing **Northern Mariposa County History Center**.

JACKSON

Placer miners – who panned for gold in rivers – first settled Jackson but the community's wealth was created by machine-worked gold mines. With some reaching a mile below ground, Jackson's mines were the deepest and, sadly, were the scene of the one of U.S.'s worst mining disasters – 47 miners losing their lives here in 1922. Sited on a hill above the pocket-sized town center, the **Amador County Museum**, 225 Church Street, outlines gold-mining techniques and the local political wranglings which created tiny Amador County, of which Jackson is the seat.

JAMESTOWN ✕

Anyone whose vision of the Old West includes a high-pitched whistle and clouds of steam as an "iron horse" thunders along railroad tracks will find

Jamestown's **Railtown 1897 State Historic Park** much to their liking. The park preserves four steam locomotives, assorted rolling-stock, and many weighty tools which belonged to the Sierra Railroad Company, which began moving people and cargo around the Gold Country in 1897.

MARIPOSA

Proximity to Yosemite National Park causes many people to pass through Mariposa, and few take the trouble to stop and explore the intriguing gold-rush paraphernalia assembled in the town's **Mariposa Museum and History Center**, corner of 12th and Jessie Streets. Interestingly, while the grand 1854 **Mariposa County Courthouse**, 5808 Bullion Street, is California's longest continuously used place of justice, the neighboring **Old Mariposa Jail** continued to house felons until 1960.

RECOMMENDED HOTELS

ANGELS CAMP

Gold Country Inn, $$; 720 *Main Street; tel.* 209 736 4611; *credit cards,* AE, DS, MC, V.

Unelaborate but comfortable motel on the edge of town, ideal for a reasonably priced one-night stopover.

SONORA

Ryan House, $; 153 S. *Shepherd St; tel.* 800 831 4897; *credit cards,* AE, DS, MC, V.

A rose garden, a library and a wood-burning stove add to the charm of this mid-19thC miners' cabin now converted to provide four antique-filled bed-and-breakfast rooms in a wonderfully quiet location.

Sonora Inn, $-$$; 160 S. *Washington Street; tel.* 209 532 7468; *credit cards,* AE, DC, DS, MC, V.

A Victorian hotel which was given a mission-style remodelling in the 1920s and recently underwent a complete interior modernization.The blend of old and new makes it a pleasant place to stay.

SUTTER CREEK

Sutter Creek Inn, $$-$$$; 75 *Main Street; tel.* 209 267 5606; *credit cards, none.*

Enthusiasts of California-style bed-and-breakfast should find a spare night to spend at the Sutter Creek, partly for the invitingly furnished rooms and no-holds barred country breakfast, but also because this was the state's first bed-and-breakfast inn, opened in the 1960s long before the concept was fashionable.

RECOMMENDED RESTAURANTS

ANGELS CAMP

Country Kitchen, $; 1246 *Main Street; tel.* 209 736 2941; *credit cards, none.*

In a town with limited eating options, the Country Kitchen is a welcome no-frills eatery plying an inexpensive line in filling breakfasts and lunches.

JAMESTOWN

Jamestown Hotel, $-$$; 18153 *Main Street; tel.* 209 984 3902; *credit cards,* AE, DC, MC, V.

The dining-room of a restored 19thC hotel, this probably has the most appealing setting of any Gold Country restaurant. With a choice of seasonal dishes, the food is not bad either.

SONORA

Hemingway's, $-$$; 362 S. *Stewart Street; tel.* 209 532 4900; *credit cards,* AE, MC, V; *closed* Sun, Mon.

Some of the Gold Country's most memorable meals are served here at a price that discerning diners in California's bigger cities can only dream about; any selection from the eclectic menu is sure to be prepared and presented to perfection.

Miners' Shack, $; 157 S. *Washington Street; tel.* 209 532 5252; *credit cards, none; closed daily, evenings.*

Plenty of high-calorie American staples – gigantic sandwiches, burgers, hunks of fried chicken, rich desserts and much more – to satisfy large appetites.

• *Railtown 1897, Jamestown.*

Beside the County Fairgrounds on Mariposa's southern edge, the quality of the area's mineral riches is shown in no uncertain terms by the **California State Mining and Mineral Museum**, which displays fist-sized diamonds and gold nuggets among 200,000 precious pieces unearthed in the state.

MOKELUMNE HILL

One of the Gold Country communities which has done little to encourage tourism, Mokelumne Hill stretches for little more than a single block off Hwy-49, its lack of commercial trappings and dusty wooden sidewalks evoking a time-locked mood and making the town one of the area's more intriguing short stops.

PLACERVILLE

See California Overall: 2.

SAN ANDREAS

San Andreas's greatest day came in 1883 when legendary frontier outlaw **Black Bart** was tried and sentenced at the town's County Courthouse, an immaculately restored building which now serves as the **Calaveras County Historical Museum and Archives**. Known as "the poet laureate of outlawry," Black Bart relieved 28 Wells Fargo stage-coaches of their gold between 1875 and 1883 and usually left a self-penned poem at the scene of the crime. Imprisoned for five years after his San Andreas trial, Bart kept a low profile following his release and was rumored to be receiving a pension from Wells Fargo on the understanding that he never steal from them again.

SONORA

As the commercial hub of the southern mines, Sonora enjoyed great prosperity and is still a busy town with the symbols of Californian suburbia – shopping malls and tract housing – encroaching on its old center. Nonetheless, Sonora retains much of note from its past, not least several elegant mansions set along Washington Street and the strikingly red-colored **St. James Episcopal Church**, built in 1860 on the corner of Washington and Snell Streets.

A leaflet describing the town's historic houses can be picked up in what used to be the County Jail, 158 W. Bradford Avenue, which now holds the **Tuoloumne County Museum and History Center** and fills the one-time cells with exhibits and some highly-regarded cowboy paintings.

SUTTER CREEK

With its primly-preserved white clapboard homes and steepled churches, Sutter Creek pitches itself firmly at the passing tourist trade. Other than strolling around and browsing the shops, the sole point of call is **Knights Foundry**, 13 Eureka Street, a water-powered foundry which has been casting iron since 1873.

Central California

The Eastern Sierra

160 miles (one way); map Kummerley + Frey California-Nevada

Doubling as a section of our statewide route between Sacramento and Los Angeles (California Overall: 4), this tour focuses on the geological oddities which lie on either side of Hwy-395 as it traverses the Owens Valley. With parts of the route likely to be blocked by winter snowfalls, this is a summer-only tour, and is easily reached from Lake Tahoe (Local Explorations: 5) in the north and from Bakersfield (California Overall: 4) in the south; it can also be joined from Yosemite National Park (Local Explorations: 13). This is a short journey: two days to cover it all. Gently ascending foothills mark the western side of the Sierra Nevadas, but glacial action has caused the mountains' east-facing slopes to rise sheerly and dramatically. They form the west wall of the Owens Valley, rising to stark and arid peaks which also mark the California-Nevada border. Navigating an excitingly raw landscape throughout, the tour also ventures a few miles off Hwy-395 to discover even more impressive natural forms – the basalt columns of the Devil's Postpile Monument and the prehistoric trees of the Ancient Bristlecone Pine Forest.

The handful of small towns scattered along Hwy-395 are largely uninteresting, but their abundant motels and diners provide inexpensive lodging and food. My sleeping and eating recommendations are in the well-placed larger centers of Bishop and Mammoth Lakes, which I suggest you use as overnight stops.

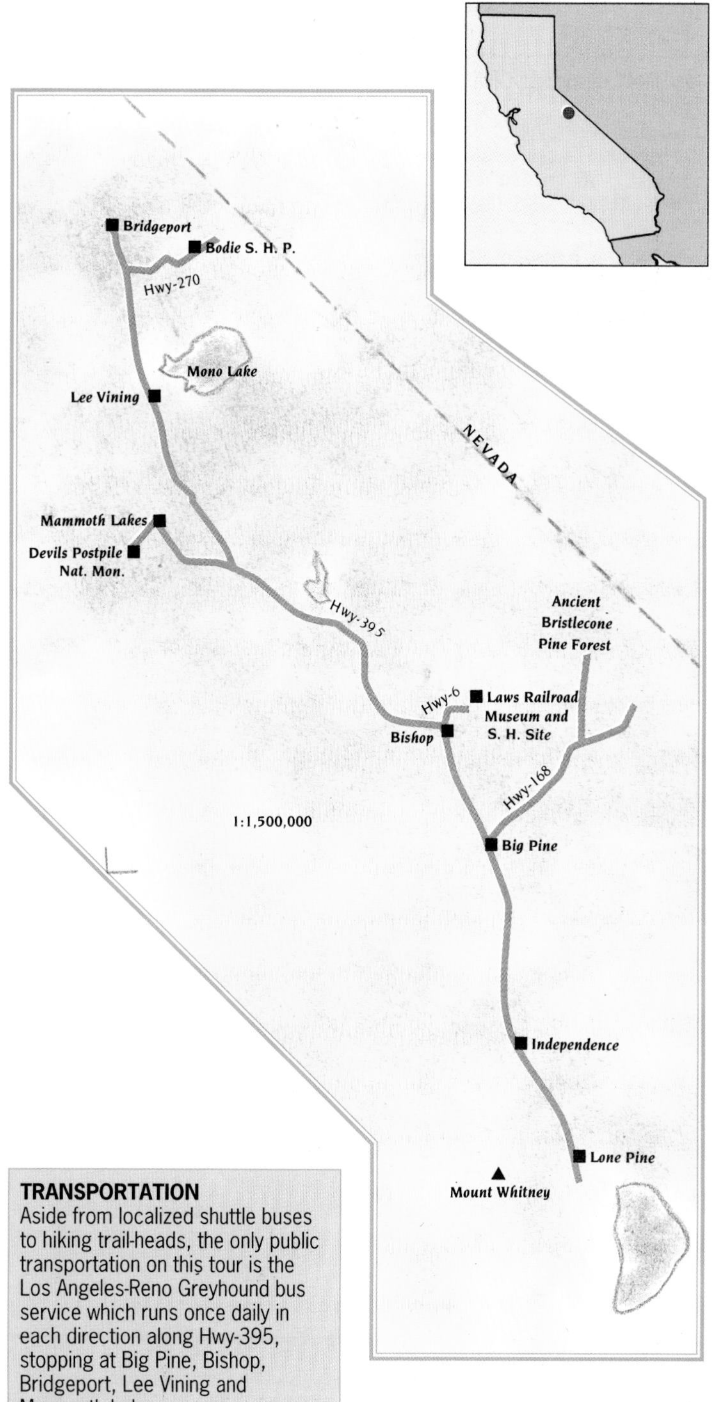

TRANSPORTATION
Aside from localized shuttle buses to hiking trail-heads, the only public transportation on this tour is the Los Angeles-Reno Greyhound bus service which runs once daily in each direction along Hwy-395, stopping at Big Pine, Bishop, Bridgeport, Lee Vining and Mammoth Lakes.

SIGHTS & PLACES OF INTEREST

ANCIENT BRISTLECONE PINE FOREST

The gnarled trees of the Ancient Bristlecone Pine Forest really are ancient: many are more than 4,000 years old and, until recently, were thought to be the world's oldest living things. Able to survive in arid conditions and in poor soil, the bristlecone pines' growing season seldom lasts more than four weeks, while a spread-out root system causes the trees to be widely spaced and therefore relatively invulnerable to forest fires.

At the end of the paved road off Hwy-168 from Big Pine, the Visitor Center at **Schulman Grove** provides an explanation of the trees' longevity and two walking trails lead into bristlecone pine groves. The most picturesque section of the forest, however, is found at the end of a bumpy, hour-long uphill drive to **Patriarch Grove**, where a scattering of bristlecones contributes to the desolate beauty of the White Mountains.

When dwelling on the haunting qualities of this 11,000-ft-high landscape, you might also ponder the fact that just 1,000 feet further up, the University of California operates a high-altitude research laboratory at what is thought to be the country's highest inhabited place.

BIG PINE

The town of Big Pine is not much more than a bend in Hwy-395 lined by motels, diners and supply shops aimed at visitors heading for the natural sights around it. These include the Ancient Bristlecone Pine Forest (see left) and, 10 miles west, the various tongues of the **Palisades Glacier** – North America's most southerly ice sheet and one whose tricky slopes present fresh challenges for experienced ice-climbers.

DETOUR – **LAWS RAILROAD MUSEUM AND STATE HISTORIC SITE**

There was a time when California was dependent on railways rather than freeways, and on Hwy-6 (branching from Hwy-395 north of Bishop) the 1880s railroad town of Laws has been recreated. The produce of local dairy farms began its journey to the Sierra mining towns by narrow-gauge railway from Laws, where history enthusiasts in period dress are now eager to dispense fact-filled anecdotes of the old days.

DETOUR – **BODIE STATE HISTORIC PARK**

The search for the ultimate California gold-rush ghost town comes to an end at Bodie State Historic Park, on Bodie Road, off Hwy-395 7 miles south of Bridgeport. Walking among what is now a collection of decaying wooden buildings with sagebrush blowing across the deserted streets, it is hard to image that a century ago nearly 10,000 people lived in Bodie and helped give the town a reputation as the wildest in the West. Inside the Miners' Union Hall, a small museum records Bodie's swift rise – and its equally swift demise.

BISHOP 🛏 ✕

Among the motels, restaurants, all-night supermarkets and adventure sports shops which fill Bishop – the Owens Valley's largest settlement and a useful base for climbing and hiking excursions into the wilderness – the **Paiute-Shoshone Indian Cultural Center and Museum**, 2300 W. Line Street, provides a welcome opportunity to discover something of the history and culture of the valley's indigenous inhabitants.

BRIDGEPORT

As the seat of Mono County, Bridgeport enjoyed 19thC prosperity on the back of the gold mines at Bodie (see above). These days, an inordinate number of bait-and-tackle shops fills the small town, serving the anglers who flock to the well-stocked rivers of nearby Bridgeport Reservoir. The reposeful **County Court House**, on Main Street, is one remnant of times past; the neighboring **Mono County Museum** holds many more.

INDEPENDENCE
Independence outdoes other Owens Valley towns by offering, besides the usual requisites of food and accommodation, excellent accounts of local life and history at its **Eastern California Museum**, 155 Grant Street. Among the museum's exhibits are a striking collection of Paiute and Shoshone basketry, and a thought-provoking exhibit on one of the darker episodes in California's past: the internment of 10,000 Japanese-Americans at the Manzanar camp, just outside Independence, following the outbreak of war between the U.S. and Japan in 1941.

LEE VINING
Another supply-center town on Hwy-395, Lee Vining gives access to Mono Lake (see page 211).

LONE PINE
It seems that everyone who comes to Lone Pine and doesn't need to eat or sleep either barrels straight through on Hwy-395, or branches west along the 12-mile Whitney Portal Road to reach the trail-head giving access to 14,494-ft **Mount Whitney**, its summit – the highest in the continental U.S. – the prize at the end of an arduous 10-mile hike.

MAMMOTH LAKES 🛏 ✕
A major winter skiing center, Mammoth Lakes lies just west of Hwy-395 in one of California's most geologically active regions, the largest earthquake ever known in the state occurring here in 1872. The **US Forest Service Visitor Center** has the facts on recreational pursuits in the area – in summer, mountain-biking is becoming as popular as hiking – and explains the causes of the locale's earthly fidgets; the **Mammoth Lakes Visitors' Bureau** is another handy source of tourist info.

Fourteen miles further on, at the end of Hwy-203, the **Devils Postpile National Monument** – an extraordinary collection of neatly arranged hexagonal basalt columns, formed as molten lava cooled and smoothed and polished by passing glaciers – can be reached by taking the shuttle bus from Mammoth Ski Center car-park and completing an easy 1/2-mile trail.

BUDGET ACCOMMODATION

Long Valley Hostel; *Lake Crowley Drive, near Mammoth Lakes; tel.* 619 935 4377.
Hilton Creek Hostel; *Lake Crowley Drive, near Mammoth Lakes; tel.* 619 935 4989.
ULLR Lodge; *Main Street, Mammoth Lakes; tel.* 619 934 2454.

RECOMMENDED HOTELS

BISHOP
Matlick House, $-$$; 1313 *Rowan Lane; tel.* 619 873 3133; *credit cards, none.*

A 1906 farmhouse, converted to an inn, now offering comfortable bed-and-breakfast accommodation in a choice of four rooms, at very attractive rates – especially so in midweek.

El Rancho Motel, $; 274 *Lagoon Street; tel.* 619 872 9251; *credit cards,* AE, CB, DC, MC, V.

Small and justifiably popular, this is the pick of Bishop's many motels for its clean, airy rooms – equipped with coffee-makers – and congenial atmosphere.

MAMMOTH LAKES
Snow Goose Inn, $$-$$$; *Forest Trail, off Hwy-203; tel.* 619 934 2660; *credit cards,* AE, DC, DS, MC, V.

A cozy mountain lodge with well-equipped rooms and a few two-bedded suites. A wholesome breakfast is served each morning, and wine and snacks are offered in the early evening.

Tamarack Lodge Resort, $$-$$$$; *Lake Mary Road; tel.* 619 934 2442; *credit cards,* AE, MC, V.

Perched on a tree-coated mountainside above a glistening glacial lake, the 1920s-built Tamarack Lodge serves as a ski resort during winter and a lovely rural base during the summer, with many quiet walks to waterfalls and spectacular vistas within easy reach.

MONO LAKE

Nine thousand feet above sea-level and almost a million years old, the heavily-saline waters (lacking an outflow, its waters evaporate leaving their salt content behind) of Mono Lake support a large insect population, which provides great delight for the many species of wading birds found here. In turn, the wading birds provide great delight for birdwatchers.

Ornithological know-nothings, however, should visit the lake for its strangely-shaped **tufa formations**. These are created by calcium, in the freshwater springs which feed the lake, mixing with carbonates. The formations became exposed as the lake's water level fell: since the 1940s, the lake has suffered a 40-ft drop – a result of the damming of local rivers to provide water for Los Angeles.

Self-guided trails weave through the largest of the tufa formations, on the lake's south side and reached by Hwy-120, east off Hwy-395. For an explanation of the tufa's creation, and the low-down on the region's ecological headaches, call at the **Mono Basin National Forest Scenic Area Visitor Center** in Lee Vining.

• *Opposite:* *Mount Whitney, highest point in the continental* U.S.
• *Right:* *Lone Pine.*

RECOMMENDED RESTAURANTS

BISHOP

Bishop Grill, $; 281 N. *Main Street; tel.* 619 873 3911; *credit cards, none.*

Classic coffee shop with smiling waitresses and a long menu of all-American favorites at prices OK for even the tightest budget.

Erick Shat's Dutch Bakery, $; 763 N. *Main Street; tel.* 619 873 7156; *credit cards, none.*

Plenty of locals swear by Shat's, which has been providing simple, inexpensive breakfasts and lunches, and a range of homemade breads and other fresh-baked goods, since 1938.

MAMMOTH LAKES

Anything Goes, $-$$; *Sherwin Plaza, Old Mammoth Road; tel.* 619 934 2424; *credit cards,* AE, MC, V.

Anything really does go at this wildly eclectic eatery, which specializes in skillfully-prepared dishes drawn from the cuisines of every corner of the globe.

Mammoth Grill, $-$$; *Mammoth Lakes; tel.* 619 934 2581; *credit cards,* AE, MC, V.

With alpine views through the windows and wooden rafters overhead, the Mammoth Grill – inside the Mammoth Mountain Inn – offers fare to fuel the longest wilderness ramble. Breakfast options include pancakes, omelettes and waffles, lunch finds a choice of sizeable salads and sandwiches, and the chef saves his best dishes for the dinner specials.

Local Explorations:12

Central California

Death Valley

240 miles (one way); map Kummerley + Frey California-Nevada

This tour focuses on the desert landscapes of Death Valley - one of the hottest, driest places in the world – while providing a link between the Eastern Sierra (Local Explorations: 11) and California Overall: 7.

Bear in mind, however, that while Death Valley stretches across a vast area, only a relatively small portion can readily be visited by car and that a great deal of driving is needed to reach it at all.

Death Valley is also an extreme and isolated region where services are in short supply and visitors will soon be facing severe problems if they fail to plan ahead adequately (see the tips in the boxes that follow). Seasons are important too: Death Valley will roast you alive during summer, and the tour should only be undertaken between November and March.

Avail yourself of the ubiquitous motels and coffee shops of the dot-on-the-map communities which line the roads leading to Death Valley, and you could easily complete the valley tour in a day. With more time to spare, I recommend that you spend a night in the valley itself and use the additional time to undertake the detour to Scotty's Castle and the Ubehebe Crater.

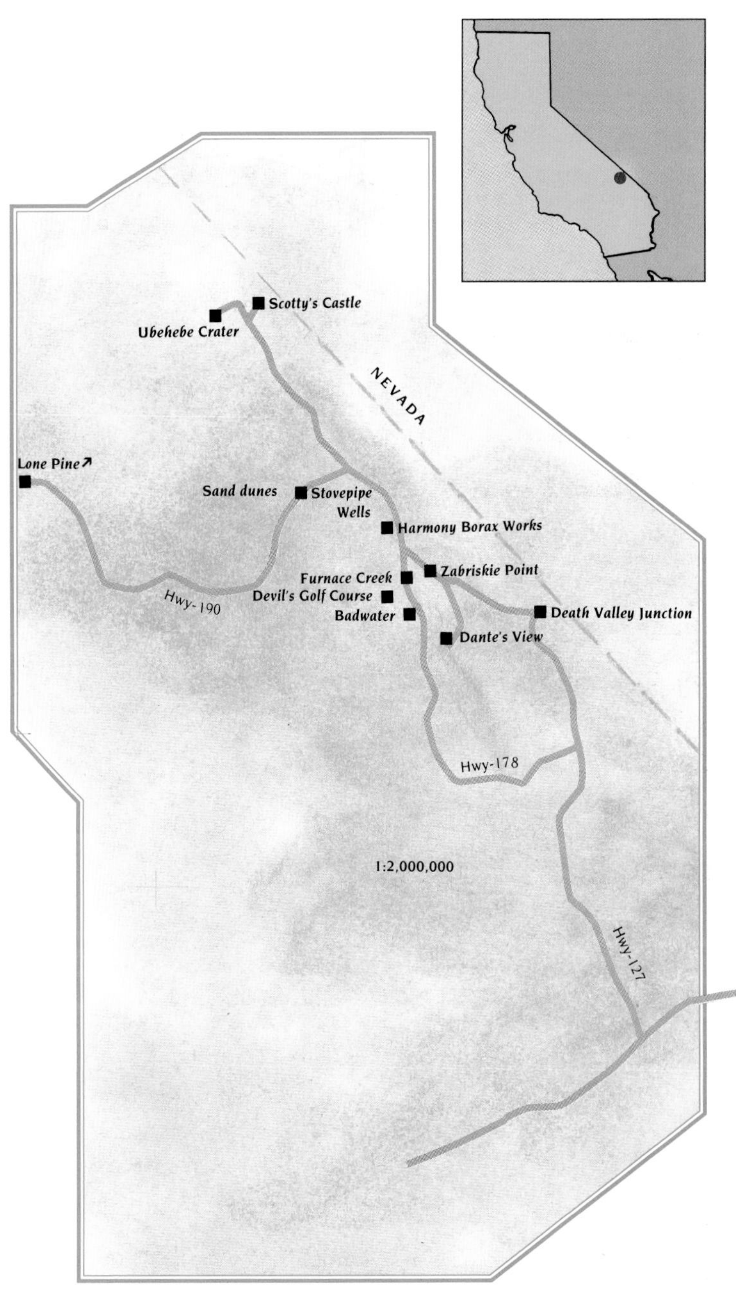

TRANSPORTATION
No public transportation services operate in or around Death Valley.

SIGHTS & PLACES OF INTEREST

ARTISTS DRIVE

On the **Artists Palette** section of Artists Drive, a 9-mile loop-road off Hwy-178, volcanic debris embedded in a series of mud hills forms a multi-colored landscape – shades of amber, red, brown, black and violet, mostly caused by the presence of oxides in the rock, which change their hue according the angle of sunlight. The most colorful display is in the late afternoon.

BADWATER

Badwater was named by a 19thC prospector whose mule refused to drink from the salt water pool here. What neither the prospector nor the mule probably realized was that they were standing at the lowest point in the U.S: Badwater reaches 282 feet below sea level. The actual low point is an unrewarding 4-mile trek from the car-park, which is just 3 feet higher.

DEATH VALLEY DRIVING

Ensure that your car is in perfect condition before embarking on this tour, and carry around five gallons of spare fuel (there are only three petrol stations within Death Valley – at Furnace Creek, Stovepipe Wells and Scotty's Castle) and a similar quantity of spare radiator water. Carry plenty of food and at least a gallon of drinking water per person per day. If your car breaks down, wait until another car passes and signal for assistance – do not leave your car. When driving, always keep to the marked roads. Useful desert touring accessories include a first-aid kit, a flashlight, and waterproof matches.

• *Scotty's Castle, Death Valley.*

• *Zabriskie Point.*

DANTE'S VIEW
More than a mile high in the Black Mountains, the view from Dante's View is one which will bring fresh perspectives to the landscapes you may already have seen from the valley floor – particularly the white carpet of the Devil's Golf Course. Dante's View also provides a chance to see the country's lowest and highest places: Badwater (see above), and the 14,495-ft high Mount Whitney, 60 miles distant in the Sierra Nevada mountains.

DEVIL'S GOLF COURSE
When the prehistoric sea which filled what is now Death Valley evaporated, it left enough salt behind to form the 200-sq-mile expanse of salt flats known as the Devil's Golf Course. Although they do indeed look flat from a distance, a close inspection reveals the "flats" to be comprised of thousands of tall and jagged salt crystals.

FURNACE CREEK 🛏 ✕
Besides a handful of shops, a few restaurants and two accommodation options, Furnace Creek also has the **Death Valley Visitors' Center**, which provides a wealth of geological, ecological and historical information on the region, plus the free maps which are an essential aid to exploring it.

HARMONY BORAX WORKS RUINS
If you find Death Valley's heat uncomfortable on a leisurely visit, spare a thought for the miners who worked deposits of borax here from the 1880s, and the 20-strong mule teams

DEATH VALLEY WALKING
Even on a short walk, drink water regularly – whether or not you feel thirsty. Keep in the shade whenever possible. Wear loose, light-colored clothing, dark glasses and a wide-brimmed hat, and use a sunscreen. On your feet, wear walking boots or trainers; don't go without socks: they won't make your feet significantly hotter, and they will reduce the risk of blisters. For extra safety, be sure that you know what to do if bitten by a desert creature. Details about dealing with the unwelcome attentions of everything from tarantulas to rattlesnakes are available from any desert visitor center or rangers' office.

• *The tiny opera house, Amargosa.*

which hauled 10-ton wagonloads of the mineral across 165 miles of unyielding desert terrain to the nearest railway station. A small museum filled with large pieces of mining machinery and explanatory displays, and some ruined adobe buildings, remain from the Harmony Borax Works, which was active into the 1920s.

LONE PINE

See Local Explorations: 11.

RECOMMENDED HOTELS

FURNACE CREEK

Furnace Creek Inn, $$$$; *tel.* 619 786 2345; *credit cards,* AE, DC, MC, V.

The rustic appearance of this stone-built inn dating from the 1920s belies its modern-day comforts. The air-conditioned rooms also have ceiling fans, and the facilities include an 18-hole golf course, tennis-courts, and an inviting swimming-pool. With alternative desert dining opportunities few and far between, the inn's rates include breakfast and a 7-course dinner.

Furnace Creek Ranch, $$-$$$; *tel.* 619 786 2345; *credit cards,* AE, DC, MC, V.

Located beside the Death Valley Visitors' Center, the Furnace Creek Ranch is a large and fairly characterless hotel but has lower rates than the Furnace Creek Inn, of which it is an annex.

STOVEPIPE WELLS

Stovepipe Wells Village, $$; *tel.* 619 786 2387; *credit cards,* MC, V.

Has the lowest rates in Death Valley. The rooms are budget-motel standard and, although they vary slightly in quality, they should provide an adequate night's lodging.

RECOMMENDED RESTAURANT

FURNACE CREEK

Furnace Creek Inn, $-$$; *tel.* 619 786 2345; *credit cards,* AE, DC, MC, V.

With fresh supplies flown in daily by light aircraft, the restaurant of the Furnace Creek Inn is by far the most enjoyable place to dine in Death Valley, both for the quality of the food and the ambience of the setting.

STOVEPIPE WELLS

A general store, a petrol station, a motel and a public swimming-pool all make a welcome appearance at Stovepipe Wells, the second of the valley's two supply centers. (The actual well after which the village takes its name is a mile or two north-east.)

Just east of the village, a marker indicates Burned Wagons Point, where a group of "49ers" – migrants travelling overland from the east during 1849 and looking for a southerly route into California – became trapped, eventually burning their wagons to smoke the meat of their slaughtered oxen, and then finding a route out of the valley on foot. Incidentally, it was another 49er who allegedly gave the valley its name, turning back to utter "Goodbye, Death Valley" as he and his party made their escape.

Slightly further east along Hwy-198, 14 square miles of sand dunes appear to the north. Formed by desert winds wearing down fragments of quartz, these shifting yellow carpets at the feet of the surrounding hillsides are fascinating to see when the sun casts moving shadows across their rippled tops. The dunes can also be viewed from a signposted vantage point off North Highway, on the detour described below.

ZABRISKIE POINT

Antonioni's 1969 film and its Pink Floyd soundtrack have not lessened the mystique of Zabriskie Point, an expanse of mustard-colored mudflats which stretch dreamily out from a 700-ft-high viewing point. Mudflats are seldom noted for their visual appeal, but these – lake-bottom sediments formed up to 12 million years ago – make up one of Death Valley's most memorable vistas.

DETOUR - **DEATH VALLEY JUNCTION**

Ballet and Death Valley are not as mutually exclusive as you might expect. At Death Valley Junction, a hamlet near the junction of Highways 127 and 190, 50 miles east of Furnace Creek, the tiny **Amargosa Opera House** finds former New York-based ballerina Marta Becket staging dance and mime performances on Friday, Saturday and Monday evenings throughout the winter. For details, tel. 619 852 4316.

DETOUR – **SCOTTY'S CASTLE AND UBEHEBE CRATER**

With a few hours, or half a day to spare, leave Hwy-190 near Stovepipe Wells and continue north along the North Highway. Thirty or so miles ahead lie two of Death Valley's more celebrated features. Nature presents itself in many curious guises in Death Valley but the region's least likely sight is a man-made one: the red-tiled roofs, balconies and arched entrances of **Scotty's Castle**, a Spanish-Moorish mansion which sits at the foot of the brown hillsides off Grapevine Canyon, 3 miles east of the North Highway.

Though named after Walter "Death Valley Scotty" Scot, a colorful frontier character who claimed to have built his castle with the proceeds of a secret gold mine, the $2.5 million which funded the mansion was actually raised by a Chicago millionaire, Albert Johnson, who moved to the desert for health reasons in the 1920s and lost most of his fortune during the Depression.

Both men lived at the mansion which, though never officially completed, boasts 18 fireplaces, a massive pipe organ, heaps of ornate wrought ironwork – and a 185-ft-long swimming-pool for cooling off in the dry desert heat – all of which are viewable on guided tours.

Half a mile wide and 800 feet deep, the **Ubehebe Crater** – turn west off North Highway a mile north of the Scotty's Castle turning – was formed in a split second by the terrific explosion which occurred when molten lava struck the valley's water table. From the rim, the sheer size of the crater is highly impressive. Take the trail leading to the crater floor for a close look at the different-colored layers of sedimentary rock in its walls, exposed by the explosion.

Local Explorations: 13

Central California

Yosemite National Park

150 *miles (round trip); map* Kummerley + Frey California-Nevada

California is richly endowed with striking landscapes but none of its natural sights quite compares with the beauty of Yosemite Valley, 7 miles long and 1 mile wide, coated by fir trees, patrolled by wild deer, and walled by towering granite cliffs.

For me, the thrill of sighting the valley as the approach road twists through the surrounding forests has yet to grow stale despite many visits. For this exploration I have selected highlights from the valley – a mixture of waterfalls; sky-high peaks and domes; startling viewpoints at the end of foot trails; and some of the more accessible portions of the rest of Yosemite National Park, such as Wawona (where you might spend the second night on a two-night stay) and the giant sequoia trees of the Mariposa Grove. To do it justice, allow at least two days.

The tour links with the town of Mariposa (on Local Explorations: 10) and Fresno (California Overall: 4) and – during the summer when the Tioga Pass Road is open – can be coupled with Lee Vining and the Eastern Sierra tour (Local Explorations: 7). Although the park is open all year, the tour is ideally undertaken during spring or fall, when the valley is free of its heavy summer crowds. Note that accommodation in the park is often fully booked, especially during summer. Cancellations can sometimes, however, be picked up on the day.

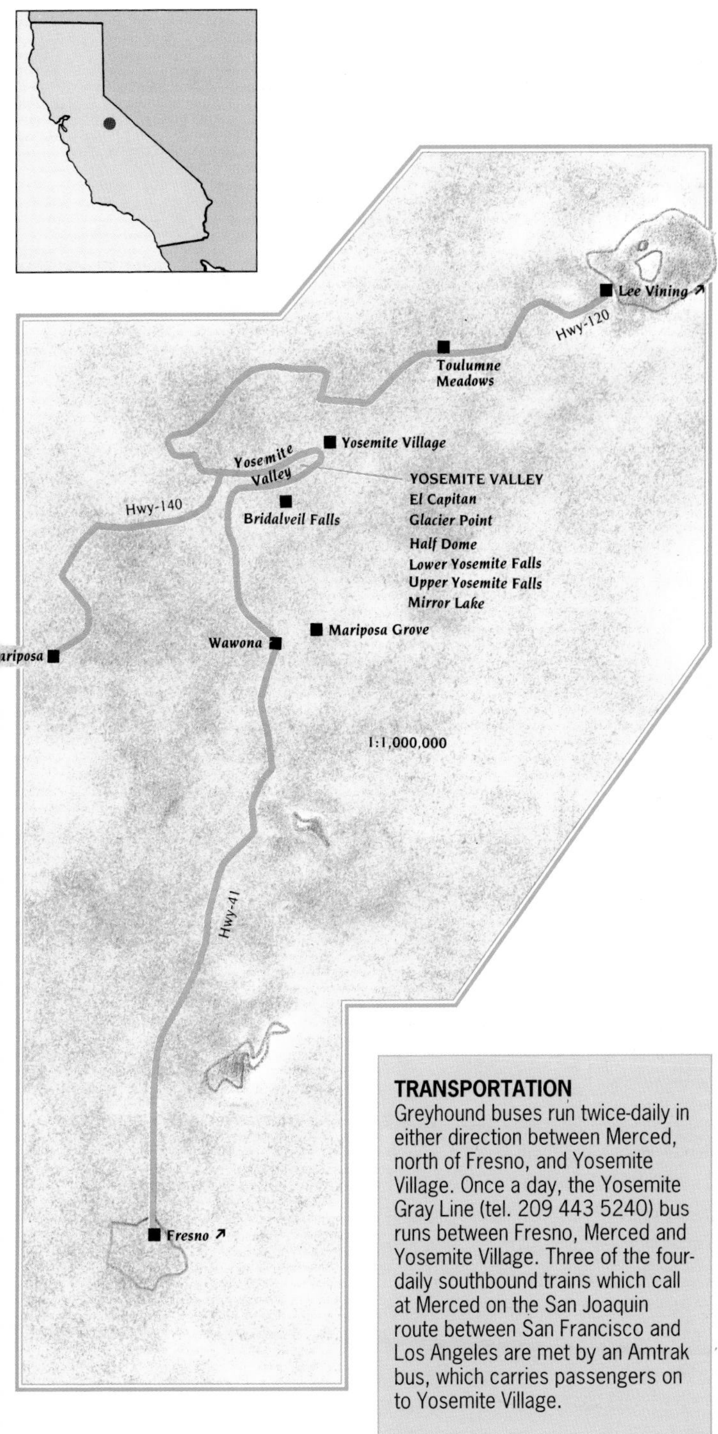

TRANSPORTATION
Greyhound buses run twice-daily in either direction between Merced, north of Fresno, and Yosemite Village. Once a day, the Yosemite Gray Line (tel. 209 443 5240) bus runs between Fresno, Merced and Yosemite Village. Three of the four-daily southbound trains which call at Merced on the San Joaquin route between San Francisco and Los Angeles are met by an Amtrak bus, which carries passengers on to Yosemite Village.

SIGHTS & PLACES OF INTEREST

BRIDALVEIL FALLS

Ribbon-like waterfalls are a feature of Yosemite National Park, though they only gush at full power during springtime when fuelled by the melting snows of the Sierra peaks – by late summer, many are nothing more than a pathetic trickle. One of the prettiest and easiest to reach of Yosemite's falls is Bridalveil Falls, cascading from 600 feet and often swayed from side to side by the wind, creating a swirling spray around its base.

EL CAPITAN

The world's tallest granite monolith, El Capitan provides a 3,593-ft sheer wall to Yosemite Valley, rising three times taller than New York's Empire State Building. Scarred by cracks and fissures, El Capitan's near-vertical face provides an irresistible challenge for advanced climbers – who mostly prefer to avoid the summer months, when the sun beats down on the rock making it hot to touch.

FRESNO

See California Overall: 4.

GLACIER POINT

The best views in Yosemite National Park are from Glacier Point, 3,200 feet above the valley and giving magnificent views of Half Dome (see right). Try to arrive early at the viewing point: later in the day, quiet contemplation of the stunning vistas is made difficult by the arrival of tour-bus crowds. Make a second visit to Glacier Point at night, when the valley is lit by moonlight and stars twinkle in the High Sierra sky.

A DAY'S HIKE – UPPER YOSEMITE FALLS

A 3-mile uphill hike leads to the base of Upper Yosemite Falls, a cascade of water dropping nearly 1,500 feet in a single leap. The trek includes some very steep sections and innumerable switchbacks and is best tackled over a full day: carry a packed lunch and plenty of drinking water.

A HALF-DAY HIKE – THE MIST TRAIL

There's little in the way of physical exertion necessary to complete the so-called Mist Trail but you're certain to get wet if making the trek during the spring, when the trail's two waterfalls love to give visitors a welcoming spray; dress accordingly.

From the Yosemite Valley's Happy Isles Nature Center, a flat mile-long path leads to the base of 300-ft-high **Vernal Falls**, beyond which lies an uphill climb to the more powerful – and much more dramatic – **Nevada Falls**, where the gushing waters of the Merced River plunge 594 feet.

HALF DOME

The aptly-named Half Dome was sliced in two by glacial action millenia ago. Its remaining half reaches 8,842 feet above sea-level and casts a distinctive presence over the western end of Yosemite Valley – especially so when the the rays of the setting sun give its face a vivid orange glow.

Half Dome was first successfully climbed the hard way in 1956, an ascent which took five days. With the aid of steel cables sunk into rock, the summit is much more accessible from the rear, though even this route entails a strenuous 12-hour trek and is not to be undertaken on a whim.

LEE VINING

See Local Explorations: 11.

LOWER YOSEMITE FALLS

A short paved footpath leads to Lower Yosemite Falls, the final section of the tallest waterfall in North America. To reach the immensely more spectacular Upper Yosemite Falls requires much greater legwork – see left.

MARIPOSA

See Local Explorations: 10.

MARIPOSA GROVE

A narrated tram ride takes you around the 2,000-year-old giant sequoia trees of Mariposa Grove, a source of tourist wonderment since the 1880s. Early in the 20thC, the ecologically-unsound

YOSEMITE ON HORSEBACK
You can save your leg muscles and learn a great deal about Yosemite National Park by taking a guided horseback tour, which might last anything from an hour to several days. The summer-only tours operate from Tuolumne Meadows, Wawona and Yosemite Village. Any park visitor center will be able to provide details, or tel. 209 372 1248.

founders of the hotel at Wawona (see right) hollowed out one of the trees to enable a road to pass through it. The **Mariposa Grove Museum**, housed in a log cabin, carries exhibits unravelling the fascinating natural history of the enormous trees – which are essential viewing if you're not visiting the larger groves at Sequoia National Park (Local Explorations: 14).

MIRROR LAKE

The silting process which transformed a prehistoric lake into the present-day floor of Yosemite Valley is being repeated on a smaller scale at Mirror Lake. Steadily filled by river-borne deposits of mud and gravel, Mirror Lake is usually completely dry by mid-summer; when replenished by the spring snow melt, however, the lake reflects the summits of surrounding peaks in its uncannily still surface.

TUOLUMNE MEADOWS

Reached from Yosemite Valley by a 60-mile drive along the steadily-climbing Tioga Pass Road (Hwy-120), Tuolumne (pronounced Twa-LUM-Nay) Meadows is the highest sub-alpine meadow in the Sierra Nevadas, its 8,757-ft elevation providing views of snow-capped mountains and endless opportunities for walks and hikes.

Not only is the top-of-the-world scenery at Tuolumne Meadows quite different from that of the granite-enclosed Yosemite Valley, the tourists are far fewer, too, and many who use Tuolumne as a base are serious back-country adventurers.

The roadside views are reason enough to make the journey from the valley but if you have sufficient energy (remember that these high altitudes will quickly sap your strength), call at the Tuolumne Meadows Visitor Center for details of the day-long hikes in the area.

WAWONA 🛏

Stunning views are not a feature of Wawona, a crossroads hamlet set amid dense forests, verdant meadows and gushing streams, providing a calm, rural contrast to the busy Yosemite Valley. Still operating today, the **Wawona Hotel** opened here in 1879 to accommodate stage-coach

RECOMMENDED HOTELS

All tourist services in Yosemite National Park are run by a single company. The telephone number given for the hotels below is the number for all lodgings in the park.

WAWONA

Wawona Hotel, $$; *tel.* 209 252 4848; *credit cards*, AE, CB, DC, MC, V.

On the main western approach to Yosemite Valley but far from the valley's maddening crowds, the Wawona Hotel provides simple (most lack private bathrooms) but attractively-priced rooms in peaceful surroundings. You can even play croquet on the lawn and walk to the Yosemite History Center.

YOSEMITE VILLAGE

Ahwahnee Hotel, $$$$; *tel.* 209 252 4848; *credit cards*, AE, CB, DC, MC, V.

Built of local stone in the 1920s, the plushly-decorated Ahwahnee Hotel is as much a Yosemite landmark as the surrounding waterfalls and granite peaks. To stay here in summer, book a year in advance.

Yosemite Lodge, $$; *tel.* 209 252 4848; *credit cards*, AE, CB, DC, MC, V.

Motel-style rooms with rustic touches in cabins spread across the grounds. Usually fully-booked far in advance but cancellations are common during the spring and fall, and spare rooms are allocated daily on a first-come, first-served basis.

• *Yosemite's higher elevations.*

travellers making their way to the valley and to the giant sequoia trees of the Mariposa Grove (see page 220), discovered by Wawona's founder, Galen Clark.

Besides poking your nose inside the elegantly-verandahed hotel, call at the neighboring Pioneer **Yosemite History Center**, which has reassembled several 19thC buildings to illustrate local life of a century ago – and offers stage-coach rides.

RECOMMENDED RESTAURANT

YOSEMITE VILLAGE
Ahwahnee Hotel, $$$$; *tel.* 209 372 1489; *credit cards*, AE, DC, MC, V.

The timber-beamed restaurant of this top-notch hotel has large windows giving views of the valley and serves enormous portions – the steak and fish dishes are the best bets. Dinner is a semi-formal affair and smart attire is required.

YOSEMITE VALLEY
See the individual entries for each point of interest listed on the map.

YOSEMITE VILLAGE 🛏 ✕
The commercial center of Yosemite Valley, Yosemite Village has shops, several relatively inexpensive eating places, a post office and an info-packed visitor center. You'll also find the **Indian Cultural Museum**, which gives a modest account of Yosemite's native inhabitants with exhibits and a reconstructed village – and sometimes with demonstrations of basket-making and ceremonial celebrations.

• *Opposite*: *Yosemite Valley.*

RENTAL

Central California

Sequoia and Kings Canyon National Parks

150 miles (round trip); map Kummerley + Frey California-Nevada

The coastal redwoods, explored in California Overall: 1 and Local Explorations: 3, are tall indeed. But in terms of bulk, no tree, nor indeed any living thing, is larger than the giant sequoia trees which grow only on the western foothills of California's Sierra Nevada mountains.

This local exploration, which can be undertaken in either direction between Fresno and Visalia (see California Overall: 4) and is best between April and October (though weekends and vacation periods can be off-puttingly crowded), reveals the great groves of sequoias which stand majestic and proud in Sequoia National Park. It continues with a spectacular descent into Kings Canyon National Park (the two parks are administered as one).

Many park visitors see no more than the largest sequoias, conveniently located a short walk from the road. In a more adventurous spirit, I have planned the tour to include one of the region's many caverns; I've also suggested one-day and half-day hikes – neither of which calls for superhuman stamina – and given the option of a detour by car to the remote southern section of Sequoia National Park. To cover it all, allow two to three days.

Food and lodging take second place to nature on this tour and my recommendations are drawn from the limited facilities offered at the parks' handful of developed centers.

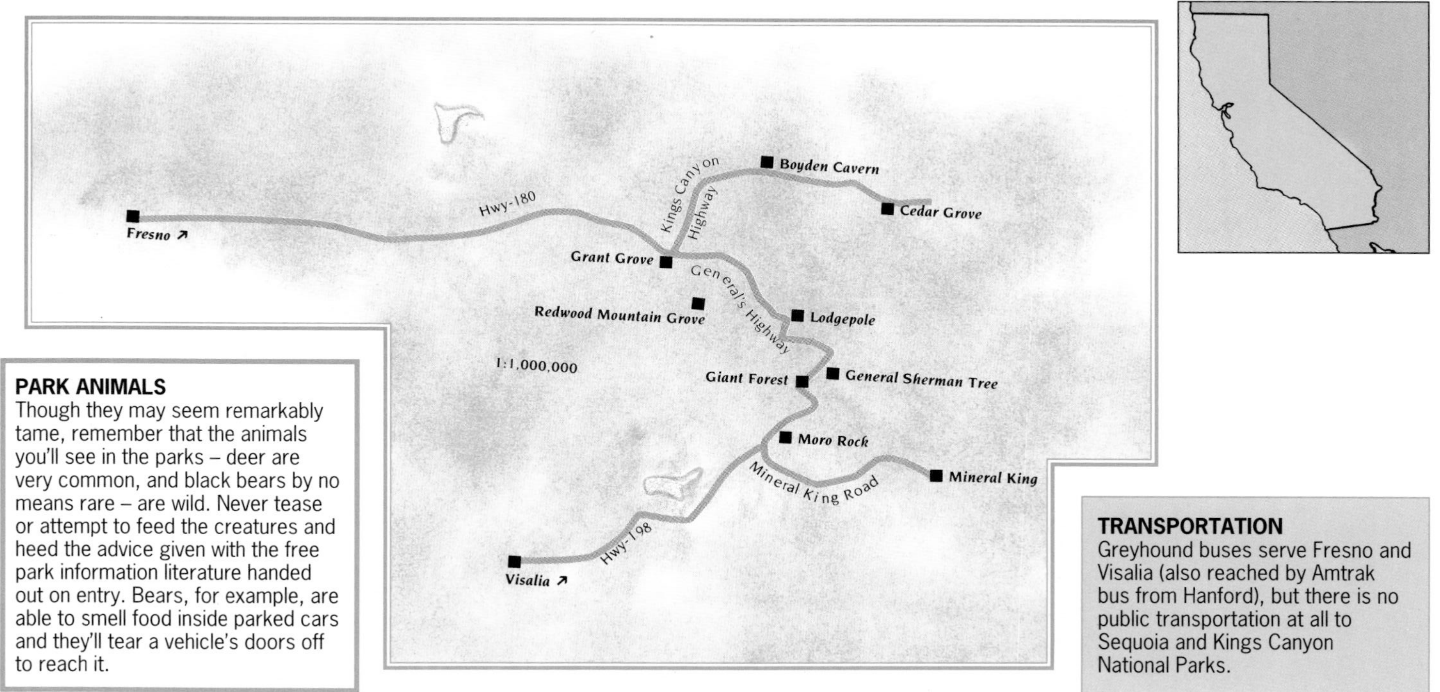

TRANSPORTATION
Greyhound buses serve Fresno and Visalia (also reached by Amtrak bus from Hanford), but there is no public transportation at all to Sequoia and Kings Canyon National Parks.

PARK ANIMALS
Though they may seem remarkably tame, remember that the animals you'll see in the parks – deer are very common, and black bears by no means rare – are wild. Never tease or attempt to feed the creatures and heed the advice given with the free park information literature handed out on entry. Bears, for example, are able to smell food inside parked cars and they'll tear a vehicle's doors off to reach it.

SIGHTS & PLACES OF INTEREST

BOYDEN CAVERN

The permanently cool innards of Boyden Cavern offer a welcome respite on a hot day, and the 45-minute guided tours which pass through the cavern provide intriguing insights into the processes which – over the last 300,000 years – have created the weird marble formations deep inside. The water responsible for these surreal sculptures still drips eerily from the cavern's roof.

CEDAR GROVE AREA @

The Kings Canyon Highway comes to an end at Cedar Grove, beyond which only backcountry hikes allow further penetration of the high-elevation wilderness areas lying to the north and south. At a lower level, much shorter and simpler treks include the **Zumwalt Meadow Trail**, leading to a lush patch of grass,

THE GIANT SEQUOIA TREE

With a fire-resistant bark and near-immunity to insect attack and tree-threatening diseases, the giant sequoia tree is virtually immortal. Many sequoias have lived for more than 2,000 years and the only natural forces likely to end their lives are abnormally heavy snowfalls and unusually strong winds. Logging decimated many of California's giant sequoia groves in the late 19thC, but the sequoias' wood was found to be a poor building material and therefore uneconomic to mill – enabling some 75 separate groves to live on unmolested.

• *Opposite and below, wonders of* Sequoia *National Park.*

DETOUR – **MINERAL KING**
The isolated southern section of Sequoia National Park is reached only by a partially paved road (Mineral King Road, open summer only) which branches off Hwy-198 from Visalia. Although only 29 miles long, the condition of the road means the journey is likely to take a couple of hours.

At Mineral King, the road terminates in a pristine mountain landscape, 7,500 feet high and with the rugged Sierra Nevada peaks seemingly close enough to touch. In fact, they can only be reached by undertaking lengthy backcountry trails.

Fortunately, perhaps, two plans for developing Mineral King came to nothing. The first was thought up by over-optimistic silver prospectors in the 1870s. The second came from the Disney Corporation in the 1960s, who schemed to turn the area into a gigantic ski resort.

speckled in spring by wildflowers and popular with deer, who show up to feed in the cool of early morning and early evening. A 2-mile continuation of the trail (and a short walk from a marked roadside stop/car-park) reaches **Roaring River Falls**, living up to their name spectacularly during the early summer.

FRESNO

See California Overall: 4.

A DAY'S HIKE – REDWOOD MOUNTAIN GROVE
Spend a day freed from the crowds which pack the easily-visited sequoia groves by taking the 6-mile loop trail into **Redwood Mountain Grove**, which begins off the General's Highway a few miles south of Grant Grove, and reaches into the park's (and the world's) largest single grouping of sequoias. Remember that there are no facilities on this route, so be sure to carry plenty of drinking water. You should also get up-to-the-minute advice – such as a weather forecast – from the nearest visitor center before setting out.

A HALF-DAY HIKE FROM LODGEPOLE
If a 2-mile uphill hike doesn't sound too daunting, tackle the **Tokopah Falls trail**, which winds sharply upwards from the Lodgepole camp site, following the course of the Kaweah River to the point where it tumbles over a glacier-carved gorge. Usually, the route turns up many pika: amusing little creatures which look disturbingly like rats but which are a species of rabbit, recognized by their rounded ears.

GENERAL SHERMAN TREE

Reached by a short paved trail from the General's Highway between Giant Forest and Lodgepole (and by an easy 2-mile foot trail from Giant Forest), the General Sherman Tree, discovered in 1879, is the largest sequoia of them all, with a circumference of 102.6 feet at its base.

Although nature's handiwork tends to make statistics irrelevant, there is something indefinably special about standing face to bark with the world's largest living thing – which the General Sherman Tree is. For good measure, the second-, fourth- and fifth-largest sequoias stand within the same grove.

GIANT FOREST AREA @ ×

From the shops, restaurants and accommodation at Giant Forest Village, Crescent Meadow Road leads south, passing a short loop road to the **Auto Log**, sawn flat enough to drive a car on to it, and another to the **Tunnel Log**, a fallen sequoia with a hole cut through it large enough to drive through.

Such crass exploitation of the forest marked the early years of tourism in Sequoia National Park. A different kind of usage can be seen just beyond Crescent Meadow (a verdant expanse of grassland framed by towering trees) at the slightly smaller Log Meadow, where cattle farmer Hale Tharp built a makeshift cabin in the 1860s by hollowing out the end of a fallen sequoia. Known as **Tharp's Log**, the cabin can still be seen on the numerous signposted short trails which begin at the end of Crescent Meadow Road.

LANDSCAPE DRIVE -- KINGS CANYON HIGHWAY
From Grant Grove, the Kings Canyon Highway – built by prison laborers during the 1930s – makes an hour-long winding descent into the canyon which gives Kings Canyon National Park its name, and concludes at Cedar Grove – see page 226. Carved by the Kings River, the sides of the steep, V-shaped canyon are marked by exposed granite and broad expanses of chaparral, studded in places by the yellow spikes of yucca plants.

GRANT GROVE AREA
At Grant Grove, the most developed section of Kings Canyon National Park, you'll find a useful visitors' center and a short walk leading to the sequoia grove holding the **General Grant Tree**, the third-largest sequoia and one known to Americans as the "nation's Christmas tree."

A more unusual walk is the **Big Stump trail**, which traverses an area littered by the stumps of sequoias felled when commercial logging was carried out here during the late 1800s. Though the logging stopped long ago, only recently have there been signs of recovery: the walk passes many young, second-growth sequoias steadily reclaiming this devastated portion of forest.

LODGEPOLE AREA
The excellent visitors' center at Lodgepole provides an informative account of the evolution of the giant sequoias, although the Lodgepole area's ecology means none of them actually grows in the immediate vicinity.

MORO ROCK
A stone staircase winds to the 6,725-ft summit of Moro Rock, a gigantic hunk of granite perched on the edge of a hillside and which, visited during the early evening, offers a fabulous view of the sunset across California's vast Central Valley.

VISALIA
See California Overall: 4.

RECOMMENDED HOTELS

All tourist services in Sequoia and Kings Canyon National Parks are run by a single company, hence the same telephone number for hotels and restaurants.

CEDAR GROVE
Cedar Grove Lodge, $$; *tel.* 209 561 3314; *credit cards*, MC, V.

Open summer only, with 18 unfussy motel-style rooms beside the Kings River.

GIANT FOREST
Giant Forest Lodge, $-$$$; *Giant Forest Village*; *tel.* 209 561 3314; *credit cards*, MC, V.

The accommodation here ranges from two-bedded cottages with wood-burning fireplaces to motel-style rooms with private bathrooms and (in summer only) rustic cabins with outside bathrooms – all are priced according to facilities.

RECOMMENDED RESTAURANT

GIANT FOREST
Giant Forest Lodge Dining Room, $$; *Giant Forest Village*; *tel.* 209 561 3314; *credit cards*, MC, V.

You'll find filling fare at reasonable prices in the cafes and cafeterias at the parks' other commercial centers – Grant Grove, Cedar King and Lodgepole – but only here does the food, setting and service reach a higher standard. The excellent fresh fish dishes and the well-stocked salad bar are a welcome treat after a day spent foraging in the wilds.Serves breakfast and dinner.

Southern California

The Los Angeles Coast

65 miles (one way); map Kümmerley + Frey California-Nevada

An obvious but very stimulating link between California Overall: 6 and 8, this tour provides a healthy taste of Los Angeles without straying from the calming influence of the Pacific Ocean. If the maelstrom that is the rest of LA really does beckon, however, it is a simple matter to interrupt this tour and venture deeper into the city using Local Explorations: 16.

Even though the tour keeps to the coast, it offers a great deal of variety. From the north, the area around Malibu will surprise you with its ramshackle and under-developed appearance. This is due to the rolling canyons of the Santa Monica Mountains, which reach almost to the ocean. Nonetheless, with scores of rich and famous faces residing in hidden-away canyon homes or in million-dollar beachside residences, Malibu fully deserves its jet-set reputation.

Should Malibu prove irresistible, I suggest you spend one of your two possible nights here, and the other in Santa Monica to the south. To me, Santa Monica looks and feels exactly like an LA coastal community should. Lined by palm trees, the town's impossibly large beach plays host to sunbathers, cyclists and joggers, and is overlooked by an historic pier.

Enjoyable though Santa Monica is, it can't match the anarchic spirit evident at Venice, a few miles south, which fulfils even the wildest expectation of what LA beach life might be all about. Take lunch beside Venice's boardwalk and you'll see the craziest parade in LA go by.

San Pedro is another possibility for an overnight stop. Long regarded by Angelenos as an uninteresting outpost, this former fishing village beside LA's busy harbour is fast developing into a vibrant and intriguing place, and is also the major departure point for ferries to Catalina Island. I've described the island as a detour because it can pleasantly consume a spare day.

On a summer weekend, this tour finds the LA beaches at their liveliest. A drawback, though, is that traffic on the coastal roads can be heavy; on weekdays, driving is more pleasant. In winter, LA can be warm and sunny but heavy rainfall is a constant possibility.

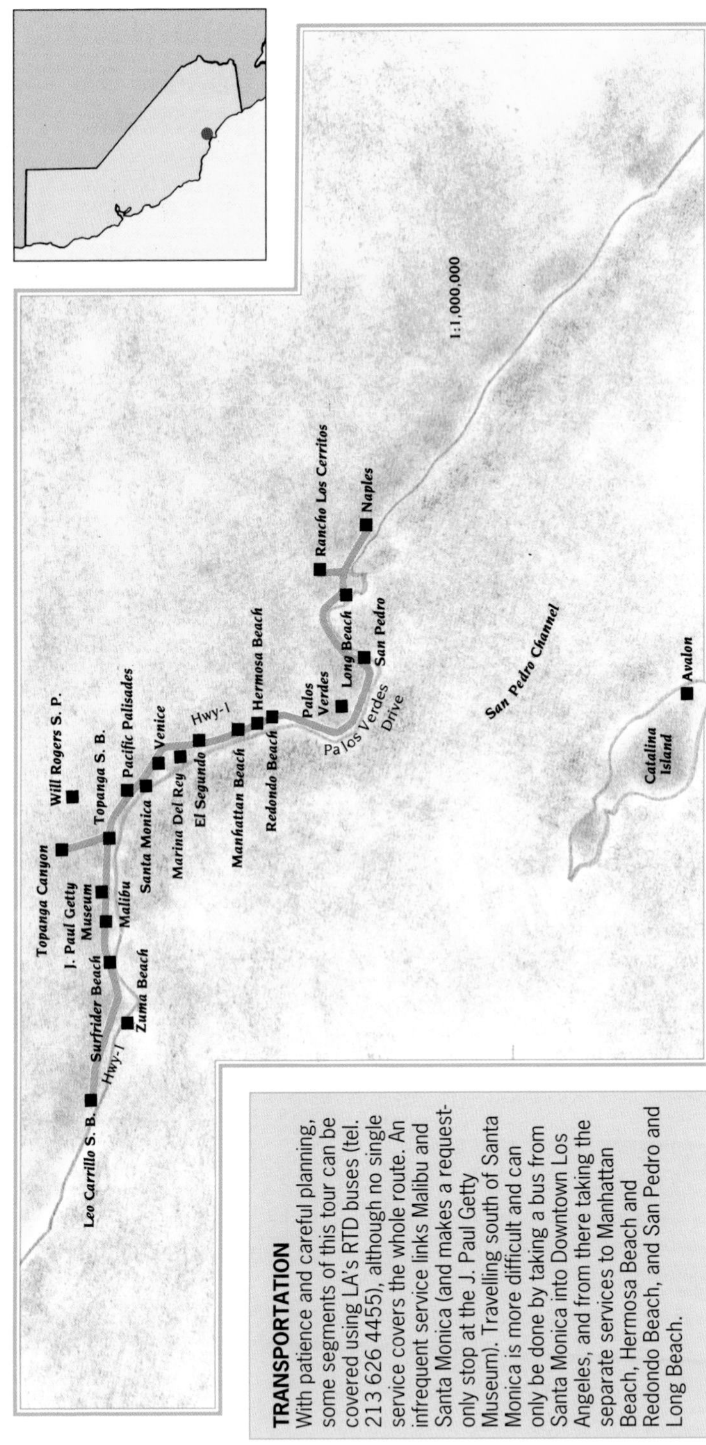

TRANSPORTATION
With patience and careful planning, some segments of this tour can be covered using LA's RTD buses (tel. 213 626 4455), although no single service covers the whole route. An infrequent service links Malibu and Santa Monica (and makes a request-only stop at the J. Paul Getty Museum). Travelling south of Santa Monica is more difficult and can only be done by taking a bus from Santa Monica into Downtown Los Angeles, and from there taking the separate services to Manhattan Beach, Hermosa Beach and Redondo Beach, and San Pedro and Long Beach.

• *Early morning, Malibu Beach.*

SIGHTS & PLACES OF INTEREST

EL SEGUNDO

A quiet residential community, El Segundo's Spanish name translates as "the Second" and refers to Standard Oil's refinery – utterly ugly and unmissable as you pass along the coastal highway – which was the company's second in California.

HERMOSA BEACH

A local surfer and youth leader is remembered by a statue at the foot of Hermosa Beach's pier, which should be proof aplenty that riding the waves is taken very seriously indeed in this slightly downbeat beachside community. Away from the sands and surf, however, the town has little to merit a stop.

LEO CARRILLO STATE BEACH

Approaching from the north on Hwy-1, Leo Carillo State Beach marks your arrival in Los Angeles County and, in keeping with LA's showbiz roots, is named after the actor who played Pancho in TV's *Cisco Kid* series. Most weekdays, bronzed beach bodies are conspicuous by their absence and attention focuses on the state beach's cave- and tunnel-ridden bluffs and the breeze-tormented fishermen who cast hopefully into its offshore kelp beds.

GONDOLA RIDES IN NAPLES

Believe it or not, the canals of Naples – dredged from a harbor bed on the southern edge of Long Beach during the 1920s by the Italy-fixated Arthur Parsons – and the extremely expensive homes which line them, can be lazily explored on hour-long gondola tours. The tours are run by Gondola Getaway; tel. 310 433 9595.

LONG BEACH

Take care to stick to the coastal section of Long Beach and the features which are described below. Just a mile or so inland lie some very mean streets – home of the Cambodian street gangs which over recent years have lately added a new ethnic dimension to LA's interminable social woes.

High-rise offices and hotels give parts of Long Beach an anodyne appearance, but within the compact town center – around the junction of Pine Avenue and 3rd Street – several pleasing examples of 1920s architecture give substance to a stroll. Also justifying a swift perusal are the souvenir shops and food outlets of **Shoreline Village**, arranged along a bay-side boardwalk. Beside Shoreline Village, the grassy acres of the thoughtfully-landscaped **Shoreline Aquatic Park** provide a tempting place for picnics or just strolling and relaxing.

For many years, Long Beach's foremost tourist attractions have been the

DETOUR – **RANCHO LOS CERRITOS**

Completed in 1844, Rancho Los Cerritos, 4600 Virginia Road, is an excellent example of California's Monterey-style architecture and one of the few remaining examples of the style in the south of the state. The furnishings of the family who lived here – over the period when ownership of California switched from Mexico to the U.S. – are arranged throughout ten rooms. You can reach Rancho Los Cerritos by driving 5 miles north along Long Beach Boulevard, off Ocean Boulevard.

1930s Cunard liner, the Queen Mary (clearly visible across Long Beach Harbor), and Howard Hughes' 1940s Spruce Goose wooden aircraft (inside a geodesic dome behind the Queen Mary). At the time of writing,the Queen Mary had reopened for free tours but the future of the Spruce Goose was uncertain.

MALIBU ✕

Malibu may suggest wealth and glamour but when passing through you might well wonder where the famous faces are hiding. In fact, the big names and big money are either concealed in the inland canyons or in luxury beachside homes carefully sited where there is restricted public access to the sands – despite the fact that all LA beaches are public property.

For many years, Malibu was the private ranch of one Frederick Rindge, who made every effort to keep the area separate and aloof from the expanding Los Angeles until the Supreme Court ruled that a road (the present Pacific Coast Highway, the local section of Hwy-1) could be driven through his land.

From the 1920s, a cast of Hollywood celebrities – including Clara Bow, Barbara Stanwyck and Gloria Swanson – moved into the luxury homes of the

RECOMMENDED HOTELS

MALIBU

Malibu Beach Inn, $$$-$$$$; *22878 Pacific Coast Highway; tel.* 310 465 6444; *credit cards,* AE, DC, MC, V.

Sited directly on Malibu Beach, this sizeable but cozy hotel offers many amenities: every room has a balcony overlooking the ocean and is fitted with a copiously-stocked minibar, a VCR, and a coffee-maker. The Inn is ideal for combining lazy hours on the beach with an exploration of the nearby canyons.

SAN PEDRO

San Pedro Grand Hotel, $$$; 111 *Gaffey Street; tel.* 310 514 1414; *credit cards,* AE, DC, DS, MC, V.

The gentrification of San Pedro continues apace and this stylish recent link in the Best Western hotel chain – its rooms spacious and decorated with Victoriana – is as good an indication as any of the area's fast-rising profile.

SANTA MONICA

Carmel Hotel, $$; 201 *Broadway; tel.* 310 451 2469; *cards,* AE, DC, MC, V.

This likeable and unpretentious hotel continues to offer the best value in Santa Monica, as it has done for years. Be sure to book early to take advantage of the excellent rates.

Loews Santa Monica Beach Hotel, $$$$; 1700 *Ocean Avenue; tel.* 310 458 6700; *credit cards,* AE, CB, DC, DS, MC, V.

The first hotel to be built in Santa Monica for 20 years, this pristine post-modern establishment promises – and delivers – luxury beside the ocean waves. Everything in Santa Monica is but a short walk away although you may well be tempted never to leave the premises, which have a fitness center and a generously-sized swimming-pool.

Shangri-La, $$$-$$$$; 1301 *Ocean Avenue; tel.* 310 394 2791; *credit cards,* AE, DC, DS, MC, V.

Lovers of art deco – or 1930s Hollywood – need look no further for a place to stay than this thoroughly renovated hotel, which first opened its doors in 1939. The rooms have ocean views and are decorated with art deco pieces and images of the great days of LA movie making. The price includes breakfast and afternoon tea.

BUDGET ACCOMMODATION

SAN PEDRO

San Pedro International-AYH Hostel; *building* 613, 3601 S. *Gaffey Street; tel.* 310 831 8109.

SANTA MONICA

Santa Monica AYH; 1436 *2nd Street; tel.* 310 393 9913.

VENICE

Venice Beach Hostel; 1515 *Pacific Avenue; tel.* 310 392 6277.

• *Malibu Beach.*

Malibu Beach Colony, a beachside area whose exclusivity is carried into the present by a household-name population of film stars, sports champions, rock musicians, TV personalities and others.

You'll find the well-guarded homes of the Malibu Beach Colony on Webb Way, off Pacific Coast Highway, but if star-spotting (or hoping to) doesn't appeal, time is better spent at **Malibu Lagoon State Beach**, which draws surfers to its southerly swells and local history enthusiasts to the **Adamson House**, a striking Spanish Colonial-style house from the time of the Rindge ranch, and the exhibitions of the adjoining **Malibu Lagoon Museum**.

MANHATTAN BEACH ×

Probably the most fashionable and style-conscious of LA's outlying coastal communities, Manhattan Beach social activity centers on the numerous cafes grouped along Manhattan Beach Boulevard.Sporting activity, however, centers on the volleyball nets lining the town's beach. In California, beach volleyball is a very serious sport with many professional players, a few of whom might be spotted exercising their perfectly-formed calf muscles along the sands. For a glimpse into the founding of the community – just 80 years ago, this was a remote outpost of LA – drop into the small **History Center**, 425 15th Street.

MARINA DEL REY

The world's largest artificial harbor, Marina Del Rey provides docking space for more than 10,000 small boats. It should therefore come as little surprise that the owners and crews of luxury yachts predominate in the expensive restaurants of Fisherman's Village – actually a collection of eating places and retail businesses – and live in the expensive, ultra-modern apartments of neighbouring Playa Del Rey.

PACIFIC PALISADES

The fact that the Pacific Ocean is steadily reclaiming more and more of the bluffs which mark the western edge of Pacific Palisades does nothing to dent the social desirability of the area, which is among LA's most affluent and well-tended neighborhoods.

A group of influential LA-based architects Ray and Charles Eames, Eero Saarinen and Richard Neutra among them – gave Pacific Palisades several houses as part of the city's much-vaunted Case Study Program which began in the 1940s. Unfortunately, public visibility wasn't high on the architects' agenda and none of the much-photographed houses can be seen adequately from the roadside.

Disappointed fans of architecture, and anyone who feels LA's urban madness is about to overwhelm them, should spend an hour or two beside the swan-populated lakes and gardens of the **Self-Realization Fellowship**, 17190 Sunset Boulevard, founded by an Indian sect in 1950 to express the universality of all religions.

PALOS VERDES

The LA coastline changes dramatically at Palos Verdes, where broad sandy beaches give way to tall bluffs. Hwy-1

• *Right, La Salsa Dude, and below, the J. Paul Getty Museum, contrasting images of Malibu.*

DAY TRIP - **CATALINA ISLAND** ×

San Pedro is one of four places (Long Beach, Redondo Beach and Newport Beach on California Overall: 8 are the others) from which ferries make an hour-long crossing to **Catalina Island**. The ferries put ashore within walking distance of Catalina's only town, **Avalon** (population 2,000), which is filled with whimsical architecture and locals getting about on bicycles and electrically-powered buggies – the cost of shipping cars to and from the mainland is prohibitive.

On one side of Avalon, the art deco **Avalon Casino** is a reminder of William Wrigley Jr.'s (Wrigley effectively purchased control of the island in 1919) successful attempt to bring mainlanders to Catalina with the promise of gambling. Guided tours of the former casino are fascinating – don't miss the luscious art deco ballroom, where big bands serenaded revellers during the 1940s. Also very interesting is the adjoining **Catalina Museum**, which outlines the demise of the Gabrieleno Indians who occupied Catalina for 4,000 years before being forcibly relocated to the mainland by white fur-trappers.

Outside Avalon, Catalina is free of development and retains the wild appearance which all of southern California had before it disappeared beneath freeways and suburbia. Catalina's upkeep is funded by the Santa Catalina Conservancy, which has also enabled much of the island's unique flora and fauna to survive. Some of the island's wild flowers can be seen inside the **Wrigley Botanical Gardens**, 1400 Avalon Canyon Road.

To penetrate backcountry Catalina, you'll need either to plan a lengthy hiking trip or to arrive on the first ferry of the day which allows just enough time to join the **Inside Adventure** (tel. 310 510 2888). Departing daily from Avalon, the anecdote-filled bus tour explores the narrow roads leading across the rest of the island and turns up many great views of buffalo- and antelope-roamed hillsides.

DETOUR - **TOPANGA CANYON**

Sixties California hippiedom is alive and well and living next door to 1990s New Age pursuits in Topanga Canyon, a rustic village on Hwy-27 (which cuts inland from Topanga Beach) dominated by health food restaurants, handicraft shops and esoteric bookstores. It was in Topanga Canyon that some of LA's psychedelic musical gurus – Canned Heat, Spirit, the Byrds among them – either lived, played or partied and made the most of bucolic surroundings only a few minutes' drive from the clubs of Sunset Strip. The hillsides above the community make up **Topanga State Park**, 9,000 acres of tree- and chaparral-coated hillsides with hiking trails rising to breathtaking views of ocean, mountains, and the enormous flat basin which holds the conglomeration of LA.

turns inland to avoid the hilly Palos Verdes peninsula, which is dotted with affluent, hamlet-sized communities reached by snaking lanes. The peninsula's coastal side is traversed by Palos Verdes Drive, a road which threads its way between rocky cliffs and the ocean. On it, keep an eye out for the many footpaths which lead from the roadside to pint-sized beaches – some of them home to surfers who are fiercely protective of what they call "their" waves. Look, too, for the short road which winds up to the **Wayfarer's Chapel**, erected in a young redwood grove by architect Lloyd Wright (son of the more famous Frank Lloyd) in 1946 as a monument to 18thC Swedish theologian Emmanuel Swedenborg.

Just before Palos Verdes Drive begins its descent into San Pedro (see page 238), the 37-acre **Point Fermin Park** is a popular spot for watching migrating gray whales and also gives aerial views of the LA harbor, and – smog permitting – across the unrelenting sprawl of LA itself.

J. PAUL GETTY MUSEUM

Since its opening in 1974, the J. Paul Getty Museum – founded by the late oil tycoon and housed in a replica of Herculaneum's Villa dei Papiri (buried by the eruption of Mount Vesuvius in AD 79) – has been at the forefront of the art world, not merely for the quality of its collections but also for its colossal spending power, deriving from Getty's $2.2 billion endowment.

Many hours are required to make even the most superficial survey of the museum's treasures, and you'll save much legwork by concentrating on your personal interests. Getty's liking for Greek and Roman statuary is evident throughout the villa's ground floor. Subsequent galleries hold paintings from the 13thC to the 20thC – Rembrandt, Van Dyck, Gauguin, Degas and Gainsborough, among the diverse artists displayed – and an immense stock of beautifully-crafted tables, chairs, clocks and ornaments and other examples of 17th-19thC French decorative art.

In the early 1980s, the museum began specializing in illustrated medieval manuscripts and now boasts a major collection: the vivid, radiant colors of many examples belie their antiquity. Elsewhere, the extensive photographic exhibits range from grainy early-19thC portraits to the experimental images of Man Ray and Walker Evans.

Apart from continuing to increase its possessions, the museum's future

RECOMMENDED RESTAURANTS

CATALINA ISLAND

Armstrong's Seafood Restaurant, $-$$; 306 *Crescent* Ave, *Avalon; tel.* 310 510 0113; *credit cards,* MC, V.

Should you make the recommended day trip to Catalina Island, stop off here for a classy but affordable seafood lunch. Whether it is swordfish or mahi-mahi, the catch is certain to be fresh and usually tastes best when it has been mesquite grilled.

MALIBU

Alice's, $-$$; 23000 *Pacific Coast Highway; tel.* 310 456 6646; *credit cards,* AE, MC, V.

Alice's has occupied a prime ocean-view site close to Malibu pier for 20 years and serves dependable seafood and pasta dishes, plus an intriguing selection of creative salads. Some Malibu residents make Alice's bar the fulcrum of their social life.

MANHATTAN BEACH

Cafe Pierre, $$-$$$; 317 *Manhattan Beach Boulevard; tel.* 310 545 1373; *credit cards,* AE, MC, V.

A would-be French bistro which, along with some very accomplished French provincial-style fare, offers tempting pasta and fresh seafood.

SAN PEDRO

Papadaki's Tavern, $-$$; 301 W. *6th Street; tel.* 310 548 1186; *credit cards,* MC, V.

A local institution as well as a hit on the tourist circuit, this lively family-run Greek eatery not only offers a lengthy menu and enormous portions, but has waiters who frequently burst into song and dance their way around the tables.

SANTA MONICA

Broadway Bar & Grill, $–$$; 1460 *Third Street; tel.* 310 393 4211; *credit cards,* AE, DC, MC, V.

The outdoor tables provide a great view of lively Third Street and the food is a classy blending of standard American favorites and California specialities: ideal for a stylish lunch or a leisurely, indulgent dinner.

Zucky's, $; 431 *Wilshire Boulevard; tel.* 310 393 0351; *credit cards, none.*

Trendy Santa Monica eaterys come and go but Zucky's – established 1946 – seems set to last for ever. Deli favorites are served around the clock to a nutty mix of old folks, youthful nightclubbers, and anyone else who fancies a quick, cheap feed.

VENICE

The Sidewalk Cafe, $-$$; 1401 *Ocean Front Walk; tel.* 310 399 5547; *credit cards,* AE, DC, MC, V.

The standard selection of omelettes, burgers and salads, plus a few pasta dishes, are much less of an attraction than a patio table – expect a line on weekends – overlooking Venice's effervescent beachside Boardwalk.

plans include the removal of all but the classical pieces to a new 450,000-acre hillside site overlooking west Los Angeles, due to be ready in 1995.

REDONDO BEACH

Like neighboring Hermosa Beach and Manhattan Beach, Redondo Beach draws its share of surfers, though high-rise condominiums and holiday apartments loom behind the sands and families on vacation are often as much in evidence as tanned beach bums. Beside the beach, the ramshackle wooden walkways of Fisherman's Wharf hold a tame selection of souvenir shops, snack bars and fresh seafood stalls.

SAN PEDRO 🛏 ✕

Situated on the LA harbor, which by the 1940s was the world's largest man-made harbor, San Pedro grew from a tiny fishing community into a vibrant enclave of ethnically-diverse seafaring migrants. Even today, the tightly-packed older streets of San Pedro evoke a mood quite unlike that in any other part of LA, though the broad avenues in the rest of town are fast being populated by the young and upwardly mobile.

San Pedro's **Cabrillo Marine**

• *3rd Street Promenade, Santa Monica.*

Museum, 3720 Stephen Wright Drive, aims its ocean-life exhibits at young minds. Older heads are better served by the accounts of the rise and rise of LA's harbor given at the **Maritime Museum**, Berth 84 (at the foot of 6th Street). Nearby stand the pseudo-New England cottages which form the **Ports O' Call Village**, a gathering of souvenir shops.

SANTA MONICA 🛏 ✕

Santa Monica's expansive white sand beach and fresh sea breezes have been refreshing citizens of LA since the "Red Car" rail transportation system linked it to the rest of the city at the turn of the century. Since the demise of the offshore gambling ships, which circumvented gaming laws and gave the community a seedy ambience in the 1920s, Santa Monica has forged a reputation as one of LA's creative and radical communities. Nonetheless, few people can afford to live here without being very securely bank-rolled with the notable exception of the many unfortunates who sleep rough in the beach-side Palisades Park.

The landmark **Santa Monica Pier**

• LA *surfers in conference.*

has withstood the poundings of storms and tourists' feet for seven decades, and the frequent attentions of TV and film crews, including those who used its 1922 carousel for a bit part in *The Sting*. Away from the beach, and the hotels and apartment houses which face it, Santa Monica's appeal centers on the trendy cafes of **Third Street Promenade** – a lively pedestrianized street often engulfed by parades or festivals. A short walk south, at 2612 Main Street, are the worthwhile historical exhibitions of the **Santa Monica Heritage Museum**. The **Santa Monica Museum of Art**, no. 2437, shows some of the latest works from the town's many highly-rated contemporary artists in a 1908 warehouse redesigned by one of its most acclaimed architects, Frank Gehry.

SURFRIDER BEACH

On any sunny weekend bikinis, biceps and surfboards are still as much in evidence at Surfrider Beach as they were in the early 1960s, when Frankie Avalon and Annette Furnicello starred in the low-budget beach party movies made here.

TOPANGA STATE BEACH

One of a string of popular surfing beaches, Topanga Beach also marks the junction of Pacific Coast Highway and Hwy-27, which continues inland to Topanga Canyon (see page 236).

VENICE

After the canals of Naples (see Gondola Rides in Naples, page 232), another set shouldn't come as a surprise. In Venice, however, most of the seven-mile system of waterways created by wealthy philanthropist Abbot Kinney were filled in to make roads or to accommodate drilling equipment when oil deposits were discovered here during the late 1920s.

Instead of the replica Italian town which Kinney envisaged, people flock to present-day Venice for its crazed beachside boardwalk. Along the half-mile walkway, fire-eaters, sword-swallowers, tap-dancers and fortune-tellers are all likely inhabitants, plying their trade as wildly-dressed roller-skaters and skateboarders whizz by. And at Muscle Beach, an open-air gym beside the boardwalk, muscle-bound physiques are tweaked ever closer to total perfection.

WILL ROGERS STATE PARK

Known as the "Cowboy Philosopher," Will Rogers first delivered his deadpan monologues on current affairs on the stage and, after moving to California in 1919 to act in Westerns, developed his homespun views on life and politics by writing a newspaper column and several books. The humorist's former home sits at the center of the 187-acre Will Rogers State Park and is packed with mementoes of his life and a short film revealing – among other things – Rogers' dexterity with a lasso.

ZUMA BEACH

However hot Zuma Beach may be in summer, it's cooler than the San Fernando Valley – the quintessential LA suburb, infamous for its smog and for its air-headed "Valley Girls" – which is why, on any summer weekend, the entire valley population appears to have relocated to the picnic tables and snack-stands here, the easiest beach to reach from the valley.

Southern California

Los Angeles: The City

40 *miles (one way); map* De Lorme *Southern & Central California*

Exciting and frightening in equal measure, Los Angeles is a city which defies the most lurid and colorful descriptions. Nowadays far more famous for the rioting of April 1992 than for being the most futuristic – and superstar-filled – city in the U.S., LA undoubtedly has major problems, but is also unrivalled as California's most stimulating urban area.

Instead of covering LA in the same way as San Francisco, I've chosen to make it a local exploration. The city has no single nucleus, but several, widely separated; wandering around on foot is unsafe and will reveal little. So, I've devised a driving route to guide you safely through the captivating sections while keeping you clear of the trouble spots.

I must stress, however, that no part of LA is entirely safe and you should take more than usual care wherever you go. Of course, you can make good use of this section without actually doing the route, but it does guide you through the confusing conglomeration of areas – many of them cities in their own right – which form this vast, flat metropolis, large chunks of which are consumed by nothing more interesting than car-repair forecourts and mini-shopping malls.

California Overall: 6, 7 and 8 all converge on LA, though I recommend that you join this tour from Santa Monica, which is on Local Explorations: 15 – coastal LA. From Santa Monica, you're perfectly placed to move inland to Westwood and the UCLA campus, and to continue the few miles east to glamor-soaked Beverly Hills, a likely base for your first night and a great place from which to send postcards – embossed with a Beverly Hills postmark – to your friends.

An alternative first-night base, just east of Beverly Hills, is West Hollywood, a lively and fashionable area with the bulk of the city's nightclubs. By contrast, Hollywood itself should only be tackled in daylight: the area has several must-see movie landmarks, but much of Hollywood is drab and tawdry and won't make you feel like lingering long.

After Hollywood, the rest of your second day should be spent in Downtown LA, the most compact and diverse part of the city. I've offered some accommodation selections in Downtown but I suggest that you consider moving directly on to Pasadena, an appealing small town ringed by suburbia and with several important museums within easy reach. Pasadena also makes a very agreeable base for the second of your two nights.

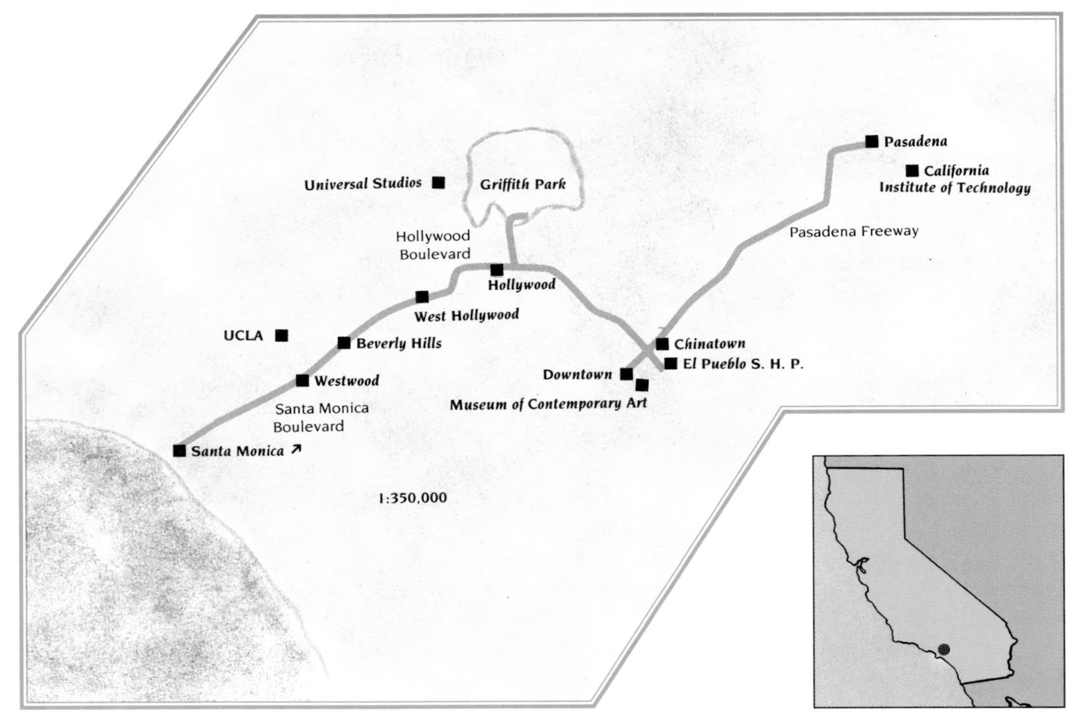

TRANSPORTATION

Problems of smog and congestion have forced the city built for the automobile to invest millions of dollars in a new subway service which it is hoped will free millions of Angelenos from their car-dependency by the year 2,000. So far, only a 22-mile stretch of the intended 150-mile Metro train line exists, and links Downtown with Long Beach. Still a much more common form of public transport are the snail-paced buses, which serve more or less every quarter of this immense city and ply almost all the main thoroughfares. Of several companies which operate bus services, the largest is RTD (tel. 213 626 4455), whose well-labelled stops can be found on most street corners and who operate a single flat fare of $1.10.

It can't be stressed enough that using public transport in LA is an extremely slow way of getting around. And, especially at night, all manner of undesirables are likely to be aboard.

• *Rodeo Drive, Beverly Hills: shopper's paradise.*

SIGHTS & PLACES OF INTEREST

BEVERLY HILLS 🛏 ✕

To enter Beverly Hills is to venture into realms of hyper-wealth that very few people even dare dream about. Rich and famous faces by the score live in Beverly Hills, though most of them are hidden from the public gaze behind tall walls and elaborate security systems in the hills above the town, an area first settled in force by the movie idols of the 1920s. You'll best feel the moneyed pulse of this unbelievably affluent community along **Rodeo Drive**, a prized shopping strip between Santa Monica and Wilshire Boulevards, where locals emerge from their fortress homes long enough to patronize top-name designer stores: Cartier, Hermès and Gucci are just three with outlets here. Another top-notch shopping stop is the **Rodeo Collection**, 421 N.

ARRIVING

All international flights and most domestic flights land at Los Angeles International Airport (LAX), 15 miles south-west of Downtown LA. All car hire firms in LA have desks at the airport and operate free shuttle buses for arriving passengers to collect their hired vehicles. If you have no car, you can use one of dozens of privately-run minibuses which call at the airport concourse and will travel to almost any address in LA, usually for a fare of $10-$20. A taxi from the airport is likely to cost in excess of $30. Local buses serve LAX but their route network is incredibly complex and is certain to bewilder first-time arrivals.

Trains into LA arrive at Union Station (tel. 800 872 7245), in Downtown. The city's main Greyhound terminal is also in Downtown, 208 E. 6th Street (tel. 213 629 8400), a very run-down area – the station is in the process of being relocated to a new Downtown address. A few arriving buses also call at smaller Greyhound terminals in Santa Monica, Hollywood and Pasadena.

Rodeo Drive, a shopping mall like no other, where the prerequisites of the jet-set lifestyle are displayed at dizzying prices.

CHINATOWN

LA's sizeable Chinese population was forcibly removed from the original Chinatown district during the 1930s to make way for Union Station (see Downtown, below) and relocated around North Broadway in an area now characterized by a heady assortment of live poultry shops, pagoda-shaped Far Eastern banks, bustling marketplaces entered by dragon-decorated gateways, and countless neon-lit restaurants. Although many LA-Chinese families vacated Chinatown for the suburbs long ago, they often return at weekends – by far the best time to visit Chinatown – to shop and to eat. Much of Chinatown's present 200,000-strong population is made up of recent arrivals from south-east Asia.

DOWNTOWN

The skyscrapers huddled together in Downtown's Financial District can be seen from far across predominantly low-rise LA and are enduring symbols of the city's immense economic power. Much of the rest of Downtown is quite different, however, often quite dangerous and always at least slightly intimidating for visitors.

Before LA clutched the automobile to its bosom, the city barely extended beyond what is now Downtown and the theater-lined **Broadway** was the city's most fashionable thoroughfare. Today's Broadway provides popular shopping territory for LA's immense Latino population, with a ceaseless procession milling around its cut-price T-shirt and electrical shops.

To the north, smaller but immeasurably more handsome than Downtown's recent glass-and-steel towers, the 1928 **City Hall**, 200 N. Spring Street, is best explored with the aid of a guided tour (reservations essential; tel. 213 485 4823). Within a short walk of City Hall, **Union Station**, 800 N. Alameda Street, was completed in

• *Downtown* LA.

DETOUR – **THE MUSEUM OF CONTEMPORARY ART**
When the frantic pace of Downtown streets saps your strength, aim to spend a relaxing hour or two inside the **Museum of Contemporary Art** (MOCA), 250 S. Grand Avenue, occupying an architecturally-acclaimed building designed by Arata Isozaki. Few famous works feature among MOCA's permanent stock, but plenty of accomplished names crop up in its survey of American and European art trends from 1940 to the present. MOCA has also staged several much talked-about temporary exhibitions in its few years of existence, and in so doing has challenged – albeit in a minor way – New York's long-standing role as the fulcrum of modern art in the U.S. Short-term large-scale exhibits are presented across Downtown at the **Temporary Contemporary**, 152 Central Avenue, to which MOCA tickets are valid on day of issue (and vice versa).

1939 during the heyday of American rail travel. Its graceful design was based on the Spanish mission style and was intended to leave cross-country rail passengers in no doubt that they had arrived in California.

EL PUEBLO STATE HISTORIC PARK
Although historians still debate the fine points, it was in or around what is now **El Pueblo State Historic Park** that LA's 44 ethnically-diverse original settlers arrived in 1781, charged with the task of growing food for California's Spanish missions.

What little there was of Los Angeles throughout the 19thC grew up around El Pueblo, but one thing which didn't exist then was the enjoyable pseudo-Mexican market of **Olvera Street**, off the park's Old Plaza, which was created in 1930 as a tourist attraction and a celebration of LA's Mexican roots. Interesting handicrafts and less interesting tourist tack stand side by side on the market's stalls, and several hole-in-the-wall eaterys offer well-priced snacks – look for those offering hand-made tortillas.

Aside from the 1818 **Avila Adobe**, 10 Olvera Street, claimed to be the oldest house in LA, with tourable rooms furnished in 1840s style, the park's real history lies around the Old Plaza and along Main Street. Most of the 19thC buildings here – notably the Merced Theater, the Masonic Hall and the Pico House can only be admired from the outside, but do explore the richly-decorated interior of the **Plaza Church**, 535 N. Main Street. Building began in 1818, took 40 years, and was partly financed by donations of cattle and whiskey.

The Olvera Street information center provides background on El Pueblo State Historic Park, although you'll learn a great deal more by joining the **walking tour**, which begins from the Visitor Information Center on the Old Plaza and winds around the area's points of interest, providing historical anecdotes by the score.

GRIFFITH PARK
Municipal parks rarely come bigger than Griffith Park, with 4,000 acres spanning everything from the quiet, leafy glade of the Ferndell to steep hiking trails which reach far into the Santa Monica Mountains. If you do fancy a day's walking in the wilds (be warned that Griffith Park can be dangerous, and you should be sure to avoid the secluded areas after dark) collect maps and relevant information from the park's Ranger Headquarters, 4730 Crystal Springs Drive (tel. 213 665 5188).

Otherwise, the expansive park – crossed by several snaking roads – is best explored by car. Be sure to visit the **Griffith Observatory**, a park feature since the 1930s and a bit player in films as diverse as *Rebel Without A Cause* and *Barton Fink*. The Observatory's Hall of Science holds briefly-divert-

UNIVERSAL STUDIOS
The thrill-a-minute rides around familiar film sets offered by Universal Studios are one of the major tourist attractions of LA. The entrance to Universal Studios, however, lies not in Hollywood but at Universal City by the junction of the Hollywood Freeway and Lankershim Boulevard, near Burbank. For details, tel. 818 508 9600.

ing exhibitions but the views across LA from its hill-top site are likely to have greater appeal. The Observatory also has a planetarium and a heavens-scanning telescope which, on clear nights, is opened for public viewings (until 10 pm; tel. 213 664 1191). If an inordinate number of long-haired youths appear to be hanging around the Observatory, they're probably arriving for the laser light shows with heavy rock music soundtracks which take place in the specially-designed

BUDGET ACCOMMODATION

For details of budget accommodation in Los Angeles, see Local Explorations: 15.

RECOMMENDED HOTELS

BEVERLY HILLS

Beverly House Hotel, $$-$$$; 140 S. *Lasky Drive; tel.* 213 271 2145; *credit cards,* AE, CB, DC, MC, V.

A great find at a great price in a Beverly Hills side-street, within easy reach of the famed Rodeo Drive. Modelled along European lines, this small hotel provides a complimentary light breakfast.

Hotel Del Capri, $$$; 10587 *Wilshire Boulevard; tel.* 213 474 3511; *credit cards,* AE, CB, DC, MC, V.

Tucked away behind high-rise condos, not many people know about the Del Capri but this modestly-sized hotel offers a high standard of service and – considering the prime location – remarkably sound value.

DOWNTOWN

Metro Plaza Hotel, $$; 711 N. *Main Street; tel.* 800 223 2223; *credit cards,* AE, MC, V.

One of the newest of the many new medium-range hotels which have appeared in Downtown over recent years. Clean and efficient, with a fridge in every room.

Westin Bonaventure, $$$$; 404 S. *Figueroa Street; tel.* 213 624 1000; *credit cards,* AE, CB, DC, MC, V.

The glass towers and city-within-a-city ambience of the Bonaventure made an exciting addition to the Downtown cityscape a few years ago but nowadays seem a trifle passé. Nevertheless, if you want to stay in an ultra-modern hotel where the (rather ordinary) rooms are reached by way of several shopping malls and numerous nightclubs and restaurants, there's no better place.

PASADENA

Days Inn, $-$$; 3500 *Colorado Boulevard; tel.* 818 792 1365; *credit cards,* AE, MC, V.

This medium-sized branch of the inexpensive nationwide chain of dependable, no-frills motels is just right for a low-cost stay in Pasadena.

Ritz-Carlton Huntington Hotel, $$$–$$$$; 1401 S. *Oak Knoll; tel.*818 568 3900; *credit cards,* AE, MC, V.

Opened as a high-class resort hotel in 1907, the recently revamped Huntington once again offers a special brand of luxury in landscaped surroundings, in a quiet residential section of Pasadena. The rooms have king-sized beds, marble bathrooms and well-stocked minibars. Stroll through the hotel and you'll find an Olympic-sized swimming-pool and several elegant restaurants.

WEST HOLLYWOOD

Beverly Laurel Motor Hotel, $$; 8018 *Beverly Boulevard; tel.* 213 651 2441; *credit cards,* AE, CB, DC, MC, V.

Its location, a short drive from the Sunset Strip and the center of Beverly Hills, helps reduce the rates at this unelaborate but perfectly useable spot.

Chateau Marmont, $$$-$$$$; 8221 W. *Sunset Boulevard; tel.* 213 656 1010; *credit cards,* AE, CB, DC, MC, V.

Plenty of top-bracket celebrities inhabit the bungalows, lesser names use the cottages, and ordinary folk with style occupy the regular rooms at this well-known and very comfortable hotel. The impressive roll call of former guests includes John and Yoko Lennon and comedian John Belushi, who checked in but never checked out.

• *Ripley's Believe It or Not!, Hollywood.*

Laserium.

In the park's north-western corner, the **LA Zoo** will meet with the approval of young travellers, but the **Gene Autry Western Heritage Museum**, which explores the settlement of the American West and lifts the lid on the Hollywood Western, offers a more thought-provoking few hours.

HOLLYWOOD ×

The American motion picture industry, which got off the ground in the then Methodist temperance colony of Hollywood in the 1910s, gave the neighborhood an aura of glamor which soon spread far and wide. Truth be told, though, the film companies and the film stars both left Hollywood as soon as they were successful (you'll find the former in Burbank and the latter in Beverly Hills or Malibu) and the district has since deteriorated into a handful of movie-era landmarks sandwiched between souvenir shops and surrounded by depressed – and dangerous after dark – residential streets.

Nonetheless, you haven't been to LA unless you've spent an hour strolling Hollywood Boulevard and combined this with a car tour of the nearby sights. On Hollywood Boulevard, the **Walk of Fame** remembers two thousand showbiz stars prepared to pay $3,500 for the privilege of adding a paving slab bearing their name to the sidewalk and deserves no more than passing glances on the way to **Mann's Chinese Theater**, no. 6925. Opened by impresario Sid Grauman in 1927, the theater's mock-Oriental form is barely noticed by the two million visitors who descend each year on the world's most popular set of foot and hand (and hoof, in the case of Gene Autry's horse) prints embedded in the theater's forecourt, bequeathed by screen stars.

Drive north along Highland Avenue and you soon reach the **Hollywood Bowl**, a renowned open-air auditorium and the summer home of the LA Philharmonic Orchestra. The Philharmonic's evening concert series here has entertained Angelenos since the 1920s, a fact borne out by the photos and exhibits stored inside the Hollywood Bowl Museum, close to the entrance, where you'll also find evidence of the Beatles' legendary appearance at the bowl in 1964.

Directly across Highland Avenue, the **Hollywood Studio Museum** is an under-valued collection of absorbing bits and bobs culled from American movie-making's earliest days and is housed in the barn in which Cecil B. DeMille made an inauspicious start to his directing career, sharing the building with a horse.

Round off your tour of Hollywood at the **Hollywood Memorial Cemetery**, 6000 Santa Monica Boulevard, a final resting place for many famous or indeed legendary names: among them Jayne Mansfield, Tyrone Power, Douglas Fairbanks, and, in the Cathedral Mausoleum, Rudolph Valentino.

PASADENA 🛏 ×

Nestled at the foot of the San Gabriel Mountains (their slopes often obscured by smog, which can be particularly bad here during the summer), Pasadena is easily the most appealing of LA's neck-to-neck inland suburbs and was founded in 1875 as a winter resort for affluent Easterners. Pasadena was considered far removed from the hurly-burly of LA until 1940, when the two communities were linked by the city's earliest freeway – the Arroyo Seco Parkway, now known as the Pasadena Freeway. The architectural firm of Greene & Greene – whose influence on southern Californian dwellings was profound – were responsible for several early Pasadena houses, including the wonderful **Gamble House**, 4 Westmoreland Place, completed in 1908 and as fine an example of the Greenes' Arts and Crafts style as you're likely to find. Guided tours of the house, parts of which are used by the University of Southern California's School of Architecture, are conducted Thursday to Sunday (tel. 818 793 3334).

Besides significant architecture, Pasadena also has one of LA's most striking art collections, the **Norton Simon Museum of Art**, 411 W. Colorado Boulevard. The museum's western art is of exceptional quality – works displayed range from Rubens and Rembrandt to Renoir and Van Gogh, and also include a comprehensive Degas collection and pieces by Picasso. But what sticks in the mind is the museum's tremendous horde of Asian sculpture: a mass of ancient religious pieces

• *Above, in Beverly Hills; below, Mann's Chinese Theater, Hollywood.*

chiefly from India, Nepal, Cambodia and Thailand, and often innovatively arranged to combine the museum's interior space with its outdoor sculpture garden.

A few minutes' walk from the museum brings you to the section of Colorado Boulevard, in the vicinity of the junction with Raymond Avenue, known as **Old Pasadena**, where many recently-renovated 1910s buildings have been taken over by small, entertaining shops and numerous cafes – a perfect spot to waste an hour or two.

Another place to admire at leisure is the 1927 **Pasadena City Hall**, a block north of Colorado Boulevard off Garfield Avenue. With its over-wrought Renaissance-style dome, the hall is difficult to miss: walk through the cloistered archways into the pleasant courtyard garden and try to imagine a more serene setting for local government offices.

DETOUR – **CALIFORNIA INSTITUTE OF TECHNOLOGY**

The Huntington Library and Gardens are a major draw on Pasadena's outskirts, but scientifically-minded visitors with time to spare will be better served by a visit to the California Institute of Technology. The Institute, better known as **CalTec**, is a small, independently-run university but one with such phenomenal resources that it can attract the nation's leading scientific minds. Twenty-one Nobel Prize winners have been based here, and CalTec is the home of the Jet Propulsion Laboratory, where the means to carry NASA astronauts into space and to the moon were devised during the 1960s. Tours of CalTec are run on Mondays, Thursdays and Fridays at 3 pm; on Tuesdays and Wednesdays at 11 am. For details, tel. 818 356 6327.

SANTA MONICA

See Local Explorations: 15.

SUNSET STRIP

As Sunset Boulevard passes through West Hollywood (see below), it mutates into the Sunset Strip, known for the best of the city's rock music clubs and a glut of fashionable restaurants. Above the Strip rise gigantic billboards touting the latest offerings from LA's entertainment industry.

WEST HOLLYWOOD 🛏 ✕

Keen to dissociate itself from run-down Hollywood, West Hollywood begins west of La Brea Avenue and is officially a city in its own right. A hip and fashionable area, West Hollywood boasts dozens of trendy shops along **Melrose Avenue**, the clubs of Sunset Strip (see above), and is a major base for LA's large and politically assertive gay population.

WESTWOOD AND UCLA

Laid out in the 1920s, Westwood is one of the few places in LA designed with the pedestrian in mind. The Italianate buildings of this would-be Mediterranean shopping village, however, hold only a routine collection of book, clothing and souvenir shops. Most people who come to Westwood are film buffs making for its cinemas, which show new releases long before they reach the rest of the world, or are among the 25,000 students enrolled at the nearby University of California at Los Angeles (UCLA).

A more deserving place than Westwood for an hour's stroll is UCLA, whose roots stretch back to 1881 though the oldest campus buildings are attractive Romanesque structures dating from the 1920s. Places of note include the characterful **Powell Library**, the **Museum of Cultural History** with its exhibitions of folk art, and the contemporary art and sculpture shows of the **Wright Art Gallery**. Much more art can be found on the edge of Westwood at the **Armand Hammer Museum of Art and Culture Center**, 10899 Wilshire Boulevard, which displays the multi-million dollar collection of the late oil magnate. Packed with the leading names of European art and devoting a special gallery to the Codex Hammer – a collection of pages from the notebooks of Leonardo da Vinci – the museum is surprisingly underwhelming, largely due to its lack of single great works. The temporary exhibitions, on the other hand, can be exceptional.

RECOMMENDED RESTAURANTS

BEVERLY HILLS

California Pizza Kitchen, $-$$; 207 S. *Beverly Drive; tel.* 310 272 7878; *credit cards,* AE, MC, V.

Where the California pizza – with toppings such as Bombay duck, Thai chicken or roasted shrimp-in-garlic – first saw the light of day. Also offers a wide assortment of pasta dishes and salads. Interesting food and usually an interesting crowd to be found here, too.

Nat'n Al's, $; 414 N. *Beverly Drive; tel.* 310 274 0101; *credit cards,* AE, V.

New York-style deli which has been serving lox, bagels, blintzes and more for many years to a devoted clientele, which includes numerous TV and movie backroom movers. Not only cheap, but one of the few places in Beverly Hills where you can eat without being dressed up.

DOWNTOWN

Original Pantry Cafe, $; 877 S. *Figueroa Street; tel.* 213 972 9279; *credit cards, none.*

Legendary down-to-earth eatery which, since 1924, has been serving generous helpings of American diner fare around the clock. The breakfast fry-ups are formidable and the dinner options include a large steak accompanied by an enormous salad.

Original Sonora Cafe, $$; 445 S. *Figueroa Street; tel.* 213 624 1800; *credit cards,* AE, MC, V.

The fiery fare of the American south-west is prepared and presented with panache – and Californian culinary invention – in this suitably-decorated restaurant.

HOLLYWOOD

Gorky's, $; 1716 N. *Cahuenga Boulevard; tel.* 213 463 4060; *credit cards, none.*

Russian specialities served canteen-style, 24 hours a day to a great mixture of Hollywood would-be rock stars, posers, and the simply hungry. Also offers home-brewed beer and has live music most nights.

Pink's, $; 709 N. *La Brea Avenue; tel.* 213 931 4223; *credit cards, none; closed Fri, Sat.*

Hot dogs in more shapes, sizes and varieties than you ever dared imagine have been the speciality of this order-pay-eat-go outlet since 1939.

PASADENA

Cameron's, $-$$; 1978 E. *Colorado Boulevard; tel.* 818 793 FISH; *credit cards,* AE, DC, MC, V.

Promises 43 varieties of seafood – including oysters – and delivers them in many mouthwatering styles. The generous Sunday buffet brunch is a must for devoted fish eaters.

Rose City Diner, $; 45 S. *Fair Oaks Avenue; tel.* 818 793 8282; *credit cards, none.*

Not the best place in town for lunch or dinner, but this 1990s version of a 1950s diner does offer value-for-money omelettes (choose your fillings from a choice of three) intended for breakfast but served, with toast or muffins, throughout the day.

Roxxi, $$; 1065 E. *Greene Street; tel.* 818 449 4519; *credit cards,* AE, MC, V.

Plenty of what California does best – exotically-topped pizzas, enormous salads, delicious pasta dishes – served in a stylish but low-key setting.

WEST HOLLYWOOD

Border Grill, $$; 7407 *Melrose Avenue; tel.* 213 658 7495; *credit cards,* AE, MC, V.

There's rarely a quiet moment at this pulsating and fashionable eatery, which takes the simple basics of Mexican and American south-western cuisine and adds only-in-LA touches to produce innovative dishes.

Johnny Rocket's, $; 7507 *Melrose Avenue; tel.* 213 651 3361; *credit cards, none.*

The trendiest of LA's many 1950s-style retro-diners, serving burgers and milkshakes to local fashion victims with a background of taped early rock-and-roll classics. The food is less interesting than the clientele. Expect a long line at weekends.

Southern California

San Diego Area

28 miles (one way); map De Lorme *Southern & Central California*

This expedition, a natural extension of California Overall: 8, provides an overview of San Diego and its vicinity. This is southern California's most welcoming city and one which couples its benevolent climate and picturesque ocean-side setting with important historical sites and one of the state's largest concentrations of museums. Allow three days to cover it all.

San Diego divides easily into several well-defined areas, each of which is best explored on foot (although you'll need more than feet to travel between the different neighborhoods). I suggest that you dispense with your car for part of your stay, not least because weekday traffic can be fierce in this busy city, and make use of the local bus network.

It could be that coastal San Diego, with its surfer-filled sands and energetic beach life, will be your major interest. If so, I recommend that you spend both your nights by the beach. I've made accommodation selections in Pacific Beach, a fine location for sipping cocktails while gazing into the sunset and for partaking of the classic Californian beach scene which prevails at adjoining Mission Beach. Otherwise, spend at least one of your nights in Downtown, where small and reasonably priced hotels are plentiful on or around the evocatively restored streets of the Gaslamp District. Staying in Downtown will also leave you nicely placed for touring the rest of the city.

San Diego's easy-going mood may make you feel like doing nothing at all, but essential things to see include Balboa Park – a vast hunk of landscaped greenery whose Spanish-style buildings hold a formidable batch of museums – and Old Town State Historic Park, where San Diego was born with the 18thC founding of California's first Spanish mission. I have also included the city's two nationally-known features – San Diego Zoo and Sea World – and the option of a ferry ride across San Diego Bay to Coronado.

The city's year-round mild climate means the tour can be enjoyed to the full at any time, but expect accommodation prices to rise by $10-$20 during the summer, and for this popular vacation city to be particularly crowded over national holidays.

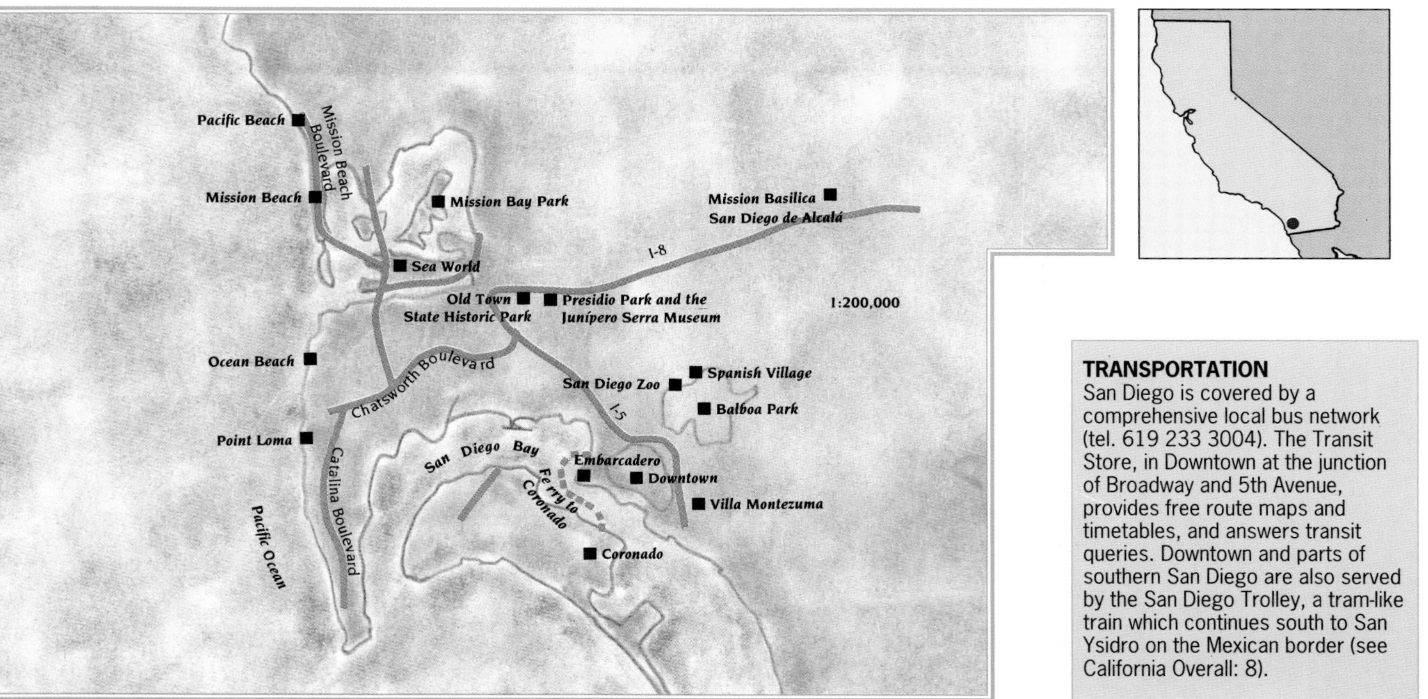

TRANSPORTATION
San Diego is covered by a comprehensive local bus network (tel. 619 233 3004). The Transit Store, in Downtown at the junction of Broadway and 5th Avenue, provides free route maps and timetables, and answers transit queries. Downtown and parts of southern San Diego are also served by the San Diego Trolley, a tram-like train which continues south to San Ysidro on the Mexican border (see California Overall: 8).

SIGHTS & PLACES OF INTEREST

BALBOA PARK
Exuberant landscaping and highbrow culture go hand-in-hand in the 1,200-acre Balboa Park. Two major expozitions held at Balboa Park, in 1915 and 1935, raised San Diego's international prestige and gave the park a series of ornate, Spanish-style buildings. Although the buildings were intended to be temporary, their elegant profile amid the park's palm trees won the hearts of locals; many have survived into the present and several of them now hold sizeable museums.

The park's major museums are located in two sites. To the south, the **Aerospace Historical Center** holds hundreds of pioneering aircraft and spacecraft, and the **Automotive Museum** stores some splendid vintage cars. If art is more to your taste than engineering, concentrate on the northern section of the park. Here, along El Prado, a call into the **Museum of Art** finds European Old Masters, Far Eastern and Asian treasures and a strong trove of American art. Complement it with a visit to the **Timkin Gallery**, which has some wonderful Russian icons alongside works by Rembrandt, Rubens and Cézanne, and by casting an eye over the contemporary works displayed in the gallery of the **San Diego Art Institute**.

Also on El Prado are the **Museum of Natural History** – with fossils and precious stones in abundance – and the **Museum of Man**, with interesting but lightweight displays on Native American cultures and in-depth accounts of anthropological expeditions. Several smaller collections – the Museum of San Diego History, the Museum of Photography, the Hall of Champions and the San Diego Railroad Museum – are also worthwhile.

Don't feel obliged to visit all of Balboa Park's museums: there's much to be said for simply strolling and picnicking, and making a leisurely exploration of the park's minor attractions, such as the Palm Arboretum, the Spreckels Organ Pavilion – with 5,000 pipes, claimed to be the world's largest pipe organ – and the arts and crafts workshops of the Spanish Village.

Balboa Park also has its share of evening activities. Diverse dramatic productions are staged at the **Old Globe Theater** – a replica of its 15thC London namesake. There's opera at the **Casa del Prado Theater**, and giant-screen IMAX films, exploring the natural world and beyond it, are shown at the **Reuben H. Fleet Space Theater and Science Center** (also open during the day).

DETOUR – **VILLA MONTEZUMA**
In a once-fashionable, now depressed area about 2 miles east of Downtown, Villa Montezuma is an impressively restored affluent Victorian house which reveals some fascinating details about its original occupant, Jesse Shepard. A cultured Englishman, interested in music, literature and the arts, and with an abiding interest in spiritualism, Shepard was brought to San Diego with the brief to raise the city's cultural tone. Despite entertaining the city's well-to-do with musical seances, Shepard eventually died broke in Los Angeles. The San Diego Historical Society keep the villa in fine condition and dispense informative snippets on Shepard and on 1880s San Diego. The villa is located at 1925 K Street.

DOWNTOWN 🛏 ✕
A mix of modern commercial architecture and turn-of-the-century brick buildings in varying stages of renovation, Downtown San Diego is an interesting blend of new and old and also reveals the city's social contrasts, sharp-suited bankers and the destitute, both likely to be spotted along Broadway, its busy main drag (avoid it at night).

The easily-walked **Gaslamp District**, 16 short blocks of restored buildings south of Broadway between 4th and 6th Avenues, is the one section of Downtown which merits a detailed exploration. The best way to tackle the area is with the **guided walking tours** which begin each Saturday at 11 am from Downtown's oldest building: the 1850 William Heath Davis House, 410 Island Avenue.

Most of the Gaslamp District's prettiest buildings are redbrick affairs adorned with intricate bas reliefs and topped by mysterious-looking towers which arose during the early years of the 20thC, as San Diego flourished at its new bay-side location. (Its former site, now Old Town State Historic Park, was abandoned in the late 1800s.)

Unusually for a major U.S. city, the San Diego authorities have actively encouraged the preservation and development of Downtown, and stimulated its leisure-time activity with **Horton Plaza**, between E and G Streets and 1st and 4th Avenues. One of California's few shopping malls not sited in deepest suburbia, Horton Plaza – completed in 1985 – is designed in a winning pseudo-Mediterranean style, with six open-air levels which invite window-shopping and people-watching.

Continuing west along Broadway, the delightful Spanish-Moorish **Santa Fe Depot**, San Diego's railway station since 1915, provides a sharp contrast to the 34-story **American Plaza**, next door. One of many Downtown buildings started during the economic boom of the late 1980s, the American Plaza's future is shrouded in doubt but plans include a glass-canopied walkway linking the building to the Santa Fe Depot and the adjacent San Diego Trolley terminal.

EMBARCADERO

Between the western edge of Downtown and the Gaslamp District, the breezy Embarcadero walkway winds along the edge of San Diego Bay, giving views of yachts sailing on the bay and – less frequently – allowing glimpses of naval vessels emerging from their bases on Coronado or Point Loma.

The busiest section of the Embarcadero is **Seaport Village**, a not particularly realistic recreation of a New England village, whose clapboard buildings hold tourist-aimed shops and restaurants. Among them, the Upstart Crow offers a promising combination of many shelves of books and magazines and several varieties of fresh coffee by the cup.

The Embarcadero also includes the **Maritime Museum**, comprising three

FERRY RIDE TO CORONADO ×

San Diego Bay and quite a lot of money divide Coronado – a place repaying a half-day trip – from the rest of the city. The carefully groomed and very suburban neighborhood sits at the head of an isthmus, which it shares with a large naval air station.

The navy keeps the present-day local economy on a sound footing, but Coronado's first taste of wealth came with the completion of the **Hotel Del Coronado** in the late 1880s, a conglomeration of wooden towers, turrets and other fanciful flourishes of Victorian architecture spread across a large chunk of a 4,000-acre site. Marketed as a "dream resort," the swish hotel drew moneyed Easterners on the new cross-country railway with the promise of luxury and sophistication at a time when the rest of California was spit-and-sawdust frontier territory.

By the 1920s, no discerning sybarite could visit San Diego without showing him- or herself at the "Del." The story of the hotel, its construction, its famous guests, and its starring role alongside Marilyn Monroe, Jack Lemmon and Tony Curtis in the 1955 film *Some Like it Hot* is outlined in a small museum. For a more thorough exploration of the hotel, join the free guided tours which begin from the lobby at 1 pm on Saturdays – and don't forget to ask about the haunted room.

From the time of the hotel's opening until the completion of the two-mile long **Coronado Bridge** in 1969, the only way to reach Coronado from Downtown San Diego was by ferry. Cunningly, the city authorities suspended the ferry service until the bridge had paid for itself (by way of the tolls collected at the Coronado end). Nowadays, the ferry makes the 15-minute ride between the Embarcadero and Coronado frequently throughout the day, and docks at Coronado's **Old Ferry Landing** which, despite its name, dates only from 1987 and is a fairly uninteresting retail and restaurant complex. A stroll along Orange Avenue, towards the Hotel Del Corondo, offers a choice of lunch places: see Recommended Restaurants, page 257.

restored sailing vessels from the 19th and early 20thC. The ships can be boarded and explored although only very salty dogs are likely to find them of abiding interest. Of greater appeal is the adjacent departure point for the ferry to Coronado.

MISSION BASILICA SAN DIEGO DE ALCALA

In 1769, Spanish padre Junípero Serra – leader of the Sacred Expedition across California – founded Mission Basilica San Diego de Alcalá on a hilltop site above what is now Old Town State Historic Park (see page 256). The first of the 21 missions which spread northwards across California, the San Diego mission was soon moved to a more convenient location and now sits amid the suburban sprawl of Mission Valley, at 10818 San Diego Mission Road. This is not the biggest nor the best of California's missions, but do pay a call if you don't have the opportunity to visit any of the others: the well-stocked museum and the simple chapel offer an arresting flavor of bygone times.

MISSION BAY PARK

Filling a 4,600-acre expanse between Downtown and Mission Beach, these one-time marshlands have developed into a series of beach-lined lagoons. Come the weekend, the grassy sections are clogged with frisbee throwers and volleyball players as jet-skiers and wind-surfers zip by on – or above – the park's waterways. Mission Bay Park is also the site of Sea World (see page 259).

MISSION BEACH ×

The epitome of Southern California beach culture, Mission Beach life really does revolve around sand and surf – not least because there's almost nothing else to see or do along this slender, 2-mile-long peninsula. You'll get

the measure of Mission Beach along the beachside **boardwalk**, thronged with cyclists, roller-skaters and others, whose clothing often covers nothing more than their genitalia. The boardwalk is always busy and so too is the single main road, Mission Beach Boulevard, which local police often close during the crazed days of summer.

At the southern end of the boardwalk, **Belmont Park** is where you'll spot two much-updated survivors of 1920s Mission Beach: the Giant Dipper Roller Coaster, and a 175-ft-long salt water swimming-pool known as The Plunge.

OCEAN BEACH

Surfing and sunbathing are the big attractions of Ocean Beach, though unlike the heavily tourist-populated Mis-

• *Opposite: Balboa Park - see page 252.*
• *Right, San Diego Harbor and below, Hotel del Coronado, San Diego.*

sion Beach (see page 254), this little community possesses a small-town charm and perches picturesquely on the hilly neck of the Point Loma peninsula, with the impressive **Sunset Cliffs** overlooking its popular strips of sand.

OLD TOWN STATE HISTORIC PARK ✕

First housing the community which settled beneath the hilltop Spanish fort – or Presidio – which followed the founding of the San Diego Mission in 1769, and the center of San Diegan life during California's Mexican period, the half-dozen adobe structures of Old Town State Historic Park provide an interesting if not always satisfying glimpse into the city's back pages.

With the exception of the marvellous 1827 **Casa de Estudillo**, which housed the commander of the Presidio, the more successful restorations – usually filled with entertaining historical debris – are the wood-and-brick buildings erected in the years between the advent of U.S. rule (1846) and the late 1800s, when the new San Diego emerged 4 miles away on the bayside – the present Downtown.

Be sure to call at the visitor center for the free and informative map, without which the layout and history of the park are difficult to comprehend. Especially at weekends, be prepared for large crowds: the park's shops and the restaurants which line the adjoining

BUDGET ACCOMMODATION

Armed Services YMCA; 500 W. *Broadway; tel.* 619 232 1144.
Jim's San Diego; 1425 C *Street; tel.* 619 235 0234.
Point Loma AYH Hostel; 3790 *Udall Street; tel.* 619 223 4778.
YWCA Women's Hostel; 1012 C *Street; tel.* 619 239 0355.

RECOMMENDED HOTELS

DOWNTOWN

Downtown Inn Hotel, $-$$; 660 G *Street; tel.* 619 238 4100; *credit cards,* AE, MC, V.

Ceiling fans are just one pleasant touch in this crisply modern hotel, where every room has a kitchenette. One slight drawback is the location: no worries by day, but be cautious if returning on foot alone at night.

Hotel St. James, $$-$$$; 830 *6th Avenue; tel.* 800 338 1616; *credit cards,* AE, MC, V.

An historic Gaslamp District hotel now entirely modernized. The rooms tend to be small but are pleasantly furnished and well equipped, and the hotel offers sound value in this prime central location.

Hotel San Diego, $$$; 339 W. *Broadway; tel.* 800 824 1244; *credit cards,* AE, MC, V.

Attentive service and spacious rooms are welcome features of this inviting hotel, located directly on Downtown's main street – choose a room at the rear if you're concerned about noise. There's a classy restaurant and bar on the ground floor; or choose a title or two from the video library and curl up in front of the VCR in your room.

La Pensione, $; 1654 *Columbia Street; tel.* 619 232 2400; *credit cards,* AE, MC, V.

Offering weekly and nightly rates, clean and comfortable La Pensione sits in a quiet residential neighborhood a few minutes' walk from Broadway. The rooms have fridges and microwave ovens, and there's a laundry for guests' use.

PACIFIC BEACH

Beach Cottages, $$-$$$; 4255 *Ocean Boulevard; tel.* 619 483 7440; *credit cards,* AE, MC, V.

A mix of one- and two-bedroom cottages, and regular motel-type rooms, grouped around a courtyard within a frisbee's throw of the beach.

Pacific Terrace Inn, $$$$; 610 *Diamond Street; tel.* 800 344 3370; *credit cards,* AE, DC, MC, V.

The wonderful ocean view from your balcony is just one of the things worth mentioning here. Other features include the comprehensively-stocked minibars and fridges found in every room, and the light breakfast served each morning.

San Diego Avenue are extremely popular. Another busy spot is **Bazaar del Mundo**, a likeable though very sanitized version of a Mexican street bazaar on the park's northern edge, with a colorfully-tiled courtyard ringed by souvenir shops, Mexican food outlets and, at weekends, often filled by the sounds of live mariachi bands.

PACIFIC BEACH ⛟ ✕

It may neighbor riotous Mission Beach but Pacific Beach is an altogether more genteel residential community, one which decorates its beach-side pathway with plants and well-tended gardens. Pacific Beach's most energetic spots are the trendy eaterys and nightspots grouped along its main street, Garnet Avenue.

POINT LOMA ⛟

The 10-mile-long Point Loma peninsula divides San Diego Bay from the Pacific Ocean and provides a sheltered location for some of the city's better-off residents, who inhabit pricey houses set along quiet, leafy lanes.

Point Loma's visitor interest lies at its southern tip, where the **Cabrillo National Monument** remembers the 1542 landing of Juan Cabrillo, a Por-

RECOMMENDED RESTAURANTS

CORONADO

Bula's Pub & Eatery, $-$$; 170 *Orange Avenue; tel.* 619 435 4466; *credit cards,* AE, MC, V.

Strong selection of quality salads, quiches and homemade soups, served informally amid antiques and well-tended plants. An ideal lunch stop on a Coronado excursion.

DOWNTOWN

Old Columbia Brewery & Grill, $; 1157 *Columbia Street; tel.* 619 234 2739; *credit cards,* MC, V.

One of the few micro-breweries in southern California, the homemade beer here is definitely worth sampling. The food – American staples such as burgers, sandwiches, along with German sausages – is less original, but will inexpensively relieve hunger pangs.

Croce's, $-$$; 802 *5th Avenue; tel.* 619 233 4355; *credit cards,* AE, DC, MC, V.

Owned by the widow of singer/songwriter Jim Croce, this is a tempting Gaslamp District lunch spot but even better for candle-lit dinners with the sounds of live jazz percolating from the adjoining bar. There's usually a broad selection of seafood and pasta dishes on the changing menu.

MISSION BEACH

Red Onion, $; 312 *Ocean Front Walk; tel.* 619 488 9040; *credit cards,* AE, CB, DC, MC, V.

An always-busy beach-side eatery, packed at night for its disco and fruit-flavored margaritas. By day, big eaters are contented by the truly enormous helpings of Mexican food.

OLD TOWN STATE HISTORIC PARK

Casa de Bandini, $-$$; 2666 *Calhoun Street; tel.* 619 297 8211; *credit cards,* AE, CB, DC, MC, V.

Other nearby Mexican restaurants are cheaper and sometimes equally good, but only here will you be able to choose from a large selection of fine food and consume it in the courtyard of a Spanish-style hacienda built in 1823, which later became a hotel for stage-coach travellers.

PACIFIC BEACH

The Eggery Etc, $; 41250 *Mission Boulevard; tel.* 619 274 3122; *credit cards,* AE, MC, V.

Big breakfasts – omelettes, waffles, pancakes in a variety of styles – are served all day at this ocean-front spot. Other options include a fairly undistinguished range of burgers and, in the evening, pasta dishes.

McCormick & Schmick's, $-$$; 4190 *Mission Beach Boulevard; tel.* 619 581 3938; *credit cards,* AE, DC, DS, MC, V.

Of San Diego's countless seafood restaurants, this one can be best relied upon for the widest choice of the freshest fare from all across the Pacific. The setting, too, is conducive to memorable eating. Reservations are recommended for dinner.

• *Old Town, San Diego.*

tuguese adventurer employed by Spain who became the first European to put ashore in California. The monument itself is unspectacular but the views – across San Diego and far beyond – are stunning.

A short walk from the monument, a visitor center carries texts on Cabrillo's arrival but devotes more energy to documenting the marine life which inhabits the **tide pools** found at the foot of Point Loma's coastal bluffs. Also nearby, the interior of an 1891 lighthouse can be visited but won't hold your attention for more than the few minutes it takes to tour its few rooms and clamber up its short staircase.

PRESIDIO PARK AND THE JUNIPERO SERRA MUSEUM

Presidio Park shows the benefits of its 1920s planting with 10,000 trees and shrubs, and rises steeply above Old Town State Historic Park. In an elaborate structure raised in the Spanish Colonial style, the park's **Junípero Serra Museum** carries odds and ends from mission-era California but is better visited for the stupendous views from its tower. Spanning suburbia and ocean, the outlook can be contrasted with ageing photographs of the same areas – then farmland from 50 years ago. From the museum, a short path leads to a cross which marks the original site of San Diego's mission.

SAN DIEGO ZOO

Zoos seldom come bigger or better than San Diego's, which began with the handful of bears, lions and wolves left behind after the 1915 Panama-California Exposition in nearby Balboa Park. It has since grown into one of the world's leading centers for zoological research. Almost 800 species are represented among the zoo's 4,000 inmates, many of them apparently enjoying life in elaborate recreations of their natural habitats – most impressively an equatorial rain forest and several thickly-vegetated canyons, complete with waterfalls – where boundaries are defined by streams or high ridges, rather than bars and fences.

Spread across 128 acres, there's plenty to see at the zoo and you'll need to allocate a whole day to do it justice. If your feet start complaining, try the "skyfari" ride, which provides not only a seat but also a bird's-eye view of the zoo from 170 feet up.

SEA WORLD

A multi-million dollar operation and one of San Diego's most visited (and most highly-priced) tourist attractions. Sea World combines behind-the-scenes marine research with a series of major exhibits which offer the chance to see killer whales, sharks and penguins at close quarters plus numerous minor displays on ocean themes and special events throughout the day.

If you're not upset by intelligent mammals being taught tricks for human amusement (one reason why Sea World has many critics) or by crowds and commercialism – there's a gift shop and over-priced snack stand at every turn – and have always wanted to stroke a stingray or feed a bottle-nosed dolphin, then Sea World could well be for you.

SPANISH VILLAGE

See Balboa Park, page 252.

• *Right, in San Diego Zoo and below, San Diego Zoo entrance.*

Southern California

Escondido, Julian, Santa Ysabel

150 miles (one way); map Kümmerley & Frey *California & Nevada*

On the face of it, this tour is a short and simple route linking Palm Springs (California Overall: 7) and San Diego (Local Explorations: 17). However, I have devised it in the certain knowledge that it will surprise you. The modest length (allow two days for everything) disguises the fact that it passes through a diverse assortment of landscapes, following winding country lanes as they climb into the hills dividing southern California's heavily-populated coastal areas from its thinly-inhabited inland deserts.

The heart of the tour lies between these extremes, among the apple orchards, woodlands and tiny rural settlements which often comprise no more than a few ranch houses grouped around a road junction. I've chosen the most sizeable of the towns, Julian, as an overnight stop, and it's one which you'll enjoy: filled with Victorian wood-framed houses and countless shops offering fresh-baked apple pies, this is archetypal backwoods California.

Elsewhere, I've included a detour to the world-famous Palomar Observatory, and a couple of branch (or *asistencia*) missions. These minor Spanish-founded churches may be ignored by the history books but they are still used by the local Native American community.

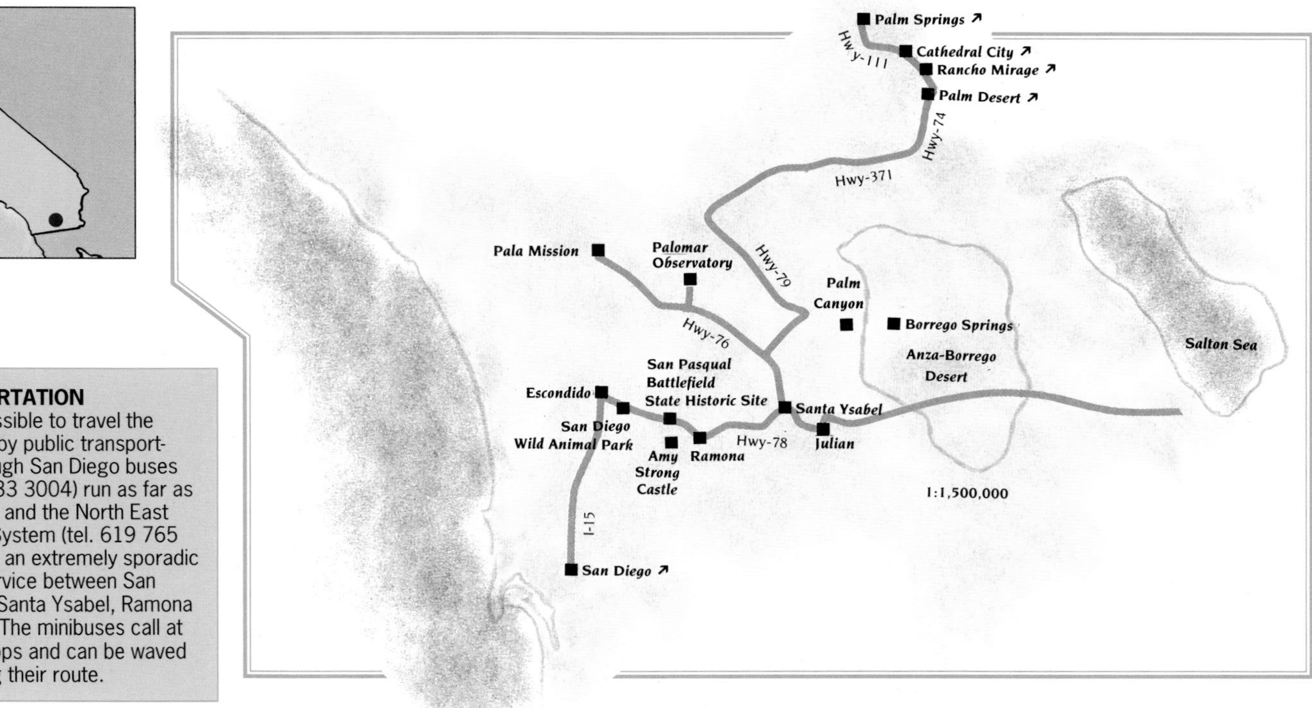

TRANSPORTATION

It is not possible to travel the whole way by public transportation although San Diego buses (tel. 619 233 3004) run as far as Escondido, and the North East Rural Bus System (tel. 619 765 0145) runs an extremely sporadic minibus service between San Diego and Santa Ysabel, Ramona and Julian. The minibuses call at marked stops and can be waved down along their route.

SIGHTS & PLACES OF INTEREST

BORREGO SPRINGS
See Detour – The Anza-Borrego Desert, below.

CATHEDRAL CITY
See California Overall: 7.

ESCONDIDO ✕
A dull but comfortable suburban town, Escondido is best-known to older Americans as the home of Lawrence Welk, a middle-of-the-road band leader whose popularity soared through a long-running TV show. Welk owns the Lawrence Welk Village Resort, a vacation center on the edge of town, where a small museum details his career and three separate golf courses occupy some of the resort's 1,000-acre grounds.

Also on Escondido's periphery are a couple of **wineries** warranting a call if you're not heading north to California's better-known wine-producing areas (see Local Explorations: 1, 6 and 7): Bernardo, off Pomerado Road, and Ferrara, 1120 W. 15th Avenue, both of which offer free tastings.

JULIAN @ ✕
These days it's apples which bring visitors to Julian: orchards cover the rolling hillsides around the town and the cafes grouped along the homey community's main street – which is called Main Street – do a roaring trade in apple pies, as well as other wholesome fare. A century ago, however, Julian was a gold-mining town and one of the largest and most prosperous settlements in the area. Off C Street, the **Eagle & High Peaks Mine Museum** stores vintage mining equipment

DETOUR - **PALA MISSION AND PALOMAR OBSERVATORY**
Travel west for some 30 miles along Hwy-76, which branches off Hwy-79 at Morettis Junction, and you'll reach the small and isolated **Pala Mission**, now in the heart of the Pala Indian Reservation. Built in 1816 as a branch of Oceanside's mission – further west on Hwy-76 (see California Overall: 8) – the Pala Mission has a run-down, unkempt appearance but some interesting native-painted frescos adorn its chapel walls.

By contrast, the high-tech **Palomar Observatory** can also be reached from Hwy-76: take Route S6, which winds its way up Palomar Mountain. The public can't peer through the observatory's 200-inch telescope but they can admire the photographs it has produced of distant galaxies, which are displayed here in a museum.

DETOUR - **THE ANZA-BORREGO DESERT AND THE SALTON SEA**
To the west of Julian, forested hills slope gently downwards towards the coastal flatlands. To the east, in contrast, high ground prevents rain-bearing clouds reaching the **Anza-Borrego Desert**, which covers 600,000 acres of bone-dry, lizard-inhabited terrain.

Though simple to reach from Julian on Hwy-78, the Anza-Borrega Desert is not a place to visit on the spur of the moment and not at all during summer. Sensible desert visitors only come here during the winter or between March and May, when colorful wildflowers bloom across these otherwise severe vistas and serve as a reminder of nature's gentler qualities. The oasis community of **Borrego Springs** holds the desert's only accommodation. Two miles west at **Palm Canyon**, a visitor center is an essential call for maps and general information.

From high points in the desert, you should be able to see the **Salton Sea** lying to the east. One of the world's largest inland seas, the Salton Sea was created in 1905 when an unusually severe winter in the Mid-west caused the Colorado River to breach the canals directing it to southern California's farmlands. The sea is much appreciated by watersports enthusiasts, anglers, and by thousands of gulls, herons, and other migratory birds, often viewable from the observation tower at the **Salton Sea National Wildlife Refuge**, off Hwy-111.

• *Fire Station, Julian.*

and keeps an old mine-shaft open to the public. Many more varied artifacts from Julian's past are gathered inside the **Pioneer Museum**, 2811 Washington Street.

There's not much to do or see in Julian, though its rural setting and preponderance of bed-and-breakfast inns – plus the historic Julian Hotel – make it a pleasant place to pass a night; see Recommended Hotels, page 264.

PALM DESERT
See California Overall: 7.

PALM SPRINGS
See California Overall: 7.

RAMONA
One of the larger of the rural communities in the area, its inhabitants tend either to be long-distance San Diego commuters or local farmers. The town holds remarkably little of interest, though the **Ramona Pioneer Society and Guy B. Woodward Museum**, 645 Main Street, with several restored frontier-era buildings and a 19thC house with many original features, might take half an hour.

RANCHO MIRAGE
See California Overall: 7.

SAN DIEGO
See Local Explorations: 17.

SAN DIEGO WILD ANIMAL PARK
An offshoot of the excellent San Diego Zoo (see Local Explorations: 17), the San Diego Wild Animal Park recreates the natural habitats of Africa, Asia, Australia and several other ecologically-diverse regions over a 2,000-acre site. Giraffes, tigers, zebras, lions, rhinos, and a host of other creatures roam the artificial plains and savannahs, while the humans who come to see them are confined either to the monorail which makes a 50-minute journey across the

DETOUR - **THE AMY STRONG CASTLE**

Turn off Hwy-67 just south of Ramona along Archie Moore Road and you'll quickly reach the **Amy Strong Castle**, a mansion created from granite boulders during the 1920s. An exploration of the 27-room "castle" (open weekends only) reveals the tale of Amy Strong, a local seamstress of great repute and considerable means.

park, or to the park's many miles of foot trails. Bear in mind that you'll need most of a day to see the park in full – and that the midday heat finds many animals snoozing out of sight behind bushes.

SAN PASQUAL BATTLEFIELD STATE HISTORIC SITE

A modest marker and visitor center beside Hwy-78 records a little-known footnote in California's history: the battle of San Pasqual, which occurred in December 1846 between a band of *Californios* (Mexican-Californians) and a force of U.S. soldiers – among them, frontier legend Kit Carson – who were advancing on San Diego. Facing defeat, the U.S. contingent withdrew from the battle but, aided by reinforcements, later took control of the region.

SANTA YSABEL

A crossroads community of a few hundred souls set around the junction of Hwy-78 and Hwy-79. Large numbers of passing motorists pause in Santa Ysabel just long enough to buy a loaf of bread from **Dudley's Bakery**. The spacious bakery shop has many shelves of warm loaves, baked in various styles to traditional recipes, as well as a tempting selection of fresh-baked cakes.

Within sight of the bakery along Hwy-79, the miniscule **Mission Santa Ysabel** was founded in 1818 as a branch of San Diego's mission though soon fell to ruin: the current church dates from 1924. Next door to the church, a one-room museum holds many intriguing objects from the original mission.

RECOMMENDED HOTELS

JULIAN

Julian Hotel, $$-$$$; *Main Street at* B *Street; tel.* 619 765 0201; *credit cards,* AE, MC, V.

Founded by freed slaves in 1897, this atmospheric wood-framed hotel is a survivor of Julian's gold-rush days and has the Victorian fixtures and fittings to prove it – telephones and TVs are nowhere to be found. As well as the rooms in the main house, some of which have shared bathrooms, there are two cottages outside. A substantial breakfast greets you each morning, and tea and cakes are laid out in the afternoon.

Julian Lodge, $$-$$$; *Main Street at* C *Street; tel.* 619 765 1420; *credit cards,* AE, MC, V.

By Julian's standards this is a large and modern hotel but, with just 23 rooms and its design modelled on a demolished Julian landmark, the mood is as rustic as any of the town's tiny bed-and-breakfast inns. All rooms have private bathrooms, some have fridges. A light breakfast is served, and there is a public room with a piano for communal sing-songs.

RECOMMENDED RESTAURANTS

ESCONDIDO

Cocino del Charro, $-$$; 525 N. *Quince Avenue; tel.* 619 745 1382; *credit cards,* AE, DC, MC, V.

Mexican food and plenty of it, served for breakfast, lunch or dinner in a lively setting. Come early for the extremely popular Sunday brunch.

JULIAN

Julian Cafe, $; *Main Street at* A *Street; tel.* 619 765 2712; *credit cards,* MC, V.

Though every inch the locals' favorite for wholesome fare served at solid wooden tables, it is worth avoiding the Julian Cafe at peak meal times, when it's likely to be over-full.

Mom's Pies, $; *Main Street at* B *Street; tel.* 619 765 2472; *credit cards, none.*

Should your stay in Julian be a fleeting one, this is the best of several dozen places offering the chance to sample what Julian is famous for: apple pies, here served fresh and warm with a choice of crusts.

INDEX

R